Gender, Sexuality, and Meaning

Gender, Sexuality, and Meaning
Linguistic Practice and Politics

Sally McConnell-Ginet

OXFORD
UNIVERSITY PRESS
2011

Oxford University Press, Inc., publishes works that further
Oxford University's objective of excellence
in research, scholarship, and education.

Oxford   New York
Auckland   Cape Town   Dar es Salaam   Hong Kong   Karachi
Kuala Lumpur   Madrid   Melbourne   Mexico City   Nairobi
New Delhi   Shanghai   Taipei   Toronto

With offices in
Argentina   Austria   Brazil   Chile   Czech Republic   France   Greece
Guatemala   Hungary   Italy   Japan   Poland   Portugal   Singapore
South Korea   Switzerland   Thailand   Turkey   Ukraine   Vietnam

Published by Oxford University Press, Inc.
198 Madison Avenue, New York, New York 10016

www.oup.com

Oxford is a registered trademark of Oxford University Press.

Library of Congress Cataloging-in-Publication Data
McConnell-Ginet, Sally.
Gender, sexuality, and meaning: linguistic practice and politics / Sally McConnell-Ginet.
    p. cm.— (Studies in language and gender)
Includes bibliographical references and index.
ISBN 978–0–19–518780–9; 978–0–19–518781–6 (pbk.)
1. Language and languages—Sex differences. 2. Semantics. 3. Semantics (Philosophy). I. Title.
P120.S48M33 2010
306.44—dc22   2010013979

9 8 7 6 5 4 3 2 1

Printed in the United States of America
on acid-free paper

For Carl

Foreword

It is an honor to include this collection of Sally McConnell-Ginet's essential feminist writings in Oxford University Press's Studies in Language and Gender. The volume is not only an indispensable introduction to the key work of this critically important scholar, but it is also a veritable biography of language and gender studies over the last three decades and more. This is no accident, for McConnell-Ginet stands as one of the foundational figures of language and gender research. Her impact has been significant both for her substantial contributions to the field as well as for her status within linguistics as a formal linguist with an international reputation for her work in semantics, independent of (but by no means unrelated to) her scholarship on language and gender. Her unwavering commitment to advancing feminist goals through her research is especially remarkable given that linguistics has never been known for its progressive views regarding gender. McConnell-Ginet's close involvement in the development of language and gender studies highlights the important truth that a feminist perspective on language is not reserved for sociolinguistics—the research area that has been most closely linked to gender issues—but can and should be brought to bear on every subfield of linguistics.

McConnell-Ginet's theoretical focus and acute political gaze have been strikingly consistent over the years. All of her feminist scholarship engages deeply with the issue of power, its diverse manifestations in language, and its consequences for the lives of women and men. Yet her research does not stop at identifying the workings of power. As an early feminist voice challenging essentialist perspectives on gender and language and advocating recognition of women's linguistic and social agency, she paved the way for more nuanced and contextualized approaches that nevertheless remain centrally concerned with issues of equality and social justice.

McConnell-Ginet is a generous and broad-minded scholar who does not impose artificial boundaries in her pursuit of interesting and important questions. Her analytic scope ranges widely in these chapters, from lexical semantics to prosody to variationist sociolinguistics. What draws together this rich and diverse body of scholarship is her attention to the question of meaning, which has emerged as the key issue for much contemporary language and gender scholarship. The bulk of McConnell-Ginet's research—both in language and gender studies and in formal linguistics—focuses on semantics, or the study of linguistic meaning. Her feminist explorations of this issue demonstrate that there is no such thing as "mere semantics." To begin with, she makes clear that semantic meaning is by no means a straightforward matter, for the meanings of words, let alone entire utterances, are always variable and often contested. The following pages document numerous instances of struggles and debates over what was said and what was meant, from the definition of *queer* to the meaning of *gender* itself. Meaning, in short, matters.

At the same time, McConnell-Ginet extends her consideration of meaning beyond the traditional mandate of formal semantics to incorporate the social and stylistic meanings that are projected through language use. This innovative move allows her to take account of contextual factors—including gender and sexuality, to be sure, but also race, age, class, and so on, as well as more interactionally based issues like the social relationship between the speakers and what they are trying to accomplish through their talk, as well as the larger social practices in which they engage. Readers will find the roots of this perspective in McConnell-Ginet's earliest writings on gender and its fullest development in the work that resulted from her long-term intellectual partnership with Penelope Eckert. These scholars' collaborative investigations of the relationship of gender, social meaning, and style are among the most influential theoretical contributions within language, gender, and sexuality studies, providing a firm foundation for the exciting new social-constructionist direction the field began to take in the 1990s. Their theoretical insights continue to bear fruit, informing the latest research developments.

The following chapters encompass some of McConnell-Ginet's best-known work on language, gender, and sexuality—such as her ground-breaking essay on gender and intonation, which first appeared in the premiere feminist journal *Signs* and which opened the gate to a now-thriving field of research—as well as some chapters that will be new to many readers, like her thoughtful discussion of how linguistic, literary, and poetic views of language can play complementary roles in understanding gender. Her most recent work incorporates issues of sexuality into her longstanding concern with gender, providing deep insights into how the large-scale cultural discourses that ideologically structure social systems begin with the simplest and most powerful of building blocks, words and meanings.

It is a joy to read the work of a writer who communicates so clearly and engagingly about complex ideas and who is not afraid to bring her personal voice and perspective to her academic writing. As a result, *Gender, Sexuality, and Meaning* is sure to find a wide and appreciative audience. Language and gender specialists will not only find great utility in the book's theoretical focus on meaning as a productive unifying theme for the entire field, but will also enjoy reacquainting themselves with their favorite pieces and discovering those they may not have encountered previously. Meanwhile, their students as well as their colleagues in other fields—both nonlinguists and nonfeminists—will learn a great deal from the volume, which provides an excellent introduction to the key issues and developments of language and gender studies as a research area.

McConnell-Ginet has been instrumental in bringing the study of language and gender and, more recently, the study of language and sexuality into the mainstream of the discipline as a course instructor on those topics at the biennial Linguistic Society of America Institute. And her stature as a former president of the LSA has lent important credibility to a small subfield that has often been stigmatized and marginalized within linguistics. Her impact on language and gender studies is due in no small part to her unflagging efforts to work from within established institutional structures to effect meaningful change, whether this means pushing formal linguists to consider the social world of language use and language users or urging feminist researchers to offer accounts of gender and language that capture the full complexity of both phenomena. It is telling, too, that change is at the center of McConnell-Ginet's intellectual and political enterprise. Her work paints a portrait of gender and sexuality as the foundation not merely for social dominance but also for individual agency and collective transformation.

By her own invaluable definition, Sally McConnell-Ginet is the quintessential feminist scholar, whose "scholarship informs feminism and feminism informs scholarship" (chapter 3). Both her groundbreaking scholarship and her passionate feminism have helped to bring language, gender, and sexuality studies into being and have helped to make it the dynamic and robust field that it is today.

Mary Bucholtz
Series Editor

Preface

This book includes twelve chapters, the first of which has been written especially for this volume and serves as a theoretical prelude. An essay written for a New Zealand conference organized by Janet Holmes (see below) on language in the workplace applies some of the theoretical points to real-life issues and is placed as a practical coda. The remaining ten essays are grouped in three parts. "Politics and scholarship" addresses the significance of both feminism and linguistics for the practice of feminist linguistics. "Social practice, social meaning, and selves" focuses on the personae people project (and accord to others) as they engage conversationally. (Two of the three essays in this section were coauthored with Penelope Eckert and invoke the notion of communities of practice; see below for an account of our collaboration on these and other works.) "Constructing content in discourse" deals with messages linguistically conveyed. Each section opens with a brief introduction. The previously published essays all appear in their original form, save for minor corrections, a few updates, and adoption of a consistent style for references. Any notes in the original appear as endnotes, sometimes with additions in brackets; I have also added a few footnotes. References appear at the end of each chapter, with newly added entries enclosed in brackets. Each section, including the prelude and the coda, opens with a few paragraphs situating the following essay or essays.

In 1973, a freshly minted PhD in linguistics, I was offered a temporary joint position by Cornell University's philosophy department and its fledgling women's studies program. Hired just a few weeks before classes began, I scrambled to put together a course on language and gender, a topic I had never thought much at all about until that summer. I could not then have imagined that I would eventually do my own research in the area. I had come to linguistics from philosophy of language and mathematics, and my PhD dissertation looked at semantic and syntax-semantics interface issues raised by English comparative constructions like *Joan is taller than Mary*. Actually, my examples were peopled mainly by *John* and *Bill*, then stock characters for linguists constructing illustrative sentences for grammaticality data. With a nascent recognition that examples have some life beyond their immediate use for generating judgments of well-formedness, I ended the dissertation "with thanks to John and Bill." But it took me a little more time before I realized the full masculinizing power of my examples and of the masculine generic pronouns I also used throughout my dissertation. And it was several years before I actually allowed myself to marry my semantic and my feminist interests— "Pronouns, prototypes, and persons," chapter 9, is the first example of my feminist-informed forays into matters of linguistic meaning.

It was my feminist interests that drew me into language, gender, and sexuality studies. I began by teaching other people's work but before long redirected some of my own research efforts toward the field, publishing a number of relatively theoretical and general articles (e.g., the essays in part I) along with others in which I applied my developing theoretical perspective to particular issues such as the place of intonation in constructing gendered speakers (see "Intonation in a man's world," chapter 6), or the use and interpretation of address forms ("Social labeling," chapter 10, owes a considerable debt to McConnell-Ginet 1978, "Address forms in sexual politics," in D. R. Butturff and E. J. Epstein, eds., *Women's Language and Style*, 23–35), or the meaning of words like *queer*, *gay*, and *lesbian* (I gave several talks in the 1980s that focused on *lesbian*; some of those ideas have been further developed in "'Queering' semantics," chapter 11).

In the mid-1980s I met Penelope Eckert (now at Stanford) and began talking with her about language and gender. Not only have I learned an enormous amount from her about variationist sociolinguistics (she was Labov's first PhD student), but our continuing conversations have developed into what has been a wonderfully productive and stimulating working partnership as well as one of the most important friendships in my life. Our first joint publications were in 1992. "Where communities of practice live" (chapter 5) is a considerably shortened and more reader-friendly version of the ideas first presented in our longer publication, "Think practically and look locally: Language and gender as community-based practice" (*Annual Review of Anthropology* 21, 461–90). (We have ordered our names alphabetically in all our publications.) It was Penny's contact with the work of Jean Lave and Etienne Wenger on social learning that introduced me to the specific notion of communities of practice, which fit well with my own emphasis on linguistic interactional strategies and practices. Penny and I were invited by Brian Joseph to give a talk together at the 1993 OSU LSA Linguistic Institute, which developed into "Constructing meaning, constructing selves" (chapter 7), and Eckert and McConnell-Ginet (1999) appeared in the special issue of *Language in Society* (edited by Janet Holmes and Miriam Meyerhoff) on communities of practice in language and gender studies. We were eventually persuaded to write a language and gender textbook, which finally appeared as *Language and gender* (Cambridge University Press, 2003); a second edition is in progress. Of course, I thank Penny for giving me permission to publish two of our jointly written articles in this book. I also thank her for much else: long walks, late nights, loud arguments, and a friendship that has survived many stresses but remains strong. Penny's Stanford students, especially Andrew Wong (on whose dissertation committee I served) and Rob Podesva (a sterling student in my Cornell undergraduate language and gender course before going to Stanford), have also been wonderful intellectual companions.

Penny and I also cotaught a course on language and gender in 1991 at the Santa Cruz LSA Linguistic Institute. Mary Bucholtz, now herself a well-known figure in language and gender studies and editor of Oxford's Language and Gender series in which this book appears, was one of our students then. It was Mary who first proposed that I think about collecting some of my writings on language, gender, and sexuality, and I thank her for that suggestion and for help with the project. I thank Elise Kramer for helping me prepare the manuscript and Adam Cooper for drafting the index. I also thank my contact person at Oxford University Press, Peter Ohlin, who was more than patient as I let other projects displace this one. Brian Hurley, Liz Smith, Philip Wolny, and Niranjana Harikrishnan have handled things capably since I submitted a typescript. And the volume would not have been possible without the kind permission to use previously published materials, which is hereby acknowledged. I want to thank especially editors Mary Bucholtz, Kathryn Campbell-Kibler, Deborah Cameron, Hester Eisenstein, Francine Frank, Cheris Kramarae, Nancy Henley, Janet Holmes, Kira Hall, Madeline Mathiot, Miriam Meyerhoff, Fritz Newmeyer, Robert Podesva, Sarah Roberts, Barrie Thorne, Paula Treichler, and Andrew Wong for their interest in publishing (or anthologizing) the work included here in volumes they were editing, for their ongoing collegial support and inspiration, and for helping me track down contacts for releasing the materials. Information about original publication appears on the first page of each chapter.

The essay I wrote on defining *marriage* is not included in this volume, but I want to thank Gregory Ward and Betty Birner for inviting me to contribute it to the Festschrift they were editing in honor of Larry Horn; that piece was anthologized in a volume coedited by Deborah Cameron and Don Kulick. Both Gregory and Larry have been longtime sources for material about language and sexuality as well as language and gender; additionally, Gregory and I cotaught a course on language and sexuality at the 2003 LSA Linguistic Institute at Michigan State, an experience from which I learned an enormous amount and which helped solidify our already close friendship. Debby, of course, has done groundbreaking work on language, gender, and sexuality, and our occasional face-to-face encounters have made me wish she were not across the ocean.

Closer to home, all this work has been influenced by my Cornell colleagues and students over the years. Editing *Women and language in literature and society* (Praeger/Greenwood: 1980), one of the first cross-disciplinary volumes of language and gender studies, with Ruth Borker (who died in 1989, then in anthropology and women's studies at Cornell) and Nelly Furman (then in romance studies at Cornell and also active in its women's studies program, now director of MLA's foreign language programs and ADFL and still a close friend) taught me an enormous amount about literary and anthropological perspectives on language and gender studies. I also had the great privilege of coteaching with both Ruth and Nelly and later with Kathryn S. March (Cornell anthropology and women's studies), who was a student in my first course on language and gender. I have never taught or written anything with Sandra L. Bem, psychology and women's studies (renamed feminist, gender, and sexuality studies during her most recent stint as director), but she has read much of what I have written in this area and has always offered strong support for all my projects. As with my collaboration with Penny, these collegial relations have been accompanied by important personal ties.

Cornell graduate students Marisol del-Teso Craviotto and Tanya Matthews both wrote dissertations with me in this area, and I have learned much from our conversations and from their research. David Silva's dissertation was in a very different area, but we talked often about the writing course he developed on matters of language, gender, and sexuality.

Finally, I thank my family. My children, Lisa, Alan, and Greg, were all living at home when I first embarked on my teaching and writing career, and they all gave me much loving support as I struggled to balance my professional and personal lives, and they continue to cheer me on. It is my life partner, Carl, however, who has been cast as chief cheerleader, continuing to bear the brunt of my short temper when I'm trying to finish a writing project, listening to me give many a talk when he might have preferred to be sightseeing, and never failing to be willing to read drafts and offer good advice, not all of which gets heeded. He'll be as happy as I to see this book finally in print. This book is dedicated to him.

Contents

Gender, Sexuality, and Meaning

Prelude

The book opens with "Gender, sexuality, and meaning," which I have written especially for this volume. Although chapter 1 does mention some of the later chapters, 'introducing' the rest of the book happens in brief essays at the beginning of each of the three multichapter parts and the one-chapter coda. What this first essay does is lay out an overview of what I see as the important issues addressed by my work on the interaction of language with gender and sexuality. It grows out of a talk I gave a few years ago sketching my current thinking about these topics.

Of course, such an overview is necessarily partial. But I try to give an introduction to such topics as the close links between gender and sexuality, why thinking about identities has been so important in this area, how ideologies about language (and about gender and sexuality) are as important as 'actual' linguistic and social practice, the distinction (and the connections) between content (message) and social (style) meaning, and the notion of communities of practice (concrete and imagined). I close with two sections that point to the complexities of content and social meaning respectively, one arguing that communicative effect has to be considered when assessing the significance of content meaning (what speakers 'intend' may not be how hearers 'construct' the message and speakers may sometimes be held accountable for such unintended effects) and the other arguing that people generally construct multiple selves and that there may be no clear answers to which are 'authentic'.

1

Gender, sexuality, and meaning

An overview

0. Introduction

What are we doing as we talk with one another during mundane, everyday activities (e.g., in the workplace or at home, at the bus stop or in the shop or in an online chat room)? As we process media productions (e.g., on TV or in the newspaper or on websites produced for large audiences)? As we engage with religion (e.g., pray privately or participate in religious rituals)? As we encounter artistic productions (e.g., read books or attend films or visit museums)? As we participate in classes or conferences? As we attend or give university lectures or conference talks? As we make small talk at parties? As we flirt or joke with friends?

There are of course many things we do as we engage in such linguistically rich social activities. We debate reports or plan work projects, chat about the weather, amuse ourselves with a recent film, eat breakfast to the accompaniment of a newscast on the radio, write something about discourse analysis in answer to an examination question, flirt with a new acquaintance. Or we deplore the American presence in Afghanistan with companions over lunch, speculate with those same companions on friends' likely romantic prospects, read *Harry Potter* out loud, comfort an ill elderly parent or a cranky infant, work on improving yoga skills under the direction of an instructor, request hotel reservations by e-mail. Just think about the few hours preceding your opening this book, and you will almost certainly recall language entering into your life at many different points and in many different ways.

Using language is fundamental to pursuing our various life projects: to coordinating actions with others, to sharing ideas, to reminding others and ourselves of plans and commitments, to amusing ourselves and others, to making sense of ourselves and our world. And beyond individuals and face-to-face networks, language is fundamental to institutional arrangements—for example, law, religion, corporations, schools, media—and to

This essay was written for this volume. An early version was the basis of a talk at Aristotle University of Thessaloniki, Greece, in March 2005, which I was invited to give by Professor Theodossia-Soula Pavlidou. I thank Soula and her graduate students for their insightful comments and their stimulating company.

the articulation, transmission, and reinforcement of cultural belief systems or ideologies. Language is also central to challenging existing structures and ideologies: political struggles of many kinds are fought to a considerable extent on linguistic terrain.

Why does language matter so much? Because it is an omnipresent and all-purpose meaning-making system. And it offers meanings at two levels: basic content or the message expressed—roughly, what is said—and style or the persona and attitudes projected, often called social meaning—roughly, how it is said. I will discuss these two levels and their connections in linguistic practice below. This opening chapter offers a general framework for thinking about what follows.

1. Gender, sex, and sexuality

Gender, sex, and sexuality are central to individual experience and social life. But what is the distinction among them and how are they connected to one another? *Sex* is the oldest of these three words. *Sexuality* and *gender* were introduced to make explicit distinctions often conflated under *sex*: *sex* was to be reserved for biological/bodily classification of living beings as female or male, *gender* for sociocultural practices, conventions and ideologies clustering around the biological classification, and *sexuality* for sexual practices and erotic desires. Yet as Cameron and Kulick (2003) note, English speakers now often use *gender* where bodily configuration is at issue (under *gender* on many forms *male* and *female* are the choices) and *sexuality* is often understood simply as sexual identity (*straight* or *gay* often presumed the exclusive and exhaustive choices) whereas *sex* still covers the full terrain. They offer this account of why ordinary usage collapses distinctions that feminist scholars and others investigating these matters have found useful:

> Partly, this may be because some speakers still cling to traditional beliefs (e.g., that the way women or men behave socially and sexually is a direct expression of innate biological characteristics). But it may also be partly because the phenomena denoted by the three terms—having a certain kind of body (sex), living as a certain kind of social being (gender), and having certain kinds of erotic desires (sexuality)—are not understood or experienced by most people in present-day social reality as distinct and separate. Rather they are *interconnected*. (4–5)

The distinctions get noted by ordinary folks mainly when there is gender or sexual nonconformity: the kid in a boy's body who wants to play with dolls, the person in a woman's body whose erotic desires and activities center on other people in women's bodies. The gender inversion theory of homosexuality—sissy boys grow up to be gay men, for example—tries to keep the connections as tight as possible. Much of what gender is about in many cultural settings is sexuality, often supporting and enforcing heterosexuality and almost always also connected to arrangements for the birth and care of children.

There are also some recalcitrant bodies that challenge the putative dichotomizing imperative of the 'biological' category of sex: as Bergvall et al. (1996) demonstrate, that babies have universally been labeled either *girl* or *boy* (or the equivalents in local languages) is a social and not a 'purely' biological phenomenon. I will use the gender labels *woman* (*girl*) and *man* (*boy*) to designate those who claim those labels for themselves and are so labeled by others. A few people fall outside these two categories: for example, someone whose body was labeled *boy* at birth but who wants to identify themself[1] as a girl or a woman yet gets rebuffed in attempts to do so. Yet the dichotomy works pretty well. Most people who do not identify as heterosexual, including those who might be gender nonconformists, nonetheless do accept the gender label assigned them in infancy. Even those relatively few people who successfully manage transition from the birth assigned to the other gender category do not reject the dichotomy: they simply have switched categories.

Many women and men, whatever their sexual orientation might be, reject gender norms and ideologies while nonetheless identifying *as* women or men. They may well not be considered 'real' women or men by others, but such criticisms leave the label while chiding its bearer for not 'properly' living up to it, for being only 'biologically' or 'technically' a woman or a man. Those rejecting social conventions for womanhood or manhood may strongly reject identification with those who adhere more closely to such conventions: identifying oneself *as* a woman does not require that one identify *with* other women. Being a woman or man is a matter of GENDER IDENTITY. What has become very clear from the past few decades of gender studies is that the precise content of that identity, the significance of womanhood or manhood, varies not only for individuals within a particular society but also cross-culturally and historically and even for a given individual situationally and over the life course.

The notion of a person's having a SEXUAL IDENTITY is a relatively recent concept. Although different kinds and circumstances of sexual activity have long been recognized, the idea that erotic orientation, like gender identity, gives rise to distinct 'kinds' of people was unknown in Anglo-American culture before the late nineteenth century. In particular, our forebears would have been surprised by the idea that being attracted to sexual partners of one's own gender rather than to those of the other gender is a fundamental and persistent characteristic central to people's sense of who they are and where they fit in the broader social landscape. This is not to say that there was no discrimination among kinds of sexual activity—sexual interactions other than intercourse between a husband and his wife were thought immoral or deviant—but engaging in nonmarital sex (or desiring to do so) with whatever sexual category of partner did not thereby give one a particular sort of socially recognized identity. In contemporary Anglo-American society, however, categories like those labeled *gay*, *lesbian*, *straight*, and *bi* now constitute for many people significant identities that interact with gender identities in some interesting ways.

Feminist linguistics and the more recent queer linguistics have both frequently focused on language as INDEXING or pointing to (gender or sexual) identity; in other words, on ways of talking as reliable pointers to the identity of the talker. How do women talk? How do lesbians talk? Both enterprises, however, have moved from taking identities as fixed and given, with ways of talk just (somehow) arising from having a particular identity, to seeing talk as one of the ways that people shape their identities, construct themselves and others as (certain kinds of) women or men, as (certain kinds of) gay men or lesbians. This SOCIAL CONSTRUC-TIONIST approach to gender and sexual identities sees these and other identities as not a matter of who or what people are but a matter of what people do: rather than *have* identities, people *perform* them.

Neither gender nor sexuality is only about individual identities. Both are also and perhaps more importantly about the ideologies, institutions, social relations, and social practices through which individuals experience and give content to these identities—about what feeds gender and sexual identity construction and makes it matter at both individual and social levels. Inoue (2006) makes a compelling case that 'women's language' in Japan has a history inextricably intertwined with that of the Japanese nation-state, of Japan's relation to 'modernity' and to the Western world, and of class and regional divisions within Japan. (See also sec. 3 below.) Identities are always part of a much larger picture. Feminist linguistics and its newer partner, queer linguistics, are scholarly investigations of linguistic practices, those that might index identities as well as many others. The goal is to enhance understanding not only of how language works but also of gender and sexuality as both personal and sociocultural phenomena. Those who would describe themselves as pursuing one or both of these endeavors would generally also say that their motives for such inquiry are both scholarly and political: they (we) hope that increased understanding of how gender and sexuality now work might ultimately help lessen male and heterosexual privilege (and inequities based on other social distinctions) in future gender and sexuality arrangements.

2. Identity work

A primary emphasis in feminist linguistics has been investigating the role of language in making sense of ourselves and our social relations. To highlight the constitutive role of language in social life, we might say that the focus is on linguistic practice as part of actually making—constructing—ourselves and our social relations. The shift here reflects the growing recognition that identities and social relations do not exist independently of engagement in linguistic and other social practices—they emerge from and are constituted by the things people do, including what they say and how they say it. This social constructionist perspective does not mean that people are simply free to construct whatever identities and social relations they might want to: language users are indeed agents, but their possible actions are constrained both externally and internally (see sec. 7 below). Nonetheless, people are constantly doing what I will call IDENTITY WORK of one kind or another.

As we use language for such various and varied purposes as making lunch dates or cheering up a friend who's down or speculating about who'll be the next appointee to the U.S. Supreme Court, we and those with whom we interact are at the same time presenting ourselves and recognizing one another as certain kinds of people with particular attitudes, interests, capabilities, responsibilities, rights, identifications with others, and also with particular histories and projected futures. Brown and Yule (1983) speak of the transactional and the interactional dimensions of language use, others (e.g., Holmes 1995) of instrumental and affective language use. Self-presentation and other-recognition might seem allied with the interactional and the affective, both of which have been associated in the literature more with women than with men. The point I want to emphasize here, however, is that making selves and recognizing others' selves is not an added frill or something extra that some folks engage in with their talk while others are just getting 'real' things done, building bridges in the physical rather than the social world. Some people do indeed construct identities that require them to take considerable account of others' evaluations of them or that involve their own attending to others' feelings, whereas other people construct identities that involve considerable indifference to others' evaluations of them and little attention to others' feelings. But for either kind of person (and for the many people fitting neither of these characterizations), identity work is done.

No one other than a hermit can avoid performing identities, relating to others, and ratifying or rejecting one another's self-presentations and relational moves: we all have to do identity work when we speak to one another. Of course, identity work is far less important in some situations than in others—someone who sees flames and yells "Fire!" is unlikely to be concerned about the persona being projected and those who hear that warning probably care little about the persona projected by its source (though even in this situation it might matter whether they take that source to be reliable). More generally, the more focused interactants are on the other work being done linguistically, the less explicit attention they will pay to identity work. Nonetheless, it still goes on, whether above or below the level of conscious awareness.

Although identity work is most obvious in face-to-face spoken interactions, it is also generally part of other kinds of language use though sometimes attenuated by things like group authorship or great distance in time and space of the production of linguistic expressions and their interpretation. And the identity work we are able to do is often informed not only by what has worked in past face-to-face interactions for us or others we've observed but also by participation in other kinds of linguistic activity—for example, reading romance novels, watching sitcoms or 'reality' shows on

TV, reading advice columns in teen or women's magazines. But for now I will focus on talking face to face. In face-to-face talk, we may perform as women or men, as Americans or Greeks, as professors or students, as young or old, as straight or gay, as Christians or Muslims or Jews or atheists, as wives or mothers or lovers or friends. Sometimes language choice—for example, English or Turkish or Arabic or Latin or Hebrew—might inflect these performances; sometimes choices within the resources of a single language (dialectal features, use of casual or taboo variants, specialized vocabulary, syntactic choices, pronunciation, and the like) give rise to stylistic meaning. Identity work is done not only through stylistic meaning, however. Sometimes content meaning or the message conveyed (taking sports or fashion as one's topic, for example, and the slant taken on the chosen topic) also contributes to presenting ourselves or taking others as certain kinds of people.

I've used labels above for some categories generally thought of as social identities or social roles (e.g., *woman, lesbian, mother, Muslim*), and labels like these are often useful for considering the social personae people build together. (See chapter 10, this book, for further discussion of labeling.) But not all labels are always relevant. Just because someone identifies herself as a lesbian, for example, does not mean she is always performing a lesbian identity: she may, for instance, be focused on and interpreted as presenting a 'distinguished scientist' or a 'concerned mother' persona. The primary gender sort into male and female is sometimes said to be always relevant: on this view, socially intelligible personae are always gendered, whatever other properties they may have. How we might actually test this hypothesis is not obvious, but certainly gender attributions and claims are more or less salient in different situations, and it seems at least possible that they are sometimes completely irrelevant for some interactants.

Possible, but perhaps unlikely, or at least infrequent. For most people in most cultures, attributing maleness or femaleness to others and claiming such an identification for themselves happens early in life and continues to loom important in most interactions. And some linguistic systems make it more difficult than others to avoid attributing gender to those of whom one is speaking. In English when I use a pronoun to refer to a specific person other than myself or my addressee, it is very difficult to avoid making a gender attribution; furthermore, most though not all English first names also attribute gender to their bearers. In languages with grammatical gender and agreement conventions (e.g., Spanish, Hindi, and other Indo-European languages), there are further cases in which one would be hard put to avoid attributing gender to self or others. There is some slight evidence that kids can go longer ignoring gender attributions if their language is like Chinese or Finnish and does not force them to make them, but there are so many other ways to do gender work in most cultures that what difference such grammatical facts make is unclear. (See chapters 9 and 10, this volume, and also Boroditsky, Schmidt, and Webb, 2003, for evidence that grammatical gender has effects.)

In any case, identities are not put together simply by linking such independent identifications as gender, sexuality, ethnicity, socioeconomic status, occupation, and local origins. Rather, different dimensions of identity inflect one another: Crenshaw (1994) speaks of the "intersectionality" of gender and race, and part of her point is that what it means to be a woman depends on racial identity, and what it means to be, for example, African American, depends on gender identity. And of course these gendered racial or racialized gender identities depend on other features of identities and of situations in which people perform those identities. One of the reasons so-called identity politics has fallen out of favor in many circles was that too often this point was lost as, for example, affluent American women of European ancestry spoke on behalf of women in general, ignoring racism and class privilege among women, and African American men spoke on behalf of the entire African American population, ignoring sexism in their own homes and communities. Noting such problems, some African American feminists called themselves 'womanists', to emphasize the particularity of their struggle to confront both sexism and racism (and the ways they intertwine). They refused to let their identity as women trump their identity as African Americans or vice versa. Another stumbling block was the question of drawing boundaries: did bisexuals and transsexuals really share identities with gay men and lesbians? The move away from gay rights to queer politics emphasizes the fluidity of sexual identities. (See chapter 11, this book, for some discussion.) Nonetheless, invoking socially shared identities can be strategically useful and politically powerful sometimes. (See Appiah 2005.) And linguists and others find that attributed social identity does indeed affect how speech is interpreted, both its form and its content.

Socially recognized sexual identities and gender identities are experienced as 'embodied' and also by most not as fluid but as inescapable and permanent. With occupation or religion, for example, we can see the possibility of choices but not, for most people, with sexuality or gender. The 'work' we (and others) do to create and maintain our gender and our sexual identities is seldom recognized as such in part because it usually has little to do with *which* socially recognized identity will be claimed (or attributed by others). Rather, gender and sexual identity work most often involves *how* a particular socially recognized identity will be manifested and *when* and *where* it will matter to what we do, including what we say (and how we are interpreted, something we can never completely control).

Sexual and gender identities do not work in exactly the same way, of course. Sexual identity, even if experienced as both inevitable and persistent over time and from situation to situation, is less pervasively made manifest than gender identity: a woman who is a lesbian is highly likely to be recognized/categorized by others as a woman in most situations, whereas that same person may often encounter others with no sexual attributions made (or perhaps with heterosexuality covertly presumed, sometimes forcing people to 'come out' in situations where they do not especially want to). And it is also the case for many people that slotting themselves and others into socially recognized sexual identities comes much later than doing the same thing for gender identities, which are generally firmly in place even for three-year-olds. Nonetheless, giving substance to these and other abstract identities is a lifetime project.

Some folks undoubtedly have basic dispositions and early important experiences that make the process of shaping themselves in ways that make them intelligible to others and themselves *as* certain kinds of people apparently effortless. But although they "walk the walk and talk the talk" with no obvious difficulty, they are nonetheless doing identity work. Those who do not fit so readily into what is expected of them on the basis of initial gender attribution—for example, transgender and transsexual people, tomboys, sissies—just make identity work more strikingly visible.

3. From identities to ideologies and symbolic values

Early work in feminist linguistics (e.g., Lakoff 1975, reprinted in Lakoff and Bucholtz 2004 with new annotations by Lakoff and short commentaries from others) drew on such constructs as 'women's language' or 'feminine style'. And what has been called queer linguistics has invoked notions of 'gay English' (Leap 1996), or 'the gay male voice' (Smyth, Jacobs, and Rogers 2003; Smyth and Rogers 2008). But what do such labels mean? If, for example, the forms and usages brought together under the rubric 'women's language' are not used by all and only women (i.e., by all and only those who identify themselves and are identified by others as women), does it make sense to call them 'women's language'?

In recent years, many analysts have observed that 'women's language' and similar putatively identity-based constellations of linguistic usage have more to do with ideology and symbolism than with reliably indexing identities. Bucholtz and Hall (1995) make this point in an essay that presents Lakoff's work as widely misunderstood:

> The distinction between ideologies of language and actual linguistic practice continues to be neglected by many researchers. . . . Lakoff states quite clearly in her introduction that she is interested not in the quantitative realization of linguistic variables but in the cultural expectations that have come to influence their use. . . . The cultural expectations that Lakoff locates through her intuitions and observations reflect the ideologically dominant socialization process of middle-class European American women, the influence of which extends far beyond this subculture. (5–6)

Cameron (2000a, rpt. in Cameron 2006) makes a closely related point:

> However inaccurate it [the stereotypical lay notion of 'women's language']
> may be as an empirical description of the way women 'really' speak, and
> however unsatisfactory it may appear from the perspective of academic
> scholarship, this notion of 'women's language' provides a powerful symbolic
> 'meaning resource' for 'stylistic agents' to draw on. (123 in reprint version)

On this symbolic view, the gendered or sexualized semiotic value of
certain ways of speaking is not a matter of who might so speak but of
what effects such speech might produce—how it is heard and what
responses it elicits, for example.

Others, also recognizing the mismatch of stereotypical and normative
characterizations of the speech of particular groups with how members of
those groups actually speak, prefer to broaden and loosen the conception
of what counts as gendered or otherwise gender-inflected speech while
still taking its gendered value to arise directly from the gender attributed
to the person from whose mouth it issues. Some analysts seem to suggest
that one is always speaking *as* a gendered person, which might involve
performing dis-identification with the other gender. So Coates (2003, 37)
says, "[I]n telling a story, a male speaker is...performing *not* being a
woman." Sometimes indeed he is, but at other times he may be performing
being a hero or a parent or not being a dupe or some other identity he
assumes or rejects, with no particular gendered significance being attached
to his speech by him or his interlocutors. On what I will call the EXPANDED
INDEXICAL view of gendered talk, whatever way a particular group of men
(i.e., people claiming and being attributed the status of man) might speak
is (one variety of) 'men's talk' just as 'women's language' includes the
wide range of ways of speaking used by women (i.e., all those claiming
and being attributed the status of woman).

One reason the expanded indexical approach to gendered talk has
appealed to many feminist linguists is that it opens space for exploring
talk by all kinds of women, including those from subordinated social
groups (in the United States, e.g., Native Americans, African Americans,
Deaf users of American Sign Language; for examples, see contributions to
Bucholtz et al. 1999) or those who resist dominant cultural values,
including pervasive gender norms for speech and other activities (see, e.g.,
Bucholtz's 1999 study of girls who adopt a 'geek' or 'nerd' identity). It is
certainly valuable to have access to a much fuller range of actual girls' and
women's linguistic practices, and feminist linguistics has helped increase
the visibility—and, importantly, audibility—of a far wider range of female
voices than attended to by previous linguistic research, which had tended
to focus not only on some ethnic and class groups but also, within those
groups, on men.

At the same time, the linguistic practices characteristic of some
particular group of women or girls in the contexts of certain activities
might play little or no role in their performances *as* women or girls. This
is possible even if gender identities are omnirelevant because it is not only

language that informs people's identity work—clothing, bodily postures, facial expressions, voice quality, as well as other features of the discourse situation (what speech activities people are engaged in, e.g.) can all help override what might otherwise be heard as 'masculine' speech or can give 'feminine' value to performances whose strictly linguistic features might be heard as gender-neutral from other mouths or in other situations. So, although it is certainly important for feminist linguistics to highlight the wide range of linguistic practices engaged in by female language users and to amplify the voices of women who have been marginalized, I would argue that 'women's language' becomes an empty notion if anything any woman says is included under that rubric.

Even when it is focused on the role language plays in people's identity work, feminist linguistics need not confine itself to the study of gendered language in the global sense. Beyond such identities as mother or actress or ballerina or nun, which are themselves gendered, there are many other identities like professor, comedian, factory worker, missionary, and the like that gendered people claim and many situated roles like interviewer or guest that they assume. In many cases, their talk as occupants of these identities may itself carry little or no gendered meaning. I will speak of gendered language only if there are specific linguistic practices associated with specific gendered identities or if nongendered identities and roles are linguistically performed in gender-specific ways. In such cases, however, we do not have what might be called globally gendered language as the gendered meaning is inextricably caught up with the other social meanings involved. 'Motherese', for example, is gendered, but we can not equate it with speaking 'as a mother' because not only do some mothers avoid it even when acting parentally but it is also audience-specific, implying a child as recipient. And, of course, linguistic styles may be indirectly gendered via their association with particular activities (e.g., child care) or interactional stances (e.g., sociability) that are themselves gendered (via ideology, stereotypes, or observation). (This possibility is mentioned in chapter 2, this book, and also figures prominently in chapter 6 on intonation; Elinor Ochs 1992 later made the same point and dubbed this possibility the INDIRECT INDEXING of gender through linguistic choices.)

But then should feminist linguistics simply abandon the notion of globally gendered linguistic practices? Consider again the ideological or symbolic view of 'women's language', 'guy talk', 'gayspeak'—identity-linked constructs. Certain kinds of linguistic practices have been interpreted in particular cultural and historical contexts in ways that evoke norms and ideologies of gender and sexual identity and relations. At the same time, the symbolic identity-linked value they have thus acquired can be exploited by those who are not thereby claiming the identities to which they are ideologically linked. For example, components of the 'women's language' described in Lakoff (1975) are sometimes drawn on and used by those whose own claimed and attributed identities do not match that symbolically associated with those linguistic resources: white, middle-class heterosexual American women who defer to men in many contexts and who embody ideals of female 'politeness' and concern for others in their personal lives, of female disempowerment in the public sphere. This can be for playacting purposes, like the workers on the sexual fantasy lines pitched to male heterosexual callers that Hall (1995) describes. It can be for entertainment value, perhaps to parody the 'ideal woman' so evoked and the gender ideology she might represent. Queen (1997) analyzes the speech of lesbian comic strip characters. She suggests that these characters sometimes draw on stereotypical features of women's speech either to mock or distance themselves from the kind of heterosexual woman canonically associated with those features ("I don't speak spritch. Now stand still so I can count the bubbles in your head," 243, fig. 13.4). They sometimes also use it affirmatively, however, perhaps making gentle fun of themselves (swooping down on a resting cat, "oh my god she's so cute I can't stand her," with typography indicating a 'gushy' sort of delivery, 251, fig. 13.12). Barrett (1997), in a study of the "homo-genius" speech of African American drag queens, argues that the performers whom he observed drew on Lakoff-style "respectable straight white lady" speech and other stylistic elements (e.g., African American Vernacular English and features associated with gay male speech) to present personae that brought together their identities as gay men, African Americans, and drag queens.

On the symbolic/ideological view of 'women's language', 'gayspeak', and other identity-linked linguistic styles, many (indeed most) of those claiming the identity in question might use the style seldom if ever and others might adopt the style in certain situations in order to evoke the identity without thereby claiming or asserting it. The style itself has acquired a social meaning that goes well beyond indexing a gender identity. The more general point is that the significance of language for gender and sexuality is not confined to indexing identities, whether directly or indirectly. Language plays a key role in creating and sustaining (and sometimes challenging and changing) all of the varied kinds of beliefs and practices that inform gender and sexual identities, relations, practices, and ideologies. This is because language is meaningful: we use it to do things with one another, to 'do' gender and sexuality as well as much more.

4. Two levels of meaning

As noted earlier, we can speak of two levels of meaning: CONTENT (the message expressed) and STYLE (the personae presented, the attitudes assumed toward others and toward the content), what I am calling SOCIAL/STYLISTIC MEANING. The linguistic subfields of semantics and pragmatics in which I was trained focus on content meaning—roughly, what is being spoken of or about. Semantics deals with meanings of morphemes—

words and other basic expressions (e.g., affixes)—and with the systematic effects that assembling morphemes into more complex expressions have on what those more complex expressions mean. Pragmatics has focused primarily on the ways in which the utterance context can contribute to content meaning or can help the interpreter see that the overt message expressed is distinct from what the speaker intends to convey. What is actually conveyed depends on interpretation, however, and speakers may not always succeed in their communicative aims (see sec. 5 below).

Social/stylistic meaning is sometimes said to be about *how* content is expressed, the formal properties of the language used to convey the basic message, *what* is expressed. Narrowly construed, the *how* is generally held to include matters of pronunciation, word and syntactic choice (and even language choice in multilingual communities), and perhaps also some less clearly linguistic features such as tempo, volume, pitch, and voice quality. Social/stylistic meaning in this narrow sense characterizes individual utterances and, when general patterns are considered, individual speakers. It is useful, however, to broaden our horizons to think about interruption, amount of speech, and other aspects of conversational dynamics: here we can see interactional styles and can appreciate that *how* can be a more collaborative and genuinely social notion than is often realized. Sociolinguistic studies of phonological or morphosyntactic variation and work in discourse and conversation analysis all have contributed to under-standing social/stylistic meaning (see, e.g., Eckert and Rickford 2001) in both the narrow and the broader senses. And, of course, social/stylistic meaning is informed by accompaniments to speech such as participants' clothing, make-up, posture, gaze, facial expression. (For written materials, we have illustrations, fonts, layout, bindings, and the like to supplement linguistic expressions. Computer-assisted communication sometimes has graphics of various kinds as well as fonts, emoticons, and other devices to supplement language proper.)

It is tempting to equate identity work with the social/stylistic level of meaning, but content can also figure in the personae we project or in the ideologies surrounding our identities. 'Ladies' don't talk about sex or (on some versions of the ideology) about politics or religion or anything pos-sibly controversial; 'real' men don't discuss household decor or recipes for quiche or their feelings. On the other hand, talk about sports may help establish credentials for dealing in such traditionally masculine domains as politics. And, conversely, many feminist linguists have argued that styles affect our success in conveying content. Lakoff (1975), for example, argued that women were handicapped in making their way in the public world if they adopted 'women's language', being unable to make their points forcefully and effectively. And many less feminist sources are still proposing that young women undermine their own credibility by using discourse particles such as *like* and *y'know* and by ending many affirmative statements with a rising intonation, so-called uptalk. In fact, many young men share these stylistic tendencies with their sisters, but the stereotypes and the criticism focus on female speakers (Valley Girl talk, e.g.). It may be that young women do engage in some of these practices more than young men (because they are differently situated in the social world), but not only do commentators typically ignore the range of goals these practices might be serving but their evaluation of the practices seems to depend more on beliefs about those whom they take to be the canonical practitioners than on any speaker-neutral assessment.

5. Communities of practice: Local and imagined

As is implied by the examples with which I began, language use is never just that but is always part and parcel of nonlinguistic activities and purposes. In our book on gender and language (Eckert and McConnell-Ginet 2003), Stanford sociolinguist Penelope Eckert and I argue for grounding the study of language and gender in investigations of social practice, with special attention to local COMMUNITIES OF PRACTICE (CsofP). Local CsofP are groups whose members regularly engage with one another face to face (or, perhaps, keyboard to keyboard in online CsofP!) in various activities centered around some goals, often only very loosely defined. Not all members need interact with all others but they must orient to one another and hold one another 'accountable' in some not very precisely defined way. The basic arguments for taking CsofP as central to language and gender studies were first presented in some detail in Eckert and McConnell-Ginet 1992a and, more briefly, in Eckert and McConnell-Ginet 1992b (chapter 5, this book; chapter 7, also coauthored with Penny Eckert, both applies and further develops our ideas about how CsofP are relevant for thinking about matters of gender and language).

Like most people, I belong or have belonged to a number of different CsofP. My workplace CofP has for more than three decades centered on the Cornell University linguistics department—its students, faculty, and support staff and various activities bringing some or all of those people together. (Being now officially retired, my 'form of membership' has changed in that CofP, and connections with linguists, philosophers, and publishers elsewhere are as or more important to my working life.) My domestic CofP now centers around my husband and me, though our children (now with their own spouses and children) could still be considered members, though relatively peripheral at this stage because of the distances that preclude regular interaction of the sort we had back when I first began my career as a feminist linguist. At Cornell, I have also been involved in a CofP that centers on the feminist, gender, and sexuality studies program, FGSS, which we pronounce 'FIGS'. And I have been very active in the work of the Linguistic Society of America; that LSA-centered CofP includes officers and other members of the society's executive committee and of the society more generally as well as the society's paid staff. Over the years, I've participated on a regular basis in political action groups, drama and music performance groups, yoga classes, and the like (even Sunday school when I was a child who had not yet renounced religion). I am now involved in a prison-education program, where I work with Cornell graduates and undergraduates and with men incarcerated in a nearby maximum security facility, and I also serve on the board of a regional theater, which allows me to participate in some rather different CsofP. There are also various friendship groups, some overlapping, in which I participate—some frequently, in others less often. And so on. Each reader can come up with similar lists.

In each CofP, practices develop, including linguistic practices. Taking the Cornell linguistics department as an example, I can note that virtually all graduate students are on a mutual first-name basis with faculty and with staff but the situation is more variable with undergraduate majors. There are also certain shorthand expressions that those entering the CofP learn: for example, the acronym CLC designates the Cornell Linguistics Circle, a grad student-run organization that sponsors departmental talks and social events, and there are many others, many not restricted to Cornell but used in the wider linguistic community as well (e.g., *LabPhon, DP, QR*). There is also, of course, a lot of unshortened technical vocabulary (*choice function, adjunction site, floating tone*), including many special uses of ordinary terminology. Being in the know about such expressions is a mark of 'full' membership for students and faculty in the CofP: a friend of mine in a new job in a larger and more complex organization than my department sometimes complains about the many acronyms her new colleagues assume she is familiar with. In well-established and smoothly functioning CsofP like my department there is often joking and also talk of shared past events; stories about the community's past can be evoked by a short tag ("the time we faced down the dean") and may become resources for interpreting current developments.

And people bring news of other CsofP: for example, I regularly exchange with the administrative staff little tidbits about our respective offspring, and my students often talk with me about problems with parents or with their romantic partners. Sometimes this is just a little perfunctory small talk before we turn to our work talk, but sometimes it is more substantial. Outside work hours, I get together socially with some of my colleagues, mostly with other faculty members but occasionally with staff or students. A workplace-centered CofP is likely to involve more multidimensional kinds of relations and interactions as well as more different forms of membership than a CofP like my Sunday morning yoga class that is in contact less frequently and with purposes less central to participants' lives.

Arguably much of sociolinguistic variation (alternative ways of saying 'the same thing') and, more generally, of social/stylistic meaning arises when people negotiate their positions and their personae as they participate in the various local CsofP to which they belong. Eckert (2003), Bucholtz (2002), and others have argued that late childhood and adolescence are especially salient times for people's developing personae and the linguistic features that characterize them, and for most people this is certainly the stage at which certain phonetic and grammatical features of their speech are likely to stabilize. Families still matter at this stage, but neighborhood, and school-based CsofP are usually even more important, at least in the United States. Matthews (2005) discusses the centrality of schools in many U.S. teens' experience—family arguably continues to be very important for the long term in some other cultural settings, and the significance of schools is also quite variable cross-culturally. Although the young are indeed more linguistically flexible than mature adults, linguistic adaptation to new CsofP or to changes in an ongoing CofP continues throughout life. Even the 'elderly' (those, like me, over 60) can develop somewhat new personae as they participate in new CsofP or assume different roles (forms of membership) in familiar CsofP. Still, as noted in several places throughout this book (see, e.g., the speculations in chapter 4), some verbal habits (both of production and of interpretation) may be hard to shift even when circumstances might make language users want to do so.

It is also possible to speak of more global CsofP whose members don't connect directly to one another. In many cases, these more diffuse CsofP might be better conceived as what political theorist Benedict Anderson (1983) has dubbed IMAGINED COMMUNITIES—for example, 'the linguistic community' or 'the feminist community' or 'the lesbian community' or nation-based 'communities' such as the United States or Morocco or Japan. Such relatively large imagined communities are often loci for dominant ideologies that feed ideas about gender, sexual orientation, and other categories that connect to the various socially recognized identities people claim and attribute to others (linguist, feminist, American, Greek, woman) and also connect to social institutions (e.g., family, religious institutions, schools, law, government, corporations). Recent work on ideologies of language in Japan (see the contributions to Okamoto and Shibamoto Smith 2004 as well as Inoue 2006) explores implications not only for the phenomenon of 'women's language' in Japanese but also for encoding content relevant to gender and sexuality.

Large and relatively diffuse imagined communities host many of what we think of as the linguistic 'conventions' that underlie the expression of content in our messages, both overt and covert. Institutions like schools, publishing companies, and dictionaries operate at relatively global levels to regulate linguistic practice at local levels though never with perfect success. For example, the word *rape* was once defined legally and in dictionaries so that it applied only to a man's penetrating a woman who is not his wife, but social change and activism have resulted in English users now speaking of both marital rape and rape of men. (See McConnell-Ginet 2006 for this example and for more extensive discussion of ongoing debates over the institution of marriage and definitions of *marriage*.) Prescriptions to use *he* and *man* to speak of people of both sex classes are losing their force (though generic masculines do still exist in some contexts), and singular *they* is widening its range in spite of continuing strictures against it. (See, e.g., chapter 9, this book.) Much of the regulation of both style and content, what Cameron (1995) calls VERBAL HYGIENE, links to ideologies and to what some linguists have called social or cultural 'discourses' that cut across local CsofP and are associated with more global imagined communities. At the same time, these global linguistic and sociocultural forces affect individuals in local CsofP and ultimately are affected and changed by actions in local CsofP (as well as by more organized global efforts).

A central question that my semantic-pragmatic research addresses is the link between, on the one hand, these more global discourses and the meanings and inferences they license and, on the other hand, concretely situated interactive discourses and the meanings generated in them, both content and style. (Chapter 8, this book, illustrates this project most clearly, though the other chapters in part III are also relevant.)

6. Content meaning and communicative effect

Issues of speaker and hearer identities and relations were mainly ignored in semantics and pragmatics as I first encountered them, assumed to be completely irrelevant. Language users were taken to be interchangeable for purposes of understanding what they and the expressions they produced and interpreted mean. If we are interested in what an English sentence like *snow is white* means and how its parts combine to produce that meaning, this may be adequate. It may also do if we are interested in understanding how it is that an English sentence like *it is raining* is understood as conveying essentially the message expressed more explicitly by *it is raining here* and not, for example, saying that somewhere it is now raining. Or if we want to understand how *she got a job and moved to Wyoming* implies that her getting the job preceded her move unless we go on to say something like *but not in that order*.

If we are trying, however, to understand something about the import of using *he* and *him* for both masculine and sex-indefinite referents (chapter 9) or why there are so many more words designating women than designating men that acquire implications linked to sexuality (see discussion of *hussy*, once 'housewife', in chapter 8), then we really do need to think about who is saying what in which context and for which purposes. Interlocutors' communicative success is closely tied to power, prestige, ideologies, and background assumptions of various kinds, matters central to social/stylistic (including interactional) meaning. It was not until I realized that semantic/pragmatic dimensions of the interaction of language with gender and sexuality could be understood only by seeing social/stylistic meaning as influencing and influenced by content meaning that I began to apply some of my own linguistic training to the significance of content meaning in this arena. "The sexual (re)production of meaning," chapter 8 in this book, is my first attempt to articulate explicitly a theoretical account of some of the connections between stylistic and content meaning.

In thinking about the mutual influences of the two levels of meaning— of the message conveyed and the personae between whom it is communicated—there are several semantic/pragmatic concepts I have found particularly useful. One is the notion of CONVERSATIONAL IMPLICATURE, originating in the work of philosopher Paul Grice (see the essays in Grice 1989) but adopted and adapted by many linguists working in pragmatic theory. The example above about getting the job and moving to Wyoming illustrates that one can systematically convey more than what is said. As Grice said, interpreters expect that speakers have good reasons for what they are saying and the way they are saying it. In addition to knowledge of the literal linguistic meanings of what is said, the interpreter, Grice suggests, uses some general default principles (in this case, perhaps something along the lines of "assume that events are related in the order in which they occur") to guide interpretation to additional (or even different) possible content. Similarly, some woman might say "I'm not dating any man at the moment" and mean that she has been dating some man or men previously. Grice did build in the intended audience of an utterance, though he never exploited its full social significance. For some audiences, perhaps for most readers of this essay, "I'm not dating any man at the moment" might, given a suitable speaker, imply the possibility that the speaker is dating a woman now. Liang (1999) discusses examples of this sort and talks about a speaker's being able to mean different things to different hearers.

The dating example illustrates the further important notion of PRESUPPOSITION. The speaker and hearer may both simply assume—presuppose— that dating is between a man and a woman and thus never entertain at all the possibility of the speaker's dating a woman. But a hearer who is alert to the possibility of same-sex dating may interpret what is said differently. There are many background assumptions conveyed as such without people being consciously attuned to what is happening. Consider someone who tells a child "You'll understand better when you get married." The utterer is presupposing that the child will marry (and probably also presupposing that the marriage will be to someone of the other gender). The presupposition that marriage will happen is triggered by *when*—its linguistic meaning tips us off. In contrast, any presuppositions about the heterosexual nature of marriage or dating are buried in conceptions of marriage and dating. Such conceptions may be triggered by the words *marriage* and *dating* but whether or not they are part of the linguistic meaning of these words is a contentious matter. In McConnell-Ginet (2006), I discuss definitional debates over the word *marriage* and the institution of marriage, and in chapter 11 of this volume I explore the meaning of *queer* and other labels for sexual minorities, developing the idea that content words are relatively empty of linguistic meaning and thus often become sites for ideological conflict. Because ideas about gender and sexuality are often presupposed, seldom explicitly asserted, and thus hard to challenge, presupposition and the sometimes contentious status of word meanings are very important for understanding such ideas and for contesting them.

Notice that the person who says "You'll understand better when you get married" might quite honestly deny having given any conscious thought to assumptions about the addressee's getting married. The assumption that marriage is inevitable is so far in the background that it operates below the level of conscious monitoring, making it all the more likely to affect what is said and how without people's noticing. At the same time, even a person who is sincere about not having thought explicitly about the presumptive inevitability of marriage is likely to agree that it would be very odd indeed to say "You may not get married but you'll understand better when you do [get married]." Once the possibility that marriage won't happen is laid on the table, an *if* is needed rather than a *when*. Choosing *when* rather than *if* is the surface linguistic symptom of assumptions that may never have been articulated consciously by many (perhaps even most) of those who have them. Hearers may pick up on the assumption, again without really even noticing that they are doing so.

A speaker's intentions certainly do matter for what content she or he means to convey, but actual success in that project is by no means guaranteed. Here is an example from relatively recent history that was widely reported and discussed a few years ago. On January 14, 2005, Lawrence Summers, then president of Harvard University, spoke at a small conference where he said the following:

> There are three broad hypotheses about the sources of the very substantial disparities...in the presence of women [as compared to men] in high-end scientific professions. One...is what I call the high-powered job hypothesis. The second is what I would call different availability of aptitude at the high end, and the third is what I would call different socialization and patterns of discrimination in a search. And in my own view, their importance probably ranks in exactly th[is] order.

Much of Summers's talk then emphasized women's reluctance to commit themselves to jobs requiring some eighty hours weekly—a not unusual time commitment for high-level research faculty at the top U.S. universities—and possible genetic bases of a sex-differentiated pool of scientific talent, with some speculation that there might also be genetic bases for sex-differentiated 'taste' for, say, child care. And he downplayed talk about socialization and discrimination as helping to explain the considerable existing sex differences in men's and women's visibility at the top of scientific professions. It is pretty clear, I think, that he did not *intend* to convey the message that no or virtually no woman could be an outstanding scientist or mathematician nor even that the 'average' man in science or mathematics is more gifted than the 'average' woman in those fields. At the same time, it is clear that many people understood him to be insulting women scientists and mathematicians and saying to girls and young women, "You might as well give up any ambitions you have to excel in mathematics or science." Many people also took him to be suggesting that there is no point to efforts to reduce biases against women in these areas or to develop programs that encourage women who show mathematical or scientific talents and interests to pursue them.

Not surprisingly, reports of Summers's comments triggered an avalanche of indignant response, and he quickly issued a number of statements vigorously denying that he intended either an insult to women in the sciences or discouragement to girls and women aspiring to become scientists. (Ultimately, he resigned his position, but that outcome is not my focus here.) Assuming the sincerity of these denials, does Summers's lack of such intentions automatically settle the question of whether he deserves blame for insults or discouragement? Although we might well agree that he did not 'mean' to insult or discourage, he could still be held responsible for having produced such effects. We could point, as many women in sciences did, to the long and continuing history of roadblocks to women in these fields, of active opposition and resistance to those who did try to make their way, and of subtler forms of discouragement that contribute to men's overwhelming dominance in this area (see chapter 12, this volume). Noting Summers's position as the head of one of the most prestigious universities in the United States, we could also argue that he should have had a far better appreciation than he showed of the forces that have hindered women's achievement in the sciences and should also have realized how his comments might be interpreted, especially by people who have themselves experienced discrimination and discouragement and also by those who have a deeper understanding than he of the complexities of the research on sex-based variability in aptitudes. The critical question is not whether there is or is not some genetic reason that more men than women might display great aptitude for scientific inquiry: as one woman scientist put it, "What about those girls whose problem with math is that they are too good at it?"

Apparently Summers himself eventually accepted at least some responsibility for the interpretations others placed on his comments. In a letter to the Harvard community on January 19, 2005, he said,

> As the careers of a great many distinguished women scientists make plain, the human potential to excel in science is not somehow the province of one gender or another. It is a capacity shared by girls and boys, by women and men, and we must do all we can to nurture, develop, and recognize it, along with other vital talents. That includes carefully avoiding stereotypes, being alert to forms of subtle discrimination, and doing everything we can to remove obstacles to success. . . . I was wrong to have spoken in a way that has resulted in an unintended signal of discouragement to talented girls and women.

And on February 17, he sent a further letter to the Harvard faculty accompanying the released transcript of the actual comments he had made at the January 14 meeting:

> My January remarks substantially understated the impact of socialization and discrimination, including implicit attitudes—patterns of thought to which all of us are unconsciously subject. The issue of gender difference is far more complex than comes through in my comments, and my remarks about variability went beyond what the research has established.... It is vital that we aggressively implement policies that will encourage girls and women to pursue science at the highest levels, and that we welcome and support them in our faculty ranks.

What Summers himself initially meant was (arguably) different from how he was interpreted, but, as he himself later acknowledged, those interpretations were not unreasonable: the content of his original message was quickly challenged and expanded on in ways that he apparently came to see were warranted. Of course, people may lie or deceive themselves about what they meant—what content they intended to communicate—but even speakers who are honest about their meaning intentions can come to see that those intentions were problematic because they ought not to have expected others to recognize them. Summers ought to have foreseen that many people would interpret his message as insulting and discouraging. Intentions are not irrelevant to the content of an utterance, but they don't settle all questions of what we might dub its DISCURSIVE MEANING, its full communicative significance, which is linked to responses and further developments in the larger discourse where its impact is felt[2]. Of course, Summers's remarks had far more impact than the same comments from someone in a different position might have had. Summers might have wanted to inhabit a social persona that did not have the privileges or the responsibilities that come with presidency of Harvard, but he could not reasonably intend to do that in the context of a conference of academics.

7. Social/stylistic meaning, capacities, and authenticity

There is even less agreement about meaning at the social/stylistic level than at the content level, many more possibilities for alternative interpretations, and much less explicit awareness of the symbolic value of resources used. How I pronounce my vowels may index my childhood origins as well as various social affiliations, but few have an explicit understanding of such details. And I am seldom aware of the precise details of my syntactic or even my lexical choices, much less of my intonation, my speech rhythms and volume, my voice quality. Nonetheless any and all of these details may enter into the social persona I construct in a particular interaction—that is, what you may infer about the kind of person I am (or purport to be) from my speech. You too are probably unaware at any explicit level what it is about my speech that leads you to take me as pretentious or unassuming, as friendly or cold, as educated or unschooled, as politically conservative or progressive, as trustworthy or unreliable.

Social/stylistic meaning is more constrained than content meaning in the following sense. Any fluent speaker of a language can express essentially any message she chooses—some messages might not be believed or have the other desired effects or they might shock her hearers, but, assuming adequate linguistic knowledge, there are no barriers in her basic capacities to expressing any content. There are, however, substantial barriers to enacting social personae. No matter how much I might want to do so, there are personae I cannot enact because I lack the requisite dramatic talents—and no matter what my dramatic talents, it would be very hard indeed for me to enact certain personae face to face because of my physical size and appearance (and my only hope in doing so would be excellent makeup and the like, not something I could readily manage at a moment's notice in a particular encounter).

As Kira Hall's (1995) research with phone sex workers shows, people with some dramatic skills can in fact vocally enact personae very different from those they most commonly project in their private lives, including enacting those claiming a different gender or different sexual orientation from what they claim for themselves away from these performances, in their off-the-job 'real' lives. All of the operators Hall interviewed prided themselves on successfully performing heterosexually desirable female personae (for the benefit of the presumptively heterosexual male callers), yet some of the operators in their personal lives did not identify as heterosexual and one identified himself as a bisexual, Mexican American man. Hall coins the term CROSSTALKING as a linguistic analogue to the sartorial 'cross-dressing' that switches gender cues. None of the operators saw themselves as simply 'doing what comes naturally': even those who claimed female identities in their personal lives performed very different female identities on the phone, identities that they thought would appeal to the man on the other end of the line. Often they had a number of characters they assumed, with different ethnic and racial backgrounds. Good actors can make you believe in multiple, very different personae: in the film *Angels in America*, actor Meryl Streep plays two very different women and one old man, and there is even a scene in which two of her different characters are shown talking to one another. She is convincing: I did not realize she was in all these roles until I saw the credits. But Meryl Streep is a person of unusual acting talent: most of us have a much narrower range of personae available to us and fewer available face to face than over a phone line, where appearance becomes a non-issue. Well, almost a non-issue. Services that target phone sex at a straight male audience often advertise using pictures that show voluptuous women, seductively (un)clothed and posed. When Hall told one of her neighbors about her research and mentioned that the operators were usually hired by employers who had not actually seen them, he responded, "What? You mean it's all a scam?" (213 n. 19).

In contexts like fantasy phone services or night club acts or films, many people do expect 'acting'—they are not surprised by a disjuncture between the personae projected in the acting contexts and those projected by the actor in 'offstage' encounters. But in everyday encounters, there is often distrust of anything that looks like acting and a strong belief by many that they are not 'doing' anything but just being themselves, acting 'naturally' or 'authentically'. In many cultural contexts, someone seen as 'inauthentic' is likely to be labeled a 'poser' or a 'phony'. Laura Miller (2004) discusses Japanese women's 'doing *burrido*', feigning a kind of helpless immaturity and vulnerability via a style that uses extremely high pitch and other hyperfeminine speech strategies. Because the women drop this style when there are no men to impress, they are criticized for their pretense. Such style shifting is less likely to be criticized in some contexts than others. Miyako Inoue (2006, ch. 6) notes that a couple of the women she got to know while doing ethnographic work in a Japanese corporation eschewed honorifics and so-called women's language utterance-final particles in talk with male peers and with one another but produced them flawlessly when representing their company on the phone to unknown callers. Less dramatically perhaps but nonetheless quite noticeably, many people shift styles when turning from talk with family to a phone conversation with a relatively superficial social acquaintance. Which of a person's many ways of speaking is the natural, authentic one? The line between authenticity and inauthenticity cannot always be drawn.

In the case of language, authenticity is often ideologically tied to origins: someone who grew up working class can be viewed as deceptive if her speech sounds upper class. Insistence on 'authenticity' provides a way for patrolling certain boundaries: outsiders who do not have the right credentials are viewed with suspicion if they do indeed "talk the talk and walk the walk." More generally, folks are expected to talk (and walk and dress and pick cars and meals and music and...) like others with whom they share certain socially significant dimensions of identity: residence during the formative primary and grade school years, ethnicity, social class, gender categorization. (Age also enters in, though of course one is expected to move through different age groups over the life span.) And certain kinds of talk are viewed as coming 'naturally' from people with certain identities. For example, Cameron (2000a, 2000b) discovered that the sort of synthetic 'friendly' tone (a 'smile' in the voice) managers would like employees at call centers to use is thought to issue with no effort at all from women. Just how much work such a tone in that work situation requires of both women and men is grossly underestimated. That many women may find its production a bit easier than most men would is probably due in part to all the practice they have under their belts. Their unsmiling girl selves heard adults say "You are so much prettier when you smile" or "No boy likes to see a frown like that," threatening heterosexual failure as the price of a smileless face, and they eventually were habituated to smiling no matter what their feelings might be, habits that some of us grown women might like to eliminate but cannot. That smile does have an effect on the shape of the vocal tract and thus the sound of the voice.

We tend to think of ourselves and others as more or less stable and consistent individuals. Even though everyone does perform somewhat different personae in different situations (no one always offers a smile to the world), we and those with whom we interact expect a certain coherence among these personae on many dimensions. And in certain cultural contexts, there is considerable investment in the assumption not just of relative stability but of a kind of rigidity that does not recognize that people might well want or need to change in various ways, sometimes temporarily and sometimes for much longer periods. In the 2004 U.S. presidential elections, George Bush scored points by projecting the image of an unchanging persona, of someone who is the same in every context, whereas John Kerry was criticized for 'flip-flopping', for sometimes changing his mind or behaving in somewhat different ways in different contexts. There are stereotypes and ideologies about women as 'changeable' and 'indirect', focused on how others view them rather than on being their 'real' selves, men as fixed like rocks in their positions and straightforward, always saying just what they mean and behaving as they want, no matter what the circumstances. Of course, deliberately misleading or deceiving others about yourself can be problematic: the spy or double agent is the classic example. But as "The Waltz," a lovely short story by Dorothy Parker (1933), illustrates, 'double lives' are often less about deception than about competing pressures and desires. The story consists of the 'inner' (unvoiced) thoughts and the 'outer' (voiced) speech of a young woman moving around the dance floor with a male partner (unheard).[3] The inner voice constantly complains about the man's dancing abilities and the general experience, fervently wishing for an end to the awful episode: "Get off my instep, you hulking peasant! What do you think I am, anyway, a gangplank?" and "I've been locked in his noxious embrace for the thirty-five years this waltz has lasted. Is that orchestra never going to stop playing? Or must this obscene travesty of a dance go on until hell burns out?" In counterpoint, her partner hears her outer voice say, "No, of course it didn't hurt. Why it didn't a bit. Honestly. And it was all my fault" and "I'd like to go on like this forever." The music stops and the inner voice exults "in my ears there is a silence like the sound of angel voices" but then he hears "they've stopped, the mean things…Oh, do you think they would…if you gave them fifty dollars?…I'd simply adore to go on waltzing." The young woman is 'trapped' by her vulnerability, her incapacity to pay the heavy social (and life) price of refusing an eligible young man's overtures. Her 'real' self is created from an array of personae, more complex and conflicted than either the inner or outer voices suggest.

Few think of themselves as 'performing' a gender identity because they do not experience themselves as choosing gender as one might choose whether or not to wear jeans a particular day. As Butler puts it, gender PERFORMATIVITY does not mean that gender identity is 'voluntaristic'. Nonetheless, within a certain range we do make stylistic choices and to a considerable extent we do so strategically. At the same time, there is a considerable constraining force that is at least partly the result of what French sociologist Pierre Bourdieu dubbed HABITUS, the ways of speaking and moving and generally being in the world that we develop early in life and which become virtually hardwired into our brains and muscles. And, as Parker's "The Waltz" suggests so brilliantly, there are also powerful social and ideological constraints as well as constraints that follow from one's general dispositions and capacities.

Gender performativity does not mean that I am any freer to intend to enact a male persona in the middle of a conversation with a friend than I am to intend to conduct our conversation in Greek: neither is a genuine possibility for me, even though both might be options I would like to have. What gender performativity does mean is that even though I settled early and relatively easily into a female gender identity (even though greatly disliking and trying to reject some of the expectations that identity seemed to bring with it at various stages of my life), and even though much of the social/stylistic meaning others infer from my linguistic performance is far beyond my intentional control, I can still make choices about the kinds of personae I will enact, and there is stylistic meaning that I can (and sometimes do) intentionally convey through my linguistic choices.

Approaching gender and sexuality as social constructions, as I and many other feminist and queer linguists now do, does not preclude the possibility of considering their possible biological dimensions. There may well be various kinds of constraints that biology places on the range of personae individuals will opt to enact, which includes, of course, the tastes they adopt and the activities they pursue. I am just too short (and lacking in athletic talent) to be (or have been) a professional basketball player. But beyond those individual factors, there were obstacles to any young woman of my pre-Title 9 generation taking basketball very seriously as a life choice: there were few teams even at high school levels for girls, and the rules confined players to one side of the center line, making the game far less demanding and also far less interesting than the male version. There are virtually always substantial social and cultural factors that push people in certain directions.

As species go, humans are not strongly sexually bimorphic. On almost every trait studied, there is, even in today's world, considerable crossover in the sexual distribution of these traits. It is true, for example, that, on average, men are taller than women. This statistical truth does not, however, allow us to claim confidently that for any man-woman pair the man will be taller. Nor does it explain why taller men are coupled with shorter women at a rate higher than would be predicted by height-random heterosexual pairings or why people tend to overestimate men's heights and underestimate women's. Heights do show statistical sex differentiation, but what is more interesting is how height is socially and culturally interpreted.

Social psychologist Virginia Valian (1998) cites a number of studies showing that people tend to notice phenomena that confirm stereotypes and ideologies and to ignore or downplay those that might threaten them. Such findings should make us somewhat wary of anecdotal observations of the linguistic practices of women and men, gays and straight folks. Biology does matter, but in thinking about the interaction of language with gender and sexuality, the biological fact that humans are social and meaning-making creatures may ultimately prove far more important than reproductive or sexual biology.

Notes

1. Here and elsewhere, I sometimes use the conventionally plural *they/them/their* with singular reference in order to avoid gender-specificity.

2. Controversy over the statements Summers made was still alive as this book was going to press. On June 7, 2010, John Tierney in a New York *Times* piece, "Daring to discuss women in science," suggests Summers was badly misunderstood and that new data support the view that men as a group have more aptitude for math and science than women. Responses to the piece were very interesting, some doubting the relevance of the studies cited, others noting that statistical tendencies do not license conclusions about individuals, and still others joining Tierney in defense of Summers's claim that the relative paucity of women in the sciences is to be explained mainly by their lesser capacity and interest.

3. Treichler (1981) first drew my attention to Parker's story.

References

Anderson, Benedict (1983). *Imagined communities: Reflections on the origin and spread of nationalism*. London: Verso.

Appiah, Kwame Anthony (2005). *The ethics of identity*. Princeton, NJ: Princeton University Press.

Barrett, Rusty (1997). The 'homo-genius' speech community. In Kira Hall and Anna Livia (eds.), *Queerly phrased: Language, gender and sexuality*. New York: Oxford University Press. 181–232.

Bergvall, Victoria L., Janet M. Bing, and Alice F. Freed (eds.) (1996). *Rethinking language and gender research: Theory and practice*. London and New York: Longman.

Boroditsky, Lera, Lauren Schmidt, and Webb Phillips (2003). Sex, syntax, and semantics. In Dedre Gentner and Susan Goldin-Meadow (eds.), *Language in mind: Advances in the study of language and thought*. Cambridge, MA: MIT Press.

Bourdieu, Pierre (1977). *Outline of a theory of practice*. Cambridge: Cambridge University Press.

———— (1991). *Language and symbolic power*. Cambridge, MA: Harvard University Press.

Brown, Gillian, and George Yule (1983). *Discourse analysis*. Cambridge: Cambridge University Press.

Bucholtz, Mary (1999). "Why be normal?": Language and identity practices in a community of nerd girls. *Language in Society* 28: 203–224.

—— (2002). Youth and cultural practice. *Annual Review of Anthropology* 31: 525–552.

Bucholtz, Mary, and Kira Hall (1995). Introduction: Twenty years after *Language and woman's place*. In Hall and Bucholtz, 1–24.

—— (2004). Theorizing identity in language and sexuality research. *Language in Society* 33(4), 469–515.

Bucholtz, Mary, A. D. Liang, and Laurel A. Sutton (1999). *Reinventing identities: The gendered self in discourse*. New York: Oxford University Press.

Butler, Judith (1990). *Gender trouble: Feminism and the subversion of identity*. New York and London: Routledge.

—— (1993). *Bodies that matter: On the discursive limits of sex*. New York and London: Routledge.

Cameron, Deborah (1995). *Verbal hygiene*. London and New York: Routledge

—— (2000a). Styling the worker: Gender and the commodification of language in the global service economy. *Journal of Sociolinguistics* 4(3): 323–347. Reprinted in Deborah Cameron (2006). *On language and sexual politics*. London: Routledge, 112–132.

—— (2000b). *Good to talk? Living and working in a communication culture*. London and Thousand Oaks, CA: Sage.

Cameron, Deborah, and Don Kulick (2003). *Language and sexuality*. Cambridge: Cambridge University Press.

Coates, Jennifer (2003). *Men talk: Stories in the making of masculinities*. Malden, MA, and Cambridge: Blackwell Publishers.

Crenshaw, Kimberlé Williams (1994). Mapping the margins: Intersectionality, identity politics, and violence against women of color. In Martha Albertson Fineman and Roxanne Mykitiuk (eds.), *The public nature of private violence*. New York: Routledge, 93–118.

Eckert, Penelope (2003). Language and gender in adolescence. In Janet Holmes and Miriam Meyerhoff (eds.), *Handbook of language and gender*. Oxford: Blackwell.

Eckert, Penelope, and Sally McConnell-Ginet (1992a). Think practically and look locally: Language and gender as community-based practice. *Annual Review of Anthropology*, 21:461–490.

—— (1992b). Communities of practice: Where language, gender, and power all live. In Kira Hall, Mary Bucholtz, and Birch Moonwomon (eds.), *Locating power: Proceedings of the Second Berkeley Women and Language Conference*. Berkeley: Berkeley Women and Language Group, 89–99.

—— (2003). *Language and gender*. Cambridge: Cambridge University Press.

Eckert, Penelope, and John Rickford (eds.) (2001). *Stylistic variation in language*. Cambridge: Cambridge University Press.

Ehrlich, Susan (2001). *Representing rape: Language and sexual consent*. New York and London: Routledge.

Grice, H. Paul (1989). *The ways of words*. Cambridge, MA: Harvard University Press.

Hall, Kira (1995). Lip service on the fantasy line. In Hall and Bucholtz 1995, 183–216.

Hall, Kira, and Mary Bucholtz (eds.) (1995). *Gender articulated: Language and the socially constructed self.* New York and London: Oxford University Press.

Holmes, Janet (1995). *Women, men and politeness.* London and New York: Longman.

Inoue, Miyako (2006). *Vicarious language: Gender and linguistic modernity in Japan.* Berkeley: University of California Press.

Lakoff, Robin Tolmach (1975). *Language and woman's place.* New York: Harper and Row.

Lakoff, Robin, and Mary Bucholtz (eds.) (2004). *Language and woman's place by Robin Tolmach Lakoff: Text and commentaries.* New York: Oxford University Press.

Leap, William (1996). *Word's out: Gay men's English.* Minneapolis: University of Minnesota Press.

Liang, A. C. (1999). Conversationally implicating lesbian and gay identity. In Bucholtz et al., 293–310.

Matthews, Tanya (2005). From category label to discourse strategies: Girls' categorization practices at Millcreek High. Unpublished PhD dissertation. Cornell University, Ithaca, New York.

McConnell-Ginet, Sally (2006). Why defining is seldom 'just semantics': Marriage, 'marriage', and other minefields. In Betty Birner and Gregory Ward (eds.), *Drawing the boundaries of meaning: Neo-Gricean studies in pragmatics and semantics in honor of Laurence R. Horn.* Amsterdam: John Benjamins.

Miller, Laura (2004). You are doing *burriko*: Censoring/scrutinizing artificers of cute femininity in Japanese. In Okamoto and Shibamoto Smith, 148–165.

Ochs, Elinor (1992). Indexing gender. In Alessandro Duranti and Charles Goodwin (eds.), *Rethinking context.* Cambridge: Cambridge University Press, 335–358.

Okamoto, Shigeko, and Janet S. Shibamoto Smith (eds.) (2004). *Japanese language, gender, and ideology: Cultural models and real people.* New York: Oxford University Press.

Parker, Dorothy (1933). The waltz. *New Yorker*, September 2, 1933. In Dorothy Parker and Colleen Breese (eds.) (1995). *Dorothy Parker: Complete stories.* New York: Penguin Books, 209–212.

Queen, Robin (1997). 'I don't speak Spritch': Locating lesbian language. In Kira Hall and Anna Livia (eds.), *Queerly phrased: Language, gender and sexuality.* New York: Oxford University Press, 233–256.

Smyth, Ron, Greg Jacobs, and Henry Rogers (2003). Male voices and perceived sexual orientation: An experimental and theoretical approach. *Language in Society* 32(3): 329–350.

Smyth, Ron, and Henry Rogers (2008). Do gay-sounding men speak like women? *Toronto Working Papers in Linguistics* 27.

Summers, Lawrence (2005). Quotations taken from the Harvard University website, http://www.harvard.edu, accessed on February 27, 2005.

Treichler, Paula A. (1981). Verbal subversions in Dorothy Parker: "Trapped like a trap in a trap." *Language and Style* 13: 46–61.

Valian, Virginia. 1998. *Why so slow?: Women and professional achievement.* Cambridge, MA: MIT Press.

Part I

POLITICS AND SCHOLARSHIP

The chapters in this section all directly address connections between academic scholarship and feminist politics. Less directly, these essays also engage with academic politics—questions of disciplinarity and of intellectual turf. What kinds of investigations are 'legitimate' linguistics? And, from a different viewpoint, what kind of work is 'truly' feminist? As I explained in the preceding chapter, my own take on what counts as feminist is not very restrictive: I include almost any work informed by a critical stance on issues of gender and sexuality. Most important, I don't assume that feminist linguistics must arrive at results that fit with my own particular tastes and desires for making the world more hospitable to women and sexual minorities.

Can linguistic research be at the same time credible as scholarship and potentially relevant to feminist concerns? All three of these papers show my own struggle to construct myself as both a committed feminist and as a serious linguist (of a relatively formal variety), two identities I embraced (and continue to embrace) wholeheartedly. I don't think I ever use the word *identity* in these papers, but it is clear that it was not just general matters about the linguistic dimensions of gender identities that concerned me but my own identity as a scholar and an activist. From early in my career, I worked hard to shape a kind of feminist linguistics to which I could usefully contribute. It is perfectly possible for someone to be a committed feminist and an excellent linguist but not engage in what I am calling *feminist linguistics*: some of the linguistic research I have done is outside the realm of feminist linguistics, not addressing matters of gender or sexuality at all. Furthermore, just as there are many kinds of feminism, there are potentially many varieties of feminist linguistics: the kinds of issues I raise by no means exhaust the possibilities for feminist linguistics, but they do reflect my interests.

These essays can also be read as trying to make linguistics more hospitable to language and gender scholarship, to help legitimate a focus on gender issues. Gender and sexuality studies in linguistics have certainly achieved a much firmer institutional status than they had a couple of decades ago when these essays were written, but legitimacy issues continue to plague this research arena, especially for younger scholars, most of whom have had career trajectories very different from mine.

Chapter 2, "Language and gender," is an overview of work on gender and language through the late 1980s. Written for a series surveying linguistics for nonlinguists, it sets out a number of the main issues dealt with by linguistically oriented language and gender scholarship. How are social and linguistic change connected? In what ways does linguistic practice enter into the sociocultural construction of gender? To what extent do speech patterns index gender? How does gender meaning piggyback on other social meanings to facilitate indirect indexing of gender? How are strategies and goals of speakers connected to their production of linguistic forms? How do gender arrangements affect what speakers mean and their success in having those meanings socially acknowledged? How is it that substantive matters (of, e.g., gender and sexuality) can undergird contests over what seem 'merely' semantic issues? My own research and that of others continues to grapple with many of these same questions. This essay, though addressed to nonspecialists, also invites linguists to make room for language and gender scholarship, to see its relevance to issues important for understanding language and languages. The message is that language and gender work has the potential to enrich not only gender studies but also linguistic scholarship.

Chapter 3, "Feminism in linguistics," derives from a talk I gave in the early 1980s at a conference at the University of Illinois on feminist scholarship in a wide range of disciplines. Most of the paper discusses what language-focused research can tell us about gender issues. The different social situations in which women and men lead their lives and the different culturally mediated evaluations of them suffice, I argue, to explain gender-differentiated linguistic practices without supposing any 'essential' differences between women and men as language users. The essay also tries to suggest how linguistic practices can help sustain gender ideologies. Although it is primarily aimed at a readership interested in feminist studies, it also tries to speak to linguists without gender interests, proposing that looking at gender and language forces a reconsideration of some of the assumptions (often not completely explicit) common to much late twentieth-century linguistic research, especially that drawing on formal models of language. There is no rejection of formal linguistics—I still think formal theories of language have much to offer—but there is an insistence that formal theorists need to consider just how their models connect to what gender-focused investigations reveal about how language seems to work in situated social interactions and in everyday thought. One could also read some of this discussion as an attempt to persuade nonlinguists that my being a feminist really has led me to a critical stance on dominant views in linguistics, even though I still am very much influenced by them.

Chapter 4, "Difference and language: A linguist's perspective," closes the section with an insistent plea to attend to linguistic differences among women and also to respect diverse kinds of voices among

feminists. This piece began life as my contribution to a panel on
language at a conference, "The Future of Difference," organized by the
feminist studies program at Barnard College in New York City and
involving not only academics but many other feminist thinkers and
activists. My copanelists were a poet, Audre Lorde, and a literary scholar,
Alice Jardine. In the essay, I point to how linguistic research can give
concrete substance to abstract discussions of differences among women.
I also argue that feminist thinking about language cannot be confined to
any single mode—that we need not only poets, novelists, and literary
scholars but also linguists and others who approach language from very
different perspectives. I try to position linguistics as a scientific
enterprise that complements rather than competes with poetry in
helping deepen our understanding of ourselves and of the complex
diversity of gender.

2

Language and gender

> Why can't a woman talk more like a man?
>   (H. Higgins, phonetician)

0. Introduction

Questions of gender are now seen as a major challenge in almost every discipline that deals with human behavior, cognition, institutions, society, and culture. Within linguistics, however, sex/gender studies have played a relatively minor role: 'feminist linguistics' is far better known in literary than linguistic circles (see e.g., Ruthven 1984, ch. 3). There are, of course, occasional publications in linguistics journals and papers at linguistics meetings. It is fair to say, however, that the recent 'feminist intervention', which is largely responsible for the increased attention to gender in so many areas of intellectual inquiry, has been little felt by most linguists, many of whom have scoffed at claims (e.g., in Spender 1980) that language is 'man made'.

Why have linguists been relatively inactive in the rapidly growing area of research on language and gender? One reason is that most of the initial impetus for investigation of this area derived from feminist thinkers' concern to understand gender, especially the mechanisms that create and maintain male dominance, and not from interest in language as such. This emphasis made the early research of limited professional interest to linguists though often of considerable personal and political interest to many of us as participants in the women's movement.

In fields like anthropology and literature, however, many leading non-feminist scholars soon saw gender studies as of great potential theoretical significance, whereas linguistic theoreticians (correctly) saw gender as irrelevant to the questions of formal grammar that have been center stage in mainstream linguistics. Many linguists do not see how to combine their linguistic interests and their feminism. Can sex and gender function as central analytical categories in linguistic thought? Can a feminist linguistics profitably interact with mainstream linguistic

This essay first appeared in F. J. Newmeyer, ed., *Linguistics: The Cambridge Survey, Volume IV* (Cambridge: Cambridge University Press), 75–99.

research traditions? Must we swim against that mainstream to explain the language component of gender phenomena? For those of us whose intellect and passion have been fired by recent feminist thinking but who are also engaged by questions in linguistic theory, there is real urgency in the project of connecting issues of gender to some of the issues we care about as linguists.

Much recent linguistics has as its primary concern the principles that constrain the possible structure of LANGUAGES—linguistic systems represented by grammars. Formal linguistics has little to say directly about LANGUAGE—the practice of using a language (i.e., a linguistic system) or languages in a community and the relation of individuals to such systems and their use. Nonetheless, the systematic study of possible properties of languages is necessary for illuminating work on language; conversely, any adequate theory of languages and grammars must ultimately be able to support or be compatible with an account of language.

The critical distinction between systems and their situated uses and relations to users, language, is often ignored by those whose main interest is gender (or more generally, society and culture). I will adopt Lewis 1975's use of the mass versus count distinction—LANGUAGE versus A LANGUAGE or LANGUAGES—as shorthand for the 'uses and users' versus 'system' distinction. The distinction between language and languages has been challenged by linguists whose primary concern is language function rather than form. But to understand just how function and form connect, and how gender systems shape and are shaped by language, I find it very useful to consider both language and languages, while keeping sight of the difference between them. The sexual politics of language can be played out, for example, in struggles over which system(s) a community should use. (See Valian 1977 and Black and Coward 1981 for discussion of the limitations of gender studies that conflate the linguistic system and its uses.)

The word *gender* in the title of this chapter refers to the complex of social, cultural, and psychological phenomena attached to sex, a usage common in the behavioral and social sciences. The word *gender* also, however, has a well-established technical sense in linguistic discussions. Gender in this technical sense is a grammatically significant classification of nouns that has implications for various agreement phenomena. In the familiar Indo-European languages for which gender noun classes were early recognized, there is some connection, albeit highly attenuated, between gender of nouns and sex of their referents. The connection is shown not only by the class labels *feminine* and *masculine* but also by the fact that gender 'agreement' can depend on sex of a deictically given referent rather than on gender class of an antecedent. Many languages, however, show a similar agreement-based categorization of nouns in which the nominal classes show no connection at all to sex. Thus as a technical linguistic notion *gender* has virtually severed the connections to sex it had when first introduced to describe languages like Latin and German.

Gender is a useful term for present purposes precisely because it suggests an arbitrariness or conventionality in the sociocultural construction of the (non-sexual) significance of sex and sexuality not unlike that involved in the construction of Indo-European grammatical gender classes with weak connections to sex. (McConnell-Ginet 1983a, sec. 4, and Smith 1985, ch. 2, discuss the relevance for language studies of the cultural construction of sexual difference.) In the title of this chapter, ambiguity does not really arise, since *gender* in its grammatical sense does not conjoin any more happily with *language* than does *ablaut* or *adjective* or *anaphora*: *language and x* suggests that *x* designates something considered separate from language—the law, race, literature—not a linguistic component or concept.

Gender studies can illumine some important questions of potential linguistic relevance, especially for understanding the connection between language and languages. How do grammars, mental representations of linguistic systems, connect to other modules of the mind (e.g., those involved in social cognition; in person perception, in the planning of intentional action)? How do minds connect to each other through language use? What do rules of phonetic realization look like, and how can they vary within a speech community and from context to context? How are social and linguistic change connected to one another? What role does language use play in social categorization and cultural evaluation of its users? More generally, to what extent are patterns of language use reflective of social structure and of cultural values, of inequality and oppression? Can language be in part constitutive of culture and society, of women and men and their relationships? If so, how? Gender-focused studies shed some light on these and other questions, although we are still a long way from providing satisfactory answers.

Gender studies have made it quite clear that language users have a wide range of beliefs and knowledge about language that go beyond the rules and representations specifying grammars. There are, for example, gender-related norms as to who should use which expressions in particular social contexts, gender differentiation in access to rules for special genres of language use such as lamentations or ritual insults, and gender-related 'frozen' patterns of expression (English *man and wife*, *#husband and woman* versus Spanish *marido y mujer*, *#hombre y marida*). Are all such pragmatic beliefs and knowledge governed by principles common to other kinds of social cognition or do some have a distinctive structure because they are about linguistic expressions and actions? How are they represented, and how do they connect to grammars?

More generally, a focus on gender raises forcefully some fundamental questions about the links between language and social and cultural patterns. How are linguistic forms endowed with significance? How do the meanings a grammar associates with an expression interact with contextual factors in constraining what speakers mean and what hearers understand them to have said by uttering that expression? What is the role of power and of conflict in constructing interpretations and in choosing among competing interpretations? Do our linguistic practices tend to sustain existing gender arrangements, to avert fundamental challenges to those arrangements? ("Obviously," says the feminist. "But tell me how," says her other self, the linguist.)

Gender is of special theoretical interest because it is so pervasive. Gender is not only implicated in race relations, social stratification, legal codes and practices, and educational institutions (language in academia is thoughtfully discussed in Treichler and Kramarae 1983), but it also affects religion, social interaction, social and cognitive development, roles in the family and the workplace, behavioral styles, conceptions of self, the distribution of resources, aesthetic and moral values, and much more. And gender is of special practical interest because it is the focus of a widespread struggle to change the material conditions and the ideological frameworks of women's (and men's) lives.

Rather than attempt a comprehensive (and necessarily sketchy) survey, I have chosen to emphasize a particular theoretical perspective on language/gender studies. Recent books in this area with some sort of linguistic orientation (and with their own rather different emphases and limitations) include Kramarae (1981); Vetterling-Braggin (1981); Thorne, Kramarae, and Henley (1983); Cameron (1985); Shibamoto (1985); Baron (1986); Frank and Treichler (1989); Philips, Steele, and Tanz (1987); Thorne et al. (1983) also includes an invaluable annotated bibliography that updates and extends the useful bibliography in Thorne and Henley (1975). [The current volume is part of a series devoted to this area, and there have been scores of relevant books published in the more than two decades since I compiled this list.] The newsletter *Women and Language*, formerly edited by Paula Treichler and Cheris Kramarae at the University of Illinois, is a useful guide to ongoing research not only in America but also elsewhere (see e.g., the winter 1984 'multicultural issue'), citing work in many different disciplines.[a]

Language (use) involves the *production* by linguistic agents (speakers or writers) of linguistic forms; in using these forms, agents are *meaning* to

a. *Women and Language* is now edited at George Mason University and sponsored by the Organization for the Study of Communication, Language and Gender (OSCLG). *Gender and Language*, affiliated with the International Gender and Language Association (IGALA), is a refereed journal that began publication in late 2006 and was first distributed at IGALA 4 in Valencia. IGALA itself began in 1999, a development of the Berkeley Women and Language Conferences, which started in the 1980s. A decade into the twenty-first century there are several good textbooks and dozens of excellent collections available that deal with language and gender (and also sexuality).

express content and to present themselves as social beings and actors in the world. I discuss first production and then meaning.

1. Production: Patterns of linguistic forms

How does gender interact with patterns of linguistic expressions produced (spoken or written)? This is often construed as a question about how the sex or gender of the linguistic agent, the speaker or writer, affects which linguistic forms are produced. Moving from sex to gender can make the investigation more subtle: gender categories are not restricted to the male/female dichotomy, females need not be feminine, and femininity can be a matter of degree [or, as I might now put it, take many different forms].

Nonetheless, focus on gender as involving just properties of individual linguistic agents can obscure important insights into how gender affects language production. For example, there might be no connection at all between agent's sex or gender and patterns of language produced but significant interactions between forms produced and sex or gender of the audience (Brouwer, Gerritsen, and de Haan 1979 discusses one such case). Production patterns might show systematic dependence on the sex/gender relations between agents and their audience, for example, same-sex versus cross-sex situations of language use, or the Yana data reported in Sapir 1929 in which what mattered was whether or not the group was male only. Or they might show dependence on other features that make gender more or less salient in particular situations of language use, for example, my colleague Eleanor Jorden reports that a Japanese woman can use a relatively low level of 'feminine' speech markers when speaking to a male classmate about their studies but a much higher level when talking with that same classmate at a party. In a real sense, agents are responsible for what is produced. But this does not mean that it is only through agents' sex or other individual gender characteristics that sex/gender systems can affect linguistic production.

There are two reasons why we might tend to view the study of linguistic production as the study of speakers. The first is a general psychological phenomenon observed in our strongly individualistic culture. Language production is a form of behavior, and the 'ultimate attribution error' (Pettigrew 1979) is to explain a person's behavior as due to intrinsic properties of the person—for example, her grammatical knowledge or her intellectual capabilities—without reference to contextual factors that might play a role. Those involved in language/gender studies have not been immune to this error. The second reason lies in linguistics itself. Linguists have primarily studied grammars, systems instantiated in the minds of the linguistic agents. Linguistic production is *prima facie* evidence only for the grammar (or grammars) in the mind of the agent responsible for the production. For many linguistic purposes (e.g., writing grammars), there is little reason to look beyond the speaker to her audience or her situation. But to look at language in interaction with gender (or with other sociocultural phenomena for that matter), it is not enough to observe how features of linguistic production connect to characteristics of the producers. The study of how gender affects linguistic production is not exhausted by the study of how the gender characteristics of speakers affect their speech (of writers their writing). Yet this is all that the prevalent sex-difference approach considers.

Even where linguistic production patterns do covary systematically with gender characteristics of speakers (e.g., with speaker sex), there are still important questions to be asked about what explains this covariation. It might be evidence of (1) gender differentiation in the grammars or systems of linguistic knowledge that underlie speakers' uses (this is what labels like 'women's language' and 'genderlect' seem to suggest), (2) grammaticized gender display, which I discuss and illustrate below under the rubric 'gender deixis', (3) pragmatic systems and expectations about how the grammar is or should be used ("Nice girls don't say *what the fuck!*"), (4) favored linguistic strategies for achieving given aims ("Get him to think it was really his idea to do what you want done"), (5) emphasis on particular aims or goals ("What's really important is sharing feelings"), or (6) some combination of two or more of the above.

Most contemporary linguists would expect no sexual differentiation in the acquisition of grammars *unless* there were differences in the grammatical systems underlying the language usage that girls and boys encounter. This is because we take core linguistic capacity to be a species-universal biological characteristic. To put it slightly differently, gender interacts with linguistic knowledge only to the extent that it interacts with linguistic exposure. Children might, of course, be exposed to multiple systems, to which they might attend somewhat differently. For example, in developing their own grammars, girls might attend specially to the linguistic productions of their older female playmates, their mothers, and other female models. It is theoretically even possible that sex has some connection to certain details of what Chomsky calls the 'language organ', although there is no evidence that this is so (a few papers concerned with neurolinguistic investigations and sex differences appear in Philips et al. 1987). But one thing that makes gender especially interesting is that in most cultures there is significant cross-sex linguistic communication at all stages of the life cycle, suggesting that there must be considerable linguistic knowledge shared by the sexes.

What I call GENDER DEIXIS provides the most explicit link between gender and linguistic units produced; here the particular form of some linguistic unit *expresses* or *means* something about gendered properties of the circumstances of language production, the gendered perspective from which an utterance is produced. Like person or social deixis (see Levinson 1983, ch. 2), gender deixis is in some sense grammaticized, part of the language system. One clear example of gender deixis can illustrate the kind of phenomena involved. Ekka (1972) reports that in Ǩurux, a Dravidian language, 'feminine' conjugations of verbs signal that the speaker is speaking 'as a woman among women'; apparently, these verbal forms linguistically express the 'femininity' of the conversational group. In contrast, GENDER STEREOTYPES (models 'of') and GENDER NORMS (models 'for') incorporate respectively the community's views about how gender *is* related to language and how it *ought* to be. The English *-fuckin-* infix (as in *absofuckinlutely*) provides an example of a gender stereotype, useful to filmmakers for evoking a certain 'macho' image, whether or not the 'macho' types in question actually are the main users of these forms; a gender norm preaches that such forms aren't to be used by women or in mixed company. GENDER MARKERS represent actual associations between occurrence of linguistic units and gender phenomena that are informative for (and thus potentially manipulable by) community members, even though the association might not be a matter of conscious knowledge. In Montreal French, the use of *tu/vous* rather than *on* for indefinite reference is strikingly sex-differentiated among younger speakers (Laberge and Sankoff 1980); this is one of many examples of a gender marker. (Smith 1979 discusses mainly what are markers in this sense, ranging over a variety of ethnographic situations.) Gender-deictic expressions will, of course, be gender markers (because of the connections between linguistic meaning and language use discussed in sec. 2.2), though the converse does not hold (e.g., the use of indefinite *on* in Montreal, though strikingly associated with female speakers does not 'mean' anything about gender and thus is not gender-deictic). Gender stereotypes, norms, and markers are matters of language and not part of a language; thus they involve production frequency, not just categorical production or non-production. (Bodine 1975 distinguishes sex-preferential or sex-exclusive distributional patterns, an important distinction but limited to surface occurrence data that do not directly indicate gender significance.)

Gender deixis is also direct, whereas stereotypes, norms, and markers may all involve either a direct or an indirect connection between linguistic phenomena and gender. For example, people might associate utterance of "Let's wash yourself now, honey" (at least preferentially) with female speakers, but make the association through a primary link with child tending and additional background beliefs about the connections between child care and women.[b] In fact, it can be argued that most links between language production patterns and gender characteristics of producers are indirect (Brown and Levinson 1979, McConnell-Ginet 1985a), many both a reflection and a component of male dominance (O'Barr and Atkins 1980 put it in almost these terms). Finding a correlation between a language feature (e.g., frequency of tag questions with a final rising intonation)

---

b. Elinor Ochs (1992) came up with the useful term "indirect indexing of gender" to talk about the kind of mediated connections I discuss here.

and a gender phenomenon (e.g., sex of speaker) does not in itself tell us anything about the social and cultural contexts, the mechanisms, that produce the correlation.

So-called women's language has often involved (pervasive) gender deixis rather than the gender-differentiated grammars suggested by this phrase. (See, e.g., Sapir 1929, Haas 1944, and Flannery 1946—reviewed in Taylor 1983—for Amerindian situations in which gender deixis was apparently enforced and pervasive.) Among the languages of the world, however, gender deixis is apparently rare: in other words, we fairly seldom find distinct ways of saying the same thing where the difference between the two means something about gender properties of the context-of-utterance. Rarer still are situations in which agents *must* express something about gender in the context (as English-using communities enforce the use of first-person forms for agent reference in speech) or in which such expression is pervasive (like social deixis in Japanese), affecting so many forms that few utterances will not express gender meaning.

Furfey (1944) argued that in none of the then reported cases of gender-differentiated speech did the sexes have distinct codes or grammars; more recent assessments of different ethnographic situations support that claim (in addition to references already cited, see Philips 1980, Borker 1980, Sherzer 1983, and Philips et al. 1987). Where quite distinct language systems are in a community's repertoire, gender is often implicated in their use (see e.g., Gal 1978 for Hungarian/German contact and many other references in Thorne et al. 1983). Languages reserved for ritual use or other specialized functions are generally accessible only to participants in these rituals and functions, such participation being frequently gender-differentiated (medieval Latin, for example, was almost exclusively 'men's language'). And Hakuta (1986) reports that among some Amazon Indians, marriage partners must be selected from a different (home or first) language group, a situation characterized by universal multilingualism.

What did Lakoff (1975) mean when she spoke of 'women's language' (WL) among English speakers? Was she claiming gender deixis in English? Certainly some people took her to be claiming that, for example, *magenta* 'means' that its user is speaking 'as a woman', feminine or effeminate. What Lakoff actually did was simply to identify a number of features as constitutive of American English WL: tag questions (in certain contexts), a set of positive evaluative adjectives, certain specialized color words, 'question' intonations on declaratives, euphemisms, hedges, indirect request forms and other 'polite' expressions (*Could you perhaps manage to pass the salt?*), prescriptively sanctioned forms (*To whom do you wish to speak?*), and others. Her method was essentially that used in grammatical investigations: elicitation of 'acceptability' judgments from herself and other native speakers. The difference was that her data involve judgments not just of a linguistic form but of that form *as produced* by a certain kind of speaker. She does note that not all women use these forms and that men sometimes do, but she does not say exactly what meaning should be attached to their presence or absence or relative frequency in someone's speech. In contrast, she does explicitly speak of women as compelled to become bilingual if they want to function in the public 'men's' world, suggesting that she is assuming (perhaps only a normative or stereotypical) dual system or 'genderlect' model. (See McConnell-Ginet 1983a for further discussion of that model.)

Whether Lakoff intended to be understood as saying that WL features involved gender deixis or constituted some sort of genderlect is not really clear. What is clear from her explicit denials, however, is that she was not proposing an account of the distribution of WL features in actual women's and men's speech. Most readers nonetheless supposed that she was claiming that her WL features were (also) what I have called gender markers, significantly gender-differentiated in their actual distribution. Lakoff herself was not unaware that acceptability judgments might well reflect systematic beliefs about how gender does (stereotype) or should (norm) affect speech better than they reflect actual usage. Edelsky (1976, 1977), Haas (1979), Kramer (1974, 1978), Siegler and Siegler (1976) and others offer evidence that certain elements of the picture Lakoff detailed have some reality as stereotypes. But even as stereotype, Lakoff's WL seems most relevant for the WASP, middle-class populations that American researchers have mainly studied. Middle-class Black women, for example, do not find "coherent images of themselves in the contemporary literature on language and gender" (Stanback 1985, 177). And one woman complained to Barrie Thorne (pers. comm.): "I'm tired of being told that I talk like a man. I talk like a Jew." As a normative model, the WL features have rather limited support, even among mainstream White women.

Although actual distribution of WL features was not what Lakoff was interested in, actual distribution is of considerable interest not only for learning whether gender-differentiated systems exist in a community but also for exploring other ways in which gender may affect production. Lakoff's ideas about WL inspired many quantitative descriptive studies of women's speech (especially in American English—see Thorne et al. 1983 for references), some of which failed to find the differences that stereotypes suggest (e.g., Dubois and Crouch 1976). Other studies find some of the suggested differences but only in certain contexts (e.g., Crosby and Nyquist 1977, Jay 1980) or connected with gender through other intervening variables like power (e.g., O'Barr and Atkins 1980). Such findings suggest that the phenomena involved are situationally sensitive rather than attributable simply to speakers' gender. There has also been recent linguistic research on the WL question in other languages (see, e.g., Light 1982 on Chinese, Shibamoto 1985 on Japanese, and a number of the papers in Philips et al. 1987).[c]

c. See Lakoff (2004) for Lakoff's own recent perspective on her early work and also for others' responses to it.

Frequential gender markers that are not generated by strategic choices or tied to other intervening variables like social status generally indicate gender-differentiated social networks. Do such markers, which are found, demonstrate the existence of 'genderlects'? There have been some sophisticated quantitative studies that find low-level phonetic and morphosyntactic variation statistically linked to speaker sex (see e.g., Nichols 1983; Trudgill 1983, chs. 9 and 10) within particular communities. Syntactic variation has been studied less often than phonological, in part due to greater difficulties in defining the unit that 'varies'. (See Lavandera 1978; the crucial point is that different syntactic constructions often differ in function, unlike alternative phonetic realizations of a single underlying phonological segment.) Some evidence has been offered, however, of statistically significant links between syntactic variants and speaker sex both in English (e.g., Philips 1983) and in other languages (e.g., Japanese, as reported in Shibamoto 1985). And Guy (1989) provides other examples of quantitative studies of systematic variation correlated with speaker sex, including lexical and intonational variants as well as differences in segmental phonology and syntax.

When systematic variation is found, some theorists incorporate it into a grammar with variable rules. Though language users clearly are capable of regulating their speech to achieve a certain frequency of realization of variable units, showing sensitivity to and tacit knowledge of statistical regularities, what underlies this capability seems to me cognitively quite distinct from what underlies (categorical) grammatical knowledge. But even if we do take frequencies of alternative variants to be specified by the linguistic system, to be part of what an individual knows (perhaps a distinct 'variable rule' module in her grammar), it would be appropriate to speak of 'genderlects' only if the frequency setting of *individual* grammars were directly linked to gender; to the extent that variationists focus on *group* data within a community, they show us nothing about what I would call 'genderlects', individual gender-conditioned grammars.

Much of the empirical research on WL, not only in English but also in other languages, suffers from the absence of any principled theory of how and why gender phenomena might or might not interact with language production. It can be useful to count surface structural features of actually occurring corpuses and correlate these with gendered properties of the speech situation: sex and (perceived) gender of speaker, sex and (perceived) gender of hearer, gender relations of participants, gender salience of situation. The more difficult and interesting step is explaining correlations that do occur, detailing the mechanisms that produce them, and it is this step that some investigators refuse to attempt, since in doing so they would have to move beyond what is directly observable. (Hiatt 1977 is an ambitious computer study of written texts that I criticize in McConnell-Ginet 1979 for such limitations.) A recurring suggestion has been that women tend to adopt the 'prestige' variant in their community more often than men, but matters are more complicated than this (see e.g.,

Nichols 1980, 1983, 1984 for useful discussion); explanations of this putative tendency are at best limited (Trudgill's, 1983, is one of the more interesting).

One of the reasons Lakoff's work has been of continuing interest is that she does link her proposals to some kind of theory of why language use might show gender differentiation, proposing that WL signals womanliness through its connections with deference and unwillingness to assume responsibility for one's assertions. There are, of course, other interpretations of the features Lakoff associates with deferring and abrogating responsibility, as I and others have pointed out many times (see e.g., McConnell-Ginet 1983a for some alternatives that present a more positive view of women as linguistic agents), but what I want to emphasize here is the importance of Lakoff's recognition of the fact that investigations limited to what is directly observable and easy to count cannot explain how gender affects production.

Brown (1976, 1980) has contributed to development of a theoretical perspective on language and gender by proposing explicit links between micro-level linguistic variables and macro-level strategic patterns of language use involved in politeness and connecting those patterns to gender-differentiated social networks and relations in a particular ethnographic setting. Brown and Levinson (1978) develop a general theory of linguistic politeness as involving attention to both positive and negative 'face needs' of conversational interactants. Positive face is connected to being identified with others and their interests and social connections. Negative face is tied to respect for others' rights, individual integrity or autonomy. It is possible to show concern for both positive and negative face (which is what the Mexican women whom Brown studied did with other women and with men), although there is tension between them. Certain forms can be seen as indicative of the agent's attending to positive-face needs of the audience (e.g., Brown so categorized a Tzeltzal diminutive particle in the Mexican community she studied) and others as indicative of attention to negative-face needs (e.g., certain adverbial modifiers that 'soften' or ameliorate directives). Given a functional analysis of the forms, counting them *can* provide information about strategies. The change of emphasis from a system one acquires simply by virtue of one's social identity to a set of strategies one develops to manage social interactions is one of the most promising developments in research on language production and producer's gender.

Looking at the significance of the forms produced, especially those whose function is primarily to handle social relations, can put WL questions in a different light. Brown and Levinson's politeness model suggests some useful hypotheses as to why and how forms produced might both reflect and maintain male dominance. In egalitarian relations, negative politeness shows mutual respect, tending to suggest distance, and positive politeness suggests intimacy or affection, associated with closeness. To give negative politeness attests to the recipient's (not the giver's) independence, whereas to give positive politeness can imply the recipient's vulnerability to the giver's good offices. In stratified relations, the

inferior is generally constrained to give (the semblance of) negative politeness and receive (the semblance of) positive, which explains, I think, why
we find again and again that the form used in situations of distance between equals (e.g., German *Sie*) is required usage from the inferior speaking
'up', whereas the one used in situations of closeness (e.g., German *du*) is
freely permitted to the superior speaking 'down'. Brown and Gilman's
classic study (1960) of the 'pronouns of power and solidarity' notes this
conjunction but does not really show why it is so pervasive and useful to
those who want to mask coercive power relations as ordinary social relations of interdependence. McConnell-Ginet (1978) [see also McConnell-
Ginet 2003, ch. 10 in this book] and Wolfson and Manes (1980) study the
sexual politics of address in light of this 'ambiguity'. What we have is less
an ambiguity than a form whose linguistic significance—perhaps in this
case something like attention to positive face—does not say what particular
aims and motives speakers have in producing it. That is, the (very) general
content is compatible with a variety of different, more specific, interactional moves. You may consider your address form or your compliment an
act of friendship, but I may hear it as condescending or manipulative; I
may intend my rising intonation to encourage you to continue, but you
may hear it as insecure or deferential (McConnell-Ginet 1983b). The
linguistic forms themselves support such sharply divergent functions.
Goffman (1977) notes that "the arrangement between the sexes" in our
culture is constructed on the model of that between parents and their
children, involving *both* affection and asymmetrical control; this observation helps explain the ambivalence of what we say to one another, the
complex significance of cross-sex power and solidarity.[d]

2. Meaning: Expressing content
   and announcing attitudes

Research on gender and language production focused initially on two issues.
How do women (and men) speak? How are they spoken (or not spoken) of?
My first course on language and gender was organized around these headings,
with little connection between them. We have seen above that the first
question is only one small part of a much larger one: how does gender affect
language production? The second question raises issues of 'sexist language';
see e.g., Schulz 1975, Stanley 1978, the papers in Vetterling-Braggin 1981,
and many other sources for documentation of the derogation, sexualization,
and homogenization of female reference, the universalization of male reference, and other aspects of the expression of misogynistic and sexually biased

---

d. Tannen (1994) makes a similar point, speaking of 'polysemy'. What is crucial for
understanding here is that, unlike truly ambiguous forms, these choices can express multiple
meanings in a single usage, just as we can both dominate and deeply love our children.

content [see Mills 2008 for discussion of complexities of understanding how language interacts with sexism].[e] But the second question is also ultimately unduly restrictive. Rather than focusing just on how we are spoken of (or not spoken of), I want to draw attention to a more general question: how does gender affect what (and how) agents *mean* by their linguistic productions?

In meaning, agents are both *expressing content* and *announcing themselves and their attitudes*, roughly the functions Brown and Yule (1983) dub TRANSACTIONAL and INTERACTIONAL, respectively. Languages, interpreted systems, assign content or content structures; we present ourselves and convey our attitudes only in situated language use. Content is the message: its expression is accompanied by meta-messages that situate the content in particular social contexts, provide guides to how that expression should be understood and acted upon, and announce the agent's stance toward the message.

Attitudes ("Women are the eternal mystery") and self-presentation (e.g., certain kinds of gender perspectives) may themselves actually be part of content, of what the speaker expresses. Content, however, is never a component of interactional meaning, an asymmetry that partly explains the focus of linguistic semantics on content. Nonetheless, the content one expresses is a powerful indicator of attitudes, and the act and form of its expression often an important element in the construction of social relations. Van Dijk (1984) notes, for example, that expression of negative attitudes toward ethnic minorities by White Dutch 'majority' speakers (whose audience is also from the same group though an unknown interviewer rather than a friend) frequently involves strategies designed to forestall negative judgments of the expresser as racist. Thus content and social significance interact.

Many analysts assume that the 'illocutionary attitudes' the agent means (e.g., whether she is performing the speech act of asserting or one of inquiring) belong to content. To mean a particular illocutionary attitude, however, is to mean the expressed content to have a particular sort of effect on the context: conveying illocutionary attitudes involves conveying a 'meta-message' about where this particular content is to fit in the whole transaction. The same linguistic expression can be used with radically different illocutionary 'forces', but such multiple functioning seems less like ordinary content ambiguity than like the tension noted above between whether the expression of familiarity stems from closeness or from disrespect. (Like any other attitudes, the illocutionary ones may themselves be part of expressed content: e.g., "I claim that...."). Illocutionary meaning, however, is different from other kinds of interactional meaning in being a virtually ubiquitous accompaniment of the expression of content and essential to an agent's meaning anything at all. It is like them in being radically underdetermined by linguistic form and thus heavily context-dependent.[f]

e. Frank and Treichler (1989), especially the editors' detailed and acute discussion of particular cases and the need for multiple strategies rather than mechanical replacement rules, is another excellent source, as is King (1991).

f. See Chierchia and McConnell-Ginet (2000), ch. 4, for fuller discussion of these issues.

Genderized expression of meaning and interpretive conflicts emerge often in interactional meaning, where assumptions about goals and about one another's personal positions are especially critical. Tag questions and rising intonations on declaratives, for example, are primarily of interactional significance and have multiple functions (e.g., indicating willingness to engage in further talk or a relatively low commitment to one's assertion); it is not surprising that the meaning recipients assign them does not always coincide with what their producers intend to convey.

Meaning and language production are, of course, intimately connected to one another: in order to mean anything at all, a person must become an illocutionary agent, a producer of linguistic expressions endowed with significance, with meaning. The basic conception of what it is for an agent, a speaker or writer, to mean something by producing some linguistic expression directed toward some potential recipient(s), hearers or readers, I draw from Grice (1957). My reformulation goes like this:

> Agent A means utterance U to express content C and a particular attitude toward that content to recipient(s) R just in case (i) A intends U to direct R's attention toward C and to give grounds for R to think that A has the attitude in question toward C, and (ii) A intends this effect on R to be produced by virtue of R's recognizing that A does so intend.

There are problems with this (and with other formulations), but it retains Grice's two central ideas. First, the agent's intentions are of crucial importance: to mean is to engage in a certain kind of intentional action. Second, however, what the agent can mean, can intend to express by some utterance U, is constrained by what effects she can reasonably expect (or hope) to produce in the recipient(s) by virtue of his (their) recognition of her so intending: to mean is to engage in a social action.

Intentions to mean—'illocutionary' aims (Austin 1962)—are fulfilled simply in being recognized, in being comprehended. In contrast, intentions to persuade, dissuade, comfort, impress, delight, frighten, or amuse— 'perlocutionary' aims—are easily recognized without being fulfilled. We are not surprised, therefore, to find sexual bias affecting accomplishment of these perlocutionary aims, a bias often reflected in evaluations of women's language productions. (Baron 1986 provides historical perspective on how women's speech has been evaluated, and Ostriker 1986 examines the genderized language of critical discourse about women's poetry.) It may be somewhat more surprising to discover that women can suffer discrimination even in obtaining understanding, in conveying what they mean, quite apart from how people judge its efficacy or the quality of its expression. We might want to say that to ensure understanding, an agent need only say exactly what she means, in other words, choose words and syntactic constructions whose linguistic meaning expresses exactly the content she seeks to convey.

My Gricean-type definition of what the speaker means makes no reference to linguistic meaning at all, says nothing about what linguistic expressions—as opposed to language producers—mean. Grice (1982) identifies linguistic meaning with social norms that regulate what agents are to mean in their productions of particular expressions. Familiar approaches to linguistic meaning analyze a language as assigning semantic values of some appropriate type to linguistic expressions, with recursive principles for combining word and phrasal meanings to yield sentential content. The Gricean definition is sometimes thought of as just delineating how agents can mean more than what they explicitly say (indirectness as in "Would you happen to know what time it is?" as a request that the addressee tell the speaker what time it is) or even something different (nonliteralness of various kinds or even mistakes). But even when the agent's intentions are to say exactly what she means, the Gricean account still does some work; the agent can be said to intend to invoke mutual knowledge of the language system assigning the desired interpretation. In fact, it will generally be presumed that the linguistically assigned meaning is part of common background (cf. the 'linguistic presumption' discussed in Bach and Harnish 1979) and that this linguistic meaning is intended to play a role in identifying what the speaker means.

The fundamental aim an agent must have in her act of meaning is to be understood, to communicate—and to direct this act (at least potentially) to an audience beyond herself. This is built into the Gricean definition. Sometimes communication of content is most crucial, whereas at other times adopting a social stance is what has primacy. But to get started at all, one must be able to speak or to write, to produce linguistic expressions for apprehension (and in the happy case, comprehension) by others. This can be problematic.

Conversation is not an equal-opportunity activity. For example, West and Zimmerman (1983) find men pushing women off the conversational floor, taking longer turns and more of them in cross-sex conversations and even disrupting the turn-taking system by interruptions that 'violate' the current speaker's rights to sole occupancy of the conversational floor until the end of her current unit. On the basis of detailed analysis of conversations of three heterosexual couples, Fishman (1983) argues that women bear a disproportionate share of the maintenance work in cross-sex conversations, helping men develop their topics through providing minimal encouraging responses (*mmhmm*), asking questions, and listening. In contrast, the men did not so help their female conversational partners, whose attempts to develop their own topics tended quickly to run out of steam through the men's nonresponsiveness. Interruptions and topic control typically mark the dominant person in overtly stratified pairs: doctor-patient, employer-employee, parent-child.

Still, what happens is not fully explained by pointing to male privilege and dominance. Edelsky (1981) has proposed that women fare much better when conversationalists suspend the 'one at a time' rule that usually prevails in favor of a 'shared floor'. Her analysis found some instances of mutual talk that was not interruptive; this occurred when participants knew one another well and were very much engaged in the conversation. Under such conditions, women and men produced roughly the same amounts of talk. There has been relatively little of this kind of analysis of single-sex conversations, although Goodwin (1980a) compared boys' and girls' play groups, with particular focus on the form in which directives were cast, finding that the boys tended to use bald imperatives whereas the girls tended to use forms like *let's* and *why don't we*.

Maltz and Borker (1982) draw from this and related research two different normative models of conversation, which, they hypothesize, girls and boys develop in their (mainly single-sex) peer groups. The boys learn to use language to create and maintain dominance hierarchies; the girls create horizontal ties through their words and negotiate shifting alliances. Drawing on Maltz and Borker's analysis, Tannen (1986, ch. 8) suggests that adult women and men bring different expectations of their conversational partners to cross-sex conversations, that we come from different 'cultures' that have shaped our views of conversation.[g]

This picture of gender-differentiated conversation models is based on limited populations and does not address the influence of ethnicity, social class, or the demands of particular situations. Nonetheless, there seems to be some support for the notion that middle-class American women and men typically learn, in their childhood social groups, to structure discourse in different ways. This may explain some of the prevalent patterns of cross-sex conversational problems. Especially suggestive is Tannen's (1986) claim that "women are more attuned than men to the meta-messages of talk," by which she means what is 'implicated' over and above what is explicitly said. Meta-messages frequently (though not exclusively) involve social and interpersonal dimensions of meaning; analysts have suggested that those dimensions often also enter into women's messages, are part of their overtly expressed content (see e.g., Harding 1975, Goodwin 1980b, Hughes 1985, Cazden and Michaels 1985).

Two main suggestions of the research on gender and conversational interaction are relevant for present purposes. First, in trying to mean, 'she' may pay more attention than 'he' to whether her intentions can be expected to be recognized by their intended recipient: she tends to be more attuned to the social dimensions of her acts of meaning and the attendant potential problems. Her cultural experience provides a less individualistic view of the world and recognizes more social interdependence. Second, to the extent that men dominate language production in which audiences include both sexes—not only cross-sex conversations but also public speaking to mixed-sex audiences and writing for mixed-sex readership—a 'woman's eye' view of the world will be less familiar to the general (mixed-sex) public than a 'man's eye' view. There is not *a*

---

g. This picture was further elaborated in Tannen (1990), which was widely read and often taken by the general public as the definitive take on language and gender.

view of the world common to members of each sex. The point is rather that men (and dominant groups generally) can be expected to have made disproportionately large contributions to the stock of generally available background beliefs and values on which speakers and writers rely in their attempts to mean and which are particularly critical in attempts to mean to an unfamiliar audience.

These observations may help us to understand charges of sexism in language and, more generally, claims that women are a 'muted' group, denied the 'power of naming' and linguistically alienated (see e.g., Spender 1980, Kramarae 1981, and from the perspective of literary theory, Showalter 1982). My aim is to suggest something of the mechanisms through which social privilege leads to a kind of linguistic privilege, making it appear that the language itself supports the interests and reflects the outlook of those with privilege (by virtue of sex or class or race), that the language itself resists threats to that privilege. The appearance is not illusory, although it is not a language (an interpreted system) but language (use) that helps subordinate women (and other dominated groups).

Socially directed intentions play a role both in cases where what is *meant* is different from what is *said* (linguistically assigned meaning) and in cases in which the two coincide. To succeed in meaning more than what one's sentences themselves express, an agent relies on general principles (e.g., that utterances will be assumed 'relevant') plus whatever can be taken as part of the mutually accessible background. For example, precedent and assumed accessibility of negative appraisals of women's intellectual powers make it easy for someone to mean to insult by an utterance of "You think just like a woman," harder to do so by an utterance of "You think just like a man" (though with the right audience, the second sentence might be the more powerful insulter). What is successfully conveyed implicitly by uttering an expression can eventually, by virtue of precedents, become conveyed explicitly by that very same expression: this has apparently happened to *sissy* and *hussy*, for example (see McConnell-Ginet 1984).[h] To understand "You think like a woman" as an insult, a hearer need only recognize the general accessibility of devaluation of women's thinking; she need not accept it. On the other hand, a speaker who means to insult through uttering "You think like a woman" and succeeds in so doing may (perhaps mistakenly) take his success to signal his hearer's agreement with the negative appraisal he depends on. Because she sees that he intends to insult, she might respond with "No, I don't" and simply mean thereby "No, I am not shallow, irrational, and so forth." He, on the other hand, might take her to accept his implicit negative evaluation of women's thinking but to be dissociating herself from the general run of women. Because that negative evaluation remains implicit when she replies "No, I don't,"

h. Chapter 8 in this book is the direct descendant of this paper.

it is likely to go unchallenged, and the subsequent discussion may even reinforce its hold.

The general point is that in order to mean, agents presuppose, take things for granted, and that what can be taken for granted depends on what has been (often and audibly) expressed and can be assumed to be readily accessible. Views that are little heard, that are not common currency, can reliably function as background only in linguistic exchanges between familiars. Such views will not contribute to general patterns of meaning more than what is said and thus they will not leave their mark on standard interpretations (the *hussy* case). Lewis (1979, 172) claims that there is a rule of accommodation for presupposition; namely, that "if at time t something is said that requires presupposition P to be accept-able, and if P is not presupposed just before t, then—*ceteris paribus* [unlikely in a world of unequal speakers] and within certain limits—pre-supposition P comes into existence." But not all speakers are assumed to be saying something acceptable, and accommodation is especially unlikely if what is said is in conflict with what might generally be thought presup-posed. Views that are common currency cannot easily be ignored, even by those who challenge or disavow them. To devise reasonable strategies for being understood, agents must take account of what their audience is likely to take for granted—not necessarily to believe, but to treat as the 'unmarked' opinion.

In attempting to speak literally and directly, agents must presuppose access to an *interpreted* language system, must take for granted standard assignments of semantic value. For words, semantic values are sometimes thought of as feature sets or 'definitions' in terms of necessary and sufficient conditions for application of the word. On this view, we can count on others to understand because we can count on their assigning the same features or applying the same definition as we do. Definitions or feature sets in individual agents' heads 'regulate' their (literal) usage of expressions. But there are problems of several kinds with this picture, among which are vagueness and instability of criteria for using expressions.

The alternative view that I want to sketch here is the radical one, devel-oped in several of the articles in Putnam 1975, that "meanings [of syntac-tically simple expressions] ain't in the head," which is to say that we can't always regulate our usage for communicative purposes by reference to our individual cognitive constructs. People use many words for which they have at best limited knowledge of criterial features, words for which they lack a definition. What guides the ordinary person in using the word *gold*, for example, is what Putnam calls a stereotype of gold, a set of widely held beliefs or presumptions about gold, that may sometimes lead to labeling as gold what is really pyrites. This doesn't mean that in the ordi-nary person's language, what *gold* means allows it to be applied to pyrites; it just means that the ordinary person talks about gold without being able to tell definitively what is and what is not gold, and thus can sometimes misapply the word. Suggestively, Putnam speaks of a 'linguistic division of labor': there is a scientific theory that distinguishes gold from pyrites, which some scientists know. The rest of us intend to use *gold* to speak about the same 'natural kind' of stuff that the scientific experts call gold, though we are sometimes fooled by the superficial appearance of pyrites.

Expertise seems straightforward in the case of identifying gold. It becomes problematic, however, when we turn to words and concepts that play a role in our informal, everyday theories of ourselves and our social world, our values and our ideologies. A fairly simple case that has been much discussed is that of the pronoun *he*, over whose interpretation there has been considerable dispute. In contexts of reference to a specific person, *he* unambiguously conveys maleness: "Someone$_i$ is at the door but I don't know who he$_i$ is" implies the maleness of the unknown person. In contexts in which femaleness has been made explicit or is especially salient, it is difficult to use *he* even where there is no reference to a specific individual: "Any boy or girl who thinks that !? he knows the answer..." is generally judged bizarre. Yet prescriptive grammar enjoins English users to use *he* when the antecedent is a sex-indefinite generic: "When the child is around two, he will..." is a familiar kind of example.

Martyna (1980, 1983) has investigated *he–man* language. One thing she has shown is that women and men tend to produce *he* in somewhat different contexts, with men more likely than women to adopt the so-called masculine generic uses. On the other hand, women interpreting *he* in such contexts are a bit less likely to infer that maleness is somehow meant. Why might it matter what interpretations are assigned to pronouns? Because the interpretations assigned play a role in what speakers can do by means of uttering sentences containing those pronouns. Allowing the same form to be interpreted so that it presumes maleness in the case of specific reference makes it problematic to connect that form to cases in which maleness is ostensibly not presumed. For such connections to work reliably requires tacit appeal to a theory that people are male unless proven otherwise, that femaleness is contrasted with maleness in being a special and distinctive form of humanness, a marginal condition. That such a theory does still operate was made clear to me once again when I heard a radio commentary on the November 1984 Mondale-Ferraro defeat. Some Democrat suggested that the party should draw the moral that it cannot identify with 'marginal' and 'special interest' groups— blacks, the handicapped, union members. Rather, this man went on, we must recognize that the "average voter is a white, middle-class male." Given that more women are registered and vote than men, we know this politician must mean *average* in a quite special normative and not a statistical sense. In other words, this man made explicit the semantic connection between typicality and maleness, which I have suggested is implicit in norms that urge us to use *he* when presumptions are not being made about sex.

The challenge to the prescriptively endorsed 'meaning' of *he* is a challenge to a view of the world in which human beings are presumed to be male unless proven otherwise, which helps us understand why it is resisted so vigorously. In principle, one can learn to apply *he* in the generic cases without accepting the theoretical perspective that connects those uses with those in which *he* refers to a specific individual. Still, it is rather difficult to *mean* a genuinely sex-indefinite *he*, simply because one cannot rely on audiences to recognize that one does not intend to suggest maleness.[i]

I want to reemphasize that I am not suggesting monolithic women's and men's views of the world. In McConnell-Ginet 1985b, I discussed how a large body of feminist discourse has been structured around the essentially semantic question of what being a lesbian means. Should we define *lesbian* as a matter of psychosocial orientation toward women, as a 'continuum' of concern with and interest in women, as a political stance in opposition to patriarchy, as an erotic choice? Women writing in the past decade or two have urged these and other meanings. Feminism has assigned multiple meanings to lesbianism, but it is not just a matter of 'ambiguity'. Much of this discourse *proposes* meanings, *urges* them, as part of constructing a theory and politics of sexuality, sexual oppression, desire. These are couched as questions of semantics but they are not thereby insubstantial.[j]

Given that a 'question of semantics' is often a 'question of values and action', we can see that linguistic agents cannot always take shared access to a particular interpreted language for granted. Indeed, one thing linguistic agents and their interpreters do is negotiate some kind of accord on interpretation, choose among what we can think of as alternative interpretations of the (underinterpreted) system they do share. I suggest that it is precisely because natural languages are themselves so relatively empty of meaning, so 'formal', that language users are able to do so very much with their words, indeed are forced to interpret those words actively. Expressions in formal systems are uninterpreted; it is their multiple interpretive possibilities that make them so useful for modeling diverse domains. Similarly, it is the multiple interpretive possibilities afforded us by natural languages that allow us to use those languages in developing our common thoughts, shaping our desires, and planning what we will do. Interpretation of natural language systems, endowing linguistic forms with significance, is not primarily a matter of identifying form-meaning links, of encoding and decoding. Interpretation is much more an active process, a socially situated and sometimes socially divisive construction of meaning.

i. Chapter 9 of this book discusses pronominal issues in more detail.

j. Chapter 11 of this book examines this and other disputes over labels for sexual minorities, and McConnell-Ginet (2006) looks at how meaning disputes can at the same time be disputes over substantial matters, using the example of defining *marriage* (and, at the same time, the institution of marriage).

The Gricean definition assigns the agent authority over what is meant; after all, it is agentive intentions that are crucial. But because those intentions are directed toward a recipient and are reflexive in the sense that the recipient is intended to recognize them and intended to recognize that he is intended to recognize them, the agent is not free to intend any meaning whatsoever. I might want to mean just something about humanity in my use of *he*, but I now have substantial reservations about the possibility of so meaning, reservations that block my forming certain intentions. And of course people can be less than candid about their intentions, sometimes even deceiving themselves. In many cases, there are established conventional meanings for linguistic expressions and often acknowledged 'experts' whom we depend on for regulating usage. What it is important to remember is that (1) those meanings are typically supported by background beliefs or 'theories', often implicit and sometimes ungrounded and biased, and (2) their being 'conventional' is a matter of social prescription to use only certain interpretations of a language system, to use only certain 'languages', prescriptions enforced by social privilege. The agent who challenges such prescriptions can succeed only when she is empowered by alternative *socially* endorsed practices (see Scheman 1980 on a new conception of anger arising in consciousness-raising groups).

In what ways does language shape the message(s), what agents mean? How do meanings get 'authorized', inscribed in the culture's collective repertoire? Is there a politics of meaning? Which messages are conveyed to whom? How is gender implicated in what is meant? In what sense does language 'construct' gender? Does language 'define' women as unimportant, properly subservient to men? If so, what are the mechanisms? Frank and Treichler (1989) include discussion of these issues (see especially Treichler's contribution). Kramarae and Treichler (1985) present some 'women's words', which offer alternative perspectives on human beings and their relations (and also on language itself). And Trömel-Plötz (1982, discussed in Mey 1984) proposes a vision of women using language to "change the world," especially the world of women's oppression. I have been able only to hint at the richness of these issues and some ways they can be fruitfully addressed.

In conclusion, three points should be emphasized. First, gender is not simply a matter of individual characteristics (e.g., sex) but also involves actions and social relations, ideology and politics. Second, patterns of language production depend on more than just the agent's intrinsic characteristics, her sociolinguistic 'identity': they also reflect her assessment of social situations—and her choice of strategies for the linguistic construction of her social relations (not just to men but to other women as well). Third, meaning interacts with gender because it links the social/psychological phenomenon of language with the abstract formal notion of a language, an interpreted linguistic system. The individual (what she means, her intentions) is also here inextricably enmeshed in the social (the constraints on the intentions she can have recognized and thereby realized, the social support required for invoking interpretations). In sum, a theory that accommodates the dual psychological and social nature of language and its relation to languages can help further understanding of gender and language.

References

Abel, Elizabeth (ed.) (1982). *Writing and sexual difference*. Chicago: University of Chicago Press.
Austin, J. L. (1962). *How to do things with words*. Cambridge, MA: Harvard University Press.
Bach, Kent, and Robert M. Harnish (1979). *Linguistic communication and speech acts*. Cambridge, MA: MIT Press.
Baron, Dennis (1986). *Grammar and gender*. New Haven: Yale University Press.
Black, Maria, and Rosalind Coward (1981). Linguistic, social and sexual relations. *Screen Education* 39: 69–85.
Bodine, Ann (1975). Sex differentiation in language. In Thorne and Henley 1975.
Borker, Ruth A. (1980). Anthropology: Social and cultural perspectives. In McConnell-Ginet, Borker, and Furman 1980.
Brouwer, D., M. Gerritsen, and D. de Haan (1979). Speech differences between women and men: On the wrong track? *Language in Society* 8: 33–50.
Brown, Gillian, and George Yule (1983). *Discourse analysis*. Cambridge Textbooks in Linguistics. Cambridge: Cambridge University Press.
Brown, Penelope (1976). Women and politeness: A new perspective on language and society. *Reviews in Anthropology* 3: 240–249.
———— (1980). How and why are women more polite: Some evidence from a Mayan community. In McConnell-Ginet, Borker, and Furman 1980.
Brown, Penelope, and Stephen C. Levinson (1978). Universals of language usage: Politeness phenomena. In Esther Goody (ed.), *Questions and politeness: Strategies in social interaction*. Cambridge Papers in Social Anthropology, vol. 8. Cambridge: Cambridge University Press.
———— (1979). Social structure, groups, and interaction. In Scherer and Giles 1979.
Brown, Roger, and Albert Gilman (1960). The pronouns of power and solidarity. In Thomas Sebeok (ed.), *Style in language*. Cambridge, MA: MIT Press.
Cameron, Deborah (1985). *Feminism and linguistic theory*. New York: St Martin's Press.
Cazden, Courtney B., and Sarah Michaels (1985). Gender differences in sixth grade children's letters in an electronic mail system. Paper presented at Boston University Child Language Conference, October 1985.
[Chierchia, Gennaro, and Sally McConnell-Ginet (2000). *Meaning and grammar: An introduction to semantics*, 2nd edition. Cambridge, MA: MIT Press.]
Crosby, Faye, and Linda Nyquist (1977). The female register: An empirical study of Lakoff's hypotheses. *Language in Society* 6: 313–322.
Dijk, Teun van (1984). *Prejudice in discourse*. Pragmatics and Beyond, vol. 3. Amsterdam: Benjamins.
Dubois, Betty Lou, and Isabel M. Crouch (1976). The question of tag questions in women's speech: They don't really use more of them, do they? *Language in Society* 4: 289–294.

Edelsky, Carole (1976). Subjective reactions to sex-linked language. *Journal of Social Psychology* 99: 97–104.

——— (1977). Acquisition of an aspect of communicative competence: Learning what it means to talk like a lady. In Susan Ervin-Tripp and Claudia Mitchell-Kernan (eds.), *Child discourse*. New York: Academic Press.

——— (1981). Who's got the floor? *Language in Society* 10: 383–421.

Ekka, Francis (1972). Men's and women's speech in Kŭrux. *Linguistics* 81: 25–31.

Fishman, Pamela M. (1983). Interaction: The work women do. In Thorne, Kramarae, and Henley 1983.

Flannery, Regina (1946). Men's and women's speech in Gros Ventre. *International Journal of American Linguistics* 12: 133–135.

Frank, Francine Wattman, and Paula A. Treichler (eds.) (1989). *Language, gender and professional writing: Theoretical approaches and guidelines for nonsexist usage*. New York: Modern Language Association.

Furfey, Paul Hanly (1944). Men's and women's language. *American Catholic Sociological Review* 5: 218–223.

Gal, Susan (1978). Peasant men can't get wives: Language change and sex roles in a bilingual community. *Language and Society* 7: 1–16.

Goffman, Erving (1977). The arrangement between the sexes. *Theory and Society* 4: 301–331.

Goodwin, Marjorie Harness (1980a). Directive-response speech sequences in girls' and boys' task activities. In McConnell-Ginet, Borker, and Furman 1980.

——— (1980b). He-said-she-said: Formal cultural procedures for the construction of a gossip dispute activity. *American Ethnologist* 7: 674–695.

Grice, H. Paul (1957). Meaning. *Philosophical Review* 66: 377–388.

——— (1982). More on meaning. In N. V. Smith (ed.), *Mutual knowledge*. New York: Academic Press.

Guy, Gregory (1989). Language and social class. In Frederick J. Newmeyer (ed.), *Linguistics: The Cambridge survey, Volume IV*. Cambridge: Cambridge University Press, 37–63.

Haas, A. (1979). Male and female spoken language differences: Stereotypes and evidence. *Psychological Bulletin* 86: 616–626.

Haas, Mary R. (1944). Men's and women's speech in Koasati. *Language* 20: 142–149. Reprinted in D. Hymes (ed.) (1964). *Language in culture and society*. New York: Harper & Row.

Hakuta, Kenji (1986). *Mirror of language: The debate on bilingualism*. New York: Basic Books.

Harding, Susan (1975). Women and words in a Spanish village. In R. Reiter (ed.), *Towards an anthropology of women*. New York: Monthly Review Press.

Hiatt, Mary (1977). *The way women write*. New York: Teachers College Press.

Hughes, Linda A. (1985). How girls play the game. Paper presented at the Annual Meetings of the Association for the Anthropological Study of Play and the Society for Applied Anthropology.

Jay, Timothy B. (1980). Sex roles and dirty word usage: A review of the literature and a reply to Haas. *Psychological Bulletin* 88: 614–621.

[King, Ruth (ed.) (1991). *Talking gender: A guide to nonsexist communication*. Toronto: Copp Clark Pittman.]

Kramarae, Cheris (1981). *Women and men speaking: Frameworks for analysis*. Rowley: Newbury House.

Kramarae, Cheris, and Paula A. Treichler, with assistance from Ann Russo (1985). *A feminist dictionary*. Boston and London: Pandora Press (Routledge & Kegan Paul).

Kramer, Cheris (1974). Stereotypes of women's speech: The word from cartoons. *Journal of Popular Culture* 8: 624–630.

——— (1978). Male and female perceptions of male and female speech. *Language and Speech* 20.2: 151–161.

Laberge, Suzanne, and Gillian Sankoff (1980). Anything *you* can do. In Gillian Sankoff (ed.), *The social life of language*. Philadelphia: University of Pennsylvania Press.

Lakoff, Robin (1975). *Language and woman's place*. New York: Harper & Row.

[——— (2004). *Language and woman's place: Text and commentaries*. Revised and expanded edition. Edited by Mary Bucholtz. Oxford and New York: Oxford University Press.]

Lavandera, Beatriz (1978). Where does the sociolinguistic variable stop? *Language in Society* 7: 171–83.

Levinson, Stephen C. (1983). *Pragmatics*. Cambridge Textbooks in Linguistics. Cambridge: Cambridge University Press.

Lewis, David (1975). Languages and language. In Keith Gunderson (ed.), *Language, mind, and knowledge*. Minnesota Studies in the Philosophy of Science, vol. 3. Minneapolis: University of Minnesota Press.

——— (1979). Scorekeeping in a language game. In Rainer Bäuerle, Uwe Egli, and Arnim von Stechow (eds.), *Semantics from different points of view*. Berlin: Springer Verlag.

Light, T. (1982). On being '*de*-ing': How women's language is perceived in Chinese. *Computational Analyses of Asian and African Languages* 19: 21–49.

Maltz, Daniel N., and Ruth A. Borker (1982). A cultural approach to male-female miscommunication. In John J. Gumperz (ed.), *Communication, language, and social identity*. Cambridge: Cambridge University Press.

Martyna, Wendy (1980). The psychology of the generic masculine. In McConnell-Ginet, Borker, and Furman 1980.

——— (1983). Beyond the *he/man* approach: The case for nonsexist language. In Thorne, Kramarae, and Henley 1983.

McConnell-Ginet, Sally (1978). Address forms in sexual politics. In D. R. Butturff and E. J. Epstein (eds.), *Women's language and style*. Akron: University of Akron Press.

——— (1979). Review of Hiatt 1977. *Language in Society* 8: 466–469.

——— (1983a). Review of Judith Orasanu, Mariam K. Slater, and Leonore Loeb Adler (eds.) (1979). *Language, sex and gender: Does 'la différence' make a difference?* and Vetterling-Braggin 1981. *Language* 59: 373–391.

——— (1983b). Intonation in a man's world. In Thorne, Kramarae, and Henley 1983.

——— (1984). The origins of sexist language in discourse. In Sheila J. White and Virginia Teller (eds.). *Discourses in reading and linguistics*. New York: Annals of the New York Academy of Sciences.

——— (1985a). Feminism in linguistics. In Treichler, Kramarae, and Stafford 1985.

——— (1985b). 'It's just a question of semantics.' Paper delivered at the Annual Meetings of the Anthropological Association of America, Session on Interpretation.

[——— (2003). 'What's in a name?' Social labeling and gender practices. In Janet Holmes and Miriam Meyerhoff (eds.). *The Handbook of Language and Gender*. Oxford: Blackwell, 69–97.]

[——— (2006). Why defining is seldom 'just semantics': Marriage, 'marriage,' and other minefields. In Betty Birner and Gregory Ward (eds.), *Drawing the Boundaries of Meaning: Neo-Gricean Studies in Pragmatics and Semantics in Honor of Laurence R. Horn*. Amsterdam: John Benjamins. Shortened version in Deborah Cameron and Don Kulick (eds.) (2006). *Language and sexuality: A reader*. London: Routledge, 227–240.]

McConnell-Ginet, Sally, Ruth A. Borker, and Nelly Furman (eds.) (1980). *Women and language in literature and society*. New York: Praeger.

Mey, J. (1984). Sex and language revisited: Can women's language change the world? *Journal of Pragmatics* 8: 261–283.

[Mills, Sara (2008). *Language and sexism*. Cambridge: Cambridge University Press.]

Nichols, Patricia (1980). Women in their speech communities. In McConnell-Ginet, Borker, and Furman 1980.

——— (1983). Linguistic options and choices for black women in the rural South. In Thorne, Kramarae, and Henley 1983.

——— (1984). Networks and hierarchies: Language and social stratification. In Cheris Kramarae, Muriel Schulz, and William M. O'Barr (eds.), *Language and power*. Beverly Hills: Sage.

O'Barr, William, and Bowman K. Atkins (1980). 'Women's language' or 'power-less language'? In McConnell-Ginet, Borker, and Furman 1980.

[Ochs, Elinor (1992). Indexing gender. In Alessandro Duranti and Charles Goodwin (ed.), *Rethinking context*. Cambridge: Cambridge University Press, 335–358.]

Ostriker, Alicia Suskin (1986). *Stealing the language: The emergence of women's poetry in America*. Boston: Beacon Press.

Pettigrew, Thomas F. (1979). The ultimate attribution error: Extending Allport's cognitive analysis of prejudice. *Personality and Social Psychology Bulletin* 5: 461–476.

Philips, Susan U. (1980). Sex differences and language. *Annual Review of Anthropology* 9: 523–544.

——— (1983). The interaction of variable syntax and discourse structure in gen-der-differentiated speech in the courtroom. Paper presented at NEH Conference on Sex Differences in Language, University of Arizona. Revised version in Philips, Steele, and Tanz 1987, 1–11.

Philips, Susan U., Susan Steele, and Christine Tanz (eds.) (1987). *Language, gender and sex in comparative perspective*. Cambridge: Cambridge University Press.

Putnam, Hilary (1975). *Philosophical papers II: Mind, language and reality*. Cambridge: Cambridge University Press.

Ruthven, Kenneth Knowles (1984). *Feminist literary studies: An introduction*. Cambridge: Cambridge University Press.

Sapir, Edward (1929). Male and female forms of speech in Yana. In D. G. Mandelbaum (ed.) (1949). *Selected writings of Edward Sapir*. Berkeley: University of California Press.

Scheman, Naomi (1980). Anger and the politics of naming. In McConnell-Ginet, Borker, and Furman 1980.

Scherer, Klaus R., and Howard Giles (eds.) (1979). *Social markers in speech.* Cambridge: Cambridge University Press.

Schulz, Muriel R. (1975). The semantic derogation of women. In Thorne and Henley 1975.

Sherzer, Joel (1983). Ethnography of speaking and men's and women's speech differences. Paper presented at the NEH Sex Differences in Language Conference, University of Arizona, January 1983. Revised version in Philips, Steele, and Tanz 1987, 95–120.

Shibamoto, Janet S. (1985). *Japanese women's language.* New York: Academic Press.

Showalter, Elaine (1982). Feminist criticism in the wilderness. In Abel 1982.

Siegler, David M., and Robert S. Siegler (1976). Stereotypes of males' and females' speech. *Psychological Reports* 39: 167–170.

Smith, Philip M. (1979). Sex markers in speech. In Scherer and Giles 1979.

——— (1985). *Language, the sexes and society.* Oxford: Blackwell.

Spender, Dale (1980). *Man made language.* London: Routledge & Kegan Paul.

Stanback, Marsha Houston (1985). Language and black woman's place: Evidence from the black middle class. In Treichler, Kramarae, and Stafford 1985.

Stanley, Julia (1978). Sexist language. *College English* 39: 800–811.

Tannen, Deborah (1986). *That's not what I meant! How conversational style makes or breaks your relations with others.* New York: Morrow.

[——— (1990). *You just don't understand: Women and men in conversation.* New York: Morrow.]

[——— (1994). The relativity of linguistic strategies: Rethinking power and solidarity in gender and dominance. In Deborah Tannen (ed.), *Gender and discourse.* Oxford: Oxford University Press, 19–52.]

Taylor, Allan R. (1983). 'Male' and 'female' speech in Gros Ventre. *Anthropological Linguistics* 24: 301–307.

Thorne, Barrie, and Nancy Henley (eds.) (1975). *Language and sex: Difference and dominance.* Rowley: Newbury House.

Thorne, Barrie, Cheris Kramarae, and Nancy Henley (eds.) (1983). *Language, gender and society.* Rowley, MA: Newbury House.

Treichler, Paula A. (1989). From discourse to dictionary: How sexist meanings are authorized. In Frank and Treichler 1989, 51–79.

Treichler, Paula A., and Cheris Kramarae (1983). Women's talk in the ivory tower. *Communication Quarterly* 31: 118–132.

Treichler, Paula A., Cheris Kramarae, and B. Stafford (eds.) (1985). *For Alma Mater: Theory and practice in feminist scholarship.* Urbana: University of Illinois Press.

Trömel-Plötz, Senta (1982). *Frauensprache—Sprache der Veränderung.* Frankfurt-am-Main: Fischer.

Trudgill, Peter (1983). *On dialect: Social and geographical perspectives.* Oxford: Blackwell.

Valian, Virginia (1977). Linguistics and feminism. Reprinted in Vetterling-Braggin 1981.

Vetterling-Braggin, Mary (ed.) (1981). *Sexist language: A modern philosophical analysis.* Totowa: Littlefield, Adams.

West, Candace, and Don H. Zimmerman (1983). Small insults: A study of interruptions in cross-sex conversations between unacquainted persons. In Thorne, Kramarae, and Henley 1983.

Wolfson, Nessa, and Joan Manes (1980). 'Don't "dear" me.' In McConnell-Ginet, Borker, and Furman 1980.

3

Feminism in linguistics

0. Introduction

Linguistics, the 'science of language', has links to feminist scholarship that seem obvious to the nonlinguist and rather obscure to the linguist. We might attribute this obscurity to the dominance of men in the profession, but many women and feminists in linguistics find themselves rather puzzled as well. This is not simply a question of sexism in linguistics, though it is certainly true that sexist examples abound in linguistics texts[1] and journal articles and that linguists have focused on varieties of language that they themselves or people like them (i.e., an educated [white] male elite) use.[2] More broadly, the question is this: how might linguistics contribute substantively to an understanding of women's experience? How might a feminist orientation illuminate those questions about language that led many of us into linguistic research? How has feminism begun to influence linguistic scholarship? Finally, perhaps most important, what further questions might a feminist linguistics explore?[3]

Disciplines are delineated not only by subject matter but also by methodology and theoretical orientation. On the first day of an introductory linguistics class and in the first chapter of our introductory linguistics texts, we say that linguistics is of great importance because language is central in human thought and in social interaction. The remainder of the course or text is then devoted to the study of language as an autonomous structured system whose use (in thought or social life) is beyond our scope. The focus on formal structures in isolation from their use reflects the important insight that linguistic systems can be elegantly described in terms that do not refer to the 'extralinguistic' context. By treating language on its own terms, linguists have been able to achieve a degree of theoretical rigor and descriptive precision unmatched by other behavioral and social sciences. Sloppiness has been excised by a strategy that abstracts linguistic forms from the sociocultural and psychological matrices in which they are embedded.

This essay first appeared in Paula A. Treichler, Cheris Kramarae, and Beth Stafford, eds., *For Alma Mater: Theory and practice in feminist scholarship* (Urbana: University of Illinois Press), 159–176.

Many critics would say that rigor in linguistics has been achieved at the price of rigor mortis. The radical operation required to 'isolate' the language system has killed it: formal rules and representations provide no insight into language as a human activity. The defense against this malpractice charge, of course, is to develop an account of the relation between abstract linguistic systems and the mental states and processes, social actions and cultural values, that infuse them with life. My own view is that the isolating strategy is the only viable first approach. It is extraordinarily unlikely that one could provide a revealing account of language uses and their relation to language users without distinguishing forms independently of the uses their users put them to. Certainly no one has. Yet the modular approach that explains complex phenomena as the product of interacting simpler systems does require that our simple modules be connectable and that their structures support the desired kinds of interaction. More specifically, an autonomous account of a linguistic system has done only part of the job of a theory of human language and linguistic communication.

Two approaches connect linguistics with feminist questions about human thought and action; each illustrates a mode of feminist scholarship conducted from the perspective of traditional disciplines. In the 'applied' mode, disciplinary tools shed light on women in culture and society, on the place of gender in human thought and social structures. Linguistic scholarship here serves to inform feminism, and the need for interdisciplinary and collaborative research quickly becomes apparent.

In the 'feedback' mode, linguistics is informed by feminism (and, ultimately, human experience). Insights and knowledge derived from women's lives and their analyses of sexism, male dominance, and related phenomena lead us to ask new questions about what language is like and how it works. For example, 'telescopic' approaches to the study of language and the sexes, to adopt Barrie Thorne's label for this work, frequently suggest that men 'control' language.[4] Since all speakers and all language systems are 'equal' in the eyes of the Great Grammarian, it is initially difficult to know how such control could be exercised and what is meant by the claim. Although there is not an all-male legislative body directing our linguistic developments, it is nevertheless apparent that our vocabulary and various aspects of our accepted and expected ways of talking are indicative of male-centered perspectives and sexist biases.[5] Few linguists doubt that vocabulary somehow bears the imprint of (past and present) sociocultural values. None, however, has proposed an account of the mechanisms through which the semantic system of a language develops in response to its users' situationally specific notions of how the world is (or is feared or wished to be). Feminist observations make it imperative for linguistic theory to address this question and, more particularly, to consider how it is that the notions of some users are more successfully encoded than those of others.[6] I will return briefly in the final section to discussion of how feminist investigations and analyses can feed back into linguistics.

There are not really two separate modes of feminist scholarship, of course, since it is in trying to 'apply' linguistics that feminists find their efforts 'feeding back' to extend or transform the conceptual frameworks and research methods of the discipline. Application and theory must go hand in hand, just like the study of language uses and language structure. But the distinction is useful for talking about the focus and implications of current research.

1. Linguistics applied in feminist scholarship

What tools can linguists offer feminist scholars for the study of language? First (and probably foremost), we can offer *precise formal characterizations of expressions speakers (and writers) use*. We describe language at a number of different structural levels: any aspect of linguistic form, ranging from the most minute details of sound patterning to the specifications of different levels of syntactic structure (connecting 'deep' and 'surface' hierarchical structuring of phrases via transformational rules), is potentially significant in an account of language and behavior.

What is meant by an utterance is not, however, specifiable with the same level of precision as its syntactic and phonological structure. Insofar as communicative significance depends on such strictly linguistic considerations as the particular semantic domain in which words occur or the syntactic relationships of words in a particular utterance, linguistic specifications of semantic structure are useful to feminist investigators. However, communicators draw on more than common knowledge of a vocabulary and syntax. Not only do they exploit what have been dubbed 'mutual contextual beliefs',[7] but in face-to-face communication their words are set in an intonational framework and accompanied by facial expressions, manual gestures, body postures, and the like. Linguists do not agree on how to describe intonational structure nor on precisely how it is integrated into the syntactic and phonological systems of a language. Nonvocal gestures receive even less attention, since most linguists view them as independent accompaniments to the specialized language system (except, of course, in cases like American Sign Language). Nonetheless, what we convey to one another when we speak face to face clearly draws on a full range of expressive behaviors: both intonation and nonvocal gesture have been the subject of feminist discussion.[8] Thus it becomes imperative for investigators to develop analyses that permit us, for example, to describe the 'same' intonational pattern as recurring in different communicative contexts (and superimposed on different sentence frames). [See ch. 6, this book, for more discussion.]

Second, linguistics offers some *methods and procedures for the collection and analysis of language uses*. Linguistic patterning often takes place below the level of conscious attention for members of the speech community. Although what people say about their language (about word meanings, for example, or relationships among sounds) is important for the linguist, it is not decisive. The linguist looks at data on actual language *use* as well as linguistic intuitions of speakers, and is trained in techniques that facilitate discovery of the abstract system(s) underlying speakers' language use. Working with informants (including oneself if the language under study is native to the investigator) in order to test explicit and detailed hypotheses about the language system is the classic method; it involves eliciting judgments about the sameness and difference of linguistic forms, 'appropriateness' of forms to a context of use, and the like. More recently, linguists have extended these methods (not abandoning the familiar techniques but adding new procedures) in order to discover fine-grained regularities governing apparent irregularities in the data collected from different speakers in different contexts and to try to dissolve what William Labov calls the "Observer's Paradox."[9] The paradox arises because the investigator needs high-quality recordings of systematically sampled actual language use, yet the process of careful observation affects (and distorts) the language used. Our job is to find ways to provide good data on speech in the social context without obscuring or distorting the effects of that context. There is no single technique that solves the problem, but the careful researcher uses a variety of techniques and kinds of data with the aim of canceling out the error inherent in any single approach. Work with isolated informants, although still important, is not sufficient because much systematicity in the community's language use can be observed only through detailed analysis of socially heterogeneous language users in situations other than the special one of interacting with a linguist.

Linguistic studies of language used by and about the sexes do not by themselves illuminate feminist concerns. The linguist's tools must be used in conjunction with other tools that help us identify language users' aims and purposes, the effects of language use on hearers (and readers), the sociocultural conventions governing particular kinds of speech events in particular settings, and similar phenomena. In other words, linguistics in feminist scholarship must be integrated into more general, cross-disciplinary investigations.

In applying linguistic tools, feminist scholars studying language have pursued three main themes: (1) language as a subtle indicator of social structure and cultural values; (2) language use as a significant factor both in maintaining and in transmitting male-centered values and views; and (3) language change as a potential instrument for achieving the far-reaching social, cultural, and political changes envisioned by the women's movement.

1.1 Linguistic indicators of women's experience in society and culture

Much careful work on language as an indicator of nonlinguistic phenomena has focused on speech varieties—that is, on the repertoires used by socially differentiated groups of speakers (women and men, for example) within a speech community—looking at frequency of use of alternative forms for saying the 'same thing', what is called LINGUISTIC VARIATION. Two related sorts of cases are easily accessible for systematic study: (1) communities with distinct codes or languages available and multilingual speakers who switch among them, and (2) communities that exhibit structured 'sociolectal' variation in the use, for example, of alternative pronunciations, especially where such variation is indicative of ongoing change. In both sorts of situations, gender appears to interact with language use and/or evaluation. The major question behind all such research can be put simply: what leads people to adopt a particular variety of speech? We do not know what is indicated by a speaker's use of a particular variety unless we have some answer to the question of how she (or he) came to use that variety rather than some other of the community's options.

How one speaks, given options in the particular community's linguistic repertoire, can indicate any or all of the following four factors:

1. *Access*. This depends on formal education and on communicative frequency. How do the people to whom you talk most often speak? Which variants from the collective repertoire do you hear most often?
2. *Social bonds*. How do your friends, the people whom you turn to for social interaction, talk? Here, quality or purpose rather than quantity of verbal interchange is emphasized.
3. *Social identity and status*. Speech differences may be maintained even where communication is frequent and personal ties exist if such differences mark distinctions that organize the life of the community. Gender identity may, for example, be marked verbally as a symbol of sexual difference.
4. *Utility*. Certain varieties of talk may be required for particular occupations or activities, the pool of marriage partners may be linked to the linguistic varieties, and so on. The instrumental value of particular varieties may differ for women and men because of their different occupational choices and options for social mobility.

All of these factors operate for both women and men, their relative weight depending on both social and psychological considerations. We need assume no inherent differences in the social psychology of the sexes but rather suppose both women and men to be rational social actors, whose choices reflect available information and likelihood of success. Information on how these factors operate in particular speech communities for women and men will help us understand speech differences and similarities.

Some examples will help. Patricia C. Nichols, reporting on a larger study of sociolectal variation in speech forms used in some South Carolina black communities, shows that differences between women and men in their use of creole as opposed to 'standard' variants are chiefly explained in terms of their differential social mobility. In one community, the better-paying jobs for women (teacher, clerk, etc.) required some facility in use of non-creole forms. Jobs held by men from this community were blue-collar occupations, not requiring any special linguistic skills. In this community, women used non-creole variants (representing innovations, a change from the traditional forms of the community) much more frequently than did men. In a nearby community where both women and men were relatively restricted in their occupational options, men were more likely than women (whose mobility was most restricted) to have some access to non-creole variants and. to use them, thus exhibiting more 'innovative' linguistic behavior.

Studies of code-switching show similar complexities in sex-differentiated patterning. Ann Farber and Susan Gal describe quite different bilingual situations. Farber studied the use of Cakchiquel, a local Mayan language, and Spanish in a Guatemalan village, finding Indian women much less likely to be fluent in Spanish than their male counterparts and less likely to admit to knowledge of Spanish even if they had it. Since Cakchiquel is the language of domestic life in the village, attempts to use Spanish are seen as forays from the domestic domain to which Indian women in the village have been traditionally confined. Men receive somewhat more formal education, though this is changing, and thus have more explicit instruction in Spanish. Spanish is essential for men's upward mobility, whereas for women, Spanish is associated with rejection of traditional Indian society and the women's roles associated with that society.

In Gal's study, the bilingual situation reflects long-term close contact of Hungarian- and German-speaking populations near the Austro-Hungarian border (within present-day Germany). Here, use of Hungarian is associated with peasant life, an option that women are more forcefully rejecting than men. People of both sexes know each of the two languages, although a few old peasant women are monolingual in Hungarian, reflecting their relatively lesser access to German as a result of limited schooling and restricted participation in nondomestic domains. Weighing industrial wage labor against small-scale farming, a Hungarian man may see certain advantages in the life of the farmer. For the young woman, however, industrial society offers clear advantages: life as a factory worker or as the wife of a worker is considerably more comfortable than the drudgery that falls to the wife in a farming household. Similar factors apparently explain the finding by Werner Leopold of women's greater use of standard German rather than local dialects as industrialization began to offer an attractive option to family-based agriculture, an option especially appealing to women, given the sexual division of labor operative in that society.[10]

Thus the linguistic map of a community may provide a signpost to previously uncharted social phenomena. Once the investigator has considered the effects of access, social ties, identities and statuses, and utility in the use of competing variants, shifts within a particular speaker's production will serve to indicate how that speaker assesses her (or his) social and occupational options, what identities are being presented, and the like. Linguistic choices reflect the speakers' own social analyses and thus provide one way to get at women's own perspective on their lives, rather than relying on the categorizations developed by androcentric social science, which is generally also biased toward the distinctions that operate for a particular class, ethnic group, and cultural setting.[11]

In these cases, we are talking about variation whose main explanation is to be found in the existence of alternatives associated with different groups and situations within the speech community. Social meaning is attached, for example, to the choice of a particular pronunciation of a word or to the use of one language rather than another; the point at issue is not the primary message but the secondary form its expression takes. In contrast, some differences in language use arise from saying something different in roughly equivalent communicative situations; there are distinct SPEECH STRATEGIES for "doing things with words" (the formulation of Austin 1960). In very similar circumstances, speakers can say something different (not the same thing in different words) as they follow distinct courses of verbal action in order to achieve their (often slightly different) social and personal goals. The alternatives used in this case represent different linguistic signaling elements or different structural arrangements of such elements.

For example, if I need to know the time and believe you can provide me with that information, I might say:

(a) Hey, man. What time is it?
(b) Excuse me. What time do you have?
(c) Oh, sir. Do you have the time?
(d) I'm sorry to bother you, but could you please tell me what time it is?

And so on. Any fluent speaker of English is able to interpret any of these utterances as a request for information and knows that the difference among them is linked to the social relationships of the speaker and addressee and the relative care being taken by the speaker to recognize the addressee's possible inconvenience in complying with such a request. In (a) and (c), the forms used to attract the addressee's attention signal a male addressee; (a) also suggests a male addressor.

The same four factors that influence patterns of linguistic variation can also help determine preferred speech strategies: what one does when one is not paying special attention to speech choices. Thus precisely what is meant by saying certain things—making certain moves—may depend in part simply on social identity. Ruth Borker and Daniel Maltz have argued that American girls and boys, who spend much of their unstructured play time in single-sex groups, develop somewhat different preferred speech strategies and thus that the same acts in what look like equivalent contexts may have quite different significance. Failure of each sex to recognize these differences in their 'habitual' speech strategizing can lead to communication breakdowns.[12]

A number of linguistic forms and constructions function primarily (sometimes in conjunction with other communicative functions) to mark social relations and how an action is to be interpreted—its significance, given the linguistic and extralinguistic context. Address forms, politeness particles, and what are sometimes called 'indirect speech acts'—in (c) and (d) above the point is not what is 'literally' conveyed—all function in this way. Mapping such linguistic forms can provide indexes of sexual stratification within the society and can illuminate the negotiating of social relations and status within particular interactions. It is often said that women are more polite in their speech, and many studies do find such results and explain them in terms of women's generally subordinate position. Yet as Penelope Brown (n. 10) shows, there are multiple reasons for choosing 'polite' speech strategies, and important distinctions among kinds of politeness, and one must investigate in detail the functions of particular speech forms in a given linguistic community in order to see, in her phrase, "how and why" women are more polite.

Turning from a focus on women and men as speakers to women and men (and their relationships) as spoken of, we find additional evidence of sex-typing in the division of labor and in expected behavior as well as indications of past (and present) attitudes toward women and men. Here we find, among other things, studies of the vocabulary of sexism. Linguist Robin Lakoff has noted asymmetries in vocabulary; she points to the sexualization of many terms for referring to women (compare, for example, *master* and *mistress*) and the linguistic chivalry that extends an originally "elevated" term like *lady* to virtually all contexts of female reference (compare *cleaning lady* with the nonoccurring male parallel, **garbage gentleman*). She argues that the chivalry and sexualization are linked: there is a need for euphemisms to use in certain contexts in lieu of the sexually explicit and degrading terms so widely used.[13]

The methodological strategy underlying such analyses is consideration of oppositions within the means of expression available to speakers and recognized by them. For example, most speakers do analyze *lady* as opposed to *woman, girl*, and possibly less neutral terms of reference such as *broad* and *chick*. It is also, of course, opposed to *gentleman* in some uses, to *fella* or *buddy* in others (as in the position indicated by the parentheses: "Look here, ( ). I had the right of way."). The linguist looks at such oppositions or alternations as well as the contexts of use, both linguistic and extralinguistic, in order to assess the 'meaning' of linguistic forms. The major problem, of course, is that the set of alternatives is not well defined nor is the range of linguistic and social contexts in which forms occur determinate. Sometimes for some speakers, *lady* is in opposition to *cunt*. For other speakers, the term *cunt* is never used to refer to a female human nor seldom (if ever) heard in such uses. Whose culture and whose conceptual world are we inferring?

Similar problems arise in considering the significance of terminology and word histories. For example, though *virtue* is historically linked with *virile* and indicates the ancient view that excluded women from the moral community, this particular connection is probably no longer operative for most speakers. On the other hand, *sissy* still conveys devaluation of women's behavior and activities so whether or not speakers link it with *sister* does not matter in terms of their being able to infer something about prevalent misogyny. A more recent example: *OTR* comes from *on the rag*, an expression referring to menstruation and used (by extension based on beliefs about menstruation and its effects) to signify irritableness. Some speakers do not know the history of *OTR* or of *on the rag*; for them, it simply means something like 'grouchy'. Even where the history of an expression is transparent to users, they may employ it in a use whose initial establishment depended on views to which they themselves do not subscribe; for example, a correspondent to *Ms.* magazine noted Robin Lakoff's use of *left-handed compliment*.[14] Although the existence of this phrase eloquently testifies to a prevalent distrust of left-handers and a preference for right-handers (as does the asymmetry between *sinister* and *dexterous*, deriving from the terms designating left and right, respectively), it is now a 'fixed' phrase. (Actually we need not suppose prejudice but simply the assumption of the right-handed majority's perspective on the relative worth of left and right.) This does not mean the expression is innocent of double messages; it simply indicates how a particular speaker may (perhaps unwittingly) convey messages about attitudes and values she (or he) does not share.[a]

If, however, we can point to certain kinds of patterns in a particular speaker's language use, we may well uncover a complex of beliefs and feelings that were not evident before, and perhaps not consciously articulated. A point on the infamous 'generic' *he* may help make this clear. Listening to a lecture on how to be a good teacher, I found myself attributing to the speaker the apparent intention to use *he* with sex-indefinite antecedents: *the good student, a conscientious professor*, and so on. Then when the speaker said, "When a student finally gathers courage to ask a question, don't intimidate her," he revealed a sex-linked stereotype of the timid student, a stereotype that he might have denied, sincerely but self-deceptively, if queried about it directly. Links of language to individual and general attitudes and values are complex, a complexity obscured by the indiscriminate use of such terms as "sexist language." We do not discover meanings only by consulting dictionaries but by looking at patterns of actual language use, the connections speakers make among linguistic forms, and similar evidence.[15]

---

a. The point about 'unwitting' triggering of inferences to which one does not subscribe is briefly mentioned in chapter 8 of this book and further developed in my notion of conceptual baggage, introduced in my "Words in the world: How and why meanings can matter," *Language* 84, no. 3 (2008): 497–527.

1.2 Language as 'conservator' of existing values

Linguists have had relatively little to say about the role of language (use) in maintaining and transmitting male-centered values, and what they have offered about the role of linguistic change in social change is often either inadequate or plain wrong. Given, however, the value of patterns of language (use) for indicating social attitudes and values, it is not hard to see how those patterns become implicated in maintaining the power of the socially dominant group (in our own culture, males of the white upper-middle class). The members of the sociocultural group read and read again and thus attach renewed significance to the indicators they have created. In particular, the child entering the system becomes a 'reader', an interpreter of the system into which she (or he) is supposed to fit. In addition, of course, we all receive subtle extra messages in addition to the not-so-subtle overt control exercised by the powerful in verbal exchanges. Because at least some uses of language *are* social actions, they do not simply indicate to us an independently existing social order but work to create that order and maintain it.

1.3 Language as instrument for social change

Thus changes in language can be part of social change. To the extent that language functions to make knowledge and experience public, it is important for feminists to arrive at some consensus on ways of articulating new insights that derive from woman's knowledge and experience. Sometimes new lexical items are helpful: labels like *sexism* and *male chauvinism*, for example, tie feminist analyses of women's oppression and exclusion from the mainstream to analyses of such related phenomena as racism and superpatriotism.[16] This provides a framework for analysis and investigation that may ultimately illuminate our understanding of women's position, perhaps eventually transforming the original framework in light of what we come to know about sexual differentiation and stratification in different sociocultural and historical settings.

Terms of address and reference shift as women (and men) adopt different social positions and roles. Changed patterns of address and reference play a role in changing views of options and roles, since they indicate alternative social maps. It is true that we can not suppose that words alone will win the war, but no feminist was ever so deceived. A determined male chauvinist may scrupulously use *chairperson*, generally with strong stress on the second part of the compound to say, "What a good boy am I," whereas many a committed feminist slips into the familiar *chairman*, with an unstressed suffix that does not sound like the independent form *man*. The linguist cannot predict the fate of particular attempts to change patterns of language use (and thus, ultimately, the system underlying those patterns). What the linguist can do and has frequently failed at is provide a careful analysis of present usage and an account of the likeliest directions of change, given the present system *and* given the present attitudes, beliefs, and values of those who would participate in propagating the changes launched. Speakers can then make individual choices (perhaps with benefit of collective strategizing) in order to maximize chances of advancing their goals.

It is sometimes suggested that women change their speech styles and strategies in order to improve their chances of achieving desired ends. Assertiveness training, for example, teaches people certain so-called assertive communicative devices to employ in particular situations.[17] Women do sometimes fall into a non-assertive trap by, for example, letting strategies of politeness and indirection become so habitual that they are used even when not suited to the situation or the speaker's aims.[18] It also may well be helpful to look closely at one's own language use to discover the sorts of attitudes and beliefs one may be unintentionally communicating, the ways in which one submits or defers without really intending such action. Nonetheless, precisely because there may be, and usually are, multiple functions assigned to a single form and thus competing explanations of particular usages, women must beware of falling into another trap: reading themselves according to a male-centered view of how people 'should' behave, and what is indicated when they don't behave that way.

2. Toward a feminist theory of language

Language is central in human life because it connects the individual mind and its stock of experience with a social and cultural order that embodies the evidence of others' perceptions, interpretations, thoughts, and beliefs. Variety among languages serves to demarcate social groupings, to mark identity, to build social structures. The conventional linguistic view of language as a system sealed off from the public world and from other psychological systems is inadequate to account for the feedback that relates language, mind, and society.

To combat views of the inherent superiority of the Indo-European languages, twentieth-century linguists have tended to accept the twin principles of linguistic optimism and linguistic egalitarianism:

1. Principle of linguistic optimism: all linguistic systems are ideally suited to meet the expressive and communicative needs of their users.
2. Principle of linguistic egalitarianism: language users have equal access to the resources of their language, equal facility in deploying them, and equal status as users and interpreters.

We needn't return to the belief that God thinks in Greek to object to this ostrich-like view of how languages serve their speakers' needs. It was always recognized that (1) might not hold at all times: a supplementary principle held that the linguistic system lagged somewhat behind the social system but eventually—without anyone's giving the matter any conscious thought—the linguistic system 'caught up'. These principles relate to two other principles implicit in most linguistic theories:

3. Principle of autonomous semantics: semantic/conceptual structures exist independently of their linguistic encoding.
4. Principle of marginality of the lexicon: changes in productive and/ or receptive lexical repertoires do not significantly change linguistic competence. Lexical creation and shift and extension of existing lexical resources to new uses are seen as essentially nonlinguistic.

Detailed examination of the actual facts of language use forces us to abandon these and related dogmas.

It is not that feminist scholarship has shown us what form an adequate linguistic theory must take. Rather, feminist scholarship shows us that the conventional approaches to the description of linguistic structures are inadequate. Recent investigations of 'linguistic pragmatics'—the contribution to 'meaning' of speech acts, language users, and contexts—move toward restoring language to the sociocultural context from which we extracted it for analysis. Cognitive theories, with attention to perceptual strategies, for example, are beginning to reconnect language with its mental environment. If linguists pay attention to the interrelationships among language, thought, and sociocultural systems that feminist scholarship is uncovering, we may be pushed to revise our theories of language, perhaps eventually to make precise and explicit the insights long ago hinted at by the linguist and anthropologist Edward Sapir. Sapir flirts with the four principles I just gave, noting also the value of language as an index to the culture of those who speak it and enunciating the view that "the form of language is the form of thought." I don't know whether Sapir would have considered himself a feminist; I do know that the most careful study of sex-based differences in speech prior to the relatively recent upsurge of attention was his "Male and Female Forms of Speech in Yana," succeeded by research of some of his students.[19]

What kinds of theories and research programs might a feminist linguistics develop? As I have already indicated, we badly need a plausible account of the mechanisms through which language use, for example, speech situated in face-to-face interactions, affects the language system. Such a theory must answer to the evidence from careful documentation of ongoing language change; detailed studies of patterns of pronoun usage, for example, could be important in helping us understand how changes occur. Studies should sample a variety of social contexts and attend to interactional phenomena as well as to the speech output of individuals. More generally, we need a closer look at the give and take between speaker and hearer, at how 'meaning' evolves, for example, during discourse.[20] More attention must be paid to the influence of contextual factors other than gender if we are to understand how gender interacts with such factors. I hypothesized that children draw some wrong inferences from what they hear, that this is a way language slows or impedes social change; such hypotheses need to be tested. Single-sex speech interactions, for example, talk in women's 'consciousness-raising' groups,[21] must be studied in some detail if one is to assess the significance of data from cross-sex conversation. And so on.

I would stress, however, that theory and observation have to develop in tandem. Stacks of cassettes and reams of text are of little value in the absence of well-articulated explanatory frameworks. Theories, of course, need to be subjected to empirical tests, but theory-free observation does not exist, and feminist scholars need to articulate explicit theoretical frameworks to guide our observations toward potentially illuminating phenomena. This is especially vital since otherwise we are unlikely to make any advance in understanding beyond the impoverished conceptual frameworks we inherit from the long tradition of male-dominated scholarship. This doesn't mean starting de novo—were that possible—but rather following the painstaking process of revising and re-forming theories and methods in order to transform scholarship.[22]

When is an academic feminist a feminist scholar? When scholarship informs feminism and feminism informs scholarship.

Notes

[1. See Monica Macaulay and Colleen Brice, "Don't touch my projectile: gender bias and stereotyping in syntactic examples," *Language* 73 (1997): 353–363.]

2. These and related points have been illustrated and discussed in numbers of papers and talks, for example, Stanley 1978; Nichols 1980.

3. McConnell-Ginet 1978 and 1984 deal most explicitly with these issues. The questions posed, however, underlie most of my research in this area. [And in this volume see especially part III—that is, chapters 8–11.]

4. Barrie Thorne (1978) talks of 'telescopic' views of language and feminism, which she opposes to 'microscopic' views.

5. Schultz 1975 documents some of the impact of sexism on the history of English vocabulary. Interesting articles dealing with this topic can also be found in Nilsen et al. 1977; Vetterling-Braggin 1981. Miller and Swift 1977 is a clear discussion for a general audience. Although the literature on apparent sexism in the vocabulary is quite extensive, there are few discussions of syntactic signals of language users' sexism; see, however, Tschudi 1979.

6. Kramarae 1980 and Blaubergs 1980 discuss the social psychology of responses to feminist-inspired changes in language use. Martyna 1980 provides solid empirical evidence that gender-differentiated patterns of comprehension and production exist. Such investigations offer valuable data and analyses against which linguistic hypotheses of mechanisms of language change and its relation to social processes must be tested.

7. See Bach and Harnish 1979 for interesting discussion of certain aspects of how this works.

8. See McConnell-Ginet, "Intonation in a Man's World" (chapter 6, this volume). See also Edelsky 1979. Henley 1977 is an illuminating study of non-verbal communication from a feminist perspective.

9. Labov has discussed this issue in a number of publications. The most accessible account is probably Labov 1972. The "Observer's Paradox" is formulated on p. 209.

10. The work discussed in the text is to be found in Farber 1974; Gal 1978; Leopold 1959.

11. Penelope Brown (1980) develops and illustrates in detail the point about women's language usage giving a 'woman's-eye' view of social phenomena. Nichols (1980) notes that most sociolinguistic studies have assumed that a woman's social status derives from that of some man (husband or father), an assumption that not only places single adult women in a no-woman's land but also distorts social status and roles of women who do happen to be part of a family unit including a male 'head of household'. Detailed analysis of language usage of women and men in the same household frequently makes it impossible to maintain this assumption. Individual women have a social identity that may be quite distinct from that of the men with whom they live; this fact seems blatantly obvious, but detailed analysis of their speech provides evidence that the skeptical sociolinguist would find hard to ignore.

12. Maltz and Borker 1982. They note especially the evidence in Goodwin 1980. McConnell-Ginet, "Intonation in a Man's World" [chapter 6, this volume], suggests that intonational choices may hold different significance in some cases for women and for men—and that men project their interpretation onto women's choices, sometimes refusing to acknowledge the possibility of alternative analyses.

13. Lakoff's work has received considerable attention and is more widely known among linguists than some of the related materials mentioned in n. 4. Most of the work mentioned in that note assumes *contra* Lakoff that such linguistic facts are not only indicative but also constitutive of sexism in society. I draw my examples from Lakoff 1975.

14. The correspondent was replying to Lakoff 1974; letter from Megan D. Price, Fair Haven, VT.

15. Of course, lexicographers can sometimes provide us with useful data on actual uses and thus helpful guides to meaning. However, it is important to bear in mind that lexicography is no less a male-dominated profession than linguistics. Wendy Martyna (1980) abundantly demonstrates that competing conventions of usage exist in the speech community: dictionaries and grammars are more likely to overlook women's interpretations and patterns of production than men's, I suspect. [Treichler 1989 is a relevant account of dictionary making.]

16. See Frye 1976 for an illustration of the intellectual fruits such neologisms can bear.

17. Henley 1979 provides a sharp feminist critique of assertiveness training programs. [Gervasio and Crawford 1989 provide empirical evidence that those who follow advice of assertiveness trainers may well be handicapped rather than helped in their dealings with others.]

18. Treichler 1980 beautifully evokes this kind of 'entrapment' history.

19. "Male and Female Forms of Speech in Yana" first appeared in Teeuwen 1929 (pp. 79–85); it is reprinted in Mandelbaum 1949 (pp. 206–212). This volume contains many interesting papers by Sapir. Sapir's student Mary Haas (1944) wrote another of the classic papers on sex-based differences in language use.

20. I am working on an account of linguistic meaning and its relation to language-in-use that will, I hope, shed some light on these issues. That study, *The Construction of Meaning*, is highly theoretical, however, and these phenomena require careful and detailed empirical investigation as well. [That projected volume

may or may not ever appear; much of the material therein has since appeared in other publications.] In McConnell-Ginet 1984 [most of which is incorporated in chapter 8 of this volume], I argue that conventionalization of conversational implicature is a central mechanism of semantic change, that power and privilege make it easier successfully to implicate one's own perspective, and thus that it is more likely not only that men's perspectives get 'encoded' but also that such 'encoding' could happen without women's "assenting" to the views so expressed.

21. See Susan Kalčik 1975; Scheman 1980.

22. Some have thought feminist linguists were discarding all 'traditional' linguistic theory; see Kean 1980 and my reply, McConnell-Ginet 1980.

References

[Austin, John L. (1962). *How to do things with words*. Oxford: Oxford University Press.]

Blaubergs, Maija S. (1980). An analysis of classic arguments against changing sexist language. In Cheris Kramarae (ed.), *The voices and words of women and men*. Oxford: Pergamon Press, 135–148.

Brown, Penelope (1980). How and why are women more polite: Some evidence from a Mayan community. In McConnell-Ginet, Borker, and Furman 1980, 111–136.

Edelsky, Carole (1979). Question intonation and sex roles. *Language in Society* 8: 15–32.

Farber, Anne (1974). Language choice and sex roles in highland Guatemala. Paper presented at the Symposium on Language and Sex Roles, Annual Meeting of the American Anthropological Association, 1974.

Frye, Marilyn (1976). Male chauvinism: A conceptual analysis. In Robert Baker and Frederick Elliston (eds.), *Philosophy and sex*. Buffalo: Prometheus, 65–79.

Gal, Susan (1978). Peasant men can't get wives: Language change and sex roles in a bilingual community. *Language in Society* 7: 1–16.

Gervasio, A. H., and Mary Crawford (1989). Social evaluations of assertiveness: A critique and speech act formulation. *Psychology of Women Quarterly* 13: 1–25.

Goodwin, Marjorie H. (1980). Directive-response sequences in girls' and boys' task activities. In McConnell-Ginet, Borker, and Furman 1980, 157–173.

Haas, Mary (1944). Men's and women's speech in Koasati. *Language* 20: 142–149. Reprinted in Dell Hymes (ed.), *Language in culture and society*. New York: Harper and Row, 228–233.

Henley, Nancy (1977). *Body politics: Power, sex, and nonverbal communication*. Englewood Cliffs, NJ: Prentice-Hall.

———— (1979). Assertiveness training: Making the political personal. Paper presented at the Society for the Study of Social Problems, Boston, August 1979.

Kalčik, Susan (1975).… like Ann's gynecologist or the time I was almost raped. *Journal of American Folklore* 88: 3–11.

Kean, Mary-Louise (1980). Comment on "Intonation in a man's world." *Signs* 5: 367–372.

Kramarae, Cheris (1980). Proprietors of language. In McConnell-Ginet, Borker, and Furman 1980, 58–68.

Labov, William (1972). The study of language in its social context. *Sociolinguistic patterns*. Philadelphia: University of Pennsylvania Press, 183–259.

Lakoff, Robin (1974). You are what you say. *Ms.* (July 1974), 65–67. Response from Megan D. Price, Fair Haven, VT, *Ms.* (Nov. 1974), 8.

———— (1975). *Language and woman's place.* New York: Harper Torchbooks.

Leopold, Werner F. (1959). The decline of German dialects. *Word* 15: 130–153.

Maltz, Daniel N., and Ruth A. Borker (1982). A cultural approach to male-female miscommunication. In John J. Gumperz (ed.), *Communication, language, and social identity.* New York: Cambridge University Press, 195–216.

Mandelbaum, David G. (ed.) (1949). *Selected writings of Edward Sapir in language, culture, and personality.* Berkeley: University of California Press.

Martyna, Wendy (1980). Psychology of the generic masculine. In McConnell-Ginet, Borker, and Furman 1980, 69–78.

McConnell-Ginet, Sally (1978). Linguistics in a feminist context. Paper presented at the Women and Language Forum, Modern Language Association Annual Meeting, December 1978.

———— (1980). Reply to Kean. *Signs* 5: 367–372.

———— (1984). The origins of sexist language in discourse. In Sheila J. White and Virginia Teller (eds.), *Discourses in reading and linguistics,* vol. 433. New York: Annals of the New York Academy of Science, 123–36.

McConnell-Ginet, Sally, Ruth A. Borker, and Nelly Furman (eds.) (1980). *Women and language in literature and society.* New York: Praeger.

Miller, Casey, and Kate Swift (1977). *Words and women.* New York: Doubleday.

Nichols, Patricia C. (1980). Women in their speech communities. In McConnell-Ginet, Borker, and Furman 1980, 140–149.

Nilsen, Aileen Pace, Haig Bosmajian, H. Lee Gershuny, and Julia P. Stanley (eds.) (1977). *Sexism and language.* Urbana, IL: National Council of Teachers of English.

Scheman, Naomi (1980). Anger and the politics of naming. In McConnell-Ginet, Borker, and Furman 1980, 174–187.

Schulz, Muriel (1975). The semantic derogation of women. In Barrie Thorne and Nancy Henley (eds.), *Language and sex: Difference and dominance.* Rowley, MA: Newbury House, 64–75.

Stanley, Julia Penelope (1978). Chomsky's "ideal" native speaker: Sexism in synchronic linguistics. Paper presented at the Women and Language Forum, Modern Language Association Annual Meeting, December 1978.

Teeuwen, St. W. J. (ed.) (1929). *Donum Natalicium Schrijnen.* Nijmegan-Utrecht.

Thorne, Barrie (1978). Language and social stratification. Paper presented at the Feminist Scholarship Conference, University of Illinois, Urbana-Champaign.

Treichler, Paula A. (1980). Verbal subversions in Dorothy Parker: 'Trapped like a trap in a trap.' *Language and Style* 11(4): 48–61.

[———— (1989). From discourse to dictionary: How sexist meanings are authorized. In Francine Wattman Frank and Paula A. Treichler, (eds.), *Language, gender and professional writing: Theoretical approaches and guidelines for non-sexist usage.* New York: MLA, 51–79.]

Tschudi, Finn (1979). Gender stereotypes reflected in asymmetric similarities in language. Paper presented at the Gender, Androgyny, and Language Session, American Psychological Association Annual Meeting, August 1979.

Vetterling-Braggin, Mary (ed.) (1981). *Sexist language.* Totowa, NJ: Littlefield, Adams.

4

Difference and language

A linguist's perspective

Rather than a single, unified topic, the title "Difference and language" points to a cluster of related issues and questions. Let me begin by quickly placing both myself and my approach. My own scholarly perspective on language has been shaped by early training in mathematical logic and the philosophy of language and, more recently and more significantly, by my training and research in theoretical linguistics. My feminism grows out of a variety of personal and political factors, ranging from relatively early marriage and motherhood to fairly active participation in New Left political organizations during the 1960s. My feminist investigation of language has developed through teaching and research in an interdisciplinary Women's Studies Program.[a] It has drawn as well from a growing network of friendships and contacts with other women (and some men) who are also approaching questions about the interaction of language and sex from a feminist starting point, though often from theoretical and methodological assumptions quite different from my own.[1] Not only has this interaction across traditional disciplinary boundaries led to new ways of looking at and finding out about women's experience; it has also been an important stimulus in leading me to somewhat different views of language and linguistics than I once had. I don't pretend to represent linguistics as a profession but only my particular subjective self, whose perspective on language owes much to the mutual influence of feminist concerns and formal linguistic training.

This essay first appeared in Hester Eisenstein and Alice Jardine, eds., *The future of difference* (Boston: G. K. Hall), 157–66 (reissued in paperback by Rutgers University Press, 1985). It is based on my contribution to a panel that also included poet Audre Lorde and literary scholar Alice Jardine and was part of a conference, "The Future of Difference," organized by the feminist studies program at Barnard College.

    a. In 2002, Cornell Women's Studies was rechristened Feminist, Gender, and Sexuality Studies (FGSS, pronounced like 'figs'). This clumsy label was adopted because the group feared that 'gender and sexuality studies' could be read as completely divorced from the feminist politics that first brought women's studies into being at the end of the 1960s. That fear is not unjustified: some such label changes at other institutions have been accompanied by an overwhelming emphasis on men's, especially but not only gay men's, issues.

Linguistics is often defined as the science of language. As a 'scientist', I ask different questions and have different aims and methods than those whose interest in language springs from more artistic or literary concerns. For example, I am interested in describing in precise detail the linguistic structures that people put to use in a wide variety of situations. Science is, of course, not only descriptive but also seeks to articulate explicitly and to test general principles that help explain the phenomena of ordinary (and extraordinary) life. We all know at some intuitive level that the socially dominant leave a more lasting imprint on the linguistic resources of their community than do subordinates. We also know that there are often 'different' patterns of language use in the community that survive in spite of not being 'approved' by those in control. *How* does this happen? What are the mechanisms through which language interacts with society and culture on the one hand, and with our inner mental and emotional life on the other? *Why*, for example, might women's relation to language be different from men's? What are the linguistic consequences of familiar and traditional arrangements between the sexes? What are the social and cultural consequences for women of familiar linguistic practices? Neither linguistics nor any other discipline can answer such questions, but it is now possible to begin to formulate them more carefully, as a first step in the systematic investigation of the connections between language and the political and psychological conditions of women's lives.

To be a scientist is not, in my view, to be 'neutral', 'objective', 'value-free'. All serious intellectual inquiry springs from human minds and feelings, develops in socially and culturally situated contexts of human activity. The questions we ask (or don't ask) reflect what we care about. Science, however, does not assume that the answers to those questions will be what we want them to be, that our feelings alone shape the world we share with other selves; or that our intuitions are always a reliable guide to understanding empirical phenomena. Hunches play a crucial role in the formulation of hypotheses. But these are seldom taken as adequate evidence in themselves because of their essentially 'private' character. We must, of course, take our experience and our convictions seriously and not be led, for example, to distort or deny women's perceptions because they don't fit what is allowed by some orthodox 'scientific' theory. Feminist scholars have suggested that many accepted theories and explanatory models are based on a male-centered view of human behavior and social life.[2] Bringing women into the picture gives a richer view of human experience, and women's own analyses of their experience offer critically important evidence which the male-dominated scientific community has too often ignored. Scientific methods and theories that cannot handle the phenomena that we recognize from our personal experiences are clearly inadequate. Feminist scholarship is beginning to reshape some of our conceptual frameworks and to develop new approaches to empirical investigation.

Science is 'objective' in the sense that it strives to adduce publicly accessible evidence in support of an intersubjective, shared understanding of our world. Scientists do not conduct their inquiries in isolation. The world is extraordinarily complex, and scientific thought develops through a cooperative exploration of various kinds of phenomena. This necessary division of intellectual labor can lead to a sterile compartmentalization of human thought, with increasingly narrow and specialized fields accessible only to a few initiates. Specialized vocabulary can be very helpful but can also hinder communication with noninitiates. There is also an unfortunate tendency for a kind of intellectual 'imperialism' to take hold, for specialists to forget that their own work provides only a partial perspective on the world. In spite of these limitations, however, specialization does make possible a much deeper level of understanding of certain kinds of phenomena. Generally available linguistic categories and informal observations provide only a relatively superficial view of many aspects of experience. Collaboration can help keep boundaries open between different approaches. Specialists can distill some of their results for generalist audiences.

As a linguist interested in women's concerns, I have found it essential to draw on ideas originating in other disciplines as well as outside of academia. Yet I retain a basically linguistic approach: a view of language as a complex structured system that is somehow represented in each language user's mind. The form will be slightly different for each user, though basically very similar; the major differences are likely to be in the vocabulary, the stock of words we have available. The basic system can be put to use in a variety of different ways: writing a poem, asking a riddle, giving a lecture on mathematics. Such uses don't comprise different languages in a linguist's sense of *language*, although at least some of the differences among them may be characterized in linguistic terms. However, the whole spectrum of language *uses* provides evidence of the language *system* that underlies them, and also helps shape the system itself.

Thus, my first reading of "Language and difference" suggests that the very concept of language, and what it means to explore it, will be different for a linguist, a poet, and a literary scholar. Our panel discussion at the conference—including all three—was self-reflexive: we exhibited differences not only in our personal starting points for thinking about language and its implications for feminist theory and practice, but also in our uses of language itself. Our vocabularies, our styles of discourse, differed. Such a panel does not—and should not—erase those differences, for it offers new potential for enriching our individual perspectives.

My second reading of "Language and difference" is a sketch of one way in which the existence of difference, of opposition or contrast, has been taken as fundamental in the analysis of language. The address title *Ms.*, for example, is not just distinguished from *Mr.* by its gender marking; *Ms.* enters into a more elaborate network of differences than *Mr.*, implying (at this particular stage in our history) a choice from the three-term set that also includes *Miss* and *Mrs*. This difference, however, is viewed against a backdrop of sameness or similarity: these forms can all serve as titles preceding a surname. Opposition, difference that 'counts' linguistically, is understood relative to what are sometimes called paradigmatic connections. Linguistic analysis proceeds by opposing or contrasting elements that share a substantial portion of their linguistic properties, that are in important ways *not* different, the same. Linguistic meaning implies choices or alternatives: differences against a background of partial sameness. In my view, language is not a fixed structure but a constant interplay of actions and reactions that are interpreted relative to multiple and changing structural possibilities. Use of a title, for instance, can also be looked at in the light of a larger system of address options—last name only, first name only, nickname, epithet, or endearment.[3] In general, linguistic choices are only partially fixed: they are continually being created and transformed in dynamic processes of speaking and hearing, writing and reading.

I want to expand on the general methodological point that difference is interpreted relative to partial sameness in discussing my third reading of the title "Language and difference": what is the relation between sexual difference and language and its use? This question generates two distinct though related questions. Do the sexes use language in systematically different ways? Is the language used about women and to women significantly different from that used about and to men? We also need to consider what is believed about such differences, what their psychological and social impact might be, how they are interpreted and evaluated within the linguistic community, and how and why they might be developed and maintained. We are just beginning to acquire some insight into such issues, but it is already clear that sexual difference and language interact in countless complex and subtle ways. Unless sexual difference is considered in the light of similarities that cut across sexual divisions, in a context of partial sameness, its interactions with language will seem either uninteresting or incomprehensible.

From one viewpoint, differences in the relation of the sexes to their language are relatively trivial. Both girls and boys acquire the language spoken around them in roughly the same way and, except in those few communities in which the sexes are rarely in contact, they come to recognize a basically common system. Still, the structural system—including the stock of vocabulary, grammatical constructions, and sound patterns—can be put to many different uses, and we can understand ways of speaking that we would never use. Thus, even within a basically common system, different people adopt characteristically different approaches to expressing themselves. In addition, and perhaps more important, the vocabulary we choose, the style of pronunciation, the sentence structures—all these formal details of *how* we say it—are potentially a part of *what* we say and are affected by such factors as the relative privacy of the occasion, the topic, how speakers assess the social relationships between themselves and their hearer, and so on. Factors of this kind operate for both sexes, and studies that look at sexual difference and language use must take into account the enormous variety of uses of language, the diverse contexts in which language users find themselves, and the vast array of aims they pursue through linguistic means. Even if the sexes had identical resources available—unlikely in most communities because of differences in social mobility, educational and occupational opportunities, networks of friends, and prescriptions on 'proper' language use—the fact that our situations and aims are so often different might lead to certain kinds of difference in how women and men tend to use language.

For the developing child, language acquisition and linguistic experience may well play a major role in establishing notions of sexual difference. They may also help create and maintain ways of behaving and thinking that keep sexual differences so important in social arrangements and cultural ideologies. We don't know much about how language and its use frame the child's beliefs and expectations, but we do know that patterns of language use provide the basis for a rich and often very disturbing set of inferences about both differences between the sexes in society and culture and the values attached to such differences. It seems likely that covert messages about sexual differences could be at least as powerful as the overt messages, especially for the child whose experience is limited.

First the child observes how people (especially adults) speak to and of women and men, girls and boys. Girls with brothers, boys with sisters may tend to receive more frequent examples of this differentiation in speech directed toward them by adults, but most children in our culture spend a considerable portion of their adult-supervised time in contact with children of the other sex. In one household I know, the male child is frequently addressed by both parents as *son*, the female as *honey* or *dear*—a small but potentially powerful message.

In general, girls and boys acquire not only very different conceptions of their roles (compare the partially similar verbs (*to*) *mother* and (*to*) *father*, for example—and the absence, in most children's experience, of (*to*) *parent*) but also different evaluations of themselves and their activities. Not only are many of the terms referring to women both specifically sexual and also negative, but, perhaps even more important, they tend to be HOMOGENIZED: that is, differences among women tend to be obscured for the child by our linguistic practices. The originally elevated *lady* might seem to the child at first to be the mate of the grand *gentleman* and indeed is in some contexts. Yet, as Robin Lakoff has pointed out, mother may be a *cleaning lady* whereas father cannot be a *garbage gentleman*.[4] Not only children but mature women are referred to and addressed as *girls*; boys, on the other hand, learn that they will one day grow into manhood. Terms referring to men, in contrast, *do* retain their power to mark difference and individuality within the sex, but they tend to lose their sex-specificity, a linguistic reflex of the false UNIVERSALIZATION of masculinity and male experience. For example, when they go to school, girls have to learn that words like *man* and *he*, which they first acquired in contexts of male reference, are sometimes to be interpreted as applying to human beings generally. Girls seem to believe this more than boys in interpreting others' uses but are more sensitive than their brothers to the potential exclusion and likely to eschew such forms in favor of options like *person*, *she or he*, singular *they*, and the like.[5] Females may arrive at a more complex appreciation of sexual differences than males—and possibly also of the connection between forms and their meanings. Males may be led to view their own sex as a relatively unimportant feature of their identity, important only in differentiating themselves from females, whose sex is seen as a personal characteristic that overrides all other qualities.

The impact on the child of acquiring ways of speaking about the sexes will undoubtedly depend on many factors. At what age, in what situation, and from whom does one first acquire *motherfucker*? Which forms become part of one's actively used vocabulary and which remain passive? In what ways does the rest of one's experience support or contradict the 'homogenization' of women, the 'universalization' of men's experience?

Children of both sexes almost always have their first, primary linguistic interactions with an adult female, usually the mother. We don't know precisely what difference this makes, although it may help shape notions of appropriate speech to women and to men. The very young child typically encounters father as a relative stranger and may speak to him more 'deferentially' and less 'intimately' than to mother. Distance may lend a measure of authority and status to father. We have no idea how extensive such phenomena are, or, more important, what role they might play in shaping our later modes of speaking to women and to men. Yet the different roles of the father and the mother in the child's world provide one of the earliest sociolinguistic lessons in the modification of speech as a function of social relationships with those to whom one is speaking. A fruitful line of investigation might be to compare the development of skills in language used in those children reared by both parents with those reared mainly by the mother. To the extent that mother and father provide different models of language use, the child may take these as typical or expected of women and men, respectively.[6]

It is important, however, not to exaggerate the influence of parents on children's acquisition of particular ways of speaking. We know that once the child moves beyond the very early stages of confinement in the home, peer influence is generally the most important determinant of speech. For most children, the natural play groups that form are single-sex (although there are various interactions between the girls' and boys' groups and occasional crossovers). The child may acquire ways of talking that are distinctive to its sex mainly through contact—just as I learned English rather than French because of my social environment. Yet the different ways are not, in these cases, sex-exclusive, and each sex interprets the other's styles, strategies, and favored patterns against its own assumptions. Some evidence suggests more collaborative strategies in girls' play groups ("Let's

go") as opposed to more competitive in boys' ("Get outa here").[7] It is possible that in later interaction the competitor may try to interpret the col-
laborator as just an unsuccessful competitor. Again, seeing masculine
experience as universal promotes the assumption that the expectations
developed in male contexts cover the entire linguistic community. One
can succeed in defining a situation as competitive without assent from
coparticipants, whereas collaboration is not possible without agreement.
Many studies of adults show that men tend in a variety of ways to 'control' conversational interactions with women.[8] Of course, this is linked to
other nonlinguistic mechanisms that support male dominance, but some
women may be easily dominated by men in part because their view of
conversation and their strategies for approaching it have been shaped in
situations in which resisting dominance was not a major concern. More
studies of girls and women talking in peer groups will help to clarify these
issues.

   Thus differences—and similarities—in the relation of the sexes to their
language have important implications for understanding not only our participation in intellectual, artistic, and political activity but also our ordinary social lives. The mechanisms through which individuals come to use
language as they do are remarkably similar. What varies are the social situations and the cultural values that frame our lives, as well as, of course,
those distinctive individual capacities and those particular experiences
that our accidental histories (including those dictated by our biology)
provide. To understand sexual differences in relationship to language, it is
essential to look at other kinds of sociocultural and psychological differences that cut across sexual boundaries and are connected to the uses of
language, by identifying factors (relative power of speaker and hearer, for
instance) that work in essentially the same ways no matter which sex they
happen to characterize. These need not work in precisely the same way:
gender meanings draw on and interact with other dimensions of significance. Linguistic indicators of hesitation, for example, may be heard as
characteristic of 'women's language' because women have learned this
self-protective strategy as a defense against attack. The indicators may
survive, however, in contexts in which the strategy is not needed or is inef-
fective, because they now also play a role in symbolizing identity 'as a
woman'. To understand how and why language is significant in our experience as women, we cannot focus on sex in isolation from the other
factors that shape our lives.

   The assumption that sexual difference outweighs all other factors
ignores and devalues the differences among women and perpetuates the
male-centered view of women as homogeneous. Some women create
beautiful metaphors and poetic images, others are skilled at establishing
and maintaining conversational ties, and others develop new vocabulary
and theoretical discourse for describing and analyzing women's experience. For an individual woman, only some of these uses are genuine
options: our abilities, concerns, and tastes will lead us to try to become

skilled at only a fraction of the possible uses of language. But all our lives are enriched if we are fully integrated into a community that offers a wide range of kinds and styles of discourse. As Audre Lorde made so clear to us, "poems are not a luxury," nor, I would add, are the personal observations we share with intimates, or the theoretical frameworks we build to interpret scientific research. Social life depends on our going beyond the resources available to single individuals. To create a society and culture that takes women's interests and concerns seriously, we cannot afford to cede to men exclusive responsibility for any of the diverse functions language serves. The challenge, of course, is to put all those functions to work *for* women rather than against us—to move from static dichotomies and rigid hierarchizing differences to ongoing interactive and dynamic processes of fruitful differentiation in a context of feminist community. Language is the major means of linking individual selves and creating a culture that transcends our personal limitations by making use of all kinds of differences among users and uses of language.

Notes

1. I cannot list everyone, but I must particularly mention Ruth Borker and Nelly Furman (in anthropology and literature, respectively), with whom I coedited *Women and language in literature and society* and with each of whom I have had the great pleasure of team teaching. Editing this book and reading many other papers, published and unpublished, greatly enriched my own thinking about language and the sexes. Correspondence and conferences have brought me into contact with many of the people involved in related work. I have had particularly fruitful exchanges with Barrie Thorne and Nancy Henley, coeditors of *Language and sex: Difference and dominance*, and with Cheris Kramarae, who coedited a revised edition (*Language, gender and society*) with them and who coauthored with them a review article, "Perspectives on language and communication." Francine Frank, whose "Women's language in America: Myth and reality" appears in Butturff and Epstein 1978, has been a close colleague from linguistics, as has Patricia C. Nichols, whom I first met as a coparticipant in the *Conference on the Sociology of Languages of American Women*, proceedings edited by Betty Lou Dubois and Isabel Crouch. Anthropologist Ann Bodine's work (see, for example, Bodine 1975) helped arouse my interest, and she organized the symposium on Language and Sex Roles at the 1974 American Anthropological Association Meetings, at which I presented the initial version of what eventually became "Intonation in a man's world" [chapter 6, this volume]. For me, as for many others, Robin Lakoff's (1975) *Language and woman's place* provided considerable stimulus when parts of it first appeared in 1972 in mimeographed form. Other books that incorporate influence from linguistics include Key 1975 and Nilsen et al. 1977. Selected papers from a section on Language and Sex, 9th International Congress of Sociology, August 1978, are being compiled by Cheris Kramarae and M. Schulz; J. Penelope (Stanley) and G. Valdes-Fallis are assembling papers presented at the December 1978 Modern Language Association; a generally perceptive nonacademic discussion of several issues is Miller and Swift 1976. [The list of both people and books would be vastly longer now; see the preface in this volume for at least some of the additional people.]

2. See Mary Brown Parlee's (1975, 119–138) analysis of work in the psy-chology of women in the inaugural issue of *Signs*, for examples. My "Intonation in a man's world" [chapter 6, this volume] and McConnell-Ginet 1978 [see now chapter 10, this volume] develop this general point with respect to analysis of the use of particular linguistic forms.

3. See McConnell-Ginet 1978; Kramarae 1975; Wolfson and Manes 1980 [and now chapter 10, this volume]. See also Stannard 1977 for an interesting discussion of the significance of women's names and titles.

4. See Lakoff 1975.

5. Wendy Martyna has done excellent research in this area, much of which is summarized in Martyna 1980. Bodine's work is mentioned in note 1.

6. See Edelsky 1977 for a discussion of children's developing sense of stereo-typic women's and men's speech. [Note that parenting has changed significantly since this essay was written some twenty-five years ago. Fathers play a much more active role in many kids' lives than was true then. At the same time, parenting is still not sexually neutral, and mothers are still the predominant parents in most young children's lives.]

7. Marjorie Goodwin 1980 reports such results. This paper is part of the much larger study of natural speech used by groups of working-class Black girls and boys in Philadelphia that comprised her PhD dissertation in anthropology at the University of Pennsylvania. [Goodwin 1990, the book that came from the Philadelphia work, gives a far more nuanced view. Goodwin has continued to explore the complexities of children's creation of their social worlds, with a spe-cial emphasis on conflict; Goodwin 2006 presents material from her post-disser-tation work with Los Angeles schoolchildren.]

8. See, for example, Fishman 1977 and 1978; Zimmerman and West 1975; and West and Zimmerman 1977.

References

Bodine, Ann (1975). Androcentrism in prescriptive grammar. *Language in Society* 4(2): 129–146.

Dubois, Betty Lou, and Isabel Crouch (eds.) (1976). *The sociology of the languages of American women*. San Antonio, TX: Trinity University Press.

Edelsky, Carole (1977). Acquisition of an aspect of communicative competence: Learning what it means to talk like a lady. In Susan Ervin-Tripp and Claudia Mitchell-Kernan (eds.), *Child discourse*. New York: Academic Press, 225–243.

Fishman, Pamela (1977). Interactional shitwork. *Heresies* 1(2): 99–101.

——— (1978). What do couples talk about when they're alone? In Douglas Butturff and Edmund L. Epstein (eds.), *Women's Language and Style*. Akron, OH: University of Akron Press, 11–22.

Frank, Francine (1978). Women's language in America: Myth and reality. In Douglas Butturff and Edmund L. Epstein (eds.), *Women's Language and Style*. Akron, OH: University of Akron Press, 47–61.

Goodwin, Marjorie Harness (1980). Directive-response speech sequences in girls' and boys' task activities. In McConnell-Ginet, Borker, and Furman 1980, 157–173.

[——— (1990). *He-said-she-said: Talk as social organization among black children*. Bloomington: Indiana University Press.]

[——— (2006). *The hidden life of girls: Games of stance, status, and exclusion*. Oxford: Blackwell.]

Henley, Nancy, Cheris Kramarae, and Barrie Thorne (1978). Perspectives on language and communication. *Signs: Journal of Women in Culture and Society* 3(3): 638–651.

Key, Mary Ritchie (1975). *Male/female language*. Metuchen, NJ: Scarecrow Press.

Kramarae, Cheris (1975). Sex-related differences in address systems. *Anthropological Linguistics* 17(5): 198–210.

Lakoff, Robin (1975). *Language and woman's place*. New York: Harper Torchbooks.

Martyna, Wendy (1980). The psychology of the generic masculine. In McConnell-Ginet, Borker, and Furman 1980, 69–78.

McConnell-Ginet, Sally (1978). Address forms in sexual politics. In Douglas Butturff and Edmund L. Epstein (eds.), *Women's language and style*. Akron, OH: University of Akron, 23–35.

McConnell-Ginet, Sally, Ruth A. Borker, and Nelly Furman (eds.) (1980). *Women and language in literature and society*. New York: Praeger.

Miller, Casey, and Kate Swift (1976). *Words and women*. Garden City, NY: Anchor Press/Doubleday.

Nilsen, A. P., H. Bosmajian, H. L. Gershuny, and J. Stanley (eds.) (1977). *Sexism and language*. Urbana, IL: National Council of Teachers of English.

Parlee, Mary Brown (1975). Psychology: Review essay. *Signs: Journal of Women in Culture and Society* 1.1:119–138.

Stannard, Una (1977). *Mrs. man*. San Francisco: Germainbooks.

Thorne, Barrie, and Nancy Henley (eds.) (1975). *Language and sex: Difference and dominance*. Rowley, MA: Newbury House.

Thorne, Barrie, Cheris Kramarae, and Nancy Henley (eds.) (1983). *Language, gender and society*. Rowley, MA: Newbury House.

West, Candace, and Don H. Zimmerman (1977). Women's place in everyday talk: Reflections on parent-child interaction. *Social Problems* 24: 521–529.

Wolfson, Nessa, and Joan Manes (1980). Don't "dear" me! In McConnell-Ginet, Borker, and Furman 1980, 79–92.

Zimmerman, Don H., and Candace West (1975). Sex roles, interruptions, and silences in conversation. In Thorne and Henley 1975, 105–129.

Part II

SOCIAL PRACTICE, SOCIAL MEANINGS, AND SELVES

The three essays in this section all address gender as embedded in social practice, how gendered and sexualized selves derive from the ways in which linguistic resources are deployed and evaluated in the course of social interactions and social practices more generally. The first and third come from my collaboration with sociolinguist Penelope Eckert of Stanford. Our joint work, begun in the early 1990s and continuing from time to time, has explicitly articulated an approach to the study of language and gender that takes social practice as fundamental for understanding how linguistic phenomena might connect to gender, emphasizing local communities of practice as critical. The middle essay is much older, originating in the mid-1970s and couched in terms of that era's emphasis on sex differences as the heart of gender. But although it ignores community connections, it does emphasize what people do using language and the multiple functions particular forms may serve as well as the pitfalls in others' interpretation of speakers' intentions.

'Selves' suggests a focus on matters of identity, and these essays do pay considerable attention to social meanings and their connections to gendered and sexualized personae. But one of the reasons that the community of practice (CofP) framework is so useful for language and gender research is that it brings together matters of social/stylistic meaning, the focus of most sociolinguistic research (including Penny's prior work), and of content/message meaning, the focus of most inquiry in semantics and pragmatics (including my own earlier work).

Social selves arise in large measure through people's drawing on linguistic and other resources to carve out meaningful niches they can more or less comfortably occupy as they engage with others in particular communities of practice. Some of those resources are a matter of ways of speaking; others have to do with what is spoken of and how. Few social selves are completely gender-neutral, primarily because gender categories are assigned early and almost always invoked in social interactions (though in different ways and to different degrees). Social practice theory shifts attention from passive indexing of pre-given demographic categories like a person's sex or age or socioeconomic status to the active creation of selves that may draw on such categories but give them new and diverse content.

Sexual identities or sexual dimensions of social selves are somewhat less omnipresent in social practice than gender. Of course, presumptive heterosexuality—the widespread assumption that boys 'automatically' grow into men who desire women as sexual partners and that girls 'automatically' grow into women who desire male sexual partners (or at least desire to be desired sexually by men)—has considerable impact on gender in its linguistic and its other aspects. For example, women sometimes find men's interactions with them focused on them as sexual (presumptively heterosexual) beings even in contexts where sexuality should arguably be irrelevant or at least ignored as distracting from the main business at hand—for example, they encounter flirtatious talk in the workplace when what they are looking for is problem-solving exchange. Such sexualization occurs primarily though not exclusively during what might be childbearing years—some women, at least, find themselves able to develop a wider range of relationships with men after menopause when they are assumed to be asexual beings. But even prepubescent children are often spoken of and to in ways that emphasize their (presumed) heterosexuality: childhood cross-sex friendships are often interpreted as romances, and there is much talk of 'when' (far more frequently than 'if') marriage and motherhood will happen. Children who are beginning to experience same-sex desire (and this reportedly happens quite early for some kids) may find it difficult to see how they can fit into the social landscape around them though many more young adolescents in the United States are openly carving out gay and lesbian identities for themselves at the end of the first decade of the twenty-first century than was true back when these essays were being written.

What is crucial is that social practice, especially in face-to-face local communities of practice, is central to shaping not only gendered but also sexualized selves. Moreover, even what seem our most private encounters play themselves out and are understood against the backdrop of social practices and ideologies. Social practice links individuals to institutions and to ongoing historical processes.

Chapter 5, "Communities of practice," started as a talk Penny and I gave at the Berkeley Women and Language Conference of 1992. What we wanted to do was briefly introduce the CofP framework articulated in much greater detail in our 1992 *Annual Review of Anthropology* article to the many graduate students and established scholars who had come to the Berkeley meeting to talk (from very diverse perspectives) about their own research on language, gender, and sexuality. Our ideas, sketchily presented in this piece, seemed to strike a chord with many working on language and gender.

A CofP is any group that interacts regularly around some concern, interest, or activity, the members of which hold one another 'accountable' in various ways for their participation in some common social practice(s). A family, a workplace group, a sports team, a church or synagogue or mosque (in some cases, smaller groups within the larger religious institution), a choir, a book club, a sorority or fraternity, a friendship group in a high school, a political organization, a volunteer social service group: all these and many more are examples of CsofP, within which different folks may be different kinds of members. To a considerable extent, we spend our lives in CsofP, most of us members of a number of them. Both language and gender enter our lives as we engage in various kinds of activities within these CsofP: ways of speaking emerge as do ways of being girls or women, boys or men. Of course we also interact across CsofP and media of various kinds enters into our lives (though even here our experience may be mediated by CsofP to which we belong). But CsofP play a critical role.

CsofP, a construct due to Etienne Wenger and Jean Lave, bring together two key notions: social practice and localized mutual accountability. Both are important for thinking about how language interacts with social phenomena like gender and sexuality. Social practice is more than just social activity: it involves activity in relation to social institutions and cultural histories, both at local and at more global levels. Mutual accountability has to do with expectations of others and of oneself in relation to those others, the assumption that we all act in ways interpretable by reference to norms that are mutually accessible. Social practice endows action with meaning.

In chapter 6, "Intonation in a man's world," I try to think about prosodic styles as fitting into a larger sociolinguistic landscape. Intonational 'style' can, I argue, involve either variation—alternative realizations of the same linguistic unit—or selection—opting for different units in similar communicative situations. Although intonation—roughly, the pitch and volume contours of speech through time, the 'tunes' of our talk—is (still) less well understood and analyzed than other linguistic phenomena, it is nonetheless clearly governed by linguistic conventions. At the same time, language users can exploit the system in various ways and do so for various ends, sometimes with full intentionality and other times with less self-conscious attention.

Two intonational phenomena are emphasized: (relative) dynamism, in other words, significant and frequent ups and downs of pitch, and final rises on noninterrogatives, dubbed 'uptalk' in 1990s media accounts of certain teen girls' speech (where final rises were heard as very frequent). My main targets were those who heard relative dynamism from women and girls as evidence of their/our hyperemotionality and those who interpreted noninterrogative final rises as signaling timidity and fear of self-assertion (at least when produced by female speakers). Intonational patterns, I observed, serve diverse functions: dynamism, for example, can help attract attention from problematic listeners (e.g., young children or adults who are ignoring the speaker), and noninterrogative final rises can signal unvoiced questions. The essay shifts the emphasis from appeals to supposed sex differences in basic psychological makeup to examination of the different material and political circumstances of women's and men's lives, to their often divergent situations as participants in social practice.

Chapter 7, "Constructing meaning, constructing selves," developed from a forum lecture that Penny and I gave during the summer 1993 LSA Linguistic Institute meetings at Ohio State. It was our first attempt to use the CofP framework for thinking about data, in this case, tapes of interviews Penny recorded during her early 1980s ethnographic study of what she calls Belten High, a Detroit-area suburban high school. Although sociolinguistic interviews are not themselves examples of everyday social practice, what these students said to Penny, who had gotten to know many of them quite well, gave considerable insight into the various CsofP to which they belonged. Penny's earlier work had identified two opposed groups in the school: the jocks, who dominated the various school-based extracurricular activities (sports, school government, musical groups, etc.) and were mainly college bound, and the burnouts, who visibly rejected such extracurricular participation in favor of urban-based friends and more 'adult' activities and who planned to enter the local work force after graduation rather than get further education. Interviewees' comments about applying social labels like *jock* and *burnout* (and the more diffuse but also important *in-between*) brought out clearly the hegemony that jocks had achieved during the years since junior high: jocks themselves treated the word *jock* as just applying to athletes (and denied its further social significance), taking only the burnouts to have distinctive characteristics, the rest being 'normal' or default kinds of people. What was especially interesting for thinking about gender was that the content of being a jock or a burnout differed significantly for girls and for boys. The quintessential 'jock' or 'burnout' was male, canonically an athlete in the first instance and a 'tough guy' in the second. Jock girls had to seek 'popularity' (though not overtly), whereas burnout girls aspired to 'coolness'. Gender and the class-based categories were tightly intertwined, as became very clear in looking at patterns of phonological variation, in which burnout and jock girls 'set the envelope', with boys much less sharply differentiated across the two groups. The Belten High data make it very clear that gender is as much or more about differences among girls and women and among boys and men as it is about sex differences. And of course it is also as much or more about interpretation and expectation as about actual differences.

5

Communities of practice

Where language, gender, and power all live

0. Introduction: Too much abstraction spoils the broth

Studies of language and gender since the early 1970s have looked at many different dimensions of language use and have offered a rich variety of hypotheses about the interaction between gender and language and especially about the connection of power to that interaction.[1] On the one hand, language has been seen as supporting male dominance; on the other, it has been seen as a resource for women resisting oppression or pursuing their own projects and interests. We have all learned a lot by thinking about such proposals, most of which have been supported by interesting and often illuminating observations. But their explanatory force has been weakened by the absence of a coherent theoretical framework within which to refine and further explore them as part of an ongoing research community.

The problem is not an absence of generalizations. Our diagnosis is that gender and language studies suffer from the same problem as that confronting sociolinguistics and psycholinguistics more generally: too much abstraction. Abstracting gender and language from the social practices that produce their particular forms in given communities often obscures and sometimes distorts the ways they connect and how those connections are implicated in power relations, in social conflict, in the production and reproduction of values and plans. Too much abstraction is often symptomatic of too little theorizing: abstraction should not substitute for theorizing but be informed by and responsive to it. Theoretical insight into how language and gender interact requires a close look at social practices in which they are jointly produced. We see work in the *Proceedings of the 1992 Berkeley Women and Language Conference* as headed in exactly this direction. What we want to do in this essay is to sketch the main outlines

This paper, coauthored with Penelope Eckert, first appeared in *Proceedings of 1992 Berkeley Conference on Women and Language: Locating power*, vol. 1, 89–99; it is essentially the text of the presentation we made at that conference. Reprinted in J. Coates, ed., *Language and gender: A reader* (Oxford and Malden, MA: Blackwell, 1998).

of a theoretical perspective on language, gender, and power that can help us continue to make progress toward a productive community of language-gender scholars who hold themselves accountable both to one another's work and to relevant developments in linguistics, social theory, and gender studies.

Why is abstraction so tempting and yet so dangerous? It is tempting because at some level and in some form it is irresistible, an inevitable part of theoretical inquiry. People and their activities, including their use of language, are never viewed in completely concrete or particularistic terms. With no access to abstract constructs like linguistic systems and social categories and relations like class and race and gender, we could not hope to engage in any kind of illuminating investigation into how and why language and gender interact. The danger, however, is that the real force and import of their interaction is erased when we abstract each uncritically from the social practices in which they are jointly produced and in which they intermingle with other symbolic and social phenomena. In particular, if we view language and gender as self-contained and independent phenomena, we miss the social and cognitive significance of interactions between them. Abstraction that severs the concrete links between language and gender in the social practices of communities kills the power that resides in and derives from those links.

The notions of 'women' and 'men', for example, are typically just taken for granted in sociolinguistics. Suppose we were to take all the characterizations of gender that have been advanced to explain putatively gender-differentiated linguistic behavior. Women's language has been said to reflect their (our) conservatism, prestige consciousness, upward mobility, insecurity, deference, nurturance, emotional expressivity, connectedness, sensitivity to others, solidarity. And men's language is heard as evincing their toughness, lack of affect, competitiveness, independence, competence, hierarchy, control. Linguists are not, of course, inventing such accounts of gender identities and gender relations out of whole cloth. Not only commonplace stereotypes but also social-scientific studies offer support for the kinds of characterizations linguists offer in explanation of language use. But the social-science literature must be approached critically: the observations on which such claims about women and men are based have been made at different times and in different circumstances with different populations from those whose linguistic behavior they are being used to explain.

The problem is too much or at least too-crude abstraction. Gender is abstracted whole from other aspects of social identity, the linguistic system is abstracted from linguistic practice, language is abstracted from social action, interactions and events are abstracted from community and personal history, difference and dominance are each abstracted from wider social practice, and both linguistic and social behavior are abstracted from the communities in which they occur. When we recombine all these abstractions, we really do not know what we have. Certainly we don't seem to find real women and men as sums of the characteristics attributed to them.

What we propose is not to ignore such abstract characterizations of gender identities and relations but to take responsibility for connecting each such abstraction to a wide spectrum of social and linguistic practice in order to examine the specificities of its concrete realization in actual communities. This can happen only if we collectively develop a community of analytic practice that holds itself responsible for language and gender writ large.

This means that we are responsible to linguistic theory and research beyond the areas of our particular specializations. Furthermore, we cannot excuse our inattention to social theory and gender studies on the grounds that we are 'just' linguists, not if we hope to make responsible claims about language and gender interactions. And perhaps the most important implication is that we cannot abandon social and political responsibility for how our work is understood and used, especially given what we know about sexism and racism and elitism and heterosexism in so many of the communities where our research might be disseminated.

Our major aim is to encourage a view of the interaction of gender and language that roots each in the everyday social practices of particular local communities and sees them as jointly constructed in those practices: our slogan, "Think practically and look locally." To think practically and look locally is to abandon several assumptions common in gender and language studies: that gender works independently of other aspects of social identity and relations, that it 'means' the same across communities, and that the linguistic manifestations of that meaning are also the same across communities. Such assumptions can be maintained only when the language-gender partnership is prematurely dissolved by abstraction of one or both partners.

1. Language, gender, and power viewed locally

We find many examples from work presented at the 1992 Berkeley Women and Language Conference of what it means to view language, power, and gender in local terms. Becoming language users and becoming gendered members of local communities both involve participating with other members in a variety of practices that often constitute linguistic, gender, and other social identities and relations at one and the same time. Many such activities have been described in the papers from the conference: instigating or taking the plaintiff or defendant role in a he-said-she-said dispute (Goodwin 1992), providing sexy talk on the 900 lines (Hall 1992), participating in "Father knows best!" dinnertime dramas (Ochs and Taylor 1992), taking a police report from a bleeding woman (McElhinny 1992), joining in a debate about rape and race and responsibility on the walls of a bathroom stall (Moonwomon 1992), smiling at the boss's "Sleazy bitch!"

(Case 1992), silencing a planned anecdote during a conference paper when you note its (male) protagonist in the audience (Lakoff 1992), criticizing or defending a colleague's bestseller (Freed 1992).

In the course of engaging with others in such activities, people collaboratively construct a sense of themselves and of others as certain kinds of persons, as members of various communities with various forms of membership, authority, and privilege in those communities. In all of these, language interacts with other symbolic systems—dress, body adornment, ways of moving, gaze, touch, handwriting style, locales for hanging out, and so on. And the selves constructed are not simply (or even primarily) gendered selves: they are unemployed, Asian American, lesbian, college-educated, postmenopausal selves in a variety of relations to other people. Language is never encountered without other symbol systems, and gender is always joined with real people's complex forms of participation in the communities to which they belong (or have belonged or expect to join).

Individuals may experience the language-gender interface differently in the different communities in which they participate at a given time or at different stages of their lives. Using *Mrs. Jones* may be important for avoiding the condescension of *Mary* when a professionally employed woman addresses the woman who cleans her house; for that professional woman, receiving address as *Mrs. Smith* (particularly from her colleagues) may seem to emphasize her subordination to a husband and to deny her individual identity as Joan Doe, who (as she sees it) simply happens to be married to John Smith. On the other hand, acquiring a new name of *Mrs. John Smith* upon marriage may have functioned thirty years ago for the young Joan Doe as a mark of her achieving fully adult status as a married woman (a possibility denied her lesbian sister who rejects marriage).[a] And the woman who with a tolerant smile receives *Mary* from the six-year-old daughter of her employer may insist in her local residential community on *Mrs. Jones* from her own daughter's friends.

Exploring any aspect of the language-gender interface requires that we address the complexities of its construction within and across different communities: what *Mrs. Jones* means, what social work is done by the use of that title, can be understood only by considering its place in the practices of local communities (and in the connections among those communities). Analysts not only jump too readily from local observations to global claims; they/we also too often ignore the multiple uses of particular linguistic resources in the practices of a given community. We can see the confusion that results by trying to put together some of the general claims about the social and psychological underpinnings of language use common in the variation literature with claims about gender such as those common in interaction studies.

a. Note that in the early 1990s we failed to think of the possibility of same-sex marriage.

A methodological cornerstone of variation studies is the notion that all speakers step up the use of vernacular variants when they are at their most emotional. It is also generally accepted that vernacular variants function to establish solidarity. If women are more emotional than men or more interested in promoting solidarity, as so many interactionists have claimed, the variationists might be expected to predict that vernacular variants typify women's rather than men's language. But the general claim in variation studies has been that men's language exemplifies the vernacular whereas women's aspires toward standard or prestige variants. The explanation offered is not men's emotionality or greater interest in social connections but women's supposed prestige consciousness and upward mobility (often accompanied by claims of women's greater conservatism). Even in situations in which some vernacular variant is more frequent in women's than men's speech, analysts do not consider how their explanations relate to their own claims about the social meanings of vernaculars. There are many other tensions and potential contradictions when we try to put together all the different things said about language, gender, and power. The standard or prestige variants are associated with the speech of those who have economic and political power, the social elite; at the same time, standard speech is associated with women and 'prissiness', and the vernacular is heard as tough and 'macho'. Once we take seriously the connections among gender characterizations and the various aspects of language that we study and try to develop a coherent picture, it quickly becomes apparent that the generalizations to be found cannot be integrated with one another as they now stand. This suggests serious difficulties in adopting as our primary goal the search for generalizations about 'women' and 'men' as groups with some kind of global sociolinguistic unity that transcends social practices in local communities.

Statements like "Women emphasize connection in their talk whereas men seek status" may have some statistical support within a particular community. Statistics being what they are, there is, of course, no guarantee that the actual women and men whose behavior supports one such generalization will overlap very much with those supporting another— say, that women prefer standard and men vernacular variants in everyday talk with their peers—and this is true even if our statistics come from a single community. The more serious problem, however, is that such generalizations are seldom understood as simple reports of statistics.

Most American women are under five feet nine inches tall and most American men are over five feet six inches tall, but it would sound odd indeed to report these statistical facts by saying, "Women are under five feet nine inches tall" and "Men are over five feet six inches tall" without some explicit indicator of generalization like *most*. Although unmodified claims about 'women' and 'men' do allow for exceptions, such claims, which we have certainly made ourselves, often seem to imply that individuals who don't satisfy the generalization are indeed exceptional *as* women or *as* men, deviants from some normative model (perhaps deviants to admire but nonetheless outsiders in some sense).[b] This is especially true when women and men are being characterized as 'different' from one another on some particular dimension. But if gender resides in difference, what is the status of the tremendous variability we see in actual behavior within sex categories? Too often dismissed as 'noise' in a basically dichotomous gender system, differences among men and among women are, in our view, themselves important aspects of gender. Tomboys and goody-goodies, homemakers and career women, bodybuilders and fashion models, secretaries and executives, basketball coaches and French teachers, professors and students, grandmothers and mothers and daughters—these are all categories of girls and women whose mutual differences are part of their construction of themselves and each other as gendered beings. When femaleness and maleness are differentiated from one another in terms of such attributes as power, ambition, physical coordination, rebelliousness, caring, or docility, the role of these attributes in creating and texturing important differences among very female identities and very male identities becomes invisible.

The point here is not that statistical generalizations about the females and the males in a particular community are automatically suspect. But to stop with such generalizations or to see finding such 'differences' as the major goal of investigations of gender and language is problematic. Correlations simply point us toward areas where further investigation might shed light on the linguistic and other practices that enter into gender dynamics in a community. An emphasis on difference as constitutive of gender draws attention away from a more serious investigation of the relations among language, gender, and other components of social identity; it ignores the ways difference (or beliefs therein) can function in constructing dominance relations. Gender can be thought of as a sex-based way of experiencing other social attributes like class, ethnicity, or age (and also less obviously social qualities like ambition, athleticism, and musicality). To examine gender independently as if it were just 'added on' to such other aspects of identity is to miss its significance and force. Certainly, to interpret broad sex patterns in language use without considering other aspects of social identity and relations is to paint with one eye closed. Speakers are not assembled out of separate independent modules: part European American, part female, part middle-aged, part feminist, part intellectual. Abstracting gender away from other aspects of social identity also leads to premature generalization even about normative conceptions of femaleness and maleness. While most research that focuses on sex difference is not theoretically committed to a universalizing conception of women or of men, such research has tended to take gender identity as given at least in broad strokes at a relatively global level.

b. Recent work on generics makes this clear; see, for example, McConnell-Ginet (2009) and Leslie (forthcoming).

Too much abstraction and too-ready generalization are encouraged by a limited view of theorizing as aimed at accounts of gender difference that apply globally to women and men. In the interests of abstraction and global generalization, William Labov has argued that ethnographic studies of language and society must answer to the results of survey studies—that generalized correlations reflect a kind of objective picture that must serve as the measure of any locally grounded studies. Others cite the objectivity of controlled experimental studies. We argue instead that ethnographic studies must answer to each other, and that survey and experimental studies in turn must answer to them (see Eckert 1990). Surveys typically examine categories so abstracted from social practice that they cannot be assumed to have independent status as sociolinguistically meaningful units, and they rely heavily on interviews, a special kind of social activity. Experimental studies also abstract in ways that can make it hard to assess their relevance to the understanding of naturally occurring social practice, including cognition. To frame abstractions so that they help explain the interaction of language and social practice, we need a focus of study and analysis that allows us to examine them each on something like an equal footing. This requires a unit of social analysis that has explanatory power for the construction of both language and gender. It is mutual engagement of human agents in a wide range of activities that creates, sustains, challenges, and sometimes changes society and its institutions, including both gender and language, and the sites of such mutual engagement are communities. How the community is defined, therefore, is of prime importance in any study of language and gender, even those that do not use ethnographic methods (e.g., survey or experimental studies).

2. Language, gender, and communities of practice

Sociolinguists have located linguistic systems, norms, and social identities within a loosely defined construct, the SPEECH COMMUNITY. Although in theory sociolinguists embrace John Gumperz's (1982) definition of a speech community as a group of speakers who share rules and norms for the use of language, in practice community studies have defined their populations on the basis of location and/or population. Differences and relations among the speakers who people sociolinguists' speech communities have been defined in terms of abstracted characteristics: sex, age, socioeconomic class, ethnicity, and others. And differences in ways of speaking have been interpreted on the basis of speculative hypotheses about the relation between these characteristics and social practice. Sociolinguistic analysis, then, attempts to reconstruct the practice from which these characteristics, and the linguistic behavior in question, have been abstracted. While participation in community practice sometimes figures more directly into classification of speakers, sociolinguists still seldom recognize explicitly the crucial role of practice in delineating speech communities and more generally in mediating the relation between language, society, and consciousness.

To explore in some detail just how social practice and individual 'place' in the community connect to one another, sociolinguists need some conception of a community that articulates place with practice. For this reason, we adopt Jean Lave and Etienne Wenger's notion of the COMMUNITY OF PRACTICE.[2] The community of practice takes us away from the community defined by a location or by a population. Instead, it focuses on a community defined by social engagement—after all, it is this engagement that language serves, not the place and not the people as a collection of individuals.

A community of practice is an aggregate of people who come together around mutual engagement in some common endeavor. Ways of doing things, ways of talking, beliefs, values, power relations—in short, practices—emerge in the course of members' joint activity around that endeavor. A community of practice is different as a social construct from the traditional notion of community, primarily because it is defined simultaneously by its membership and by the practice in which that membership engages. Indeed, it is the practices of the community and members' differentiated participation in them that structures the community socially.

A community of practice might be people working together in a factory, regulars in a bar, a neighborhood play group, a nuclear family, police partners and their ethnographer, the Supreme Court. Communities of practice may be large or small, intensive or diffuse; they are born and they die, they may persist through many changes of membership, and they may be closely articulated with other communities. Individuals participate in multiple communities of practice, and individual identity is based in the multiplicity of this participation. Rather than seeing the individual as some disconnected entity floating around in social space, or as a location in a network, or as a member of a particular group or set of groups, or as a bundle of social characteristics, we need to focus on communities of practice. Such a focus allows us to see the individual as an actor articulating a range of forms of participation in multiple communities of practice.

Gender is produced (and often reproduced) in differential membership in communities of practice. People's access and exposure to, need for, and interest in different communities of practice are related to such things as their class, age, and ethnicity, as well as their sex. Working-class people are more likely on the whole than middle-class people to be members of unions, bowling teams, or close-knit neighborhoods. Upper-middle-class people, on the other hand, are more likely than working-class people to be members of tennis clubs, orchestras, or professional organizations. Men are more likely than women to be members of football teams, armies, and boards of directors. Women, on the other hand, are more likely to be members of secretarial pools, aerobics classes, and consciousness-raising groups.

And associated with differences in age, class, and ethnicity are differences in the extent to which the sexes belong to different communities of practice. Different people, for a variety of reasons, will articulate their multiple memberships differently. A female executive living in a male-dominated household will have difficulty articulating her membership in her domestic and professional communities of practice, unlike a traditional male executive 'head of household'.[c] A lesbian lawyer 'closeted' within the legal community may also belong to a women's community whose membership defines itself in opposition to the larger heterosexual world. And the woman who scrubs toilets in the household 'managed' by the female executive for her husband and also in the home of the lesbian lawyer and her artist lover may be a respected lay leader in her local church, facing a different set of tensions than either of her employers does in negotiating multiple memberships.

Gender is also produced and reproduced in differential forms of participation in particular communities of practice. Women tend to be subordinate to men in the workplace, women in the military do not engage in combat, and in the academy, most theoretical disciplines are overwhelmingly male with women concentrated in descriptive and applied work that 'supports' theorizing. Women and men may also have very different forms of participation available to them in single-sex communities of practice. For example, if all-women groups do in fact tend to be more egalitarian than all-men groups, as some current literature claims (e.g., Aries 1976), then women's and men's forms of participation will be quite different. Such relations within same-sex groups will, of course, be related in turn to the place of such groups in the larger society.

The relations among communities of practice when they come together in overarching communities of practice also produce gender arrangements. Only recently, for example, have female competitive sports begun to receive significant recognition, and male sports continue to bring far greater visibility, power, and authority both to the teams and to the individual participants in those teams. The (male) final four is the focus of attention in the NCAA basketball world every spring, with the women's final four receiving only perfunctory mention. Many a school has its Bulldogs and Lady Bulldogs, its Rangers and Rangerettes. This articulation with power and stature outside the team in turn translates into different

---

c. The situation is shifting; on June 18, 2010, Tara Parker-Pope proclaimed in the *New York Times*: "Now Dad feels as stressed as Mom." Drawing on recent studies, she noted the greatly increased involvement of fathers in their kids' lives, which is leading many men to struggle with balancing work and home, a challenge once pretty much confined to employed women. At the same time, different workplace and home CofP expectations for women and for men have not vanished, complicating the picture.

possibilities for relations within. The relation between male varsity sports teams and female cheerleading squads illustrates a more general pattern of men's organizations and women's auxiliaries. Umbrella communities of this kind do not offer neutral membership status. And when several families get together for a meal prepared by the women who then team up to do the serving and clearing away while the men watch football, gender differentiation (including differentiation in language use) is being reproduced on an institutional level.

The community of practice is where the rubber meets the road—it is where observable action and interaction do the work of producing, reproducing, and resisting the organization of power in society and in societal discourses of gender, age, race, and so on. Speakers develop linguistic patterns as they engage in activity in the various communities in which they participate. Sociolinguists have tended to see this process as one of acquisition of something relatively 'fixed'—the linguistic resources, the community, and the individual's relation to the two are all viewed as fixed. The symbolic value of a linguistic form is taken as given, and the speaker simply learns it and uses it, either mechanically or strategically. But in actual practice, social meaning, social identity, community membership, forms of participation, the full range of community practices, and the symbolic value of linguistic forms are being constantly and mutually constructed.

And so although the identity of both the individual and the individual community of practice is experienced as persistent, in fact they both change constantly. We continue to adopt new ways of talking and discard some old ways, to adopt new ways of being women and men, gays and lesbians and heterosexuals, even changing our ways of being feminists or being lovers or being mothers or being sisters. In becoming police officers or psychiatrists or physicists or professors of linguistics, we may change our ways of being women and perhaps of being wives or lovers or mothers. In so doing, however, we are not negating our earlier gendered sociolinguistic identities; we are transforming them, changing and expanding forms of femininity, masculinity, and gender relations. And there are many more unnamed ways of thinking, being, relating, and doing that we adopt and adapt as we participate in different ways in the various communities of practice to which we belong.

What sociolinguists call the LINGUISTIC REPERTOIRE is a set of resources for the articulation of multiple memberships and forms of participation. And an individual's ways of speaking in a particular community of practice are not simply a function of membership or participation in that community. A way of speaking in a community does not simply constitute a turning on of a community-specific linguistic switch, or the symbolic laying of claim to membership in that community, but a complex articulation of the individual's forms of participation in that community with participation in other communities that are salient at the time. In turn, the linguistic practices of any given community of practice will be continually changing as a result of the many saliencies that come into play through its multiple members.

The overwhelming tendency in language and gender research on power has been to emphasize either speakers and their social relations (e.g., women's disadvantage in ordinary conversations with men) or the meanings and norms encoded in the linguistic systems and practices historically available to them (e.g., such sexist patterns as conflating generic human with masculine in forms like *he* or *man*). But linguistic forms have no power except as given in people's mouths and ears; to talk about meaning without talking about the people who mean and the community practices through which they give meaning to their words is at best limited.

3. Conclusion: A scholarly community of practice

Susan Gal (1992) has called for the integration of the wide range of endeavors that come under the rubric of language and gender. This comes up over and over in papers that range from Japanese morphological variation (Okamoto and Sato 1992) to girls' verbal disputes (Goodwin 1992; Sheldon 1992) to teenage girls' magazines (Talbot 1992) to phone sex (Hall 1992) and the Thomas-Hill hearings (Mendoza-Denton 1992; O'Connor 1992). Are these all loosely joined together simply by a shared interest in gender? Or is there an integral and indispensable connection that we must recognize and construct in order even to begin our work?

We have here the nucleus of a community of scholarly practice within which there is the real possibility of undertaking more ambitious collaborative inquiries. Mary Talbot (1992) shows us how a teen magazine attempts to create an imaginary community around the consumption of lipstick. It provides many of the requirements of a community of practice—knowledge, membership, history, practices—inviting the readers to become engaged in lipstick technology and to form their own real communities of practice around the consumption of lipstick. Many people studying gender dynamics in everyday conversation may not immediately see the relation between their work and studies of the discourses of gender as revealed in teen magazines. But just as gender is not given and static, it is also not constructed afresh in each interaction or each community of practice. Those of us who are examining the minutiae of linguistic form need to build detailed understanding of the construction of gender in the communities of practice that we study. But part of the characterization of a community of practice is its relation to other communities of practice and to the wider discourses of society. Thus while we do our close examination, we need to work within a consciously constructed broader perspective that extends our own necessarily limited view of the communities we study.

Significant advances in the study of language and gender from now on are going to have to involve integration on a level that has not been reached so far. The integration can come only through the intensive collaboration of people in a variety of fields, developing shared ways of asking questions and of exploring and evaluating possible answers. Language and gender studies, in fact, require an interdisciplinary community of scholarly practice. Isolated individuals who try to straddle two fields can often offer insights, but real progress depends on getting people from a variety of fields to collaborate closely in building a common and broad-based understanding. We will cease to be a friendly but scattered bunch of linguists, anthropologists, literary critics, and the like, when we become mutually engaged in the integration of our emerging insights into the nexus between language, gender, and social practice.

Sometimes our mutual engagement will lead us to controversy. And some have been concerned about the development of controversy over the cultural-difference model. It is true that argument that is not grounded in shared practice can reduce to unpleasant and *ad feminam* dispute. But rich intellectual controversy both requires and enhances mutual engagement. Without sustained intellectual exchange that includes informed and detailed debate, we will remain an aggregate of individuals with vaguely related interests in language and gender. With continued engagement like that begun at the 1992 Berkeley Women and Language Conference, we may become a productive scholarly community.

Notes

1. Many of the ideas expressed in this paper have appeared also in Penelope Eckert and Sally McConnell-Ginet 1992.
2. See Etienne Wenger (1990 and 1998); and Jean Lave and Etienne Wenger (1991).

References

Aries, Elizabeth (1976). Interaction patterns and themes of male, female, and mixed groups. *Small Group Behaviour* 7: 7–18.

Case, Susan (1992). Organizational inequity in a steel plant: A language model. In Kira Hall, Mary Bucholtz, and Birch Moonwomon (eds.), *Locating power*, vol. 1. Berkeley: Berkeley Women and Language Group, University of California, 36–48.

Eckert, Penelope (1990). The whole woman: Sex and gender differences in variation. *Language Variation and Change* 1: 245–267.

Eckert, Penelope, and Sally McConnell-Ginet (1992). Think practically and look locally: Language and gender as community-based practice. *Annual Review of Anthropology* 21: 461–490.

Freed, Alice F. (1992). We understand perfectly: A critique of Tannen's view of cross-sex communication. In Kira Hall, Mary Bucholtz, and Birch Moonwomon (eds.), *Locating power*, vol. 1. Berkeley: Berkeley Women and Language Group, University of California, 144–152.

Gal, Susan (1992). Language, gender, and power: An anthropological view. In Kira Hall, Mary Bucholtz, and Birch Moonwomon (eds.), *Locating power*, vol. 1.

Berkeley: Berkeley Women and Language Group, University of California, 153–161.

Goodwin, Marjorie Harness (1992). Orchestrating participation in events: Powerful talk among African American girls. In Kira Hall, Mary Bucholtz, and Birch Moonwomon (eds.), *Locating power*, vol. 1. Berkeley: Berkeley Women and Language Group, University of California, 182–196.

Gumperz, John J. (1982). *Discourse strategies*. Cambridge: Cambridge University Press.

Hall, Kira (1992). Women's language for sale on the fantasy lines. In Kira Hall, Mary Bucholtz, and Birch Moonwomon (eds.), *Locating power*, vol. 1. Berkeley: Berkeley Women and Language Group, University of California, 207–222.

Lakoff, Robin Tolmach (1992). The silencing of women. In Kira Hall, Mary Bucholtz, and Birch Moonwomon (eds.), *Locating power*, vol. 2. Berkeley: Berkeley Women and Language Group, University of California, 344–355.

Lave, Jean, and Etienne Wenger (1991). *Situated learning: Legitimate peripheral participation*. Cambridge: Cambridge University Press.

[Leslie, Sarah-Jane (forthcoming). The original sin of cognition: Fear, prejudice and generalization. *Journal of Philosophy*.]

[McConnell-Ginet, Sally (2009). Generic predication and interest-relativity. Paper presented at Non-Canonical Predication Workshop, University of Waterloo.]

McElhinny, Bonnie S. (1992). "I don't smile much anymore": Affect, gender, and the discourse of Pittsburgh police officers. In Kira Hall, Mary Bucholtz, and Birch Moonwomon (eds.), *Locating power*, vol. 2. Berkeley: Berkeley Women and Language Group, University of California, 386–403.

Mendoza-Denton, Norma Catalina (1992). The Anita Hill/Clarence Thomas cross-examination discourse: Variation in gap length. In Kira Hall, Mary Bucholtz, and Birch Moonwomon (eds.), *Locating power*, vol. 2. Berkeley: Berkeley Women and Language Group, University of California, 404–408.

Moonwomon, Birch (1992). Rape, race, and responsibility: A graffiti text political discourse. In Kira Hall, Mary Bucholtz, and Birch Moonwomon (eds.), *Locating power*, vol. 2. Berkeley: Berkeley Women and Language Group, University of California, 420–429.

Ochs, Elinor, and Carolyn Taylor (1992). Mothers' role in the everyday reconstruction of "Father knows best." In Kira Hall, Mary Bucholtz, and Birch Moonwomon (eds.), *Locating power*, vol. 2. Berkeley: Berkeley Women and Language Group, University of California, 447–462.

O'Connor, Peg (1992). Clarence Thomas and the survival of sexual harassment. In Kira Hall, Mary Bucholtz, and Birch Moonwomon (eds.), *Locating power*, vol. 1. Berkeley: Berkeley Women and Language Group, University of California, 463–468.

Okamoto, Shigeko, and Shie Sato (1992). Less feminine speech among young Japanese females. In Kira Hall, Mary Bucholtz, and Birch Moonwomon (eds.), *Locating power*, vol. 2. Berkeley: Berkeley Women and Language Group, University of California, 478–488.

Sheldon, Amy (1992). Preschool girls' discourse competence: Managing conflict. In Kira Hall, Mary Bucholtz, and Birch Moonwomon (eds.), *Locating power*, vol. 2. Berkeley: Berkeley Women and Language Group, University of California, 528–539.

Talbot, Mary (1992). A synthetic sisterhood: False friends in a teenage magazine. In Kira Hall, Mary Bucholtz, and Birch Moonwomon (eds.), *Locating power*, vol. 2. Berkeley: Berkeley Women and Language Group, University of California, 573–580.

Wenger, Etienne (1990). *Toward a theory of cultural transparency*. Palo Alto: Institute for Research on Learning.

——— (1998). *Communities of practice: Learning, meaning and identity*. Cambridge: Cambridge University Press.

6

Intonation in a man's world

0. Introduction

> If one were to examine the literature on men's and women's speech, one
> would conclude that it was a rare phenomenon, found mostly among extinct
> American Indian tribes. It has been reported mostly by linguists who were
> also anthropologists, for cases in which the grammar or phonology of the
> language could be stated only by taking it into account. Working out from
> ordinary linguistics then, one would have to conclude that in most societies
> men and women talk alike. That is a strange conclusion to arrive at, if lan-
> guage is a social instrument, given the importance of role differentiation
> along sexual lines in most times and places and it is a false conclusion of
> course. (Hymes 1971, 69)

When Dell Hymes made these comments, the literature on women's
and men's way of speaking could probably have been read in a fortnight.
Since that time, there has been an explosion in the study of sex-
differentiated linguistic behavior, and few people interested in language
use any longer assume that women and men "talk alike" in most societies.
We are still, however, at a very early stage in our understanding of how
women and men speak, why they speak as they do, and the importance of
language use for women in 'a man's world'. We have only recently begun
to realize that social constraints on speech behavior may restrict women's
and men's options and that such constraints function in the control of
women. Recent investigations in this area are largely the product of feminist scholars' concern to understand how talk works to create and maintain sex stereotyping and male dominance.[1] Our speech not only reflects
our place in culture and society but also helps to create that place.

"Ordinary linguistics," as Hymes calls it, provides theories and descriptions of structured language systems—for example, an account of the

This is a revised version of a paper that appeared in *Signs: Journal of Women in Culture and
Society* 3 (Spring 1978): 541–559. I want to thank Cheris Kramarae and Barrie Thorne for
their helpful suggestions on this version, which was published in Barrie Thorne, Cheris
Kramarae, and Nancy Henley, eds., *Language, gender and society* (Rowley, MA: Newbury
House, 1983), 69–88. The *Signs* paper developed from a talk I gave at the 1976 meetings of
the American Anthropological Association.

regular syntactic relation between English declaratives ("Joan *ate* the spinach with gusto") and interrogatives ("*Did* Joan *eat* the spinach with gusto?") or of the processes involved in pronunciation of *want to* as *wanna*. Such general features of English are part of the system acquired by both women and men, although one sex might, for example, more frequently choose to use an interrogative form or a verbal contraction in certain contexts. If women always said *wanna* and men *want to*, we would speak of sex differences in a low-level phonetic rule for speech production, but if each sex understood the equivalence of the forms, the basic structural systems underlying women's and men's linguistic knowledge would be identical. What I call 'extraordinary' linguistics—the explicit and detailed characterization of the actual utterances of people situated in real social contexts— relies on standard linguistic accounts of the language systems in which those utterances are cast. In other words, we can't make much progress in describing socially significant differences in language use (the case of present interest to us being the interaction of language and sex) without a framework within which we can say explicitly what it is that 'differs'.[2]

Intonation—the tune to which we set the text of our talk—functions prominently in stereotypes of female and male speech in American English. In 'ordinary linguistics', intonational structures are far less well understood than, for example, syntactic structures.[a] This is connected to the fact that members of the speech community have a less well-developed and clearly articulated conscious awareness of tunes than of texts. Our writing system, for example, ignores intonation. (A small caveat is in order: punctuation and italics are sometimes rough indicators of intonational features.) We also don't find parents 'correcting' children's intonational patterns as they sometimes do syntax or word choices. This somewhat peripheral status of intonation in the linguistic system may help to explain why speech melodies seem to be sex-typed. Over and above literal message content, tunes and their variations do apparently convey (cultural) values of femininity and masculinity as well as other traits that are culturally linked to gender (emotionality, for example).

Although not all aspects of how speech melodies are performed are relevant to describing the structured language systems, some certainly are. What we do know about the linguistic structure of intonation in American English also makes plausible the hypothesis that the basic intonational system might be used differently by women and men. Analysts agree that intonational patterns in American English are frequently used to convey 'illocutionary force'—whether, for example, the speaker is framing an

---

a. There has been significant progress made in intonational phonology since this paper was written. See Ladd (2008) for thorough discussion, including an account of Janet Pierrehumbert's influential notational system, which was first proposed in Pierrehumbert (1980). The analysis of intonational structure is still not a topic in introductory linguistics texts, however.

utterance as a question or as an assertion—and certain other aspects of the speaker's 'attitude'. Thus, intonational choices will be among the primary indicators of a speaker's aims and of the speech strategies used to pursue those aims. Given a sociocultural system in which women and men are in different social networks and positions and in which their behavior is differently evaluated, we might predict that intonational usage would be an important constituent of sex-differentiated 'styles' of speaking.[3] This applies whether such styles are normative ideals, disparaged stereotypes, or attested actualities. Many actual sex differences in favored strategies of language use in particular contexts are due to male dominance of women; they often represent women's attempts to cope with social restrictions. Women's lives consist of more than their relations to men, however, and thus women's ways of talking will be influenced by factors unconnected to male dominance.[b] Intonational studies help shed light on the complex interaction of language and women's experience.

A single speech melody can be performed as part of a number of quite different strategies, and thus its occurrence is not definitive evidence of any particular strategic orientation. Similarly, there can be many different reasons for performing a particular melody in a certain way, for selecting one 'variant' rather than another. A major thesis of this essay is that most discussions of intonational usages have assumed an androcentric perspective. The significance attributed to women's tunes has typically failed to take into account the complex range of possibilities that emerge when women's experiences and their viewpoints are seriously considered.

This androcentric perspective is manifest in two distinct but related ways. First, male-created stereotypes of what women are like are relied on both to shape beliefs about what tunes occur and to interpret and evaluate the tunes that are actually heard. Second, frameworks for analyzing the significance of particular speech melodies do not take account of women's distinctive experiences; in particular, there is a tendency to assume that men's behavior is paradigmatic of human behavior. On the one hand, women are seen as fundamentally unlike men—'feminine' speech melodies are heard as signaling women's instability (often, incompetence) and as symbolic of their devalued 'naturalness'. On the other hand, such interpretations rest on the untenable assumption that women's and men's life histories are identical, that there are no differences in the ways they have come to speak as they habitually do and have come to adopt the strategies they typically employ.

Women's speech is discounted in a man's world primarily on the basis of *how* it is said—the tunes used (and other features of 'style'). The substance of female texts—*what* is said—is frequently ignored or (mis)interpreted in

---

b. And, of course, women's relations to men are far more complex than 'male dominance' conveys.

light of hearers' assessments of the significance of the forms in which those texts are delivered. The problem, of course, is not in the melodies or their performers but in the interpreters. The following section reviews both empirical research and anecdotal suggestions about how the sexes 'sound' and, in particular, how both women and men use and interpret intonational patterns. The final section sketches a framework for explaining these observations and for further refining and testing specific hypotheses about the interaction of intonation and speaker/hearer gender.

1. Intonation: "It's not what she says but how she says it"

Many distinct phenomena are included under everyday uses of the term 'intonation' (often equated, in nontechnical discussions, with 'tone of voice'). Intonation does not characterize segments of sound but is perceived as a rhythmic structure 'overlaid' on a complete utterance. The main perceptual cues are pitch and volume changes over the course of an utterance. The language system does not recognize absolute values of pitch, volume, and duration but rather a number of abstract relational patterns, each of which can be 'realized' in different registers, in different volumes, and at different rates. These VARIANTS— alternative ways of performing basic intonational contours—play a role (only partly conventionalized) in communication. What variant is used may tell us, for example, where the speaker is from, or whether she just woke up, or whether he is lecturing to a class or talking to a friend, or how interested in the conversation the speaker wishes to appear.

Sex differences in speech are basically of two kinds. The first is what I have just called *variation*: alternative ways of uttering the 'same' linguistic unit. For intonation, this amounts to different ways of playing a single tune. The English 'question intonation' ends with a pitch rise to a point higher than earlier pitch levels in the sentence. There are, however, many variations possible on this one basic pattern. We might investigate whether women tend to make this final pitch rise relatively larger than men (rising more tones) in certain contexts. When answering the phone, perhaps she says

```
    o
    |
    |
   e
 H
```

whereas he says

These are different versions or VARIANTS of the general pattern often notated as "Hello ↑," a pattern some analysts call 'high rise' to indicate that it may occur on utterances that are not questions.

The second kind of sex difference that can be manifest in speech involves different SELECTION among the basic structural units—that is, different uses of the common system. By this I mean that women and men might tend to choose somewhat different strategies for speaking in roughly comparable situations. For example, a woman might more often than a man answer the phone with a "Hello ↑." He might, however, tend to prefer "Hello ↓" (the fall or 'neutral' intonation). These two intonational contours or tunes are quite distinct linguistically—they are *not* variations on a single melodic frame but different tunes altogether. To use one rather than the other is to engage in a different linguistic action; to act differently in roughly comparable situations is to pursue different strategies.

To put it slightly differently, we can think of the intonational system as including a 'dictionary' of meaningful tunes, an inventory of meaningful contours. Two people with the same internal dictionary can nonetheless have different patterns of usage. Where different pronunciations of a single intonational 'word' occur in different frequencies in the speech of two individuals, their usage reflects VARIATION-BASED differences. Where the frequency of occurrence of particular 'words' differs in some context, then the difference is SELECTION-BASED. Frequencies of '↑' compared to '↓' reflect selection; in contrast, the 'slope' of the rising (or falling) contour is subject to variation. (The distinction is by no means always easy to draw, but I confine attention to clear cases.)

Since any basic linguistic unit can be acquired by any speaker, all intonational (and other) differences in the speech of the sexes with a physiological explanation are variation-based. There are probably a few such differences. Adult men tend to be larger than adult women and thus their basic instrument for speech is pitched in a somewhat lower register. The larger vocal cords tend to vibrate more slowly, producing sounds that are lower in fundamental frequency (measured in units called hertz, abbreviated Hz) and thus heard as lower pitched. There is actually considerable overlap between the physiologically determined pitch ranges of adult female and male voices, but individuals seldom use in speech the full gamut of pitches they are capable of producing.

Still, although certain components of intonational differences between the sexes are a function of anatomical differences, it is clear that sociocultural factors also contribute significantly to establishing parameters of variation. Overt SPEECH STEREOTYPES of 'feminine' or 'masculine' speech (either believed typical of women and men, respectively, or desirable for them) rely most heavily on variants. This is probably because distinctions among variants do not alter overt referential meaning and are thus readily available as explicit signals of social meaning. What variants a speaker favors (within the range anatomical constraints permit) will depend on a number of factors: for example, which variants are most frequently heard and under what situations, or which variants are favored by the people with whom one identifies.

Even dimensions of variation that are quite constrained by individual physical characteristics can be affected by social and cultural factors. For example, different cultures settle on different parts of the possible pitch range for actual use in speaking by each sex. The studies of H. T. Hollien and his colleagues suggest that the speaking pitches of American males are, on the average, lower than those of some of their European counterparts by more than differences in size would predict.[4] Devereux (1949) observes that the Mohave pay no attention to the male 'voice change' at the time of puberty and that men do not shift pitch when imitating women. In our own culture, however, high-pitched voices are devalued and labeled 'shrill' if they are loud. The fact that our speech melodies are sung in different registers, then, reflects not simply the biological fact of our different physical size but is also a product of our *learning* to sound like women and men, although we have relatively little information on exactly how this works.[5]

If average speaking pitch is an important cue to speaker sex, reflecting both biologically based differences and cultural stereotypes overlaid on that biological base, it is apparently *not* the primary cue for stereotyping speaker's gender. Sachs, Lieberman, and Erickson (1973), Sachs (1975), and Coleman (1976) show clearly that pitch is not crucial to the identification of speaker sex and that other vocal tract characteristics play an important role. Sachs and her colleagues first played recordings of elicited sentence imitations from preadolescent children to judges and found sex of child quite reliably assigned, although overall the average fundamental frequency was higher for the boys' voices than for the girls. Matching girls and boys for height and weight (as a rough guide to probable vocal tract size and fundamental range), they found that vowel formant structure differed significantly for voices judged most reliably as 'girl-like' or 'boy-like'. In subsequent studies, Sachs found judges able to discriminate sex on the basis of isolated vowels and of backward speech but less reliably than from sentences, which suggests that intonational characteristics may also be operative.

Support for this hypothesis is provided by Bennett and Weinberg who found that "monotonicity had a deleterious effect on the perception of femaleness and an enhancing effect on the perception of maleness" (1979, 183) for judges (all female) of children's speech. Fichtelius, Johansson, and Nordin (1980) isolated intonational features by filtering speech to eliminate segmental information. The result is a signal in which words are no longer recognizable but rhythmic and pitch features of the original speech signal—the 'suprasegmental' or 'melodic' characteristics—are unaffected. Although they are tentative in reporting results on the basis of their limited study of Swedish-speaking children, they note that "[t]he acoustic variable showing the greatest covariation with the respondents' judgment of sex as well as the speakers' actual sex is the number of large frequency variations per time unit" (1980, 223). Again, both actual and perceived femaleness correlate with changing frequencies; in other words, with nonmonotonicity.

Perhaps even more startling is Terango's (1966) finding that adult males whose speech was heard as 'effeminate' by judges had, on the average, slightly *lower*-pitched voices than a matched group of males whom judges heard as nonremarkably 'masculine' in their speech. Terango did find significant acoustic differences between the two sets of voices: the group heard as effeminate used a significantly wider *range* of speaking pitches and changed pitch more frequently.[c]

My own informal observations suggest that when they imitate female speech, males (including young boys) emphasize intonational contours. Mimicry of female tunes shows pronounced and rapid pitch shifts (and probably also exaggerated shifts in intensity levels). Central to the stereotype of 'feminine' speech is the use of a relatively wide pitch range with frequent and rapid long glides. To imitate a woman by using an extreme version of this sort of pattern may be seen as a hostile act, and Austin suggests that to imitate a man by assuming the 'swoopy' patterns of the feminine stereotype is an extreme example of "derogatory imitation, one of the most infuriating acts of aggression one person can commit on another" (1965, 36).

Male intonational patterns do not seem to be imitated in a derogatory way, either in mocking of females or males. There are two possible reasons: (1) male intonations are heard as neutral—just as both sexes wear pants yet only women wear dresses, some patterns are heard as female while the rest are 'unmarked' for sex; (2) men lose by sounding woman-like, whereas women do not lose (perhaps they even gain in some contexts) by sounding man-like.[6] This does not mean that the male patterns are necessarily highly valued. Nonetheless, there is an asymmetry in imitative behavior to be explained.

Impressionistic accounts of men who are self-consciously rejecting a prescribed masculine role often refer to the use of special intonations. Newton says of a female impersonator, "The impression of femininity is conveyed more by the intonation, stress, and pronunciation than by the pitch itself. This intonation is parodying sweetness, rather mincing. It is a convincing imitation of affected female speech style" (1972, 72). Crystal (1971), a leading authority on English intonation, claims: "Intuitive impressions of effeminacy in English, for example,...are mainly [based on] non-segmental [features]: a 'simpering' voice, for instance, largely reduces to the use of a wider pitch-range than normal (for men), with

---

c. Gaudio (1994) did not find such differences in the speech of gay and straight men he recorded. But of course Terango was talking about perceptual judgments rather than about how actual gay and straight men might talk.

glissando effects between stressed syllables, a more frequent use of complex tones (e.g., the fall-rise and the rise-fall), the use of breathiness and huskiness in the voice, and switching to a higher (falsetto) register from time to time" (1971, 189). From the Terango study and other accounts of speech effeminacy and derogatory imitation, we can hypothesize that certain intonational variants are stigmatized markers of 'feminine' speech, indicating in male usage either overt flaunting of the code for sex-appropriate behavior (presenting oneself as 'gay', for example) or a derogatory imitation of women. Informal observation in the language laboratory indicates that male students are sometimes loath to reproduce patterns in a second language that involve the long and rapid glides (especially if reversed on a single syllable) that they associate with female or effeminate speech in American English.[7]

Comparing male speech perceived as effeminate to characterizations of global differences in female/male speech suggests the likely intonational cues for judgments of speakers on a femininity/masculinity dimension. Overall, without reference to particular contexts or to individual differences, female and effeminate male speech are apparently distinguished from 'ordinary' male speech in the following ways: the male pitch range is narrower than the female/effeminate and shows slower and less frequent pitch shifts.[d] Amplitude changes—linked to loudness—are not mentioned but are probably also important, with female/effeminate speech registering more and greater shifts in amplitude. We can call this cluster of factors DYNAMISM and say that female and effeminate male intonational variants are characteristically more dynamic than typical male patterns. By this I mean that we 'hear' dynamism as 'feminine', that dynamism is an especially salient cue to speaker gender.[8]

But do women (as a group) actually show different patterns of intonational variation from men? Is the stereotype of female speech a reflection (albeit exaggerated and distorted) of actual female speech melodies? The answer seems to be affirmative within a relatively small amount of systematically collected data. Takefuta, Jancosek, and Brunt (1972) had twelve female and twelve male speakers record ten sentences each, reading each sentence with different intonations, and found a significantly greater pitch shift in the female reading voices. Other reading studies suggest similar results, although it is unclear what the relation of oral reading styles is to ordinary speech.

Brend (1975), a linguist working in a tradition begun by Pike's (1946) landmark study of American English intonation, is one of the few to have

---

d. As Henton (1989) points out, I neglected in discussing pitch range to note that fundamental frequency range and perceived pitch range are distinct. The difference between 50 and 100 Hz is heard as the same difference in pitch as that between 100 and 200 Hz and that between 200 and 400 Hz. Clearly assessing relative dynamism has to take account of this exponential relation to fundamental frequency; the other component of dynamism, frequency of pitch shifts, is more straightforward to determine.

addressed the question of sex differences in intonation from a linguist's perspective. She does not specify how her data were obtained or whether she considered the interaction of sex with other sociolinguistic variables to arrive at her findings. Following Pike, she characterizes the patterns purportedly used by women as "polite and cheerful," "unexpectedness and surprise," "hesitation" (a pattern Pike suggests can indicate endearment, especially if used by a woman), and "incomplete and unexpected." She summarizes her results as follows:

> Men consistently avoid certain intonation levels or patterns. They very rarely, if ever, use the highest level of pitch that women use. That is, it appears probable that most men have only three contrastive levels of intonation, while many women, at least, have four. Men avoid final patterns which do not terminate at the lowest level of pitch, and use a final, short upstep only for special effects....Although they also use short downglides...they seem in general to avoid the one-syllable long pitch glides, and completely avoid the reverse glides on one syllable. (Brend 1972, 86–87)

Brend's way of describing the differences implies that the sexes have different language systems. In particular, the suggestion that few men but many women use four contrastive levels (implying distinct inventories of basic units) is probably more accurately put in terms of sex-preferred modes of variation. Some of the differences she points to, however, almost surely do involve sex preferences in selections among available basic tune forms. The variation-based differences noted by Brend fit with the dynamic complex already described.

Intonational tunes are a major means by which speakers express their emotional involvement in a particular exchange, their attitudes, and their general 'stance' in the discourse. Bolinger (1970) has noted the difficult interpretive problem created by the fact that the same acoustic features can result either from a speaker's conscious manipulations or from internal phenomena not under the speaker's control. Thus, when we are judging data from groups of speakers who show differences in the intonational features associated with the expression of emotion, it is impossible to identify causal factors.

Keeping this in mind, it is noteworthy that the dynamic complex associated with the speech of women and effeminate males is also associated with emotional expressiveness. The degree of perceived emotion is strongly correlated with pitch range (at least for male speakers): the greater the range of pitches used, the greater degree of expressed emotion hearers perceive.[9] Thus, when compared as a group to men, women may well (simply on the basis of their dynamic pitch patterns) be heard as emotional. The patterns themselves may originate quite independently of their use in emotional expression, serving other purposes and having other causes. However, to be emotional is (in part) to express one's emotion. It is possible that part of women's *being* emotional in our culture derives from our *sounding* emotional. And we sound emotional because our everyday 'tunes'—the patterns we use in ordinary circumstances when no extremes of emotion are felt or expressed—show a degree of dynamism found in men's tunes only in extraordinary circumstances of heightened emotional expression. Of course, the problem is that the culture does not simply categorize us as emotionally expressive (a positive and useful trait whose lack handicaps many males as well as some females) but also views us as unstable and unpredictable.

Whether or not expressed emotionality really bears any relation to the 'predictability' of one's behavior is one unanswered question. Even were that relation to exist it would not imply a deficiency (unpredictability) to overcome; after all, behaving predictably is not necessarily desirable. However, though emotional expressiveness and its possible concomitants might not be handicaps if androcentric biases were eliminated, the fact remains that one's intonational patterns are not really adequately expressive of emotions if they are heard in reference to a presumptive 'ideal' that inadequately reflects usage of the entire speech community. The young male apparently learns to 'sound masculine' (as he learns to 'sound cool'), whereas the culture believes that the young female is destined by her biological endowment to be at the mercy of inner psychic upheavals which produce her dynamic tunes. To some extent, such a belief simply reflects ignorance of the fact that intonational patterns are basically cultural constructs (different cultures using their own distinctive patterns and 'meanings'), although they are 'internalized' very early and not easily subject to conscious modification.

To make matters more complicated, intonation does have a 'natural' base as well. The quickened breathing and muscular tension that accompany certain kinds of heightened emotion can have an effect on our speech melodies: increased fluctuations in respiration and muscular activity will produce more dynamic tunes. And many of the culture-specific 'meanings' associated with particular melodies represent conventionalized metaphors that refer to the nonlinguistic ('natural') significance associated with certain features of melodies. For example, to keep the voice level, to speak in a 'flat' monotone, requires suppression of certain 'natural' physical impulses. It is thus a 'natural' indicator of 'control' over one's internal mechanisms. By extension, the style can come to signify 'control' more generally and can be thus heard and evaluated that way. As Bolinger (1964) puts it, intonation is "around the edge of language." Because of this interplay between the natural and cultural 'meanings', intonation is readily available and perhaps especially effective as a cultural symbol of woman's perceived greater 'naturalness', one important aspect of which is the 'free' expression of her emotions.[10] This is easily perceived by male-dominated culture as a failure to control emotion and a reflection of her innate inferiority to the male. Of course, one could equally well emphasize the positive side of dynamic and expressive communicative behavior and suggest that many males apparently fail to achieve the expressive versatility of most females.

The connection of the female/male dynamic intonational stereotype with stereotyped emotionally expressive behavior could conceivably be explained as either physiologically based (e.g., due to purported inner homeostatic mechanisms that keep most males on a more even keel than most females) or socioculturally based (due to learned sex typing of other kinds of emotionally expressive behavior such as crying) or both.[11] Note that I refer to "purported" homeostatic mechanisms; Barrie Thorne has reminded me that there is evidence from male pathology that it's not some inner 'even keel' but a bottling up or repression. It is still, of course, possible that females have a tendency to more internal volatility and that males are handicapped by a tendency toward internal stagnation. My own guess is that the contribution of biological factors is likely to be minuscule here. Whatever the ultimate finding on that score, it is clear that society and culture have played an enormous role in shaping our emotional expressiveness. The point of interest in the present discussion is that women *are* (culturally) emotional because they sound that way.

Dynamism, by and large, seems to derive from variation-based differences in women's speech compared to men's, although it is possible that selection-preferences also contribute to the general dynamic picture. (There are too little data to even begin to decide just what factors are involved.) Because of the significance attached to variants (e.g., as expressive of emotionality), however, it is quite possible for speakers to include variation preferences as well as unit selections as part of a particular strategic orientation toward speech. In particular, dynamism can be used as a positive resource for speakers. To sound highly emotional might enable one to attain ends not reachable by calm behavior if one is a subordinate, such as a child interacting with an adult or a woman with a man. And of course certain situations promote the expression of emotion: the care of a child puts greater demands on emotional expressiveness than repairing telephone lines.

In addition to dynamism as a dimension on which female intonations are said to differ from male, it is said that the sexes tend to favor different endings (often called "terminals" by linguists) for their tunes. According to Brend (1972), men avoid final patterns that do not terminate at the lowest level, using rising terminals only for special effects (whatever that might mean—they certainly do use such patterns). Pike (1946) also suggested that women were primary users of many patterns with final rise. In her informal descriptions, Eble (1972) mentions the "'whining, questioning, helpless' patterns, which are used predominantly by women." To use a rising terminal rather than a falling terminal is, as discussed above, to select a different basic 'tune'. A syntactic analogy is the choice between issuing directives in an interrogative form ("Would you put out the garbage?") or an imperative form ("Put out the garbage"). We impute different intended structural messages on the basis of the selection of units. Patterns of such differences indicate strategic orientations. The difficulty, of course, is determining what the intended messages are, since intonational 'words' can either provide a 'frame' for the text they carry or can have a meaning that is superimposed on (and largely independent of) that text. The discussion of a particular example that follows will illustrate these points.

The English high-rise or 'question' intonational pattern, as noted earlier, ends with a rising terminal that reaches a level higher than earlier parts of the utterance. Lakoff (1975) has claimed that women are more likely than men to use what she calls an "inappropriate question intonation," as in the following:

> HUSBAND: When will dinner be ready?
> WIFE   :   Six o'clock?

Lakoff claims that the wife's rising terminal indicates her failure to make a statement when discourse requires it, thus signaling uncertainty or lack of self-assertiveness. However, as was argued in McConnell-Ginet (1975), there are many alternative functions that this high-rise tune can be serving. The wife in the scenario may be heard as both stating and questioning. Her unexpressed question may be "Why do you need to know?" or "Are you listening to me?" or "Do you want to eat earlier?" or any of a host of other possibilities. Or, less specifically than questioning, she may be simply indicating desire for a continuation of the discourse. Ladd (1980) argues that we need not appeal to 'implicit' questioning but should understand the high rise as conveying nonfinality or incompleteness (of which tentativeness, doubt, and questioning are simply special instances).

Men certainly do use the high-rise intonational pattern to respond to questions for which they have the answer, and there is no evidence that such uses are heard as 'effeminate' or even particularly hesitant or indecisive. Not surprisingly, those who favor this tune for virtually all utterances are probably heard as somewhat hesitant and nonassertive.[12] Although there may be more women than men with this habit, the reasons are unlikely to be found in the pattern's being associated with 'femininity'. If there are sex differences in this usage, they will arise because one sex has more need or liking than the other for this particular communicative ploy: accompanying one explicit speech act (roughly, declaring) with another, which is implicit questioning, or more generally, requesting some additional input from the other party to the exchange.[e]

Do women and men actually tend to answer *Wh*-questions with different contours? (*Wh*-questions include "*When* will dinner be ready?" "*Where*

---

e. McLemore 1992 is an extensive ethnographic study in a Texas sorority that looks at final rises in some detail and finds that the young women in charge of the sorority use them extensively—they did not convey in these contexts any kind of timidity or insecurity but often occurred as part of authoritative speech in house meetings. At the same time, these young women told McLemore that outside the sorority they had to modify their speech in order to be taken seriously.

do you live?" and "*What's* your name?") The answer seems to depend, as one might expect, on the nature of the communicative context. Edelsky (1979) compared use of high rise, fall, and another pattern that she calls fall rise. This fall-rise, called 'low-rise' in McConnell-Ginet (1978), is heard as having a definite rising terminal, but it is not perceived as at all 'incomplete' or 'questioning' like the high-rise. Acoustically, its final rise usually stops at a point below some earlier high in the utterance. Schematically, we can contrast the three patterns as follows:

A. Hel   Fall
      lo

B. Hel   Fall Rise or Low Rise
      lo

C. Hel   High Rise ('Question')
       lo

Edelsky's female and male subjects were not differentiated in their use of the high rise. In contrast, pilot studies I have been conducting (McConnell-Ginet 1978 gave a preliminary report) show women using more high rise and more low rise. Edelsky's study had interviewers approach people in a student union and ask "Where were you born?" or "What's your favorite color?" whereas our interviewers asked (in front of a campus landmark) "What building is this?" The Edelsky questions were survey in type; ours were the kind one expects from strangers. Whether or not this difference in the communicative context explains the different findings, it is clear that we need considerably more data from real communicative exchanges if we are to have any real insight into 'how she says it' or, for that matter, 'how he says it'.

   In addition, we need more systematic study of how tunes are interpreted. Edelsky's research has begun this by investigating the contribution of the three contours to evaluation of persons using them in response to the "Where were you born?" question. She found high-rise and fall associated with stereotypically 'feminine' and 'masculine' qualities, respectively, with the low-rise in between. For instance, judges heard a high rise response as sociable whereas the fall was self-centered. (The study used the matched-guise technique so that, unbeknownst to experimental subjects, judgments were made of the same voice with different tunes.) How do judges arrive at such evaluations? My conjecture is that they figure out what sort of strategy would lead someone to speak like that in the hypothetical situation. Then they evaluate people on the basis of their opting for that strategy (and, thus, for that mode of speaking). This is, of course, an unsubstantiated claim that requires considerable elaboration and investigation. It is important, however, to consider somewhat more carefully than we have in the past the possible bases on which judges evaluate speech samples.[13] It is also important to find more direct tests of what speakers intend and hearers attribute to uses of particular tunes in a given situation.

   Clarion calls to further research are easier to sound than to obey. One of the reasons intonation continues to baffle linguistic investigators—we still cannot adequately characterize 'how she said it'—is that the tunes of speech shade into one another rather than being sharply distinguished like the sounds of speech. Traditional linguistic research—"ordinary linguistics" in Hymes's terms—deals with discrete entities, in other words, with either-or oppositions rather than more-or-less gradations. Where continuously varying parameters are significant, it is helpful to supplement human observations with instrumental measurements. We can also take advantage of such sophisticated machines as speech synthesizers to subject explicitly formulated hypotheses to controlled tests. I do not suggest that technology yields insight or that carefully collected data are the magic key to understanding the role of intonation in women's and men's lives. But I do argue that, in order to understand the ways in which 'how she said it' can work for and against her, we need to widen our descriptive base. Women certainly do not at all times in all places "talk in italics," to use Lakoff's characterization. We need to know when, where, and why does someone talk 'like a woman', and, an obvious but often overlooked question, who talks 'like a woman'? We also need to know how sex differences in intonation develop and what their consequences are for women's and men's lives.[14]

2. Toward a theory of sex differences in intonation

'Ordinary linguistics' leaves unanswered many of the most interesting questions about the function of language in people's lives. Linguists have recently, however, expanded the horizons of 'ordinary linguistics'. This expansion is partly due to social and political pressures (originating in the civil rights movement of the 1960s and continuing in the women's movement) to understand how language is used to support the status quo and to serve the interests of the powerful. Such understanding can suggest strategies to change the status quo and can be used to increase appreciation of speech styles of subordinates. Even apart from such practical concerns, however, many linguists have begun to see that the 'ordinary' linguistic practice of abstracting from the social context and focusing on a mythic 'ideal' speaker in splendid isolation from other human beings, though a necessary part of linguistic analysis, is not enough to explain how language works. Unless language is put back into the social setting from which it is extracted for initial analysis, the processes of language change, for example, cannot be properly understood.[15] But even an expanded and 'extraordinary' linguistics will not be able to answer all the issues raised by examining sex differences in language use. We must turn to other disciplines such as psychology, sociology, anthropology, and, more generally, women's studies scholarship. Because it requires sophistication in all these areas, a comprehensive theory of intonation (in a man's world or anywhere else) awaits future collaborative research. The following outlines a preliminary theoretical perspective on sex differences in intonation.

1. In oral communication, speech melodies are primary cues of speaker sex.

2. The speech community explicitly associates certain intonational patterns with the speech of women. These patterns function as part of a cultural stereotype and can be used in derogatory imitation directed against women or men. The negative connotations of the stereotype are the products of misogyny in an androcentric culture. But 'feminine' patterns can also be adopted by males to express a rejection of socially imposed canons of sex-appropriate behavior. American English speakers do not appear to exploit a masculine intonational stereotype for purposes of negative imitation or rejection of gender identification by females; stereotyped tunes are 'feminine' only (more precisely, 'non-masculine').[16] Sex-stereotyped tunes are not universal, however: what is perfectly ordinary for men in one language may sound effeminate in another.

3. In addition to the overt stereotypes, there are certain general features of intonation that correlate with speaker sex. To present oneself as feminine or masculine, one shifts speech melodies (probably not consciously) toward the extremes identified with female and male speech, respectively. It is not the sex of the other conversational participants that determines how strongly feminine or masculine a speech style will be used, but the speaker's need or desire for a particular mode of self-presentation. A woman may wish to deemphasize or emphasize her sex in working with male colleagues, and she may wish to express her 'solidarity' with or dissimilarity to female colleagues.[17] These factors are not necessarily articulated in a conscious way, and some uses of particular tunes may be attributable to a particular individual's idiosyncratic habits. Hence, it is difficult (in some cases, impossible) to determine the speaker's attitudes and aims from the evidence of her (or his) tunes. However, clear-cut cases (where nonlinguistic knowledge can inform us of participants' attitudes toward and interests in a particular interaction) can permit us to identify the intonational markers of speaker sex that function as gender symbols for the speech community.

4. Our culture, overtly espousing sexual egalitarianism and providing many shared spheres of activity, predisposes us to believe that learned behavior is androgynous and that actual sex differences in behavior must be due to biological rather than social and cultural factors. The belief that intonation directly reflects internal states promotes its use to mark gender. Because certain features of intonation are in fact affected by a speaker's internal state, those features are often (incorrectly) believed to be consistently reliable indicators of speakers' attitudes and emotions.

5. Intonational 'habits' are established without conscious consideration of available options and perhaps partly in unreflective response to available models.[18] The differences in dynamic range that have been observed in some studies probably arise chiefly from male efforts to restrict range. The extreme of 'masculine' intonation in American English is a complete monotone,[19] whereas there are (theoretically) no limits at the other end of the scale. Masculine speech melodies can thus be heard as metaphors for control, for 'coolness', and feminine speech melodies as uncontrolled, untamed by culture. The association of feminine and masculine extremes with the full disclosure of emotion and with its repression, respectively, reflects the general connection of the masculine extreme with constraint.

6. The 'feminine' habit of keeping pitch and loudness changing may serve the important function of attracting and holding the listener's attention. Women may need this device more than men because of (1) their relative powerlessness (dynamic rendition of the text is invaluable in holding the listener's attention if one lacks the authority to require that attention) and (2) their frequent contact with young children who are not yet socialized to attend reliably to verbal signals.[20] If these suggestions are viable, increased or relatively great dynamism should be a feature of 'powerless' speech and also of interaction with young children.[f]

7. Because the primary linguistic function of intonation is to indicate how an utterance 'fits' in a discourse—what the speaker is doing by means of uttering a particular text in a particular context—women and men will typically use different patterns for equivalent situations because they have different strategies for speech action. In speech as in other areas women and men frequently 'act' differently, because of differences in their early socialization and their access to power and because of the general expectations attached to their social positions. In a particular case one may not know the complex of causes of a person's intonational strategies—some people 'wheedle' because of a vocal habit established in early childhood, others because they calculate that it is most likely to bring the ends they desire, still others because no other means of attaining their goals has occurred to them. Specific tunes are virtually *never* selected at a conscious level. It should be noted that a particular individual may have one strategy or general

---

f. In retrospect, I may have overemphasized relative lack of power or authority here, although that certainly can be a factor. Dynamism can indicate engagement, and this can help hold listeners' attention. Delph-Janiurek (1999) found male teaching staff in an English university using much more restricted—less dynamic—intonation than their female colleagues, but he also found that students tended to judge the resulting almost monotonic lecture styles boring.

communicative goal in mind yet be interpreted by her (or his) addressee as motivated by some quite different factor. This possibility of miscommunication is a consequence of the fact that the same forms serve multiple functions.

This sketch of a theory of sex differences in intonation raises rather than answers questions.[21] For example, if subsequent investigation should establish that women are hurt by their use of intonational patterns that male culture devalues, ought we try to train ourselves in new melodic habits or strategies? Not necessarily. To accept the values set by the man's world is to continue residence in woman's place. Recognition of the positive values of some now generally negatively valued tunes can help women (and other subordinated speakers) develop their own speech powers as they choose. Women's tunes probably can be interpreted to keep her in her place: on her back and out of power. But views of women's intonational styles as uncontrolled (uncontrollable) and ineffectual (lacking in authority) can be challenged once the androcentric origins of these views are clearly understood.

Notes

1. See, for example, the essays in Thorne et al. (1983) and in the earlier Thorne and Henley (1975). In addition to such studies, my own approach to the study of language in social life owes much to such work as that in Ervin-Tripp (1973), Goffman (1969), Labov (1972), and Gumperz and Hymes (1972).

2. For further discussion of these issues, see McConnell-Ginet (1979), which is a reply to Kean (1979).

3. Brown (1980) develops the notion of sex-typed 'styles' as generated by strategies women and men develop from their distinct social experiences, drawing on the detailed and very interesting theory of universals of politeness in Brown and Levinson (1978).

4. See Majewski, Hollien, and Zalewski (1972); Hollien and Jackson (1973); Hollien and Shipp (1972); also relevant is Michel, Hollien, and Moore (1965).

5. Aronovitch (1976) found little correlation between personality judgments and average pitch, but his study was not designed to allow isolation of pitch from other variables. That high pitch tends to be devalued, especially if combined with relative loudness, is suggested by the unquestioned assumption of von Raffler-Engel and Buckner 1976 that women's high-pitched voices are intrinsically unpleasant if loud.

6. That the second explanation has force is suggested by the fact that male subjects, asked to read a passage "as you think a woman would" in one of the studies reported in McConnell-Ginet (1978), were very reluctant to do so; whereas women were much more cooperative in reading "as you think a man would" (and tended to comply by monotonizing their reading voice). Cheris Kramarae (personal communication) notes that courtship is a context in which women might lose by sounding 'like a man'. Barrie Thorne (personal communication) observed monotonic intonation in the speech of a fourth-grade girl who had been disparagingly described by another girl as "like a boy." The comment mentioned "looks," but Thorne noted that the girl in question had long hair and suggested that the impression of "like a boy" might well have been based in part on "sounds," even though only "looks" got noted explicitly by the other girl.

7. Suggested to me by Richard Leed, Professor of Slavic Linguistics at Cornell University, on the basis of his experience with students learning Russian.

8. Both Bennett and Weinberg (1979) and Terango (1966) provide significant empirical support for this view of our perception of dynamism.

9. See, for example, Huttar (1968) and Soron (1964). Literature on intonational expression of emotion is voluminous but not methodologically very sound. See, however, Uldall (1960), Greenberg (1969), and Reardon (1971). See also the section on intonation and emotion in Bolinger (1972). A problem often ignored is that the specific import of a tune depends on the text it carries and the context in which it occurs, a point made in Ladd (1980). See also Gunter (1974) and Liberman and Sag (1974).

10. See Ortner (1974) for discussion of connections between nature/culture and female/male dichotomies. Liberman (1975) suggests that certain global features of intonational patterns can play a role as incompletely conventionalized vocal symbols.

11. There are people who automatically assume sex differences in behavior are our anatomical destiny. See Aronovitch (1976) for mention of some psychologists' belief in "physiological differences in homeostatic mechanisms" leading to "less emotional balance in the female than in the male." Whether or not biological differences are involved, the important point is the significance of cultural and social influences and the existence of great individual variation among individuals of each sex.

12. My mail indicates that women's supposed 'timidity' is indeed a popular explanation of the high rise on declaratives. In response to a quotation from me in a recent newspaper article suggesting that the high rise is a way of asking a question whose content is not made explicit, I received a number of letters from people who wanted to 'help' with my research, suggesting that the explanation was women's "fear of asserting themselves." My guess is that people are more likely to offer the 'fear' account if a woman's usage is involved than if interpreting the high-rise pattern on a man's declarative. The classic study of how the same behaviors are differently labeled if ascribed to female rather than to male is Condry and Condry (1976).

13. Sachs 1975 (167) addresses the issue of the basis of speech evaluations. Drawing on research by Frederick Williams and his colleagues, she suggests the possibility that judges label speech on the basis of social stereotypes. Although her discussion deals primarily with the characterization of the speech rather than with attributes imputed to the speaker on the basis of the speech (the subject of most research on evaluation of women's speech), similar questions are involved. For examples of attribution to women of personal characteristics on the basis of their speech, see Giles et al. (1980), who report on the contribution of a regional accent to people's first impressions of a woman's attitudes and behavioral style. They also found that women with different outlooks on feminist issues 'sounded' different to judges. What features of speech were involved we don't know, but it is at least plausible that intonational characteristics play a role.

14. For several years I have been conducting exploratory research with the help of a number of Cornell University students to test some of the hypotheses presented in this paper. We have acoustic data from reading studies and from naturalistic observation that support the "dynamism" hypothesis above. We have also used the "matched-guise" technique first described in Lambert et al. 1960 to

test contribution of different contours to judgments of speakers' traits, and our results are similar to those reported in Edelsky (1979). Our goal eventually is to devise more direct tests of conveyed meaning and to use synthetic speech to manipulate particular acoustic variables more systematically. I have been assisted in this research by Dr. Susan Hertz, who has developed the Cornell speech synthesis system; David Walter, phonetics laboratory technician; and the following undergraduate research assistants: Susan Costello, Lisa Fine, Elizabeth Kaplan, Jennifer Klein, Cynthia Putnam, and Daniel Segal. McConnell-Ginet (1978) reported some initial results, but the research is really still in early stages and will not be ready for publication for several more years.

15. See Weinreich, Labov, and Herzog (1968) for this viewpoint. I want to emphasize again that the view that abstraction from the social context is inadequate does *not* imply that such abstraction is dispensable as a component of linguistic analysis. See Kean (1979) and McConnell-Ginet (1979) for further discussion.

16. Barrie Thorne has raised the possibility that some women may also announce a rejection of socially imposed canons of sex-appropriate behavior through their linguistic choices. However, the asymmetry in intonation seems similar to that between dresses (a 'feminine' mode of clothing, carrying a strong message when worn by men) and pants (though not 'feminine' by any means, their being worn by a woman need not convey any special message about attitudes toward sexual norms). For a woman to eschew markedly 'feminine' practices is not equivalent to a man's adopting these same practices.

17. Using the stereotypical 'feminine' tunes is only one way available to women to 'bond' with one another. Barrie Thorne (personal communication) observes extensive use of the high rise intonation in California among feminists speaking to one another. As she suggests, it probably functions as an invitation to others to speak, emphasizing the collectivity of the group and underscoring a speaker's desire not to present herself as a 'heavy'. There is much to be learned about how we deal with one another as women and how those 'dealings' are changing as feminism transforms the contexts in which they occur.

18. See account in Lieberman (1967: 45–46) of a thirteen-month-old girl and a ten-month-old boy who used higher fundamental frequencies when 'talking to mother' than when 'talking to father', presumably in imitation of their parents' speech. Very young children also show intonational 'style-shifting': the use of certain varieties of speech melody to mark the nature of an interaction; see Weeks (1970).

19. I have observed some adolescent males using an extremely monotonic style, especially in peer interactions, and decreased dynamism in adolescent males has been noted by many observers though never, so far as I know, systematically studied. For adult male speech, it appears to be the case that any variation in dynamism is seen as significant, whereas female speech is already presupposed to be dynamic. See Aronovitch (1976) for this interpretation of his results (esp. 218).

20. See, for example, Kaplan (1970), a study that found infants attended to pitch shifts and suggested that intonation plays an important role in aiding the child's language acquisition.

21. In addition to the works already cited, my own understanding of English intonation has drawn much from Crystal (1969). Future studies must also take account of Waugh and van Schooneveld (1979), a collection of essays on late 1970s research on intonation.

References

Aronovitch, Charles D. (1976). The voice of personality: Stereotyped judgments and their relation to voice quality and sex of speaker. *Journal of Social Psychology* 99: 207–220.

Austin, William (1965). Some social aspects of paralanguage. *Canadian Journal of Linguistics* 2: 31–39.

Bennett, Suzanne and Bernd Weinberg (1979). Sexual characteristics of pre-adolescent children's voices. *Journal of the Acoustical Society of America* 65: 179–189.

Bolinger, Dwight (1964). Around the edge of language: Intonation. *Harvard Educational Review* 34: 282–293. Reprinted in Bolinger 1972.

—— (1970). Relative height. In P. R. Leon, G. Faure, and A. Rigault (eds.), *Prosodic feature analysis*. Montreal: Marcel Didier. Reprinted in Bolinger 1972.

—— (ed.) (1972). *Intonation*. Harmondsworth, UK: Penguin Books.

Brend, Ruth M. (1972). Male-female intonation patterns in American English. *Proceedings of the Seventh International Congress of Phonetics Sciences, 1971.* The Hague: Mouton. Reprinted in Barrie Thorne and Nancy Henley (eds.), *Language and sex: Difference and dominance*. Rowley, MA: Newbury House, 1975.

Brown, Penelope (1980). Why and how are women more polite: Some evidence from a Mayan community. In Sally McConnell-Ginet, Ruth Borker, and Nelly Furman (eds.), *Women and language in literature and society*. New York: Praeger.

Brown, Penelope, and Stephen Levinson (1978). Universals of language usage: Politeness phenomena. In Esther Goody (ed.), *Questions and politeness: Strategies in social interaction*. Cambridge Papers in Social Anthropology, vol. 8. Cambridge: Cambridge University Press, 56–311.

Coleman, Ralph O. (1976). A comparison of the contributions of two voice quality characteristics to the perception of maleness and femaleness in the voice. *Journal of Speech and Hearing Research* 19: 168–180.

Condry, John, and Sandra Condry (1976). Sex differences: A study of the eye of the beholder. *Child Development* 47: 812–819.

Crystal, David (1969). *Prosodic systems and intonation in English*. Cambridge: Cambridge University Press.

—— (1971). Prosodic and paralinguistic correlates of social categories. In Edwin Ardener (ed.), *Social anthropology and language*. London: Tavistock.

[Delph-Janiurek, Tom (1999). Sounding gender(ed): Vocal performances in English university teaching spaces. *Gender, Place and Culture* 6: 137–153.]

Devereux, George (1949). Mohave voice and speech mannerisms. *Word* 5: 268–272. Reprinted in Dell Hymes (ed.) (1964). *Language in culture and society*. New York: Harper & Row.

Eble, Connie C. (1972). How the speech of some is more equal than others. Paper presented at Southeastern Conference on Linguistics, University of Tennessee, Knoxville, TN.

Edelsky, Carole (1979). Question intonation and sex roles. *Language in Society* 8: 15–32.

Ervin-Tripp, Susan (1973). *Language acquisition and communicative choice*. Stanford, CA: Stanford University Press.

Fichtelius, Anna, Irene Johansson, and Kerstin Nordin (1980). Three investigations of sex- associated speech variation in day school. In Cheris Kramarae (ed.), *The voices and words of women and men*. Oxford: Pergamon Press, 219–226. Also in *Women's Studies International Quarterly* 3 (2/3): 219–226.

[Gaudio, Rudolf P. (1994). Sounding gay: Pitch properties in the speech of gay and straight men. *American Speech* 69: 30–57.]

Giles, Howard, Philip Smith, Caroline Brown, Sarah Whiteman, and Jennifer Williams (1980). Women's speech: The voice of feminism. In Sally McConnell-Ginet, Ruth Borker, and Nelly Furman (eds.), *Women and language in literature and society*. New York: Praeger.

Goffman, Erving (1969). *Strategic interaction*. Philadelphia: University of Pennsylvania Press.

Greenberg, S. Robert (1969). An experimental study of certain intonational contours in American English. *UCLA Working Papers in Phonetics* 13, Los Angeles, California.

Gumperz, John J., and Dell Hymes (eds.) (1972). *Directions in sociolinguistics*. New York: Holt, Rinehart & Winston.

Gunter, Richard (1974). *Sentences in dialog*. Columbia, SC: Hornbeam Press.

[Henton, Carolyn (1989). Fact and fiction in the description of female and male speech. *Language and Communication* 9: 299–311.]

Hollien, Harry, and B. Jackson (1973). Normative data on the speaking fundamental frequency characteristics of young adult males. *Journal of Phonetics* 1: 117–120.

Hollien, Harry, and T. Shipp (1972). Speaking fundamental frequency and chronological age in males. *Journal of Speech and Hearing Research* 15: 155–159.

Huttar, George (1968). Relations between prosodic variables and emotions in normal American English utterances. *Journal of Speech and Hearing Research* 11: 481–487.

Hymes, Dell (1971). Sociolinguistics and the ethnography of speaking. In E. Ardener (ed.), *Social anthropology and language*. London: Tavistock.

Kaplan, Eleanor L. (1970). Intonation and language acquisition. *Papers and Reports on Child Language Development* 1: 1–21.

Kean, Mary-Louise (1979). Comment on McConnell-Ginet's "Intonation in a Man's World." *Signs: Journal of Women in Culture and Society* 5: 367–371.

Labov, William (1972). *Sociolinguistic patterns*. Philadelphia: University of Pennsylvania Press.

Ladd, D. Robert (1980). *The structure of intonational meaning: Evidence from English*. Bloomington: University of Indiana Press.

[——— (2008). *Intonational phonology*. 2nd ed. Cambridge: University of Cambridge Press.]

Lakoff, Robin (1975). *Language and woman's place*. New York: Harper & Row.

Lambert, Wallace E., R. C. Hodgson, and Stephen Fillenbaum (1960). Evaluational reactions to spoken languages. *Journal of Abnormal and Social Psychology* 60: 44–51.

Liberman, Mark (1975). The intonational system of English. Doctoral dissertation, MIT, Cambridge, Mass.

Liberman, Mark, and Ivan Sag (1974). Prosodic form and discourse function. *Papers from the 10th Regional Meeting of the Chicago Linguistic Society*. Department of Linguistics, University of Chicago.

Lieberman, Philip (1967). *Intonation, perception, and language*. Cambridge, Mass.: MIT Press.

Majewski, W., H. Hollien, and J. Zalewski (1972). Speaking fundamental frequency characteristics of Polish adult males. *Phonetica* 25: 119–125.

McConnell-Ginet, Sally (1975). Our father tongue. *Diacritics* 5: 44–50.

———— (1978). Intonation in the social context: Language and sex. Paper presented at the 9th International Congress of Sociology, Uppsala, Sweden.

———— (1979). Reply to Kean. *Signs: Journal of Women in Culture and Society* 5: 371–372.

[McLemore, Cynthia (1992). *The Interpretation of L*H in English*. Linguistic Forum 32, ed. Cynthia McLemore. Austin: University of Texas Department of Linguistics and the Center for Cognitive Science.]

Michel, J., H. Hollien, and P. Moore (1965). Speaking fundamental frequency characteristics of 15, 16 and 17-year-old girls. *Language and Speech* 9: 46–51.

Newton, Esther (1972). *Mother Camp: Female impersonators in America*. Englewood Cliffs, NJ: Prentice-Hall.

Ortner, Sherry B. (1974). Is female to male as nature is to culture? In Michelle Zimbalist Rosaldo and Louise Lamphere (eds.), *Woman, culture and society*. Stanford, CA: Stanford University Press.

[Pierrehumbert, Janet (1980). *The phonology and phonetics of English intonation*. MIT PhD dissertation, distributed in 1988 by Indiana University Linguistics Club.]

Pike, Kenneth (1946). *The intonation of American English*. Ann Arbor: University of Michigan Press.

Reardon, R. C. (1971). Individual differences and the meanings of vocal emotional expressions. *Journal of Communication* 21: 72–82.

Sachs, Jacqueline (1975). Cues to the identification of sex in children's speech. In Barrie Thorne and Nancy Henley (eds.), *Language and sex: Difference and dominance*. Rowley, MA: Newbury House.

Sachs, Jacqueline, P. Lieberman, and Donna Erickson (1973). Anatomical and cultural determinants of male and female speech. In Roger W. Shuy and Ralph W. Fasold (eds.), *Language attitudes: Current trends and prospects*. Washington, DC: Georgetown University Press.

Soron, Henry I. (1964). On relationships between prosodic features and lexical content of speech. *Journal of the Acoustical Society of America* 36: 1048.

Takefuta, Y., E. Jancosek, and M. Brunt (1972). A statistical analysis of melody curves in intonations of American English. *Proceedings of the Seventh International Congress of Phonetic Sciences* (1971). The Hague: Mouton.

Terango, Larry (1966). Pitch and duration characteristics of the oral reading of males on a masculinity-femininity dimension. *Journal of Speech and Hearing Research* 9: 590–595.

Thorne, Barrie, and Nancy Henley (eds.) (1975). *Language and sex: Difference and dominance*. Rowley, MA: Newbury House.

Uldall, Elizabeth (1960). Attitudinal meanings conveyed by intonational contours. *Language and Speech* 3: 233–234.

von Raffler-Engel, Walburga, and Janis Buckner (1976). A difference beyond inherent pitch. In Betty Lou Dubois and Isabel Crouch (eds.), *The sociology of the languages of American women*. San Antonio, TX: Trinity University, 115–119.

Waugh, Linda R., and C. H. van Schooneveld (eds.) (1979). *The melody of language: Intonation and prosody*. Baltimore, MD: University Park Press.

Weeks, T. (1970). Speech registers in young children. *Papers and Reports on Child Language Development* 1: 22–42.

Weinreich, Uriel, William Labov, and Marvin Herzog (1968). Empirical foundations for a theory of language change. In Winfred Lehmann and Hakov Malkiel (eds.), *Directions for historical linguistics*. Austin: University of Texas Press.

7

Constructing meaning, constructing selves

Snapshots of language, gender, and class from Belten High

0. Introduction

During the course of their lives, people move into, out of, and through communities of practice, continually transforming identities, understandings, and worldviews.[1] Progressing through the life span brings ever-changing kinds of participation and nonparticipation, contexts for 'belonging' and 'not belonging' in communities. A single individual participates in a variety of communities of practice at any given time, and over time: the family, a friendship group, an athletic team, a church group. These communities may be all-female or all-male; they may be dominated by women or men; they may offer different forms of participation to women or men; they may be organized on the presumption that all members want (or will want) heterosexual love relations. Whatever the nature of one's participation in communities of practice, one's experience of gender emerges in participation as a gendered community member with others in a variety of communities of practice.

It is for this reason that we (Eckert and McConnell-Ginet 1992a [chapter 5, this volume], 1992b) argued for grounding the study of gender and language in detailed investigations of the social and linguistic activities of specific communities of practice. Following the lead of a number of feminist social theorists (see, e.g., Bem 1993; Butler 1993; Connell 1987; Thorne 1993; di Leonardo 1991), we warned against taking gender as given, as natural. A major moral we drew is that the study of sex differences in language use does not automatically give insight into how gender and language interact in particular communities of

This chapter, coauthored with Penelope Eckert, descends directly from an invited talk Penny and I gave on July 20, 1993, at the Linguistic Society of America's Summer Institute, Ohio State University, Columbus. A significantly revised version appeared in Kira Hall and Mary Bucholtz, eds., 1995, *Gender articulated: Language and the socially constructed self* (New York: Routledge), 469–507.

practice. Rather, we proposed, the social and linguistic practices through which people construct themselves as different and as similar must be carefully examined.

Gender constructs are embedded in other aspects of social life and in the construction of other socially significant categories such as those involving class, race, or ethnicity. This implies that gender is not a matter of two homogeneous social categories, one associated with being female and the other with being male. Just as important, it also implies that no simple attributes of a person, however complex a combination is considered, can completely determine how that person is socially categorized by herself or by others, and how she engages in social practice. Suppose, for example, we categorize someone as a heterosexual middle-class African American professional woman. The attributes that make up this particular characterization—*heterosexual, middle-class, African American, professional*, and *woman*—all draw on reifications that emerge from and constitute conventional maps of social reality. These reifications structure perceptions and constrain (but do not completely determine) practice, and each is produced (often reproduced in much the same form) through the experience of those perceptions and constraints in day-to-day life.

Language is a primary tool people use in constituting themselves and others as 'kinds' of people in terms of which attributes, activities, and participation in social practice can be regulated. Social categories and characterizations are human creations; the concepts associated with them are not preformed, waiting for labels to be attached, but are created, sustained, and transformed by social processes that importantly include labeling itself. And labeling is only part of a more complex sociolinguistic activity that contributes to constituting social categories and power relations among members of a community. How people use language—matters of 'style' that include grammar, word choice, and pronunciation—is a very important component of self-constitution. How people talk expresses their affiliations with some and their distancing from others, their embrace of certain social practices and their rejection of others—their claim to membership (and to particular forms of membership) in certain communities of practice and not others. And within communities of practice, the continual modification of common ways of speaking provides a touchstone for the process of construction of forms of group identity—of the meaning of belonging to a group (as a certain kind of member). It is a resource for the orientation of the community and its participants to other nearby communities and to the larger society, a resource for constructing community members' relation to power structures, locally and more globally.

To give concrete substance to these abstract musings, we will examine some social and linguistic practices within several communities of practice related to one another and to a particular institution, a public high school in suburban Detroit. Our data come from Penny's sociolinguistic study[2] of a speech community as defined by that high school, which we shall call Belten High. For this study, Penny did three years of participant observation in the early 1980s, following one graduating class of six hundred students through their sophomore, junior, and senior years. (More detailed reports on various aspects of this project appear in, e.g., Eckert 1988, 1989, 1990b [and now Eckert 2000]). Her research yielded a taped corpus of about three hundred hours of speech, including one-on-one interviews, group discussions, and a variety of public events. The original study did not focus on gender issues, and the fact that so much material relevant for thinking about gender construction emerged anyway is testimony to its pervasiveness in this community's practices. In this chapter, we draw on eighty of the one-on-one interviews, emphasizing phonological variation (in particular, pronunciation of certain vowel sounds) and sample stretches of students' talk with Penny about social categories and socially relevant attributes. We use a combination of linguistic and ethnographic data to give a partial picture of how gender, class, and power relations are being mutually constructed in this particular setting. What kinds of identities and relations are the students making for themselves and for others? How does this construction of their social landscape happen? How do different communities of practice get constituted, and what is their relation to one another and to the institution of the school? Being female or male, athletic, studious, popular, a cigarette smoker, a beer drinker; staying out all night; wearing certain kinds of clothes and makeup; owning a car; using a certain vocabulary and style of speech; engaging in heterosexual activities such as cross-sex dating; wearing a constant smile; using illicit drugs—constellations of such attributes and activities constitute the raw materials from which the social categories of the school are constructed. It is the significance attached to these constellations and their constituents—their socially recognized meaning—that turns them into socially relevant categories mediating power, affiliation, desire, and other social relations.

Who lunches with whom? Who talks to whom about what? Who touches whom and how (and where)? Who controls which resources? Who is admired or despised by whom? When the answers to such questions depend systematically on people's being classified as belonging to one category rather than another, the social categories involved can interact with communities of practice in two ways: (1) they often form the basis for the formation of category-exclusive communities of practice, defined by their mutual orientation to the school and engaged in finding a mutual life in the school based in this orientation; and (2) the categories themselves and the opposition between them can become the object of practice, defining a larger but more loosely connected community of practice focused on conflict over the practices of everyday life in the shared space community members inhabit. Thus, communities of practice can overlap in significant ways. What makes them all communities of practice is not any shared attributes of their members but the orientation of those members to joint participation in some endeavor, and in a set of social practices that grow around that endeavor.

1. Schooling in corporate practice

The U.S. public high school is designed to dominate and structure the lives of the adolescent age group—not just to provide academic and vocational instruction but to provide a comprehensive social environment. The school organizes sports, musical and dramatic groups, social occasions such as dances and fairs, some social service such as canned-food drives, and governing activities in the form of such things as class offices and student government. These activities are not simply organized by the school for the students. Rather, the school provides the resources and authority for the students themselves to organize these activities, and institutional status and privilege for those who do the organizing. Although an organizational framework with adult supervisors is provided—for example, athletic teams have coaches, bands and choirs have directors, clubs have faculty sponsors—students themselves play substantial organizing roles (e.g., as team captains or club officers).

It is important to emphasize that although participation in this extracurricular sphere is optional, it is also expected. Extracurricular activities are viewed as integral to one's participation in school, and indeed, one's extracurricular career constitutes an important part of an entrance dossier for colleges and universities. The school is the community in which adolescents are expected to participate—a community extracted from the larger adult-dominated community that it serves. It is seen as a community designed especially for—and in the interests of—adolescents, and adolescents are expected to base not only their academic lives but their informal social lives in that institution. Adolescents who do not embrace this community are, therefore, seen as deviant, as 'not caring'.

Students are expected to compete for control of roles and resources in the production of extracurricular activities, and to base their identities and alliances in this production. This leads to a tight student hierarchy based on institutional roles and on relations with others (both student and adult) in institutional roles—in short, a hierarchy based on control of aspects of the institutional environment, and on the freedoms and privileges associated with this control. Those who participate in this hierarchy are not simply participating in individual interesting activities; they are building extracurricular careers and engaging in a corporate practice that has as much to do with visibility in and control over the school environment as with the content of the individual activities that constitute their careers.

For students participating fully in the extracurricular sphere, then, social status is constructed as a function of institutional status, personal identities are intertwined with institutional identities, and social networks are intertwined with institutional networks. Embedded as they are in a mobile hierarchy, social relations are competitive, and they change with institutional responsibilities, alliances, and status. Students are constrained to monitor their behavior carefully in order to maintain a 'responsible' public persona, and to focus their interactions on the network of people in the same school and even the same graduating class who are engaged in this endeavor. In this way, the school offers an introduction into corporate practice. Of course, corporate status and its concomitant freedoms and privileges come at a price. Participating in this hierarchy requires a certain acceptance of the institution's rules and values as articulated by the ultimate institutional authorities, the adults who occupy official positions in the school.

In schools across the United States, communities of practice develop around participation in parts of the extracurricular sphere (a cheerleading squad, a 'popular' crowd, a class cabinet), and a broader overarching community of practice develops around engagement in the extracurricular sphere and the mutual building of extracurricular careers. Participants build careers in the extracurricular sphere and achieve a merging of their personal and school networks, their personal and school-based identities. This is a community based on an adolescent version of corporate, middle-class social practice. Although this specific community of practice arises in response to the school institution, it is based to some extent in communities that have been emerging since childhood. Indeed, across the country, the students involved in the school's corporate affairs tend to be college-bound and to come from the upper part of the local socioeconomic range. Many of them have already learned aspects of corporate practice at home, both through exposure to their own parents' participation in such practice and through the middle-class family practices and values that support corporate practices. (For example, middle-class parents generally do not encourage their children to 'hang out' in the neighborhood but to cultivate friendships through school; and they commonly discourage their children from having a best friend in favor of having a more fluid network.)

At the same time that these students base their activities, networks, and identities in the corporate sphere of the school, others reject the school as the basis of social life. Indeed, in polar opposition to the corporate community of practice, there is a community of practice based on autonomy from the school. These students base their social lives not in the school but in the local neighborhoods and in the urban-suburban area more generally. Their friendships are not limited to the school or to their own age group, and their activities tend to arise from their alliances rather than vice versa. These students are largely from the lower end of the local socioeconomic hierarchy and embrace, strongly and consciously, working-class norms of egalitarianism and solidarity. They consciously oppose the norm of corporate practice in the school, and they reject the institution as a locus of identity and social life. Because they are bound for the workforce immediately after high school, furthermore, the extracurricular sphere has no hold on them as qualification for future success; rather, it appears to them as a form of infantilization and as a hierarchy existing only for its own sake. Their focus is more on the local area and its resources for entertainment, excitement, and employment; they reject environments developed especially for their own age group and seek to participate in what they see as the real world. Furthermore, in this rejection of the school's adolescent environment, they seek independence from adult control over everyday life, their bodies, activities, and consumption practices. This latter oppositional category always has a name: *hoods, greasers, stompers, stoners, grits* (depending on the region and the era) and, in the school in question, *burnouts* (or *burns*) or *jellies* (or *jells*, from *jellybrain*). The two main local names reflect the symbolic status of controlled substance use for the oppositional category in this particular school at this particular time. These names are used by all in the school, and embraced by those to whom they apply as well as by those who choose to apply them to others. On the other hand, the activities-oriented category in schools is not always given a name, a point we will discuss in the next section. The group may, however, be called something like *collegiates, preppies, soshes* (from *socialite*), or, as in the school in question and other schools around the region, *jocks*, drawing on the symbolic status of athletic achievement for this social group.

In general usage, *jock* designates a committed athlete, and the prototypical jock is male. Except for the jocks themselves, students in Belten High use *jock* to designate a network of girls and boys who achieve visibility through their committed engagement in school-sponsored activities. (As we explain in the next section, this labeling dispute connects to the absence of a name for the activities-oriented category in some schools.) Although sports do provide the surest route to jockdom, especially for boys, other activities also confer that status.

The name *jock* points, then, to one important way in which school corporate culture constructs male dominance. The male varsity athlete is seen by the school institution as representing the school's interests, and this gives him institutional status and privilege. Interscholastic competition affords boys' varsity athletics the most direct way of establishing and defending the school's status and honor. Thus, the status that a boy gains in varsity sports is connected directly to the luster he brings to the school—not to himself personally. This is a useful lesson to learn. Achieving individual status through one's efforts on behalf of an institution—being able to identify one's own interests with institutional interests—is a hallmark of much successful competition in adult corporate practice.

Athletics is also the route that boys are expected to take to prominence. In a conversation with Penny, a group of male athletes extolled the skill, 'coolness', and hard work of a male student-government officer. But they pointed out that he had had no choice but to seek a key student office because he wasn't athletic. In general, male athletes see nonathletic activities as an aside: as something one can do casually—because they require no special skill—but possibly as one's civic duty. And the status associated with varsity athletics can be a tremendous advantage for a star athlete who chooses to seek student office, an advantage that can overturn the candidacy of a nonathlete with a long history of experience and service.

Although male varsity athletes can count on their accomplishments to establish their value to the community, their status, there are no parallel accomplishments in school that lend the same kind of status for girls. Because sports still do not yield the same payoff for girls as for boys (in the section "Sports and toughness" we discuss some of the reasons for this, and also note some changes in progress), the domain in which girls are expected to achieve prominence is already designated as second-best. Girls may receive recognition through prominence in student government, through cheerleading, or through participation in musical or dramatic activities. But for both girls and boys, achieving recognition through these activities seldom if ever evokes the kind of vicarious pride of schoolmates that gives good athletes their special distinction. The female supportive role is formalized in high school in the pairing of such activities as girls' cheerleading and boys' varsity athletics, and in the feminization of organizational activities such as holding bake sales, organizing dances, and the like. Girls tend to do most of the behind-the-scenes work for school activities; boys predominate in top managerial roles (class president, student-body president, and so on).

Thus, in a number of ways school corporate culture continues students' education in the male dominance that is characteristic of most American institutions and American society at many levels. It also continues and indeed intensifies education in what Rich (1980) dubbed "compulsory heterosexuality." High school brings an institutionalization of traditional gender arrangements, heterosexuality, and romance. The institutionalization of the heterosexual couple is embodied formally in the king and queen of the high school homecoming and prom. Heterosexuality and romance are also publicly constructed in high school through formal activities like dances and informally in the status of dating and in each class's 'famous couple'. When the yearbook depicts a 'cutest couple', the relation between social status and success in the heterosexual marketplace is made visible.

Although adult corporate practice does not recognize the 'cutest couple' in an institution, socializing outside the workplace is still largely driven by business and professional alliances and organized around heterosexual marriage partners. The support role of female cheerleaders for male athletes is succeeded by wifely hosting and presumptive willingness to follow wherever a husband's career trajectory leads. But there are signs of rupture in this conflation of the personal and the institutional in both adolescent and adult practice, and it is driven by ongoing larger-scale changes in gender relations. Just as girls are beginning to reject cheerleading at boys' sports events in favor of playing on their own teams, corporate wives' own careers are making them unavailable to host dinner parties. Gender transformations have begun to challenge the all-encompassing character of corporate practice, albeit on only a small scale. And in a few places, openly gay or lesbian high schoolers are beginning to resist the heterosexual imperative of traditional mixed-sex schools. For example, in the early 1990s a group of Los Angeles high schoolers organized an alternative 'gay prom', which was reported nationally. Fifteen years ago gay and lesbian students were not 'out' at Belten High. We don't know to what extent this may have changed, but it is a safe bet that when the yearbook depicts a 'cutest couple', they still won't be of the same sex.

The names of the categories that correspond to *jock* and *burnout* at Belten High, and the specific styles and activities that signal their opposition (use of controlled substances, leisure activities, clothing, musical tastes, territorial specialization, and the like), vary regionally and locally and change through time. But it is close to universal in U.S. public high schools for two opposed social categories to arise that represent some kind of class split and that constitute class cultures within the school. And so far as we know, the construction of these cultural groups always interacts in interesting ways with the construction of gender identities and relations (although of course the nature of that interaction may vary significantly). In most U.S. schools, race and ethnicity also enter into the interaction, but in this particular virtually all-White school such social dimensions are salient only inasmuch as they provide the overarching discourse within which whiteness is constructed and differentiated. Indeed, everything that we have discussed and will discuss is at the same time part of the construction of White hegemony.

The jocks and the burnouts arise as class-based communities of practice in response to the school institution. Each is based in the endeavor to build a way of life in and out of school that makes sense and that provides the means to construct valued identities. The jocks emerge out of many students' shared desire to build lives within the school institution and to develop identities and careers based in the extracurricular sphere. The burnouts emerge out of many students' need to find ways to exist in the school that neither implicate them in corporate practice nor cost them their participation in the institution, ways that at the same time allow them to foster a strong sense of identity and participation in their own broader community.

The jocks' and burnouts' opposed orientations to the school, to institutions, and to life are the terrain for daily struggle over the right to define school, adolescence, values. Both categories seek autonomy, but in different places. Jocks seek autonomy in the occupation of adultlike roles within the institution, in building individual identities through school-based careers, and in benefiting from the kinds of institutional freedoms and perks that are the rewards for participation in these careers. Burnouts seek autonomy in the avoidance of adult-run institutions, in laying claim to adult prerogatives, and in the development of networks and activities in the local community, which will be the site of their adult lives. The jocks work the center of the school institution; the burnouts work its margins.

Because it is so basic to life in school, the jock-burnout opposition comes to define the landscape of identities at Belten. Those who are neither jocks nor burnouts commonly refer to themselves as *in-betweens*, and nuances of identity throughout the school are described in the same terms that construct these two categories. Thus, the jock-burnout opposition constitutes the dominant discourse of identity in the school, and one could say that orientation to that opposition engages almost every student in the school in an overarching community of practice. But although both communities emerge from strongly held and positive values, they do not emerge as equal within the school. The jocks embody the institution—their personal relations are inseparable from formal institutional relations and their activities are inseparable from school activities. This bestows an institutional legitimacy and function on their activities and their alliances, including their heterosexual alliances, that stand in stark contrast to the illegitimate status accorded to burnouts' activities and alliances. The co-construction of social category and gender is indeed intimately connected to the construction of institutional power, a power in which girls and boys do not share equally.

2. Labeling, conflict, and hegemony

Gender and social category are not constructed independently of each other, nor do they exist independently of practice; rather, they are continually co-constructed in the course of day-to-day practice. In the same way, labels do not exist independently of the social practice in which categories are constructed; the use of labels is not simply a matter of fitting a word to a preexisting category. Rather, labels arise in use in relation to real people in real situations: people label as they chat, make observations and judgments about people, point people out to others, challenge people, and so on. It is through such activities that labels are endowed with meaning. We have already referred to some students as *jocks*, others as *burnouts*. But this is misleading inasmuch as it obscures the very important fact that labeling is a socially significant and contested practice within the school and is part of the continual construction of the categories it designates. The use of the term *jock* or *burnout*, and of terms related to the salient issues around which these categories are constructed (e.g., *slutty, cool, snobby*), is part of the process of constituting categories and identities.

Students coming into the school see the institution as unchanging— they see institutional roles waiting to be filled. But they see their participation or nonparticipation in the school as a creative endeavor. Even though there have 'always been' jocks and burnouts, girls and boys, students coming into high school are actively and mutually engaged in constituting selves within the constraints of what has, in their view, always been—and engaging with those constraints in the process.

The jocks and the burnouts seek to define right and appropriate practices, given their relation to the institution of school. Each sees the other community of practice as embodying wrong and inappropriate practices. For the burnouts, the jocks are 'about' competition, hierarchy, advantage, elitism, ambition, and image building. Girl jocks especially are seen as phony, as obsessed with popularity. For the jocks, the burnouts are 'about' drugs, trouble, hedonism, and lack of ambition. And girl burnouts are often seen by jocks as sleazy, if not slutty. This conflict about category 'content' can present itself as a dispute over what category labels 'really' mean, but of course words as such are never the real issue. The real issue is the normativity of particular practices and the deviance of others. In the following sections, we will examine labeling practices as part of the construction of social category and gender (along with other aspects of identity such as class, age, and so on). We begin with the issue of what it means to have a label at all.

Because of the deep ideological nature of the split between jocks and burnouts, it is not surprising that the terms *jock* and *burnout* are used differently by people in different places in the school. As we have noted, jocks resist accepting this label—or indeed any label—as a name for a social category defined by extracurricular orientation. Jocks, and particularly male athletic jocks, promote exclusive use of the term *jock* to refer to someone as an athlete. This is illustrated by the following response by a male varsity athlete to Penny's question, which calls the very term into question (*I don't know really...what that means*):[3]

(1)   DO YOU CONSIDER YOURSELF A JOCK? Somewhat I guess, yeah. Just—I
         don't know really what, you know, what that means. Just, I play sports
         and stuff I guess, you know.

In accepting a self-designation *jock* purely on the basis of athletics, jocks reject any 'derivative' meanings. This has more than one effect. Although "playing sports and stuff" might in principle be socially no more consequential than preferring apples to oranges, the status of *jock* is not a socially neutral one. The jock (male) athletes' use of the term *jock* to refer to someone as 'simply' being involved in sports suppresses the connection of that involvement to social status, membership, and opportunities. At the same time, given that within the school this term is used to refer to a more generally powerful group in the institution, laying claim to it for athletes alone can have the effect of emphasizing the centrality of athletes to the institution. This latter effect depends, of course, on others' use of the term as a label for the socially dominant activities-oriented group.

The relation between corporate participation and athletics is brought home particularly in the following quotation from one of the outstanding athletes in the school. He had been participating in an independent soccer league, in which the level of play was far above that in the school; here he explains why he gave up the league to play for the school:

(2)   WHEN YOU HAVE A TEAM LIKE THAT WHY DO YOU GO INTO HIGH SCHOOL
        SOCCER? I don't, well, because—because that's—it's—you know, you
        want to play—recognition, I don't know. We should have stayed but what
        you do is, when—you—there's high school sports, more people are apt
        to play that than play in another league, you know, because you have the
        recognition, scholarships, like that.

In spite of the male athletes' insistence on the narrow meaning, most
people in Belten do not use the term *jock* to refer to a person in school
simply as an athlete. Rather, they use it to talk about a community of
practice: all the people, female and male, who build their lives around
school activities. In example (3), a burnout boy directly challenges the
equation of jockdom and participation in sports proposed by the (athletic)
jock:

(3)   I—well—some kids uh who went out for football in seventh grade turned
        into jocks. Pretty much. But it doesn't—you can—it doesn't make you a
        jock if you go out and play a sport. Because I played in football in junior
        high and I wasn't considered a jock. I used to get high before the
        games.

Being an athlete doesn't make you a jock if you don't adhere to jock
values. Here we see that jocks ought not to get high—or at least not be so
overt in their defiance of school regulations (the ambivalence of jocks
in relation to substance use is discussed in the section "Sports and
toughness.")

Only one male jock in the corpus explicitly admitted that the label
could legitimately cover more than athletes. He was a former class
president and a talented musician but not an athlete. Note that he does
not call himself a *jock* but does acknowledge that athleticism is not all
there is to jockdom:

(4)   You get your super jocks that—hell they play track and basketball and
        baseball, and I'm sure those people are going to—"Hey, jock!" That's
        their middle name practically. But, um, I think you don't have to play
        sports to be a jock.

In fact, this boy, a leading singer in the school, recognizes that he is frequently referred to as a *choir jock*. The choir, which travels internationally, is
a prestigious activity in the school and is similar to sports in bringing recognition to the school through competition with representatives of other
schools. As described by two different choir members, students have specified a difference between a member of the choir and a choir jock: a choir
jock is a choir member who gets involved in more than just the singing:

(5)   …that's that clique. That's what everybody knows about, the concert
        choir jocks…I guess it's the officers, you know, the people that are
        involved, like Dan Smart, our president. I don't know, he's, you know, he's
        always involved in choir. Then there's Cheryl Smith. Herbie Jackson, he's
        always, you know, that's his highlight of our school.

(6)   IS THERE A CROWD OF PEOPLE THAT ARE CHOIR JOCKS? Oh, yeah.
       Definitely. We always talk about them, Kim and I . . . We're not involved in
       choir that much. Yeah I mean we go to a few activities once in a while,
       but we don't make sure we attend all of them.

But why do so many jocks protest being labeled as members of a social
category? Why do they keep trying to explain their being called *jocks* as
just a matter of describing athleticism, a socially neutral attribute? A plausible explanation lies in the near-hegemony jocks achieve during the
course of the transition from junior high to the senior year of high school.
That ascendancy is threatened by being seen as such; jocks' interests
require obscuring the social processes that subordinate nonjocks generally
and burnouts in particular. It is important for jocks not to see themselves
as denying others access to valuable resources by exclusionary processes.
It is also important for them to constitute as normative the activities on
which their community of practice centers and from which they reap
advantage, with those not so engaged defined as socially deviant and thus
directly responsible for any disadvantages they may suffer in the school. If
the dominant category is not even labeled (and, as we noted earlier, in
many schools it is not), then its distinctive interests are somewhat easier
to ignore, its hegemonic control over social values and institutional norms
more readily established. Two category labels in direct opposition reflect
a live ongoing social struggle.

The jocks' status became unmarked in the course of junior high school.
The jock and burnout categories reportedly emerged in seventh grade as
apparently equal rivals, with core people in them pursuing different activities and espousing different values. In the following quotation, one
burnout girl describes the original split in junior high as just such a matter
of competing values and choices; she notes explicitly that category labels
were used by each group to 'put down' the other:

(7)   Yeah, OK, there was, you know, kids that got high and smoked and
       thought they were really cool like us ((laughter)) and then the other ones
       that didn't party or anything, were always getting into sports and being
       goody-goodies and, you know, all that stuff so we just started putting
       down those people, calling them *jocks* and everything, and they call us
       burns, and that was just going on for a while, while we were all at [junior
       high].

A self-designated 'in-between'—a girl with primary burnout connections and interests but also with many jock ties and interests—describes
quite poignantly the regulative power of the polarized labeling and the conflicts, internal and public, that those labeling practices helped produce:

(8)   That's—that's where all the—the jock/burn or the jock/jelly thing started.
       Because I didn't hear anything about it in elementary school. But once I
       hit [junior high], you know, that's all you heard was, "She's a jock," "She's
       a jell," you know. And that's all it was. You were either one. You weren't
       an in-between, which I was. I was an in-between ((laughter)) because

here I was, I played volleyball, now what, three years. Baseball, I'll be going on my eighth year, OK? So, I get along really good with, quote, jocks, OK, and I get along really good with jellies, because I'm right—I'm stuck right in the middle. And in my ninth-grade and tenth-grade year, that kind of tore me apart a little bit too. Because I didn't—my parents wanted me to make a decision. "Now which way are you going to go?"

Near hegemony had, however, been achieved by the beginning of high school. Early on in her fieldwork, one of the burnout boys asked Penny whether she'd yet talked to any 'normal' people, reflecting his (perhaps wry) admission of being relegated to deviant status. With apparently less ironic distance, a girl who is a star athlete and a popular jock denies hearing people insult one another by labeling. Rather, according to her, the categories keep enough distance that there is no call for such activity:

(9)   The jocks sort of stayed to themselves, and the burnouts stayed to themselves and everybody else kind of stayed to themselves too. So you really—if you didn't have to you didn't mix.

She then responds to Penny's query as to whether she thinks of jocks and burnouts as separate groups:

(10)   The burns, yes. Well, not so much in high school. Like jocks—you're not really aware of it.

Though jock hegemony is not total, there is every indication that jocks often manage to present themselves and be taken as the 'unmarked' or 'default' category, of which "you're not really aware." Only the opponents of the institution are seen as taking a stand with respect to the institution. Although jocks are highly visible, many no longer see themselves as actively orienting toward institutional values in opposing burnouts. Rather, their own attitudes and choices seem 'normal' or inevitable in the absence of some kind of social pathology. They no longer see burnouts as in serious conflict with them, presumably at least in part because they now are more or less sure that burnouts will never 'lead' them, will not be in controlling positions. In the following example, a jock girl from a burnout neighborhood talks about being the only jock at the bus stop:

(11)   But, you know, it doesn't really bother me, I just figure ((laughter)) who cares what they think of me, you know, they're not—they're no uh, you know, president, that they can cut me down.

Early on in the process of constructing institutional affiliation and opposition and the other aspects of class and gender practice found in the school, jock ascendancy was being asserted more directly, according to this jock boy:

(12)   There was like—at least once a week it was, "Jocks are going to fight jells after school," you know. DID THEY REALLY? DID YOU GET IN FIGHTS OR WAS IT JUST A LOT OF TALK? Never. Talk. They started it every time.

> We'd about kill them. Because we had the whole football team, and
> they wanted to fight the football team. You know. DO YOU REMEMBER
> WHICH GUYS WANTED TO GET IN FIGHTS? None of the guys on the foot-
> ball team, really, you know—they didn't care.

The quotation reveals an awareness of *jock* as a category label used in
conflict. It also indicates the speaker's bravado and (retrospective) claim
of fearlessness. We now turn to the matter of this focus on physical prowess in constructing class-based male social relations.

3. Sports and toughness: Category meanings
and male power

Although the jock boy quoted in example (12) asserts that physical
strength was concentrated in jock hands, the jock-burnout split really
became visible and contentious when some excellent athletes among the
burnouts refused to play on school teams (cf. example (3)). Both jock and
burnout boys staunchly asserted that their group could beat the other in
any physical contest, whether a game or a fight.

As a number of writers have observed (see, for example, Connell 1987
and Segal 1990), practices aimed at developing and displaying confidence
and superior physical strength and skill play a central role in constituting
a hegemonic masculinity in the United States and many other Western
nations. *Hegemonic* here implies not pervasiveness in fact but power as a
(partly fantasy) ideal of manliness. The body aimed at is muscular and
tough, able successfully to withstand physical attacks and to defend others
against them, able to win in attacks on others. Competitive sports are a
primary arena in which such a masculinity is constituted, at least as an
ideal.

Organized sports continue to enter into the practices constituting adult
masculinities. Even relatively inactive men watch and talk about football
games every week of the season. A number of writers have noted the
prominence of sports metaphors in business talk, politics, and other areas
of corporate life. That 'level playing fields' have generally not been thought
of as having females running down them is clear. The 'locker-room talk'
that prototypically occurs among teammates before and after games constructs women as men's sexual prey. Male camaraderie excludes women
and includes other men as fellow 'tough guys', to be slapped on the back,
playfully punched around in certain contexts.

Such kinds of talk and bodily demeanor are, of course, not confined to
the corporate world but are part of many male-dominated workplaces.
The form in corporate lunchrooms is different from that in factory cafe-
terias, but a 'macho' style of masculinity and male-male interaction rooted
in sports and, more generally, physical toughness is common. Indeed,
working-class men are often taken as exemplary of this ideal. Jobs that
institutionalize force, strength, and even violence—such as building trades,

police and prison work, and military combat—are low on the class hierarchy but high on the scale of hegemonic masculinity.[4]

Although the burnouts in this school are certainly not the super-tough gang members that are so frequently studied in the city, they are urban-oriented and pride themselves on their relation to the streets: to fights, encounters with the police, the criminal justice system. Much of the early oppositional behavior between jocks and burnouts in elementary school involved contests of physical prowess, both athletic and combative challenges. The burnouts were viewed as 'tough', and the jocks were hard-pressed to maintain their own prowess in the face of the burnout challenge.

Hegemonic masculinity emphasizes the possibility of physical force. It has been a central symbolic component in constructing heterosexual men as different from both women and homosexual men—in principle able to beat up either. Of course, both women and gay men have begun to challenge this view of straight men's superiority in physical strength, as attested by the enormous increase, in recent years, in female participation in organized sports and such activities as bodybuilding and by the emergence of the 'clone' style among gay men since the gay liberation movement began. But a focus on physical strength remains prominent in constituting heterosexual masculinity and, albeit in different ways, in constructing the picture of a prototypical jock and a prototypical burnout.

For the jocks, then, this physical prowess centers on participation in school-sponsored sports, violence that is tamed and put into service for the institution. The notion that jocks have tamed their violence is a crucial aspect of a more general emphasis on the control of one's urges that is an important component of corporate practice. This control is seen as requiring additional strength and autonomy. (In the section "Snobs and sluts," we discuss how this control translates into control of sexual urges for jock girls.)

Although girls' varsity athletics is increasing in importance at Belten High as elsewhere, it still has not achieved the same institutional importance as boys'. This is only partly because girls' sports are less well attended and thus girls are less able to bring glory to the school and vicariously to those who identify with it. It is also important that the association of the athlete with physical prowess conflicts with feminine norms, with notions of how a (heterosexual) girl 'should' look and behave. Heterosexual femininity is constructed as directly contrasting with the superiority in physical strength embodied in hegemonic masculinity. Too much athleticism and physicality in a girl suggests a 'butch' style of femaleness. Thus, it is problematic for an athletic girl to refer to herself as a *jock* because of the 'unfeminine' image that the label implies. In example (13) an accomplished female athlete who is part of the popular crowd denies being a jock:

(13)   ...like there's some girls that play baseball and basketball and track,
         and they're just always—they play football and they just do everything,

you know, the real you know, girl—you can tell, they walk down the
halls pushing each other, and, you know. That kind of jock. Yeah, yeah,
those kind you know? I wouldn't call my—myself a jock, I'd say. I can be
athletic or something like that, but, like people don't call me *jock*, you
know.

The disassociation of femininity and athletic prowess presents a powerful double bind for girls, for varsity sports are seen as the ultimate dem-
onstration of accomplishment (and as a kind of accomplishment with
greater institutional status than a superb artistic performance). The
association of sports with accomplishment is commonly contrasted to
other visible school activities, particularly those that are associated with
female status, which are seen as relying on popularity. This emerges in the
conversation of both female and male jocks, as in the following female
athlete's observation, when discussing whether it is necessary to know the
right people in order to participate in many activities in high school:

(14)   You can't say that for the team sports and stuff—you have to be good.
         But it is nice to know those people, and to be in the committees and
         stuff you still have to be interviewed, but if you're interviewed by kids
         and they like you, you're probably in. The uh student council, that's—if
         you know a lot of people, that's just like popularity, sort of. Yeah. I don't
         know if it is all popularity, but—

Being the girlfriend of a star male athlete is at least as sure a route to
female achievement in the jock network as being a star athlete oneself
(and perhaps less risky, given the possibility of jeopardizing success in the
heterosexual marketplace through being too athletic). We discuss jock
girls' pursuit of popularity in the next section. Popularity draws not on
the athleticism and physicality associated with prototypical male jockdom but on its visibility.

For burnouts, the labels at Belten focus on substance use rather than
physicality. But being a burnout invokes an orientation away from school
and toward urban streets and the toughness to walk them freely, to be able
to protect oneself in a fight. The image is decidedly not feminine. Although
burnout girls can fight, they do not gain the same status as burnout boys for
doing so. On the contrary, being tough in a fight is seen as somewhat admi-
rable for boys and men, but girls' (and women's) fighting is quite generally
looked down upon and viewed in terms of kicking and scratching rather
than 'real punchouts'. Further, and more important, although girls can fight
among themselves, and a few do, they cannot and do not fight boys. Thus,
they cannot walk the urban streets with the same sense of personal
autonomy that boys can. Burnout girls remain vulnerable to male violence.
They cannot really establish their anti-institutional burnout status through
being skilled fighters who need not fear others' attacks on their persons.
They can, however, draw on other components of burnout toughness to
constitute themselves as true 'bums'. In the next section, we discuss the
important place of 'coolness' in burnout girls' construction of themselves.

4. Popularity and coolness: Category meaning and female agency

The fundamental meaning of being a jock is orientation toward the institution and the possible rewards for ascending its hierarchical structures. The fundamental meaning of being a burnout is resisting the institution and its regulative constraints. These fundamental category meanings are, as we have already seen, overlaid with many other issues. In particular, girls are effectively barred from the practices most central to establishing category membership: the pursuit of athletic achievement, on the one hand, and of urban toughness on the other. They must therefore engage in other practices to construct their identities as jocks or as burnouts. The pursuit of popularity for jock girls and of coolness for burnout girls allows them to constitute themselves actively as embodying the same basic meanings as the prototypical category members, their male peers. Going out with a jock boy helps the jock girl achieve popularity; going out with a burnout boy or, even better, someone already out of school, reinforces the burnout girl's claim to coolness. Jock girls are not the only ones pursuing popularity; burnout girls do not monopolize coolness. But popularity and coolness do play central roles in constructing class-based ways of being female. We will start with popularity, but coolness enters in almost immediately as connected to burnout popularity in junior high.

Popularity is a complex that combines some kind of likeability and good personhood with visibility, community status, and a large number of contacts. The pursuit of the latter three are integral parts of corporate practice, necessary for gaining control of (and strategically dispensing) resources. Inasmuch as the jocks embody the school institution, their networks in some sense define the school community. Thus, their institutional positions not only lend them opportunities for visibility, contacts, and status but center them in a community circumscribed by the school. A burnout or in-between may well have as many social contacts as a jock, but to the extent that these contacts extend outside the school, they remain 'unfocused' and do not contribute to a communally constructed visibility. Furthermore, even if one's many ties are in the school, to the extent that they do not include those in power in the school, they cannot provide the opportunities for visibility that contribute to school popularity.

Burnout girls do sometimes talk of themselves or others in their network as 'popular'. The rubric, however, is always applied in the past tense when the girls are reminiscing about early junior high and the days when burnouts were still in active competition for school-based prominence. Although this prominence was being constructed within the school population, its focus was not on access to school resources but on access to activities outside and 'around' school. A girl whom all the burnouts point to as having been popular in junior high, for example, explains why her crowd was the 'big shit crowd':

(15)   I just think that we used to have a lot of fun, you know, and a lot of-
         you know, I mean things going outside of school, you know, and a lot of
         people, you know, looked up at us, you know—"it's really, cool," you
         know, "I wish I could."

Another burnout girl tells Penny why she wanted to hang out with this
same crowd during junior high school:

(16)   HOW DID YOU GET TO BE FRIENDS WITH THOSE PARTICULAR PEOPLE?
         Um, popularity. They—they were the popular ones.... By ninth grade,
         they were the popular ones and, you know, I wanted to be known, I
         wanted to be known by the guys, and I wanted to be known by this—
         and I started, you know, hanging around them.

Popular burnouts were highly visible in school as people to hang around
if one wanted to join in their fun and 'cool' activities outside school.
Coolness, as we will see later, is quite overtly aspired to, and the early
burnout popularity was as well. In response to Penny's query about how
she started hanging around the popular burnouts in junior high, the
speaker we just heard above explains:

(17)   Um, well, if I'd hear about, "Well, we're all going over to so-and-so's
         house tonight," you know, I'd say, "You think you guys'd mind if I came
         along?" you know, and, you know, just slowly, you know, I started to get
         to know them. I was—I'm not shy but I'm not outgoing either. I'm
         in-between. So I could really, in a way, ask them, and in a way, try to be
         accepted. That's why I think I started smoking cigarettes. That's when I
         started drinking beer, and all of that stuff.

In the following quotation, a burnout girl talks about two other burnout
girls who set out intentionally to become popular in junior high. The
speaker is an admirer of Joan, the second girl she mentions, and considers
her attempts to become popular to be funny but not reprehensible:

(18)   I know that one girl, Sally Stella, she's a—I don't know, she was just
         trying to make friends with everybody so she could be really popular,
         you know? And she thought she was so beautiful, and she had so
         many friends, and—I don't know—and Joan Border, like—you
         know, she can talk to anybody, and she was making a lot of friends
         too, like—it was like they were competing or something, her and
         Sally . . . trying to see who could get the most friends and ((laughter))
         I don't know.

In junior high school, when the jocks had not yet come to dominate
status in the school, they and the burnouts were two separate visible
popular crowds competing to define 'the good life' in school. Both participated in school activities—burnout girls were cheerleaders, burnout
boys played on school teams, and both burnouts and jocks attended
school dances and athletic events. However, the two categories engaged
in these activities on very different terms. The burnouts viewed school
activities as opportunities to 'party', and their mixing of school activities

with 'illicit' activities eventually disqualified them from participation. At the same time, the school's insistence on monitoring these activities as a condition of participation led those who had not been sent away to back away. One might say that the issue of popularity—prominence within the school as someone to hang out with—was closed for the burnouts when they left junior high. This analysis is articulated by two burnout girls:

(19)   Girl 1: Well, nobody's really popular

          Girl 2: anymore

          Girl 1: Yeah, but like they were popular then.

          Girl 2: Then they were, yeah.

          Penny: WHAT DID THAT MEAN?

          Girl 1: To have them be popular?

          Girl 2: They were the coolest.

          Girl 1: Yeah. They were the ones that had girlfriends and boyfriends first. They were the ones to try everything new out first. They hung around all the junior high kids first. And uh, that's—

          Penny: THEY WERE THE ONES EVERYBODY WANTED TO BE WITH?

          Girl 1: Yeah, yeah, every time I tried to be with them.

But by high school, the burnouts are firmly oriented outside the school and many refer to jocks in general as *the popular crowd*. Just as jockdom is denied as a social category by those in it, so is the pursuit of popularity by jock girls. In example (20), a girl on the outskirts of the central jock crowd talks about an upwardly mobile friend who left her group to try to get in with the right people:

(20)   WHO DO YOU SUPPOSE SHE THOUGHT WERE THE RIGHT PEOPLE? Um, the popular, the jock people, I think. That's what I think.

Yet, the pressure to deny an interest in popularity for girls aspiring to jock success is so strong that some will use the term *jock* to mask a concern with popularity, as shown by this extract in which the girl spoken of in example (20) is (on a different occasion) talking with Penny:

(21)   My girlfriends, we kind of tend towards the—I don't know, I—and none of my girlfriends are going out with, um,—I don't, I don't like to label people, but, burnouts. We, I guess we, we mainly go ((laughter)) out with, I guess, the, the athletes, the jocks and stuff. And, um, or the, um, the—I wouldn't say popular crowd, but, you know.

As we discuss further below, jock girls need to be circumspect about their interest in popularity, but jock boys have a different orientation. For jock boys, popularity is overwhelmingly viewed in terms of contacts, visibility, and community status. For them, it is clearly tied up with institutional influence, as shown in one class president's discussion of the inevitability of wanting to be popular. He articulates the separation between popularity and likeability:

> (22)   It starts in sixth grade, I think. You—you want to be popular because
>   you're the oldest in the school. You want people to know you. And then
>   once you get into junior high, you just have to be. I mean just—not
>   because—see, you want to because you—you feel it's the right thing to
>   do. You want to—you know, it's a big thing to be popular, but a lot of
>   people want to be popular for the wrong reasons. They want to be
>   popular because they think it's going to get them friends, or, uh, they
>   think things will be easier if they're popular. But it's not like that. In
>   fact, it could backfire. You—you create a lot of resentment if you
>   become popular for the wrong reasons.

This boy has a clear sense of the connections among popularity, contacts, and institutional effectiveness. He displays the sense of institutional responsibility that won him his position and that indeed made him an unusually effective student-government officer. One should become popular because "it's the right thing to do"; it doesn't bring one friends or make life generally "easier." The following jock boy told Penny that although there is no formula for becoming popular, the sine qua non is getting to know people:

> (23)   I think—be really outgoing you know, and don't just stay with one
>   group of friends, you know—if you just stay really—if you don't ever go
>   out and talk to anybody else, then, you know, nobody's never going to
>   know who you are or anything if you're just really—stay home all the
>   time, so—be outgoing, I think.

Jock boys will admit to the pursuit of prominence—high visibility—as a means to the end of playing a leadership role in the school, winning in the competitive governance game. Still, prominence achieved through selection to the all-state football team takes much less social effort; achieving for the school is all that is necessary for people to "know who you are" and is much less risky than having to take active steps to get to know people. (We discuss some of these risks in the next section.) Above all, this prominence is clearly based on skill and achievement, not on looks, charm, or some doubtful social 'manipulation'.

For girls, institutional success derives less from individual achievement than from the kinds of relations they can maintain with others. In the adult corporate world, wives still frequently derive status from their husbands' occupations, secretaries from the institutional positions of their bosses. School-based prominence for girls depends very heavily on ties of friendship or romance with other visible people. The pursuit of popularity for girls involves a careful construction of personhood, although this is not generally acknowledged (Eckert 1990a). Hence the cultivation of attractiveness, both beauty and a pleasing personality, becomes a major enterprise, to which cultivation of individual accomplishment typically takes a back seat. This enterprise, we might point out, is supported by a multibillion-dollar teen magazine industry aimed specifically at adolescent girls, providing them with the technology of beauty and personality (see Talbot 1995). The adult successors are women's magazines and self-help books (including those to help with communication; see Cameron 1996). Thus trained, women are far more likely than men to be obsessed with being the perfect spouse, the perfect parent, the perfect friend—the perfect person, the most loved and liked. They are far less likely to be obsessed with being the highest-paid CEO or the winningest lawyer or the world's top theoretical linguist—the top star in an openly competitive 'game'. Personal ambition is not, of course, completely out of the question for girls and women. Feminist challenges since the early nineteenth century to give middle-class women access to educational and occupational equity have opened some alternative routes for women's success. For adolescent girls, as for women in later stages of life (Holland and Eisenhart 1990), however, such ambition has an uphill battle to wage against the 'attractive-person' obsession.

The following description by a 'second-tier' jock girl of what constitutes popularity and her account of her fear of really popular people foreground the importance (and fragility) of a carefully constructed persona and especially one that the 'right' boys will find appealing:

(24)   I think personality has got to be the number one, you know—personality is probably the most important. If you've got a really good personality, you know, make people laugh all the time, then you're pretty much popular. Good looks is probably second runner up, real close up there! BUT WHEN YOU'RE TALKING ABOUT PERSONALITY...YOU SAY YOU GOT TO MAKE PEOPLE LAUGH AND SO ON, BUT WHAT ELSE IS—Well, just so that when you're around them you feel comfortable and not, you know, really tense or anything—That's probably the best. ARE THERE PEOPLE THAT MAKE YOU REALLY TENSE? Yes ((laughter)) LIKE WHO? Um, boys in particular. Really popular ones. I get really tense around them. I'm not—I don't know. The boy atmosphere is just kind of ((laughter)) I've really been close to girls all my life. I've really had really close friends, so it's kind of hard for me—I get really tense around people like that. But—even still—really popular people, I'm still really tense around. Maybe I'll say something wrong, maybe, you know, I'll do something wrong, and then they'll hate me, and then ((laughter)) you know.

What is essential for jock girls is approval from those already prominent, especially but not only boys. To be seen by those able to grant entry to the inner circle as desiring such entry is to jeopardize the chances of getting it.

Coolness, we have already seen, is central to burnout girls' popularity when being the center of a visible crowd in the school is still an issue. But even after concern with such popularity is left behind, coolness persists as the core of burnout status for girls. Coolness is a kind of toughness without the added implication of physical power associated with male burnouts. Coolness is a viable alternative to institutional popularity: it asserts independence of institutionally imposed norms, willingness to flaunt the injunctions of authorities and claim all the privileges of adulthood if and when one so desires. Treating conservative or conventional (especially, in this case, school-centered institutional) norms with disdain is one way to constitute oneself as cool, to stake out the territory of burnout status. Just as institutional status is essential to social status for a jock, female or male, coolness is essential to social status for a burnout, female or male. And although a burnout girl may not have access to full burnout status through fighting or other displays of physical toughness, she can be cool, verbally and emotionally tough. In example (25), a burnout girl describes how she and another friend gained status during junior high as the 'biggest burnouts':

(25)   But like we got along with everybody and uh we partied every day and that was the cool thing. And uh we'd smoke in school and that was cool. We used to get E's in classes [a failing grade], that was cool. You know? So, I don't know. I guess that's how.

Coolness stands in stark opposition to the jock girls' squeaky-clean image and their concern with being liked by the appropriate people and respected as 'responsible' school citizens. But of course jock girls are not cowering goody-goodies, and this opposition poses a threat to their own sense of autonomy. Thus, just as burnout girls view the quest for popularity as part of their childish past, jock girls relegate the pursuit of coolness to childhood. The only time a jock girl mentioned coolness in the entire corpus of interviews was in accounting for burnouts' behavior in junior high school:

(26)   Most of the people that were in junior high doing these kind of things ended up in high school ((laughter)) doing them even worse, so ((laughter)). WHEN DO KIDS START DOING THAT? Probably fifth and sixth grade when you think you're really cool—that's your cool age. Seventh—sixth, seventh, and eighth grade is your cool age, and everybody thinks, "Hey, I'm really cool, man! I'm gonna smoke! I'm gonna be real cool!" So that's what—where it starts probably.

Here, disparagingly, smoking is seen as putatively 'cool' because it represents defiant assertion of adult privilege. Notice, however, that the speaker in example (26) stresses the immaturity of those vigorously pursuing coolness, implying that their claims to adult-style autonomy are sham. She is implicitly defending herself against charges of sheeplike obedience by constituting herself as having been able to uphold norms when "everybody" was urging defiance.

Jock girls are the only ones who do not embrace the notion of coolness. Burnout boys, and the more-partying in-between boys, talk occasionally about coolness as something to be cultivated, as in example (27), when an in-between boy told Penny why he could give up cigarettes at any time:

(27)   Because I don't need them. I only do them for, you know, the coolness.

And burnout girls talk with humor, but not with shame, about coolness's affecting their decisions, as shown in example (28):

(28)   I would have liked to done cheerleading or volleyball or something. AND WHY DIDN't YOU? Some of it was uncool, you know, it was kind of uncool for—because I was considered a big burnout. ((laughter))

Just as jock boys want to insist on their physical toughness, a fair number find coolness appealing. For American boys, there are tensions in jock status connected with the need to assert a certain independence of institutionally imposed strictures on activities while at the same time using the institutional resources for enhancing their personal status. It is important for them to be seen as independent actors who are not institutionally ruled. Being labeled *squeaky-clean* can suggest a meek deference to school (or parental) regulations, whereas there can be a positive value attached to coolness—a stance of disregard for others' assessments, a willingness to engage in practices adults have forbidden, an assertion of disregard for possible negative judgments from others, a kind of social courage. So, although jock boys do not speak of actively pursuing coolness, apparently because they don't want to appear to be 'trying', they do sometimes speak of it as a desirable quality and one that influenced their choice of friends in junior high. At the time of this study in Belten High, smoking, alcohol consumption, and (other) drug use were of great importance for defining burnout status. As we have already noted, the name *burnout* and the more local name *jell* or *jelly* (from *jelly brain*) refer directly to drug use. And burnouts, both girls and boys, freely define themselves in these terms. After all, drug use is a powerful symbol of their rejection of adult authority and their assertion of adult autonomy. Thus, although drug use in itself does not establish someone as a burnout any more than athletic skills confirm jock status, it is important for the burnouts to try to hold the jocks to squeaky-cleanness and to reserve drug use for themselves. If one can violate institutional norms and still reap all the institutional privileges, it becomes hard to see what is gained by eschewing institutionally endorsed roads to success. Thus, the well-known fact that many jocks drink and that a number of jock boys do some drugs leads some to assert that such people are not actually jocks, or that the category itself no longer exists (again suggesting its becoming unmarked, as discussed earlier). This is illustrated by another quotation from the girl who described herself as 'in-between' in example (8):

(29)   I've come to believe that there isn't such a thing in Belten, or anybody
           that I've met, that is a jock. Because I know for a fact that my volleyball
           ((laughter)) team, after games and after tournaments, we'd have parties,
           and we'd be drinking. And some of us, you know, I—I play volleyball,
           and I smoke, and there's a few others that do. And I thought back, and
           I said, "You guys are supposed to be jocks, what's the problem here?"
           ((laughter)) you know. And they said, "Hey, you know, we have a good
           time too," you know.

The opposition that locks jocks and burnouts into these quite divergent identity practices extends its terms into both communities of practice as well. Within the broader jock network, there is a good deal of
diversity in behavior: there are clusters of girls who are truly squeaky-clean,
and there are clusters of girls who party. The salience of partying in the
jock-burnout split leads many jocks to refer to this latter partying cluster
as *kind-of burnout*. Similarly, among the burnout girls, there are degrees of
'burnout-ness'.

The main cluster of burnouts is an extensive neighborhood-based network that goes back to early childhood. The girls and boys in this cluster
originally engaged in school activities in junior high school, until, as discussed earlier, their noncorporate orientation came into obvious conflict
with school norms. Quite distinct from this large cluster is another, smaller,
cluster that is not neighborhood-based but consists of a group of girls who
got together in junior high school. These girls were never interested in
school activities in junior high except for attending dances, from which
they were quickly excluded for drinking and getting high, and they pride
themselves on being quite 'wild' in comparison with the rest of the
burnout girls. They stand out from other burnout girls as extreme in dress,
demeanor, substance use, illegal behavior, and so on. One of these girls, in
describing the social organization of space in the school courtyard, which
constitutes the smoking section and the burnout territory, demonstrates
the strategic nature of labeling. (The speech in parentheses in this
quotation is directed to passersby.)

(30)   OK, us, you know like the burnout (yeah, 'bye—wait, bum me one) the
           burnout chicks, they sit over here, you know, and like jocky chicks stand
           right here....And then there's like um the guys, you know, you know,
           like weirdos that think they're cool. They just stand like on the steps
           and hang out at that little heater. (Say, hey!) And then the poins are
           inside in the cafeteria, because they're probably afraid to come out in
           the courtyard.

In this quotation, by referring to a group of burnout and in-between girls
who smoke as *jocks*, the main group of burnout boys as *weirdos*, and other
in-betweens and all the jocks as *poins* (from *poindexters*), the speaker positions herself and her friends in relation to the rest of the school population.
She is defining her group as normative burnouts, and it is not surprising
that others have referred to them, in turn, as *burned-out burnouts*.

There are many fault lines in the neat divisions we have made between jocks and burnouts, and many in the school find identification with either group deeply problematic. Some of the strongest disapproval of jocks by nonjocks and of burnouts by nonburnouts is reserved for what are seen as typically female modes of seeking popularity and asserting coolness.

5. Snobs and sluts

A major character flaw that many in the school associate with jocks is being stuck-up or snobby. Boys can, of course, be snobs. But it is far easier for boys than for girls to achieve institutional prominence without drawing the charge of being stuck-up. The easiest way is simply to shine on the football field. But not all boys have this option. The successful class president quoted in example (22) clearly saw the potential for others' resentment when one cultivates prominence. He recommends inclusiveness and tolerance of others as the best strategy for not raising others' hackles:

(31)   ... if you're not snobby about it, the people tend to—you t—you tend to overcome, and win a lot more people if you become popular but still at the same time not too snobby. I try to talk to a lot of people now, and like right now, you know, because—because I'm president of the class, there's a lot of people that, sort of like, may know me by name or something, but there's not like really a—a group of people I won't talk to. Because a lot of people, they'll say, "Well, I don't like to talk to people in the courtyard" ((burnouts)), you know. YEAH. RIGHT. That's just the way it is. But I don't see what's wrong with it. It's not like you're s- you're- you're becoming one. Which is not, you know—what they do, it doesn't bother me. If they want to do what they do with their life, it's fine. And you shouldn't distinguish between certain types of t- people. You should just want to relate to as many people as possible.

But for jock girls, pursuit of a wide range of contacts carries with it a threat to the persona they struggle so hard to develop. To talk to a burnout girl "in the courtyard" is indeed to run the risk of "becoming one." Why? Because, as we have said in many different ways, jock girls are judged primarily by their associates and only secondarily by their achievements. For boys, in contrast, the achievements come first. It is overwhelmingly girls who describe other girls as excluding people, as pursuing recognition by the school's stars at the expense of those who are outside the star circle. This is how one burnout girl accounts for not trying out for cheerleading in ninth grade (note that this is not the same girl quoted in (28)):

(32)   DID YOU GET INVOLVED IN ACTIVITIES AND STUFF LIKE THAT? Um, ninth grade, I was involved in volleyball, because that's when it started. Um, dances, here and there. I just went to talk to people. I wasn't dancing or nothing. I went to listen to the band and that. Um, uh, I can't say I really

went to any basketball games or anything like that. DID YOU GO OUT
FOR CHEERLEADING OR ANYTHING LIKE THAT? Now that started in the
ninth grade. And that's when I—well, how—[I don't] really know how
to explain how I felt. I felt that at that time, I didn't have to do that to
be popular. And I thought, "Hmm, cheerleaders—everybody's going to
look up at them, and they're going to, you know ((laughter)) they're
going to be stuck-up, and I don't want to be known as a stuck-up cheerleader," and—so I steered away from that. I wanted to be one though.
YOU WANTED TO BE ONE—That's—that's what was, that—I did, you
know, because I knew I'd enjoy it. And I thought, "Well, look at the ones
that were last year. All the girls look down on them. 'She's a stuck-up
cheerleader,'" you know. So—

Here a quintessentially jock activity for girls—cheerleading—is equated
with being seen as stuck-up (and thus to be avoided whatever its other
attractions might be). In example (33), a burnout girl describes how she
assumes jocks view people like her:

(33)   I think of like jocks as like sort of higher up, you know, so you think that
         you know, they'd be saying, "Hey," you know, "let's get rid of these like
         diddly little people," you know?

The management of social visibility, as we have seen, preoccupies girls
seeking status as jocks. It does not, however, endear a jock girl to those
who are not welcomed to her orbit, or to her old friends whom she has no
time for because she is so busy networking. Even for a girl who cares only
about her status among the activities-oriented crowd, the twin projects of
cultivating a pleasing personality and pursuing prominence are hard to
balance successfully. If the pursuit of prominence is too evident, even
other institutionally minded people may well reject as stuck-up and
snobby the personality thereby produced. Likeability within the jock
crowd cannot be sacrificed, because one needs social ties of friendship or
romance for success as a jock girl: one must be someone others want as a
friend or sweetheart. Good personhood ought to make others feel
welcome, not excluded.

Girl jocks, then, face considerable difficulty. They must regulate their
social alliances with care in order to attain the social visibility they need.
But this regulation tends to involve excluding many, which leads naturally
to charges of being a snob. Being a stuck-up snob, however, is inconsistent
with the pleasing personality the successful jock girl needs. And of course
the good personhood the jock girl constructs is itself seen as laudable, a
special kind of achievement compared implicitly to the not-so-good personhood of others who have not made the same effort to seek such
goodness. Such invidious comparisons, however silent they may be, also
tend to lead those put down by them to view jock girls' pride in their personae as more evidence of their being stuck-up. Thus, part of burnout
girls' explicit rejection of popularity by the time they reach high school
derives from their despising what they see as the snobbery and sense of

superiority of jock girls. But that is not the only reason for their rejection of popularity.

Part of the presentation of a corporate being is as a person who is 'in control' of both her professional and her personal affairs. In the interests of presenting an image of corporate competence, jocks uniformly hide personal and family problems from their peers (see Eckert 1989). In addition, they strive to maintain an image of control over their 'urges', and for jock girls, this involves importantly a control over their images as heterosexual beings. Burnouts, on the other hand, emphasize 'being your-self' and value the sharing of problems. And while burnout girls do not necessarily flaunt heterosexual engagement, they certainly are not concerned with presenting an abstemious image, a concern that would be decidedly 'uncool'.

It is important to emphasize that it is above all the heterosexual image that is at issue in this opposition rather than sexual behavior itself. Although a jock girl's unpublicized engagement in sexual relations with a boyfriend may be considered her own business, any appearance of pro-miscuity is not. Indeed, anything that contributes to such an appearance, including styles of hair, dress, and makeup, as well as demeanor, will be seen as 'slutty' and can seriously threaten a jock girl's status, costing her female friends as well as the possibility of being judged an inappropriate public partner for a jock boy. One jock girl even considered dating too many boys to be dangerous for one's reputation:

(34)   Well, maybe there's some, I don't really know, that go out with a differ-
        ent guy every week. Because I—I don't—I don't think that's so much
        true, because you can—that—that would kind of give you a bad repu-
        tation ((laughter)) I think. I don't know. I'd leave a little space in
        between.

To be labeled a *slut* is to fail in the school's corporate culture. It is not surprising, then, that jocks view the prototypical burnout girl as slutty, and that burnouts view the prototypical jock girl as phony and uptight. The crucial difference is not so much in sexual behavior but in the fact that burnouts, in opposition to jocks, are not concerned with sluttiness— either in image or in behavior. Burnout girls view so-called slutty patterns of dress and demeanor as simply personal characteristics, which they may or may not think problematic, but certainly not as making someone an unsuitable friend. *Slut* is a category label that fuses gender and class.

Both burnout and jock girls actively construct their social statuses and they do so in ways that allow them to cooperate with their male peers in constituting the basic social orientation of their respective categories: resistance to institutional norms in the one case and participation in the hierarchical institutionally sanctioned practice in the other. In both cases, however, the girls lack access to the full repertoire of practices that can constitute category status for boys. And the practices open to girls in each category are highly likely to evoke great hostility from girls in the other

category. Burnout girls vigorously reject the relation-cultivating popularity so important to jock girls; they hate the snobbiness and
'holier-than-thou' attitudes that they associate with it. Jock girls in turn
are contemptuous of the lack of 'self-control' associated with coolness.
They see coolness as all too easily leading to sluttiness, which they roundly
condemn—and work hard to keep at bay.

Burnout girls and jock girls construct strikingly different solutions to
the dilemma created for them by the overarching gender structures they
all experience, structures characterized by male dominance and heterosexist preoccupation with sexual differentiation. And each group judges
the other's strategic moves in response to these constraints very harshly.
One result is that the overall differences in normative patterns of practice
between burnout and jock girls are far greater than those between burnout
and jock boys. After junior high, opposition—and conflict—between
burnouts and jocks centers on opposition—and (primarily) symbolic conflict—between burnout and jock girls. This is reflected with startling
clarity in patterns of phonological variation, to which we now turn.

6. Pronouncing selves

The depth of the jock-burnout opposition in Belten High is borne out by
differences in speech between the members of the two categories: differences in vocabulary, in grammar, in pronunciation. But more important,
these speech differences are not simply markers of category affiliation.
They carry in themselves complex social meanings, like tough, cool, slutty,
casual, or mean, and these meanings are part of the construction of categories like those labeled by *female, male, jock, burnout*. Finding these
meanings through correlations between the use of linguistic variables and
indicators of social practice is a major challenge for sociolinguists. In this
section, we focus on several phonological variables that enter into the
construction of social identities in Belten High, and that simultaneously
are part of what constitutes a 'Midwest', or Detroit, or Michigan accent.
The production of linguistic styles is part of the production of identities,
and local and regional pronunciations provide some of the resources that
can be put to stylistic use.

The following discussion focuses on two vowels that have symbolic
significance in this community. The symbolic significance is associated
with recent innovations in pronunciation, innovations that reflect sound
changes in progress:

- (uh) as in *fun, cuff, but* (phonetically [ʌ]), is moving back so that it
  comes to sound like the vowel in *fawn, cough, bought* [ɔ].
- The nucleus [a] of the diphthong (ay) as in *file, line, heist* raises to
  [ʌ] or [ɔ], so that the diphthong may sound more like the
  diphthong in *foil, loin, hoist*.

For each of these vowels, pronunciations in the stream of speech will vary from the conservative to the innovative with several stages in between. Most speakers in the community use the full range of pronunciations, generally within the same conversation. However, speakers will vary in the frequency with which they use the more conservative and more innovative pronunciations. It is in the speaker's average pronunciation or in the strategic use of one or the other pronunciation that this variability comes to have social meaning.

The changes described for the vowels above represent linguistic changes in progress, and certain social principles about such changes have emerged over the years (see Chambers 1995; Labov 1972, 1994). In general, sound change originates in locally based, working-class communities and spreads gradually upward through the socioeconomic hierarchy. In this way, new sound changes tend to carry local meaning and to serve as part of the local social-symbolic repertoire. This means that the speech of locally based working-class groups will generally show more of the innovative variants discussed above than that of middle-class groups in the same community. Middle-class speakers, on the contrary, are more likely to avoid clearly local pronunciations inasmuch as they are engaged in corporate institutions that strive to transcend local resources and loyalties. It is to be expected, then, that burnouts, with their heightened locally based identities and loyalties, might use more of the advanced variants for these vowels than do the institutionally identified jocks.

Gender, on the other hand, does not correlate quite as consistently with linguistic variables as class does. Female speakers quite regularly lead in sound change, but there are cases in which they do not.[5] More interesting, gender commonly crosscuts class, so that although working-class women may lead working-class men in a particular sound change, middle-class women may lag behind middle-class men in the same change. Such patterns can emerge only from a co-construction of gender and class, and this co-construction emerges quite clearly in the speech of the students of Belten High.

In across-the-board correlations of (uh) and (ay) with sex and social-category membership, we find that although the backing of (uh) as in *fun*, *cuff*, and *but* correlates only with social category, with the burnouts leading, the raising of the nucleus in (ay) (*file*, *line*, *heist*) correlates only with sex, with the girls leading. Are we to stop with these correlations, and declare that the backing of (uh) 'means' burnout and the raising of the nucleus in (ay) 'means' female? Are they markers of gender and category membership, or are they symbolic of some aspects of social practice and identity that are part of what jocks and burnouts, and females and males, are about? In fact, when we dig deeper, we will see that these data reflect a great complexity of social practice.

Tables 7.1 and 7.2 show figures for correlations of speakers' sex and social-category affiliation (as assigned on the basis of network positions and descriptions by self and others) with the backing of (uh) and the

Table 7.1. Correlation of Backing of (uh) with Combined Sex
and Social Category

Female jocks	Male jocks	Female burnouts	Male burnouts
.43	.40	.62	.54

raising of (ay).[6] The correlations in these and subsequent tables are
significant at the .001 level, indicating the minimum likelihood that the
correlations could be the result of chance. In each table, a probability
value is shown for each group of speakers. The absolute numbers are not
important, only their relative values; innovative pronunciation is most frequent among the group of speakers for whom the number is highest, least
frequent among those for whom it is lowest. When we tease apart sex and
social-category membership in the data for (uh), as shown in table 7.1, we
find that within each social category, the girls lead the boys, although particularly among the jocks this lead is not large enough to be significant in
itself. We also find that the burnouts' lead over the jocks is somewhat
greater among the girls than among the boys. Correlations for extreme
raising in (ay) show a pattern similar to those for the backing of (uh), as
shown in table 7.2.

What can be drawn from the tables is that whatever distinguishes jocks
and burnouts also distinguishes boys and girls within those categories; or
whatever distinguishes boys and girls also distinguishes jocks and burnouts
within those sex groups. One would be hard pressed to establish whether
the backing of (uh) or the raising of the nucleus in (ay) is associated with
femaleness or burnout-ness. And indeed, what distinguishes gender from
sex is that femaleness and maleness cannot be imagined independently of
other aspects of identity, such as jock- and burnout-hood.

If these vowels serve to construct meaning in the high school, and if
category and gender interact in as complex a way as shown in the earlier
sections, we might expect to find some of this complexity reflected in the
vowels as well as in labeling practices. Let us turn to the division among
the burnout girls discussed earlier, in which burned-out burnout girls distinguish themselves from the 'jocky' burnouts. It turns out that these girls
are overwhelmingly in the lead in the use of innovative variants of both
(uh) and (ay).

Table 7.2. Extreme Raising of the Nucleus of (ay) with
Combined Sex and Social Category

Female jocks	Male jocks	Female burnouts	Male burnouts
.38	.28	.79	.50

Table 7.3. Correlation of Backing of (uh) with Combined Sex and Social
Category, Separating Two Clusters of Burnout Girls

Female jocks	Male jocks	Main female burnouts	Burned-out female burnouts	Male burnouts
.41	.38	.53	.65	.52

Table 7.3 separates the burned-out burnout girls from the 'regular' burnout girls. Although the 'regular' burnout girls still back (uh) more than the jock girls, the burned-out burnout girls are far more extreme. A similar pattern shows up for the raising of the nucleus in (ay), in which the burned-out burnouts are overwhelmingly in the lead (see table 7.4).

Vowels such as these do not simply fall into a neutral linguistic space. Consider the following segment of conversation with a burned-out burnout:

(35)   ...we used to tell our moms that we'd—uh—she'd be sleeping at my house, I'd be sleeping at hers. We'd go out and pull a all-nighter, you know (laughter)) I'd come home the next day, "Where were you?" "Jane's." "No you weren't." Because her mom and my mom are like really close—since we got in so much trouble they know each other really good.

Interactions are situations in which social meaning is made. When this girl says to Penny, for example, "We'd go out and pull a all-nighter," raising the nucleus of (ay) in *all-nighter* so that it clearly sounds like *all-noiter*, Penny associates what she perceives about this girl in general and what the girl is saying in particular, with this element of linguistic style. Presumably, in speaking to Penny in this way, the speaker presents herself as a burned-out burnout—as someone who gets around, does pretty much what she wants, gets in trouble, has fun, doesn't clean up her act too much for an adult like Penny, and so on. In the course of this mutual construction, the variable (ay) takes on meaning—perhaps not in isolation, but at least as a component of a broader style. In their extreme speech, then, the burned-out burnout girls are not simply using phonetic variants with a meaning already set and waiting to be recycled. Rather, their very use of those

Table 7.4. Extreme Raising of (ay), Combining Sex and Social Category,
Separating Two Clusters of Burnout Girls

Female jocks	Male jocks	Main female burnouts	Burned-out female burnouts	Male burnouts
.42	.32	.47	.93	.54

variants produces a social meaning. They are simultaneously creating meaning for (ay) and for being burned-out burnouts. Thus, as in the labeling discussed in the earlier sections, the use of phonetic variation and the construction of identities are inseparable.

7. Conclusion

Belten High provides some glimpses of communities of practice at work. Their members are engaging in a wide range of activities through which they constitute themselves and their social relations and project their future life histories. Language, gender, and class are all produced through such social practices. These practices have locally distinctive features, but they show patterns reflecting the influence of a larger society and its institutions. They also reflect a historical location with its particular pasts and prospective futures.

Readers may wonder just which communities of practice exist. Do girls and boys form separate communities of practice? Do jocks and burnouts? What about in-betweens? Jocky jocks? Burned-out burnouts? Does the student body of the whole high school constitute a community of practice?

Questions like this miss a critical point about communities of practice: they are not determined by their membership but by the endeavors that bring those members (and others who have preceded or will succeed them) into relations with one another (which may or may not be face-to-face and by the practices that develop around, and transform, these endeavors. So certainly most—perhaps all—of the student-body members belong to a community focused on the issues of school-sponsored curricular and extracurricular activities or other practices involving students that occur at school or are relevant to what is going on there. The practices toward which community members are oriented focus on the issues we have briefly discussed, some high level and others more mundane: how and whether to compete in the school-based hierarchy; how and whether to participate in the heterosexual marketplace; relation to school and family authority; post–high school prospects; who to hang out with during school; what to do directly after school (and with whom); what to do in the evenings and on weekends; where to eat lunch; whether to use drugs; what to wear; how to talk; and so on. Athletic boy jocks and burned-out burnout girls, for example, have different forms of membership in this large community of practice. And in the process of pursuing these different forms of membership, they attend to communities of practice of their own, based on and constituting specific places and points of view within the larger community.

We do not actually have to worry about delimiting communities of practice in advance. Rather, we look at people and the practices mediating their relations to one another in order to understand better the raw materials through which they constitute their own and others' identities and relations. There is no community focused on linguistic practice, no community focused on gender practice, no community focused on class practice. As we have seen, seeking popularity (or refusing to), aspiring to coolness (or refusing to), and similar practices of various kinds are saturated with implications, at one and the same time, for language, gender, and class. And the constitution of socially significant communities—both their membership and the actual content of the practices that make them into a community—has an ongoing history.

We have explored two aspects of language use at Belten: labeling and other kinds of talk about social categories and relations; and variation in the pronunciation of certain vowels. The first gives us a perspective from linguistic content on how gender and class practices and the struggles centered on them proceed. Social labeling discriminates among people and is used as a weapon to divide and to deride. Attempts to define and delimit what labels mean are really attempts to delimit what people and the social structures they build can or should be like. Unequal power in general social processes translates into unequal power in succeeding in definitional projects.[7] The prize, of course, is not controlling what this or that word means, but controlling the immediate direction of this or that aspect of social life, perhaps continuing existing social structures and relations or perhaps transforming them in some way. Social talk helps in the process of institutionalizing power and gender relations, and it helps give local force and bite to larger-scale social constructions.

Investigations of phonological variation offer a way to view similar phenomena but at a different level. Actual uses of language always have a formal aspect as well as content, and form always enriches (and sometimes contradicts) what is conveyed in social talk. Formal properties of utterances in many cases are the only source of social meaning. Of course, how one pronounces a particular vowel on a particular occasion seldom receives the same conscious attention that shapes the content of answers to questions about popularity and coolness. Nor are ordinary people as well able to say what someone else's vowels sounded like as they are to report the content of what she said. But as shown above, the low-level details of pronunciation can give a great deal of information about how people are actively constituting their own social identities and relations. And it is such subtle variations and the social meanings they express that are the stuff of which long-term and large-scale changes in conventions of linguistic practice are made.

Social talk at Belten made it clear to us that there were no separable processes constructing gender and class. Male dominance and class relations are both involved in issues of physical prowess; forms of female agency and class practices link critically to popularity and coolness; and heterosexism informs the content of class-linked femininities and masculinities. General patterns emerge only when we stop trying to partition off matters of class from matters of gender. Similarly, patterns of vowel pronunciation are clarified when we try thinking about class-gender complexes rather than class and gender as independent. Our extracts from interviews also suggest, however, the messiness of practice, its failure to fit perfectly with neat structural analyses, the social ambiguities and contradictions it embodies. Only by continuing to examine different communities of practice and the complexities within them can we really begin to come to grips with the historicity of language, gender, class, and their interactions.

Notes

1. We thank the audience that heard our summer 1993 LSA talk and the many others who have been interested in our ideas for their comments and questions. We thank Kira Hall and Mary Bucholtz, for their excellent editorial advice and for their patience as we prepared the paper for publication. Finally, we thank each other for finishing this project. As in all our publications, our names appear alphabetically.

2. This study was funded by the National Science Foundation (BNS 8023291), the Spencer Foundation, and the Horace Rackham School of Graduate Studies at the University of Michigan.

3. All quoted speech is taken from tape-recorded interviews. Penny's speech is printed in upper case. Hesitations, false starts, and so on are not edited out of these materials.

4. See McElhinny (1995) for discussion of ways women now being hired as police officers are finding to share in normative conceptions of what it means to be a good police officer without jeopardizing their sense of themselves as 'feminine'.

5. See Eckert (1990a) and Labov (1991) for a piece of the debate about gender and variation.

6. The statistics in this and all following tables were calculated using Goldvarb 2, a Macintosh-based version of the variable-rule program, which is a statistical package designed specifically for the analysis of sociolinguistic variation. For information about the analysis of variation, see Sankoff (1978).

7. See, for example, McConnell-Ginet (1989) for a discussion, albeit more narrowly linguistic, of how social contexts affect definitional success.

References

Bem, Sandra L. (1993). *The lenses of gender: Transforming the debate on sexual inequality*. New Haven: Yale University Press.

Butler, Judith (1993). *Bodies that matter*. New York: Routledge.

Cameron, Deborah (1996). The language-gender interface: Challenging cooptation. In Victoria Bergvall, Janet Bing, and Alice F. Freed (eds.), *Rethinking language and gender research: Theory and practice*. New York: Longman, 31–53.

Chambers, J. K. (1995). *Sociolinguistic theory*. Oxford: Basil Blackwell.

Connell, R. W. (1987). *Gender and power: Society, the person and sexual politics*. Stanford: Stanford University Press.

di Leonardo, Micaela (ed.) (1991). *Gender at the crossroads of knowledge: Feminist anthropology in the postmodern era*. Berkeley: University of California Press.

Eckert, Penelope (1988). Sound change and adolescent social structure. *Language in Society* 17: 183–207.

————— (1989). *Jocks and burnouts: Social categories and identity in the high school.* New York: Teachers College Press.

————— (1990a). The whole woman: Sex and gender differences in variation. *Language Variation and Change* 1: 245–267.

————— (1990b). Cooperative competition in adolescent girl talk. *Discourse Processes* 13: 92–122.

[————— (2000). *Linguistic variation as social practice: The linguistic construction of social meaning in Belten High.* Oxford: Blackwell.]

Eckert, Penelope, and Sally McConnell-Ginet (1992a). Communities of practice: Where language, gender, and power all live. In Kira Hall, Mary Bucholtz, and Birch Moonwomon (eds.), *Locating power: Proceedings of the Second Berkeley Women and Language Conference.* Berkeley: Berkeley Women and Language Group, 89–99.

————— (1992b). Think practically and look locally: Language and gender as community-based practice. *Annual Review of Anthropology* 21: 461–490.

Holland, Dorothy C., and Margaret A. Eisenhart (1990). *Educated in romance.* Chicago: University of Chicago Press.

Labov, William (1972). On the mechanism of linguistic change. In *Sociolinguistic patterns.* Philadelphia: University of Pennsylvania Press, 160–182.

————— (1991). The intersection of sex and social class in the course of linguistic change. *Language Variation and Change* 2(2): 205–251.

————— (1994). *Principles of linguistic change: Internal factors.* Oxford: Basil Blackwell.

McConnell-Ginet, Sally (1989). The sexual (re)production of meaning: A discourse-based theory. In Francine W. Frank and Paula A. Treichler (eds.), *Language, gender, and professional writing: Theoretical approaches and guidelines for nonsexist usage.* New York: Modern Language Association, 35–50.

McElhinny, Bonnie S. (1995). Challenging hegemonic masculinities: Female and male police officers handling domestic violence. In Kira Hall and Mary Bucholtz (eds.), *Gender articulated: Language and the socially constructed itself.* New York: Routledge, 217–243.

Rich, Adrienne (1980). Compulsory heterosexuality and lesbian existence. *Signs* (5): 631–660.

Sankoff, David (ed.) (1978). *Linguistic variation: Models and methods.* New York: Academic Press.

Segal, Lynne (1990). *Slow motion: Changing masculinities, changing men.* New Brunswick: Rutgers University Press.

Talbot, Mary (1995). A synthetic sisterhood: False friends in a teenage magazine. In Kira Hall and Mary Bucholtz (eds.), *Gender articulated: Language and the socially constructed itself.* New York: Routledge, 143–165.

Thorne, Barrie (1993). *Gender play.* New Brunswick: Rutgers University Press.

Part III

CONSTRUCTING CONTENT
IN DISCOURSE

It was with some trepidation that I first began thinking about the semantic and pragmatic dimensions of language, gender, and sexuality. My background in analytic philosophy of language and formal semantics and pragmatics did not seem to equip me even to understand issues like 'sexist' or 'homophobic' language or some activists' claims that women and sexual minorities were handicapped in expressing their thoughts, in giving voice to their own perspectives. In teaching my first course on language and gender, I spent a lot of time on standard sociolinguistic issues, safely outside my own realm of expertise and thus nonthreatening to my views about my particular domain of linguistic inquiry, formal semantics and pragmatics. Gender, sexuality, and other social matters seemed reassuringly distant from matters like quantificational scope or the semantics of comparative constructions. Together with my students, I explored the gendered dimensions of multilingualism and the pronunciation of vowels, the choreography of conversations (who interrupts, who takes responsibility for keeping the ball rolling, who sets the agenda), vocal effects and their role in indexing gendered and sexual identities, linguistic ideologies ("nice girls don't say *f****," "it is shameful for women to speak in church," "men do, women speak," and so on), and even, cautiously, inventories of expressions for speaking of women and of men. But I was careful to insist that only language use or users and not language itself could be sexist. I was also confident that there was no principled reason to accept any version of linguistic relativism, the view that some languages might be better suited than others to express certain ideas, to explore certain conjectures and theories, or to adopt certain perspectives. After all, I continued to think, languages just paste formal labels on concepts and combine them systematically. No one is precluded from using the available forms to convey whatever conceptual combination might strike their fancy or from attaching new forms to concepts not already encoded. I myself, I acknowledged, had long followed the prescription to use *he* for generic or sex-indefinite antecedents and *man* for humanity in general (using models like Samuel Johnson's "when a man is tired of London, he is tired of life"), and was I not committed to working for gender equity and did I not manage to express critiques of male privilege?

Yet from my students, as well as from theorists in other disciplines and from those engaged in liberation struggles outside the academy, I kept hearing other views of language and its incorporation of bias, continued to encounter folks who experienced language as limiting and sometimes even wounding. I began to realize that perhaps content meaning was more complex and also more consequential than I (and many other linguists and philosophers of language) had thought. Where formal semantics has made great strides is in analysis of combinatorial semantics—for example, how verbs combine with their objects and verb phrases with their subjects—and of the semantic contribution of very abstract expressions like quantifiers (*some, every*), logical connectives (*and, if...then*), tense and modality (past *–ed*, future *will, must*), and so on. But the first semantics classes I taught, like most formal semantics classes, included little indeed on the meaning of basic content words such as *sex, woman, man, kiss, kick, marry, sweet*. Some linguists, of course, have done significant and illuminating work on the contributions of words to the meaning associated with linguistic exchanges, including my dissertation advisor, Adrienne Lehrer (see, e.g., her *Wine and conversation*, 2nd ed. [New York: Oxford University Press, 2009]). I learned and continue to learn much from this work and from that done by so-called cognitive linguists, of whom George Lakoff is perhaps most widely cited (see, e.g., his *Women, fire, and dangerous things: What categories reveal about the mind* [Chicago: University of Chicago Press, 1987]). But work of this kind, interesting though I found it, did not seem as much about linguistic meaning as about patterns of language use and other phenomena outside the linguistic system itself.

Increasingly, however, I began trying to connect conditions of discursive practice with what people might mean or try to mean and with what others might interpret them as meaning or might infer on the basis of what was said. Rather than seeing content as firmly attached to linguistic forms, I began to view those forms as being filled with content (at least to a significant extent) in the course of language-using social practices. And I also began to realize that content was contentious: the meaning a speaker aimed to construct might be different from the construction(s) others made of what was said. Cases involving explicit disagreements over what words could or should mean seemed to me more and more important: why weren't there clear meaning criteria, on the one hand, and why in certain cases did people care so much about pushing their own favored meanings?

Chapter 8, "The sexual (re)production of meaning," is my initial attempt to bring together certain features of discourse conditions with changing meanings. In it, I offer a 'just so' kind of story about the word *hussy* and its change in conventional meaning from something roughly like 'housewife' to something like 'wanton or forward woman.' I draw on philosopher Paul Grice's important insight that speakers and hearers go beyond the linguistic system itself by taking speech to be motivated action and reasoning about the motives that might underlie particular utterances in a given context. What Grice does not say but I do is that in interpreting utterances hearers draw not only on general principles of clear communication and on manifest features of the particular discourse setting but also on their beliefs about speakers, including unwarranted prejudices about their capabilities and their interests (some of which may arise from their inadequate attention in earlier encounters). I speculate that women and men are typically in different positions as they deploy existing linguistic forms to accomplish their various ends. I am trying in this essay to begin to understand how a language might in principle be 'sexist' in the sense that it serves women's interests less well than it does men's. What I don't do is consider the diversity of interests among women and among men, which would make it problematic to attach advantage to one sex as such. The important point that does emerge, I think, is that conditions of discursive practice are critical for constructing content and participants in the discourse may not be equivalently situated.

In chapter 9, "Prototypes, pronouns, and persons," I explore certain features of the (late 1970s) usage of English pronouns. I offer evidence that *he* cannot always, as some English teachers and grammars used to suggest, take antecedents of unknown or indefinite sex and that the so-called generic *he* ("the wise politician pays attention to his constituents"), which contrasts with generic *she* ("the careful parent will be sure that she knows her child's friends"), is often more 'masculine' and less 'generic' than traditional accounts recognized. Generics, I suggest, often refer to fictive 'prototypes', for example, in the cases above to an imagined exemplary politician or parent, who is almost always seen as a man or as a woman and seldom as a person for whom sexual categorization doesn't matter. Singular *they*, I argue, is part of the same paradigm but is limited in occurrence by being less 'personalized', a fact I link to its gender neutrality. (Some medical personnel working with people engaged in transitioning from one sex to the other use *they* to refer to individuals during that time of transition; trans folks sometimes encounter resistance from family and longtime friends for using the 'new' pronoun, and being referred to after transition as *they* does not satisfy most individuals.) I have added references to more recent studies of pronouns, and I note that usage has shifted somewhat in the more than three decades since this work was done. Although I would take a somewhat different approach to this topic now and would look more explicitly at discursive practice rather than isolated judgments of acceptability, the chapter offers ideas that are still relevant and shows something about the complexity of pronominal 'gendering'.

"Social labeling and gender practices," chapter 10, argues that the answer to Shakespeare's "What's in a name?" is "A lot—and many different things." Though it draws on work done a couple of decades ago, this article also builds on the 'communities of practice' framework described in chapters 5 and 7. It was in teaching about address and reference that I first fully realized that one could not talk about labels and their meanings without examining who might be using them, in what contexts, and for what purposes. Without considering discursive practice, it made little sense to ask what such labels 'meant.' This chapter emphasizes labeling as a kind of social practice that plays an important role in constituting social categories and in people's positioning and repositioning themselves with respect to one another. In labeling, social meaning and content are intertwined.

"'Queering' semantics," chapter 11, also focuses on labels and in particular on certain labels for sexual minorities: *queer, gay, lesbian*. Looking at some of the discursive history and the range of ongoing discursive practice involving these words leads me to try to articulate a view of the linguistic meaning of words being (relatively) empty, social practices filling in and also transforming content over time. On this picture much of content lies outside the linguistic system as such: content is constructed in the course of discursive practice, with that construction constrained but certainly not determined by earlier discursive history. Constructing meaning, I argue, is itself a social act and as such affected by sometimes conflicting interest of interactants and by their power relations. I have added references to more recent work that develops these ideas further.

8

The sexual (re)production of meaning

A discourse-based theory

Scholarship on women and language has addressed two main topics: (1) how women (and men) speak (and write); (2) how they (and other gender-marked topics) are spoken of. In each case, feminists have argued, some kind of linguistic sexism is at work. Sexism in how we speak has many aspects. Women's favored styles of language use are often negatively evaluated by the larger community, for example, and women are frequently the victims of male oppression in discourse, suffering interruptions and inattention to their conversational contributions. In more public arenas, similar problems exist on a larger scale: women speaking from pulpits or podiums are still rare, and their writings are viewed as somehow tainted by their sex. Sexism in how women are spoken of manifests itself in a variety of ways, such as "the semantic derogation of women" (in the words of Schulz 1975) in the vocabulary and the so-called generic masculines that contribute to women's relative 'psychological invisibility'.

Extensive annotated bibliographies in Thorne and Henley 1975 and in Thorne, Kramarae, and Henley 1983 attest to the wealth of empirical research on both issues. Later in this essay I discuss specific investigations of the first question—how women speak; Julia Penelope Stanley (1977) and Muriel Schulz (1975) are among those who have studied the second question—how women are spoken of. Each topic has also been explored by many other feminist thinkers: see, for example, Daly 1973; Rich 1979; and the many collections concerned with language from a literary or psychoanalytic viewpoint (including Eisenstein and Jardine 1980; McConnell-Ginet, Borker, and Furman 1980; Abel 1981; Garner, Kahane, and Sprengnether 1985; and Benstock 1987). Other recent writings are cited by Paula Treichler (1986a, 1986b). Thorne, Kramarae, and Henley (1983) suggest the need for investigating the interaction between language use and what they call *language structure* (our semantic resources), a subject

This essay was first published in Francine W. Frank and Paula A. Treichler, eds., *Language, gender and professional writing: Theoretical approaches and guidelines for non-sexist usage* (New York: Modern Language Association, 1989), 35–50. Reprinted in slightly abridged form in Deborah Cameron, ed., *The feminist critique of language: A reader*, 2nd ed. (New York: Routledge, 1998).

that Kramarae 1980 develops somewhat further. The popular term *sexist language* is generally applied to the second topic, which I call SEXIST SEMANTICS for the sake of brevity, but it sometimes is also construed to cover the first, which I call SEXIST DISCOURSE. (Some of the papers in Vetterling-Braggin 1981, for example, are more directly concerned with the ways women and men act as speakers than with the ways they are spoken of, despite the book's title. [Mills 2008 observes that terms like 'sexist language' or, for that matter, 'sexist semantics' or 'sexist discourse', tend to obscure the complexity of how gender arrangements and bias connect to language.])

My major aim in this essay is to give a brief theoretical account of the roots of sexist semantics in sexist discourse. This way of putting it is, of course, somewhat oversimplified. By SEXIST SEMANTICS I mean not only such phenomena as the sexualization and homogenization of words denoting women (e.g., *mistress* and *girl*) and the universalization of words originally denoting men (e.g., *guys*) but also subtler aspects of the relative absence of a 'women's-eye view' in the most readily accessible linguistic resources. What I mean by SEXIST DISCOURSE also goes beyond the more blatant kinds of male oppression of women in conversation, though I include some examples of these. More generally, I am interested in how sex differences [I would now emphasize gender ideologies and social practice] influence both communication and interpretation in discourse.

Whatever we may think of the merits of particular studies, it is relatively easy to see how sexism in a community could have implications for how its members speak and how their speech is evaluated. Because using language is a socially situated action, it is clearly embedded in the same sociocultural matrix that supports sexual bias in the work we do, the wages we receive, the expectations we have of ourselves and others, and so on. More difficult to understand are the connections between a sexist society and the semantics of a language; the most familiar theoretical models of linguistic meaning do not illumine the question of how particular meanings become attached to particular forms.

Stated like this, however, the question is misleading, for it suggests that meanings somehow exist independently of their articulation, as though languages merely paste linguistic labels on the semantic furniture of the universe, tagging an independent realm of concepts with sounds (or, in the graphic medium, strings of letters). Not all the possible semantic stock is tagged by a particular language-using community, but no theoretical barrier prohibits its members from adding labels whenever they choose. Or so a common line of thinking goes, a line that I refer to as the CODE VIEW of language (see McConnell-Ginet 1980, 1984). This view finds popular expression in such comments as "Oh, that's just a question of semantics" (which implies the triviality of the connection between forms and their meanings) or in such familiar adages as "A rose by any other name would smell as sweet" (see McConnell-Ginet 1984 for a discussion of this Shakespearean line and its often forgotten context).[a] What the code view fails to address is the significance of the tagging process itself and the possibility that this process shapes and gives coherence to the sometimes inchoate stuff that we seek to wrap our tags around. To understand the source of sexist semantics, the way sexism in society and culture interacts with the system of linguistic meanings, we really need to ask how meaning is produced and reproduced.

The production of meaning designates the processes through which speakers mean something by what they say (or writers by what they write) and through which hearers (or readers) interpret what is said (or written). The reproduction of meaning refers to our dependence, in producing meanings, on previous meanings or interpretations, to our dependence in particular on one another's experience with the linguistic forms being used. I argue that to understand the ways that meanings are produced and reproduced and the significance of sex and gender in these processes, we must consider the conditions of discourse. The key to explaining so-called sexist semantics and, ultimately, to reclaiming the "power of naming" (see Spender 1980) lies in analyzing the sexual politics of discourse. Macropolitical structures play a significant role, of course, in genderizing discourse. Who writes and who reads? Who preaches sermons to large congregations? Who publishes books? Whose speeches are beamed by satellite around the world? Although these are important questions, I will not consider them here but will focus instead on the micropolitics of daily discourse between ordinary individuals. Because most of what we say about daily discourse is more widely applicable, however, this restriction is not so severe as it might seem.

I am indebted to the work of the philosopher H. Paul Grice for my basic framework, though I use his ideas in a somewhat special way. Grice bases his account of meaning on what speakers intend to accomplish by speaking. (See the Grice studies listed under "References" and Lewis's (1969) and Schiffer's (1972) related theoretical analyses, which Bach and Harnish (1979) draw on in attempting to develop a general theory of linguistic communication.) The crucial feature of the Gricean account for my purposes is that meaning depends not just on the speaker but on a kind of relation between the speaker and the hearer. It is this potentially social perspective that gives insight into the (re)production of meaning.

What is involved in this account? Grice's explanation goes something like this: in saying A, a speaker means to express the thought B if the speaker intends to produce in her hearer a recognition of thought B by virtue of his recognizing that she is trying to produce that recognition in him by saying A. (Grice does not restrict his account to female speakers and male hearers,

---

a. McConnell-Ginet (2008) argues that meanings can and do matter in ways not fully appreciated by those dismissive of 'just semantics', and McConnell-Ginet (2006) discusses Shakespeare's "What's in a name?" in the context of debates over whether to deny the word *marriage* for same-sex unions.

as the pronouns I have used may imply that he does. I am following many other authors in using both *she* and *he* as 'generic' singular pronouns; but since I later discuss in more detail the hypothetical case of a woman talking with a man, the choice of pronouns is not entirely arbitrary.) This back-and-forth intending and recognizing and thinking is, of course, not usually a conscious process. In informal speech, coordination adequate for the purpose is generally taken for granted and not reflected on. The more complex (and the more novel) the thoughts one seeks to express, the more conscious the attention given to the meaning process. There is generally greater self-awareness in writing and reading than in speaking and hearing, because the memory and time constraints are less severe.

In linguistic communication, the speaker typically takes as common ground with the hearer certain beliefs about the language system and, in particular, about familiar connections between linguistic forms (signifiers) and thoughts and concepts (signified). It would seem safe to assume this common ground in most conversations. The assumption can certainly not be maintained, however, in linguistic transactions with very young children. How then do children come to manipulate sounds (and ultimately other means of signaling) to express thoughts? The issue of how much the development of this ability depends on the child's experience and how much it reflects the biologically controlled maturation process does not concern us here. What I do want to stress is that parents usually act as if their child intentionally behaves in certain ways to express thoughts, even though they may well know better.

Let us imagine the bizarre case of a child whose exposure to language involved no social interaction. We might suppose that a loudspeaker intoned English sentences into the nursery and that the child's needs were attended to with no accompanying speech. This child might indeed begin to speak, matching the loudspeaker's output, but there would be no reason to assume that the child *meant* anything by articulating "I love you, Mommy." This child would be like the parrot that produces linguistic forms with no appreciation of how the wider speech community uses those forms.

In contrast, most children in English-speaking families have a radically different experience. When the child produces something like *ma* or *mama*—whether to imitate the language of others or just to attempt vocal control—the parents attach significance to the sounds: they treat the child as if the utterance meant 'mama'. That is, they begin to make it possible for the child to give this meaning to the sounds by showing that they have attended to those sounds, using the same or somewhat similar sounds themselves in conjunction with such actions as pointing to Mama or having Mama present herself to the child. The crucial thing is that children thus start to participate in a coordinative activity, recognizing their own and others' articulations as somehow the same. The motives they begin to attribute to others' articulations can also serve to guide their own. Let me emphasize that much of this development may well be guided by children's prewired or innate capacities and dispositions, including access to a fairly rich and highly structured conceptual system as well as a natural bent to coordinate their own speech with the articulations of their community. That is, children may have a preexisting stock of concepts waiting to have tags affixed; nonetheless, as tags are placed, some of those concepts are modified or joined with others in various ways that we do not yet clearly understand but that nonetheless result in the production of new conceptual systems. The conceptual systems that children evolve will to a considerable extent reproduce those prevalent in the community.

We cannot, in this essay, follow the child's entire linguistic development. What matters for our purposes is that the child and those around the child manage to *mean* something by what they say because (1) they jointly take the saying to be aimed at triggering a common recognition of thoughts and (2) they jointly take themselves to be relying on shared resources to achieve this coordinated recognition—a common language system plus a certain amount of shared experience. To a considerable extent, the coordination is achieved through the child's adapting to what is customary for the community. Those in the community, however, may also adapt to the child's productions—perhaps accepting novel forms or understanding the child as giving certain standard forms nontraditional meanings. But, by and large, the child and its parents do not endow language forms with meaning by coordinating their uses of them de novo. Rather, the parents (and all the other language users whom the child encounters) exploit the basic consensus achieved in earlier uses, and the meanings the child manages to produce in exchanges basically reproduce those already familiar in the community.

For certain concepts—especially for talking about perceptions of the external world—the reproduction of meaning is probably almost literally that, for the simple reason that children are evidently predisposed to note certain distinctions, to attend to certain sorts of environmental stimuli, and to ignore others. Their innate conceptual systems need only be aligned with the language system in their community. Apparently, for example, children who learn the *up-down* word pair through spatial uses do not need to be taught to apply it to ascending and descending melodies: psychologists have found that even very young prelinguistic infants make this connection between the visual and auditory domains. Nonetheless, most linguistically encoded concepts are not preformed but are produced, in at least their fine detail, as children familiarize themselves with the particular perspectives, beliefs, and practices of the community.

It is by no means clear, for example, that children initially give high priority to sorting people by sex rather than by other characteristics. In languages like Finnish, where *hän* is the only singular third-person pronoun, third-person [pronominal] reference is not differentiated by sex. There is no evidence I know of that Finnish children start by trying to introduce a marking of sex difference here. There is evidence, however, that some English-acquiring children do not find the *she-he* distinction

particularly congenial. Whether or not children find it natural to gender-
ize references to a person—to choose between *he* and *she* even where the
sexual information plays no particular role in what is communicated—
probably depends on how strongly genderization has figured in their
experience. In a household with children of both sexes, for example, the
special importance of sex sorting is likely to have established itself fairly
well by the time the youngest child is working at pronouns. But some
children do resist, perhaps because their rearing has been what Sandra
Bem (1983) calls *gender-aschematic*. Such children, acculturated into an
atypical framework, use the same form for everyone or use the masculine
and feminine pronouns in somewhat random fashion, not bothering to
attend to the distinction where it does not matter for their purposes. But
even they eventually go along with the larger community, and it seems
plausible that learning to make the required distinction can serve to
heighten the conceptual salience of sex sorting.

The main point here, again, is that endowing linguistic forms with
meaning is a socially situated process. The statement applies not just to
children learning to communicate but also to more mature speakers strug-
gling to convey increasingly complex thoughts. A major insight of the
Gricean perspective is that we can manage to mean much more than
what we literally say. How? By relying on what we take to be shared or
readily accessible beliefs and attitudes in a particular context.

We can suggest a framework for understanding how cultural biases
leave their mark on language systems, and, more generally, we can begin
to see why and how social inequality results in linguistic inequality. Our
focus will be on discourse inequalities created by the sexual division of
labor in producing situated meanings. Empirical research on conversational interaction among white middle-class Americans has convincingly
demonstrated the influence of sexual stratification on discourse, and I
want to extend these results to support an account of how sexual bias can
affect the (re)production of meaning.

The major findings on discourse are hardly surprising. Basically, in
cross-sex conversation men tend to dominate women in the following
ways: (1) they actually do more of the talking; (2) they interrupt women,
in the sense of seizing the floor, more often than women interrupt them;
and (3) they more often succeed in focusing the conversation on topics
they introduce (see, for example, Eakins and Eakins 1976; Fishman 1983;
Kramarae 1981; Swacker 1976; West and Zimmerman 1983; the sum-
mary in Treichler and Kramarae 1983; and the many other studies cited in
Thorne and Henley 1975 and in Thorne, Kramarae, and Henley 1983.) In
all these respects, the conversational relation between women and men
parallels that between children and adults, employees and employers, and
other power-differentiated groups. Not surprisingly, matters are more
complex than this thumbnail sketch implies; for example, neither interruption (of which there seem to be different kinds) nor amount of talk is
always indicative of control over a conversation, and correlation with sex

is affected by many contextual factors.[b] Certainly the proposed picture runs counter to some stereotypes—notably, that women are more talkative than men. If there is any truth to this notion, it may lie in situations other than those on which research has focused to date. For example, female groups may spend more of their time in talk than do male groups. Studies of single-sex conversation do suggest that women regard conversation more as a cooperative enterprise than as a competition, enlarging on and acknowledging one another's contributions, responding to co-conversationalists' attempts to introduce topics, and signaling active listening by nods and *mmhmms* during a partner's turn (see Edelsky 1981 and Kalčik 1975). In contrast, men generally view conversation more individualistically and less socially, with each participant's contribution self-contained and the 'right' to one's own turn taking priority over any 'responsibility' to others during their turns.

To some extent, women and men simply operate with different expectations about how linguistic interactions ought to proceed. For example, men are far less likely than women to give signals that say "I read you loud and clear." This is true not only when they talk with women but also when they talk with one another. A man may interpret another's *mmhmm* as agreement with what's been said, whereas a woman hears another's *mmhmm* as registering comprehension. One young man in a classroom where these differences were being discussed decided he sometimes might be assuming that his girlfriend agreed with him when indeed she was merely signaling that she was still receiving his communication. He resolved to try to distinguish the genuine signals of assent from those of simple connection. When he thought he had an affirmative response, he would stop and say, "Oh, so we're agreed about that." More often than not her reply was "Of course not." (I owe this anecdote to Ruth Borker.) Still, what is involved here is more than different expectations; it is also an exercise of power, whether intentional or not.

Daniel Maltz and Ruth Borker (1982) argue that women and men have different models of friendly conversation. Their account draws on such work as Kalčik's (1975) study of women's rap groups and Marjorie Harness Goodwin's (1980) analysis of directives issued by girls and boys to each other. From a somewhat different perspective, Carole Edelsky (1981) contends that in addition to the SINGLY HELD FLOOR that is normative in most conversational studies, there is in some conversations a COLLECTIVELY HELD FLOOR (these are my terms for her "F1" and "F2"); she observes that women participate on a more nearly equal basis with men under collective floor conditions. Undoubtedly, the full account of sexual differentiation in discourse will be far more complex than our current picture. For example, the more interactive orientation that women and girls have toward conversation does not mean that men and boys have

---

b. That the picture is indeed much more complicated emerges from Tannen 1989 and the reviews in James and Clarke 1993 and James and Drakich 1993.

a monopoly on conflict and disagreement—a point the Goodwins (1987) make very clear. Nonetheless, whatever the explanation, the evidence shows that men generally aim at individual conversational control, whereas women aim at social conversational collaboration.[c]

Male conversational control and female conversational collaboration are, of course, only tendencies: there are women who successfully interrupt men to steer the conversation in their own direction, and there are men who work at helping their female co-conversationalists develop a topic by asking questions, elaborating, or simply by actively indicating their continuing engagement in the listening process. Still, a common pattern involves the man's controlling and the woman's supporting cross-sex conversation. Nor is there any reason to believe that this behavior is somehow biologically rather than culturally produced. Early on, children are identified by others as girls or boys and learn to identify themselves in the same way. Tied to this identification is a process that typically leads them to acquire roughly the practices of linguistic communication that prevail among their same-sex peers (see Goodwin 1980). And linguistic communication, as one kind of social interaction, is embedded in more general political structures that children are, in some sense, being prepared to reproduce. Whatever the precise mechanisms, the net result is that sex is of considerable significance in the politics of talk among adults.

How does inequality in discourse affect what can be meant and by whom? First, men are more likely than women to have a chance to express their perspective on situations, not only because they have more frequent access to the floor but also because they are more actively attended to. This distinction is especially important, since comprehension goes well beyond simple recognition of the linguistic structures used. In other words, where the sexes have somewhat different perspectives on a situation, the man's view is more likely to be familiar to the woman than hers is to him. This observation leads directly to the second point: men are much more likely than women to be unaware that their own view is not universally shared. As a result, women and men may well be in quite different positions regarding what they believe to be commonly accepted (or accessible) in the speech community. This disparity in turn can have important consequences for what each is able to 'mean' when engaging in linguistic communication. Why? Because what is meant depends not just on the joint beliefs about the language system and its conventional—that is, standard or established—interpretations but also on what interlocutors take to be prevalent beliefs in the speech community about everything else besides language.

'New' or nonconventional meanings involve a speaker's intending the hearer to infer a purpose to the words beyond that of directing attention

---

c. Or at least at the appearance for men of a certain independence and for women of a certain considerateness.

to the thought 'literally' expressed. Let us take as an example the semantic development of *hussy*, a word that was once merely a synonym for *housewife*. How did it acquire its present meaning? And, once the sexual slur was produced, how was it reproduced and attached to the form so insistently that present generations do not even connect the two words? The example is not in itself important, since *hussy* hardly figures prominently in contemporary discourse, but it is useful for illustrative purposes because its historical development is well documented.

While we cannot, of course, recapture the discourse conditions in which this particular sexual insult was produced, we can sketch what may have happened and reconstruct the course of the word's shift in meaning. It seems plausible that some members of the speech community considered sexual wantonness a salient characteristic of the housewife. Such people could say *huswif* (or, perhaps, the somewhat shortened and familiar form *hussy*) and rely on their hearers to bring that characteristic to bear on interpreting the utterance. Thus they might say something like "What a hussy!" and try to mean just what such a comment conventionally means today. Of course, if they were wrong in supposing that their hearers would recognize this appeal to the negative stereotype, the attempted communication would fail. But the mere fact that the putative common belief was not universally shared would not in itself spell doom. So long as the negative stereotype of housewives was widely known, even hearers who did not accept it could recognize an appeal to it and understand that the term *hussy* was intended as an insult.

A contemporary example of semantic derogation can be found in what some younger speakers are now doing with the term *gay*. Elementary school children who do not connect the adjective with sexuality simply understand it as a word used to belittle. They will, of course, soon learn that *gay* refers to homosexuality and that the belittlement they rightly recognized in older speakers' use of the word is based on attitudes and emotions about sexuality. Often the early connotations will persist and become associated with homosexuality, tending to reinforce the pervasive heterosexism and homophobia in mainstream social groups.[d]

Or consider a somewhat subtler example. A man who means to insult me by saying "You think like a woman" can succeed. He succeeds not because I share his belief that women's thinking is somehow inferior but because I understand that he is likely to have such a belief and that his intention is not just to identify my thinking as an objectively characterizable sort but to suggest that it is flawed in a way endemic to women's thought. The crucial point is that I need not know his particular beliefs: I need only refer to what I recognize (and can suppose he intends me to recognize) as a common belief in the community.

---

d. In the couple of decades since this was first written, the word *gay* as an all-purpose insult, applied not only to people but to inanimate things and actions, has become even more widespread.

In contrast, it is much more difficult for me to mean to insult him by saying "You think like a man," because to recognize my intention he would not only have to know that my opinion of men's thinking is low, he would also have to believe that I know he so knows (or that I believe he so believes); though such an understanding is not unimaginable in a conversation between old acquaintances, it is quite unlikely in more general communication. And even where the intended insult works, it is construed as something of a joke or as a special usage, unless the stereotype disparaging women's thought (or at least elevating men's) is not familiar to both interlocutors. Thus it is easy to reproduce notions with widely established currency and difficult to produce unexpected or unfamiliar ones. I need not actually believe some commonplace, or even know that my interlocutor does, in order to attribute to him (my choice of pronouns here and throughout this essay is deliberate) the intention to treat it as a view we share. Indeed, even if I explicitly deny that view, I may end up doing so by acknowledging that it is generally believed. Thus, as Finn Tschudi (1979) observes, to say "Women think as well as men do" is already to acknowledge that the standard for comparison is men's thought. No matter how much I might wish to insult someone by saying that *she* or *he* thinks like a man, I could not so intend without relying on more than general linguistic and cultural knowledge.

There are complications, of course. We may each be aware that the general stereotype is under attack. Until it is decisively destroyed, however, the possibility remains that someone will purport to take it as a shared belief—and thereby succeed in relying on it to convey meaning, unless the 'purporting' is exposed. As the stereotype fades, however, the meaning it conveyed may remain but become reattached to the linguistic form as part of its literal meaning. Thus the view of housewives as hussies might not have been robust enough to sustain all the intended uses of *hussy* to insult, but so long as enough of these uses succeeded, subsequent language users could be directed immediately to the insult without a detour through the extralinguistic attitudes. In other words, when enough such insults work in situations that the speakers can take as precedent-setting, where the insult is recognized and associated with the term rather than with the negative view that initiated the term's derogatory connotation, the facilitating stereotype becomes superfluous. One can rely on earlier language experience to reproduce the meaning formerly produced by the stereotype.

This discussion leads to the related issues of what speakers take as background beliefs about the interpretations 'standardly' assigned in the speech community, that is, the literal meanings that can be assumed as 'defaults' in talking with others (operative unless something special in the discourse triggers alternative interpretations). One could, once upon a time, call someone a *hussy* and not intend to insult her. One can no longer do so, however, since a contemporary speaker who is familiar with the form can hardly fail to know how it is now standardly taken—and certainly

cannot count on an unfamiliar interlocutor to ignore the negative evaluation. As we probably all realize, for example, it is becoming harder and
harder to make *he* mean 'she or he' because only incredibly isolated
speakers can have missed the controversy over the so-called generic masculine, the dispute over whether users of *he* in sex-indefinite contexts
indeed intend to refer to both sexes and, if they do, how well they succeed
in getting their hearers to recognize that intention. (The introductory
essay in Frank and Treichler 1989 describes this debate at length.) Given
the doubts raised, one cannot say *he* and mean 'she or he' because one
cannot generally expect hearers to make this identification. Humpty-
Dumpty said to Alice, "When I use a word it means exactly what I choose
it to mean," but that was, to a considerable extent, wishful thinking.
Suppose we intend others to recognize a certain thought or concept just
by understanding the linguistic forms we have used. This intention will be
reasonable only if we can expect our listeners to believe with us that the
speech community indeed associates that thought or concept with those
linguistic forms. That is, we must get others to cooperate with us in giving
our words the meaning we want. At the very least, our listeners must recognize our intention and help us by acknowledging that recognition.

It may well be that women play a major role in reproducing meanings
that do not serve their own purposes or express their own perspectives.
They are fully aware that female perspectives are not viewed as commonly held (indeed, are often not recognized at all) and, in the interests
of facilitating communication, they allow men to continue to believe that
a distinctively male view of things is actually not particular but universal.
"This is the oppressor's language," says Adrienne Rich (1971), "yet I need
it to talk to you." Indeed, some have argued that language is so little
'woman's language' that women cannot even manage to mean what they
say, much less achieve success in meaning more.

This view has been persuasively elaborated by the philosopher Sara
Ann Ketchum (1979). How, she asks, can a woman manage to mean 'no'
to a man's "Would you like to go to bed?" She says *no* with sincerity but
he interprets her through a filter of beliefs that transform her direct negative into an indirect affirmative: "She is playing hard to get, but of course
she really means 'yes'." But of course she does not mean 'yes'; assent is not
what she intends to convey. I would contend that indeed she does mean
'no', even though she faces an extraordinary problem in trying to communicate that meaning to someone ready to hear an affirmative no matter
what she says. (I am not, of course, claiming that one never means 'yes' by
uttering *no* but only that one often does not; this is the case we are now
considering.) Only if she knows that he will never take her *no* to mean
'no' can she not intend the negation. Yet she still would not mean 'yes'; his
refusal to cooperate in her attempts to communicate 'no' might reduce
her to a desperate silence, but his unreasonableness, his unwillingness to
apprehend her as someone who might mean 'no', can never compel her to
mean 'yes'. Even though what my words mean does not depend solely

on my intentions, Humpty-Dumpty is right that it does require those intentions.

Nonetheless, Ketchum's main point certainly stands: meaning is a matter not only of individual will but of social relations embedded in political structures. A positive moral can be drawn from this observation as well: it is possible to produce new meanings in the context of a community or culture of supportive and like-thinking people. I can mean 'no' if my intention is supported by a feminist network that recognizes the sexual double standard and articulates male myths regarding female sexual behavior: I am not a single, isolated individual refusing to submit but, rather, part of a collectivity resisting sexism and violence against women. More generally, women are together challenging the view that 'the' culture is what men have told them it is or that 'the' language is what is available and what women must reproduce on pain of being condemned to a solitary silence. Rather, women are uncovering the myth of univocality and discovering new voices, their own and their sisters'.

The philosopher Naomi Scheman has illustrated how a feminist community can produce new meanings. Scheman (1980) looks at how consciousness evolves—is in some sense created—in a women's consciousness-raising group: using a mass of internal inchoate stuff, women can work together to form something coherent, to build conceptual structures that allow them both to interpret their own experience and to express that interpretation to others. In other words, they do not just tag preexisting concepts but generate new ones. They are able to think new thoughts, to realize, for example, that they may have been angry without recognizing what they felt. This thought is new not just in particular instances but also in its broader implications—enabling women to interpret an earlier emotion as anger when they did not do so at the time, because their language use did not then offer that possibility. This new interpretation matters because it connects past emotions to the option of purposeful current actions. Women cannot 'mean' alone but they can collaborate to produce new meanings and support the reproduction of those meanings in the community.

The research contrasting women's and men's approaches to discourse suggests, in fact, that women may be especially well suited to producing significantly new meanings. Because this possibility depends on the development of a shared new outlook, it might be better promoted in the cooperative mode of discourse than in the competitive, where less attention is paid to the other (and where one extracts meaning by assuming that the speaker reproduces earlier linguistic habits and familiar modes of thinking). It is true, of course, that women will find it harder to express their distinctive perspectives to men than vice versa so long as sexist patterns and practices persist. Nonetheless, women might collectively reshape their conceptual systems, particularly the ways they think about women and men, about individuals and social relationships, and about language and its connection to the individuals and their communities.

Is this possibility what the French feminists mean when they speak of an *écriture féminine*, what English-speaking feminists like Mary Daly mean when they talk of a new 'gynocentric' ['woman-centered'] language? Perhaps, though calls urging women to produce their own meanings are sometimes interpreted as implying that they must leave the old and familiar language to 'him'. But they cannot begin de novo. Just as the child must start somewhere—and presumably draws heavily on a conceptual structure that is biologically endowed—so must women. It was because the women in Scheman's consciousness-raising group could assume they all had access to a common language system that they could evolve together views that differed in important ways from familiar interpretations of that system. No matter what women intend to mean by their new language, they can convey that meaning only if they can expect others to recognize the thoughts to which the language aims to direct attention. And if there are indeed new meanings to be reproduced after they are initially produced in specific contexts, then women must find a community both able and willing to apprehend those new meanings.

It is a matter not just of what women manage to mean but also of what all of us, women and men, interpret others as meaning and, ultimately, of what we help or hinder others to mean. As I pointed out earlier, feminist research has established that *he*, no matter what its user intends, is not unproblematically interpreted as generic, and the consequent shift in the community's beliefs about how *he* is interpreted has influenced what one can intend the pronoun to convey. There are now many contexts in which those who are aware of these developments cannot expect *he* to be understood as 'he or she', no matter how much they might wish they could. A footnote explaining one's generic intentions does not suffice, since some readers will doubt the sincerity of that announcement and others will forget it. This is not to say that now no one ever means 'he or she' by using *he*: my point is just that it is much harder to convey that meaning than it used to be, in large measure because we now know that many earlier attempts were unsuccessful and that many purported attempts were, in fact, spurious. (Martyna [1978, 1980a, 1980b] provides empirical evidence that the actual use and interpretation of so-called generic masculines are quite different from what grammar books prescribe.)

Language matters so much precisely because so little matter is attached to it: meanings are not given but must be produced and reproduced, negotiated in situated contexts of communication. Negotiation is always problematic if an inequality of resources enables one negotiator to coerce the other. And because negotiation involves achieving consensus about beliefs and attitudes, it is not surprising that dominant groups have an unfair advantage in working out ways of meaning that are congenial to their beliefs and attitudes. The picture is much more complex than I have indicated here, but the basic point should be clear. Meanings are produced and reproduced within the political structures that condition discourse: though a sexist politics may have helped some men to "steal the power of naming," that power—a real one—can be reappropriated by feminist women and men building new language communities.

References

Abel, Elizabeth (ed.) (1981). Writing and sexual difference. Special issue, *Critical Inquiry* 8: 173–403.

Bach, Kent, and Robert M. Harnish (1979). *Linguistic communication and speech acts.* Cambridge: MIT Press.

Bem, Sandra Lipsitz (1983). The developmental implications of gender schema theory: Raising gender-aschematic children in a gender-schematic society. *Signs: Journal of Women in Culture and Society* 8: 598–616.

Benstock, Shari (ed.) (1987). *Feminist issues in literary scholarship.* Bloomington: Indiana University Press.

Daly, Mary (1973). *Beyond God the Father: Toward a philosophy of Women's Liberation.* Boston: Beacon.

——— (1978). *Gyn/ecology: The metaethics of Radical Feminism.* Boston: Beacon.

Eakins, Barbara Westbrook, and R. Gene Eakins (1976). Verbal turn-taking and exchanges in faculty dialogue. In Betty Lou Dubois and Isabel Crouch (eds.), *Proceedings of the Conference on the Sociology of the Languages of American Women.* Papers in Southwest English. San Antonio: Trinity University, 53–62.

Edelsky, Carole (1981). Who's got the floor? *Language in Society* 10: 383–421.

Eisenstein, Hester, and Alice Jardine (eds.) (1980). *The future of difference.* Boston: Hall.

Fishman, Pamela (1983). Interaction: The work women do. In Thorne, Kramarae, and Henley 1983, 89–101.

Frank, Francine Wattman, and Paula A. Treichler, eds. (1989). *Language, gender, and professional writing: Theoretical approaches and guidelines for nonsexist usage.* New York: Modern Language Association.

Garner, Shirley Nelson, Claire Kahane, and Madelon Sprengnether (eds.) (1985). *The (m)other tongue: Essays in feminist psychoanalytic interpretation.* Ithaca: Cornell University Press.

Goodwin, Marjorie Harness (1980). Directive-response speech sequences in girls' and boys' task activities. In McConnell-Ginet, Borker, and Furman 1980, 157–173.

Goodwin, Marjorie Harness, and Charles Goodwin (1987). Children's arguing. In Susan U. Philips, Susan Steele, and Christine Tanz (eds.), *Language, gender, and sex in comparative perspective.* Cambridge: Cambridge University Press, 200–248.

Grice, H. Paul (1957). Meaning. *Philosophical Review* 66: 377–388.

——— (1967). William James Lectures. Harvard University. Cambridge.

——— (1968). Utterer's meaning, sentence-meaning and word-meaning. *Foundations of Language* 4: 225–242.

——— (1969). Utterer's meanings and intentions." *Philosophical Review* 78: 147–177.

[James, Deborah, and Sandra Clarke (1993). Women, men and interruptions: A critical review. In Tannen 1993, 231–280.]

[James, Deborah, and Janice Drakich (1993). Understanding gender differences in amount of talk: A critical review of research. In Tannen 1993, 281–312.]

Kalčik, Susan (1975). '...Like Ann's gynecologist or the time I was almost raped': Personal narratives in women's rap groups. *Journal of American Folklore* 88: 3–11.

Ketchum, Sara Ann (1979). Reflections on meaning and power. Eastern Division, Fall Meeting, Society for Women in Philosophy. Ithaca, November 1979.

Kramarae, Cheris (1980). Proprietors of language. In McConnell-Ginet, Borker, and Furman 1980, 58–68.

———— (1981). *Women and men speaking: Frameworks for analysis*. Rowley, MA: Newbury.

Lewis, David (1969). *Convention*. Cambridge: Harvard University Press.

Maltz, Daniel N., and Ruth A. Borker (1982). A cultural approach to male-female miscommunication. In John J. Gumperz (ed.), *Language and social identity*. Cambridge: Cambridge University Press, 195–216.

Martyna, Wendy (1978). "What does 'he' mean? Use of the generic masculine." *Journal of Communication* 28(1): 131–138.

———— (1980a). Beyond the he/man approach: The case for nonsexist language. *Signs: Journal of Women in Culture and Society* 5: 482–493. Rev. and rpt. In Thorne, Kramarae, and Henley 1983, 25–37.

———— (1980b). The psychology of the generic masculine. In McConnell-Ginet, Borker, and Furman 1980, 69–78.

McConnell-Ginet, Sally (1980). Linguistics and the feminist challenge. In McConnell-Ginet, Borker, and Furman 1980, 3–25.

———— (1984). The origins of sexist language in discourse. In Sheila J. White and Virginia Teller (eds.), *Discourses in reading and linguistics. Annals of the New York Academy of Sciences* 433: 123–135.

[———— (2006). Why defining is seldom 'just semantics': Marriage, 'marriage', and other minefields. In Betty Birner and Gregory Ward (eds.), *Drawing the boundaries of meaning: Neo-Gricean studies in pragmatics and semantics in honor of Laurence R. Horn*. Amsterdam: John Benjamins, 223–246. Shortened version anthologized in Deborah Cameron and Don Kulick (eds.), *Language and sexuality: A reader*, 227–240. London: Routledge.]

[———— (2008). Words in the world: How and why meanings can matter. *Language* 84(3), 497–527.]

McConnell-Ginet, Sally, Ruth Borker, and Nelly Furman, eds. (1980). *Women and language in literature and society*. New York: Praeger.

Rich, Adrienne (1971). *The will to change: Poems 1968–1970*. New York: Norton.

———— (1979). *On lies, secrets, and silence: Selected prose 1966–1978*. New York: Norton.

Scheman, Naomi (1980). Anger and the politics of naming. In McConnell-Ginet, Borker, and Furman 1980, 174–187.

Schiffer, Stephen (1972). *Meaning*. London: Oxford University Press.

Schulz, Muriel R. (1975). The semantic derogation of women. In Thorne and Henley 1975, 64–75.

Spender, Dale (1980). *Man made language*. London: Routledge.

Stanley, Julia Penelope (1977). Paradigmatic woman: The prostitute. In D. L. Shores (ed.), *Papers in language variation*. Birmingham: University of Alabama Press.

Swacker, Marjorie (1976). Women's verbal behavior at learned and professional conferences. In Betty Lou Dubois and Isabel Crouch (eds.), *Proceedings of the Conference on the Sociology of the Languages of American Women*. Papers in Southwest English. San Antonio: Trinity University, 155–160.

[Tannen, Deborah (1989). Interpreting interruption in conversation. In Bradley Music, Randolph Graczyk, and Caroline Wiltshire (eds.), *Papers from the 25th Annual Regional Meeting of the Chicago Linguistic Society. Part two:*

Parasession on language in context Chicago: Chicago Linguistics Society, 266–87.]

[——— (ed.) (1993). *Gender and conversational interaction*. New York: Oxford University Press.]

Thorne, Barrie, and Nancy Henley (eds.) (1975). *Language and sex: Difference and dominance*. Rowley, MA: Newbury.

Thorne, Barrie, Cheris Kramarae, and Nancy Henley (eds.) (1983). *Language, gender and society*. Rowley: Newbury.

Treichler, Paula A. (1986a). Language, feminism, theory: Entering decade three. *Women and Language* 10(1): 5–36.

——— (1986b). Teaching feminist theory. In Cary Nelson (ed.), *Theory in the classroom*. Urbana: University of Illinois Press, 57–128.

Treichler, Paula A., and Cheris Kramarae (1983). Women's talk in the ivory tower. *Communications Quarterly* 31: 118–132.

Tschudi, Finn (1979). Gender stereotypes reflected in asymmetric similarities in language. Paper presented at the annual meeting of the American Psychological Association in New York, September 1979.

Vetterling-Braggin, Mary (ed.) (1981). *Sexist language: A modern philosophical analysis*. Totowa, NJ: Littlefield.

West, Candace, and Don H. Zimmerman (1983). Small insults: A study of interruptions in cross-sex conversations between unacquainted persons. In Thorne, Kramarae, and Henley 1983, 103–117.

9

Prototypes, pronouns, and persons

0. Introduction

The science of linguistics has emphasized that linguistic categories and rules are not prescribed by authorities or created by fiat but represent shared principles, some of which may be biologically determined, underlying the actual speech of the community. Speakers themselves may not be able to articulate these principles, and even linguists may disagree on how best to describe the system underlying observed linguistic behavior. But linguists of all theoretical persuasions agree that a grammar of a language constitutes an empirically testable theory of how the language is structured at some particular stage in its history. And most linguists also want a grammar to give some account of the systematic variation exhibited in the realization of certain structural elements, since such variation plays a critical role in the development of new linguistic systems, new stages in the history of the language.

This essay has two main aims: (1) to provide a set of observed usages and elicited judgments of acceptability for constructions involving anaphoric personal pronouns with singular antecedents, and (2) to account for these data by presenting a partial semantic analysis of the pronoun set consisting of *he, she,* and *they.*

Recent discussions of the sexist implications of pronoun usage have done relatively little to enhance our understanding of the semantic structure of pronouns. Feminists who claim that the generic use of the masculine *he* is unclear or unfair or both have often uncritically accepted an overly simple view of linguistic structure and functioning. On the other hand, linguists have mainly responded in a prescriptivist tone by trying to set people straight on what the pronouns 'really' mean or by knocking down straw women espousing absurdly naive views of the relation between language, culture, and cognition.[1]

Some possible ways of misunderstanding and some shaky defenses of the claim that lack of a common-gender pronoun supports sex-based

This essay was first published in Madeleine Mathiot (ed.), *Ethnolinguistics: Boas, Sapir and Whorf Revisited* (The Hague: Mouton, 1979), 63–83. An earlier, shorter version was presented January 27, 1976, to the Linguistics and Women's Studies Programs of the University of Arizona.

discrimination can be easily set aside. (1) Lack of sex-based distinctions in third-person pronouns does not guarantee a nonsexist social order. Chinese and Eskimo cultures, for example, establish this point. It is not clear that anyone has ever believed otherwise, but because responses to allegations of sexism implicit in pronominal usage often fish up this red herring, we had better kill it off at the outset. (2) Nor is it obvious that only a sexist culture could support such distinctions, although in the absence of any nonsexist cultures, this claim cannot really be tested. It is probably true that only in a culture giving substantive significance to sex differences could such a pervasive marking of those differences develop and be retained. (3) Suppose that *she* is marked for a feature (femininity or sexuality) that *he* simply lacks (i.e., is unmarked for). This fact in itself would not show any implicit derogation of women. Dravidian languages have two gender classifications for nouns, the marked category reserved for men and deities, with women, cabbages, and sealing wax falling into the unmarked class. The situation is slightly more complicated than this and varies among these languages, but the point is clear: linguistic markedness need not denote a low cultural valuation relative to the unmarked category. (4) Speakers who attempt (and more or less succeed) following the prescriptive norm—"*he* must be used for indefinite or mixed-sex singular reference"—need not thereby be behaving in a sexist fashion. Those who come to believe that some features of this usage do enter into the maintenance of sex stereotyping may decide to attempt to change this pattern, substituting *he or she* or singular *they*, and meet with only mixed success.

Although some feminists have seemed to believe that the generic use of *he* is simply the figment of the androcentric mind, accustomed to identifying humanity with (male) men, there is evidence that *he* really is still less sex-exclusive than *she*.[a] On the other hand, *she* is not restricted to female sex reference and neither *he* nor *she* but only the phrase *he or she* or a singular *they* fits in certain contexts. These facts plus the facts of pronouns used to refer to specific individuals strongly support the folk wisdom that *he* is indeed masculine and not simply unmarked for femininity.

A first approximation of a semantic feature analysis of the personal pronoun set is given in table 9.1. In this view, *he or she* will receive positive markings for both the gender features MASCULINE and FEMININE. This is so simple as to seem simple-minded, but the bulk of the essay will be devoted to supporting and amplifying this analytic schema.[b] Section 1 sketches briefly the history of gender as a linguistic category in English

---

a. Although sex-indefinite *he* is somewhat less frequent in 2010 (and singular *they* found in a wider range of contexts) than in the late 1970s, it is still encountered and is more common than sex-indefinite *she*.

b. Even when this paper was originally written, I was not a fan of semantic features but set myself the challenge of using them in analyzing English pronouns. Although I would frame things differently from my current viewpoint, many of the observations made still hold and are still, I think, underappreciated.

Table 9.1

	MASCULINE	FEMININE
He (him, his)	+	0
She (her, hers)	–	+
They (their, them, theirs)	0	0

pronouns, and sections 2, 3, and 4 consider the patterns of usage of *she, he or she* and singular *they*, respectively. *It* has not been included in this study.[2]

In section 5, I suggest that singular generics are generally treated as denoting some possibly nonexistent prototype of the genus in question. Prototypes need not be common to the linguistic community, but definite generics do presuppose a specific prototype available for reference. Definite singular generics thus seem to parallel in interesting ways literary personifications, representations of abstract concepts as individual fictive persons in some sense 'embodying' the concepts so treated. Definite singular generics that represent some human prototype are only with difficulty interpreted as gender-indefinite. Attempts to avoid reference to a gendered prototype are resulting in increased numbers of references to prototype pairs (*he or she*) and to gender-indefinite but more abstract, less fully 'personified', prototypes (*they*).

The implications of the analysis are explained and developed in more detail in section 6. Conditions governing pronoun interpretation and production are outlined; some of these are probably not part of the linguistic system as such but rather underlie more general cognitive and cultural processes being brought into play by speakers. Certainly, speakers' attitudes and beliefs about the world and the communicative situation in which they find themselves help determine what linguistic resources they will use to try to accomplish a particular communicative task. Whether or not success is achieved depends, in part, on the extent to which addressees and speakers share knowledge about the world as well as on linguistic competence.

Linguistic meaning is fairly narrowly interpreted in this study. I am taking linguistic meaning to be conventional and shared by the members of the speech community even though their worldviews may differ dramatically. In particular, in trying to isolate the linguistically significant features determining the meaning of the utterance, I avoid arguments over what a particular speaker may or may not 'have had in mind' on the occasion of some utterance. This is not to say that meanings, any more than phonological or syntactic systems, are invariant and immune to change, nor is it to deny that semantic distinctions relate in important ways to cognitive processes, mental states, and speakers' intentions. But it is to claim that two different utterances, or utterance-partials, can be identical in linguistic meaning even if on one occasion of utterance the speaker's aims, mental images, and the like are completely different from those of the speaker on the occasion of the other utterance. Linguistic meaning is basically determined negatively: the meaning of a linguistic form is a matter of its opposition to other forms. A single form usually enters into opposition with a number of other forms in different linguistic and extralinguistic contexts. All systematic formal distinctions recognized by the community on the basis of knowledge of the linguistic system and its characteristic uses as communicatively significant are linguistically meaningful.

Understood loosely, the meaning of a linguistic item is the conventional or public communicative potential it has: the range of its actual and possible usages and the paradigmatic oppositions into which it enters. Knowledge of a particular speaker's habits and circumstances is mainly useful in determining the paradigmatic oppositions that need to be taken into account to understand that instance of use of some linguistic item. For example, if a particular speaker virtually always uses *he* in reference to a sex-indefinite or mixed-sex singular antecedent, more significance can be attached to the choice of *she* or *he or she* for such an antecedent than if the speaker were someone who habitually avoided *he* for such antecedents or made some conscious effort to try to avoid such uses of *he*. There is considerable variation in individual speakers' choices of forms along with similar variations in elicited judgments of what can sensibly be said, given an hypothesized context and communicative aim. At some level, such variation is consistent with a shared semantic system. We can try to accommodate the variation within the system in much the same way that phonological and syntactic variation are handled in current sociolinguistic studies.[3] Indeed, what I have called semantic variation may be syntactic variation at its lowest level: the relation between syntactically significant units and communicative function.

For a group of speakers with the same paradigmatic repertoire, we can suppose a common system if the relations among the different usages are in some sense explained in terms of the same rule or classificatory features differentially employed or realized. And it must be emphasized that different habits of production are quite consistent with a common pattern for interpretation or understanding. Jakobsonian semantic theory speaks of an invariant meaning, the basic meaning common to all usages of a form. This meaning is characterized in terms of classificatory features that can have a wide range of contextually realized variants. The classificatory features of the invariant meaning take only the values MARKED and UNMARKED, where markedness denotes the necessary presence of a feature. A form unmarked with respect to a feature is simply not marked with respect to it: that is, it does not necessarily have the feature in question. In context, a form unmarked with respect to some classificatory feature may connote the absence of the feature (this variant is known as the GRUNDBE-DEUTUNG, or basic meaning) or, alternatively, imply nothing about the presence or absence of the feature (the GESAMTBEDEUTUNG, or general meaning).[4] The analysis offered in this essay distinguishes the personal pronouns in terms of features that are classificatory in the Jakobsonian sense but also includes some semantic rules, which could be compared to phonological rules, that describe in part the mapping of contexts into contextual variants. The observant reader will note that the feature MASCULINE takes three basic values, +, −, and 0, in table 9.1. This will be eliminated from the final analysis but provides a convenient way to represent the facts at a glance.

An alternative view might use semantic functions rather than features to represent the contribution a linguistic item makes to the meaning of utterances in which it occurs. Such functions could be thought of as mapping linguistic items and contexts of an utterance specified linguistically and extralinguistically to determine the publicly available meaning of the entire utterance. Since features are more familiar to linguists and anthropologists than functions, I will not pursue this alternative approach further.

The main points of interest in the present study are independent of the theoretical framework adopted to explain the empirical evidence. The critical cases and their linguistic significance are hard to dispute: I have taken pains to use only unequivocal data. The hypothesized parallel between definite singular generics and the poetic device of personification discussed in section 5 goes somewhat beyond the linguistic data and requires further support from a supplementary psycholinguistic study. That prototypes and conceptions of personhood play a role in our understanding of singular definite generics and that their anaphoric pronoun substitutes play some, probably minor, role in the perpetuation of sex-stereotyping can be definitively established only by a careful empirical study that uses nonlinguistic paradigms and methodologies. Whatever their cognitive correlates turn out to be, prototypes do appear to provide a means of distinguishing the singular definite generic from indefinites and from bare plurals and also capture the parallelism between such constructions and personifications.

1. Feminine/masculine in the history of English pronouns

Gender, in a common use, is roughly equivalent to *sex*. In current anthropology, sociology, and psychology, gender is taken to embrace sociocultural conceptions of sex and sex differences as distinguished from biological sex conceptions. The terms *feminine/masculine* are in principle reserved for gender categories, and *female/male* for sex. In practice, the gender terms tend to be used when speaking of matters in which actual sex diverges somewhat from sociocultural expectations, beliefs, and the like. Sex is a matter of anatomy. Destiny is gender, reflecting culture-specific views of the significance of a person's sex for personality, social roles, and political participation.[c]

c. See chapter 1, part 1, of this book for discussion.

This useful distinction between gender and sex was developed in the context of the linguistic distinction between the biological or physical category of sex and the symbolic or linguistic category of gender.[5] All histories of the English language note that English, like the other Germanic languages, inherited the Indo-European system of 'grammatical' gender, distinguishing three gender classes of nouns. These are traditionally called masculine, feminine, and neuter. This sex-based terminology reflects the fact that most nouns referring, by virtue of their meaning, exclusively to male humans fell into the masculine class and no such nouns fell into the feminine class, that most nouns referring exclusively to female humans fell into the feminine class and that none of these was in the masculine gender. An obvious counterexample is the compound form *wifman*, which was masculine; the basic female element here, *wif*, is simply neuter, however. Gender classes determined, of course, the form of articles and demonstratives and, to some extent, adjectives occurring with the noun. It is a linguistic commonplace to point out that there was no semantic consistency to these gender classes beyond the rather limited connection with sex just noted. For example, OE *hand*, *giefu*, and *duru* (hand, gift, door) were all feminine. *Mearh* (related to the word whose modern reflex is *mare*), *fōt* (foot), and *stān* (stone) belonged to the masculine class, and *wīf*, *cild*, and *scip* (woman, child, and ship) were neuter.[6] It would be patently silly to suppose that masculine gender for nouns denoting horses, stones, and feet rested on English speakers' thinking of such things as significantly more like male beings than hands, doors, and gifts, somehow assimilated to femaleness.[7] (Compare, however, the quotation from Jakobson in section 5 below.)

OE anaphoric pronouns were generally selected in agreement with the gender class of the antecedent noun. Perhaps the most important reason that the sex-based terminology seemed so natural is that referential use of a pronoun lacking a linguistic antecedent was determined by the extralinguistic facts about sex, where that was relevant. The change from this system of syntactically significant gender classification of nouns to the present system of 'logical' (semantically relevant) gender was accomplished when nouns, adjectives, and articles lost gender-distinguished inflectional endings and a semantically consistent basis of selection for anaphoric pronouns was established. A seldom-noted fact is that OE, and apparently virtually all other languages with sex-related syntactic gender, allowed anaphoric pronouns to be chosen optionally in accord with actual sex of referent rather than in agreement with syntactic gender, where the two conflicted. To a lesser extent, this appears also to have been true of the animacy, or humanness, dimension of the gender system. The following example is by no means atypical:

(1)   pa *pæt wif* a loh   wereda drihtnes
       nalles glredlice   ac *heo* gearum frod

       then *the woman* (neuter article) laughed at the lord by no means kindly
       for *she* (feminine pronoun) was advanced of years

One linguist summed it up nicely: "natural gender did not *replace* grammatical gender in Middle English but survived it."[8]

What, however, is natural gender? It is sometimes argued that English nouns can still be seen as divided into gender classes, a categorization only covertly realized when the noun is replaced by an anaphoric pronoun.[9] A formulation of this view that struck me especially when I first encountered it is the following:

> The distinction, then, between the pronoun-forms *he* and *she*, creates a classification of our personal nouns into *male* (defined as those for which the definite substitute is *he*) and *female* (similarly defined by the use of the substitute *she*). Semantically, this classification agrees fairly well with the zoological division into sexes.[10]

Leonard Bloomfield was an astute linguistic observer. Why did he seem to ignore the existence of generic *he*? For instance, on the basis of his own text, *child* and *speaker* are put into the male class.

(2)   Suppose, for instance, that day after day *the child* is given *his* doll (and says *da, da, da*) immediately after *his* bath. (p. 30)

(3)   Even if we know a great deal about *a speaker* and about the immediate stimuli which are acting upon *him*, we usually cannot predict whether *he* will speak or what *he* will say. (p. 32)

The correlation with 'zoological sex' is not as close as it was when social roles were mostly sex-exclusive, but pronouns do impose semantic masculinity or femininity on their nominal antecedents. So although Bloomfield's formulation is clearly inadequate in important ways (why, for instance, should all nouns denoting roughly equal numbers of males and females get assigned to the masculine class rather than having such clearly common-gender nouns distributed roughly between the two genders?), if we understand 'semantically' broadly enough and incorporate gender as a pronominal feature, Bloomfield is basically right.

The view of gender as a covert grammatical category was challenged by Hall (1951, 172), who claims that "the apparent instances of gender agreement cited by Whorf are simply examples of sex reference (realistic or conventionalized) as one aspect of nominal and pronominal meaning." Hockett (1958) suggests that one way to treat gender as a formal classification of nouns is to recognize seven classes, corresponding to all combinations of one or more of the three singular pronouns *he, she,* and *it*. The main problem with this approach and other attempts to treat gender as a nominal feature copied onto pronouns is the absence of any principled explanation for choice among the pronouns where a noun belongs to a class associated with such choice.

Gender in contemporary English seems best described as a semantic principle governing pronominal oppositions. Formal properties of noun phrase antecedents do not determine anaphoric pronoun replacements. Rather, the anaphoric pronoun contributes to the interpretation given the antecedent. This view is neutral as to the relation between syntax and semantics. What it denies is that inherent syntactic or semantic features of the antecedent noun phrase determine gender of the anaphoric pronoun.

Gender must still, however, be kept distinct from sex reference. Gender in the pronouns is a linguistic category that is closely related to the category of sex reference but clearly not identical with it. Masculine and feminine are, in Bloomfield's terms, 'semantically' male and female, respectively. Hall appeals to 'conventionalized sex-reference'. If grammar is held to include linguistic semantics, as it generally is in current usage, then gender in contemporary English remains a grammatical category.

2. *She*

Although gender is to be distinguished from sex reference, the two coincide closely in standard uses of pronouns to refer to specific individuals. Utterances of sentences like (4) or (5) must be taken, in the absence of specific contextual cues to the contrary, to be intended as references to a male person or female person, respectively.

(4)   My roommate is a bore, and I don't want to room with him again next year.
(5)   My roommate is a bore, and I don't want to room with her again next year.

Where reference is established by extralinguistic means (pointing, for example), the same restriction holds:

(6)   He is a bore.
(7)   She is a bore.

Counter-instances do not arise in 'standard' usage and are completely unknown to many speakers. Yet they do occur. Newton (1972, 79) notes that "[d]rag queens almost invariably refer to each other as *she* among themselves, and often as *she* in gay company. The use of *she* reflects intimacy and social comfort. It is not professional—distant, formal—to refer to a man as *she* on stage."

She also occurs in reference to males in the speech of other homosexual men, but lesbians (according to my informants) do not refer to one another by using *he*. I have heard claims that such usages do occur, but all available empirical evidence strongly supports the view that pronoun 'switching' is overwhelmingly more common among male than female homosexuals. Why such an asymmetry should exist is an important and interesting question but beyond the scope of this essay.[11]

Mathiot and Roberts (1979) report *he* used by male professors in reference to a *female* college student:

(8)   I don't know about him. The way he writes is very strong and yet seem-
        ingly without emotion. It is very strange to have a woman write like that.
        It gives me the shakes.
(9)   This is what I told them: In contrast to many of the students today, he is
        alive and vibrant.

Mathiot accounts for these instances in terms of a male view of men as
intellectually competent as opposed to women and suggests that *he* may
also be used of a woman to express camaraderie or friendship: "a college
professor…when asked by one of his female students why he constantly
referred to her as 'he,' answered: '*Because you a regular fellow, a good guy.*'"
It is not clear from Mathiot's account whether such uses of the opposite-
sex pronoun in reference to a person whose sex was known occurred frequently in her data or whether we are dealing with the experience of
some one female student who, for whatever reasons, struck her professors
as eligible for admission to the male club.[12]

What does seem clear is that, in general, references to specific individuals whose sex is known or believed to be known choose the sex-
appropriate pronoun. Deviation from this pattern is relatively rare and is
generally viewed as an inverted use for some special purpose. In the most
common case, male homosexuals appear to be ascribing femininity (or, at
least, nonmasculinity) and asserting their own membership in the homosexual subculture. Most typically, use of either the masculine or the
feminine pronoun to refer to a specific individual is taken to be an attribution of male or female sex, respectively. And where speakers use either
he or *she* to refer to a person who turns out to be of the other sex, they
recognize themselves to have made a mistake. Clearly such mistakes often
reflect stereotypic conceptions of masculinity and femininity. One
example for each pronoun:

(10)   A: I've got to drive one of the kids to judo practice.
        B: How long has he been taking judo?
        A: *He's* a *she:* it's my daughter.
        B: Oh, I'm sorry. I didn't know girls, I mean I didn't think…oh, you
           know.
(11)   A: I talked to one of your students who is really worried about the
           exam.
        B: What does she know about it?
        A: It wasn't a *she* (laughing).
        B: (Trying to pretend nothing had happened) So how did he find out
           what the exam was like?

Such mistaken assumptions are encountered frequently, but the point is
that speaker B in dialogue (10) does not, cannot, claim a nonmasculine
use of *he*. Speaker B in (11), a male, was bothered by having revealed
unwittingly a sex-stereotyping assumption. Thus *he* and *she*, used to refer
to definite individual persons, attribute male and female sex, or sexuality,
respectively.

Therefore, a speaker who refers to someone cannot conceal sex of a female referent by choosing *he*. That is, to refer to someone known by the speaker to be a female with *he* is to deceive, not simply to leave the issue of sex indefinite. If *he* were simply unmarked for the feature FEMININE, one would expect that such uses would be possible. Of course, this does not establish that *he* is marked as MASCULINE: to cling to the view that *he* contrasts with *she* by virtue of its 0 FEMININE value, one could simply note that contexts involving reference to a specific individual allow only the GRUND-BEDEUTUNG (−FEMININE). Such a condition would be possible but is not usual with, for instance, nominal pairs that differ in markedness for some feature. Note that B in dialogue (12) is an inappropriate response to A since it unjustifiedly attributes to A a false statement.

(12)   A: Jane lost one of the shoes I lent her.
         B: No, it was your sandal she lost.

Although a sandal is a special kind of shoe and automatically included in talk of shoes, *she* is not just a special kind of *he* and saying *he* does not automatically include someone who could be designated by *she*.

Since references to specific individuals are the earliest kinds of uses children encounter, kids really have no evidence for supposing any difference in markedness between the pronouns and it seems unlikely that the child would hypothesize anything different from a masculine *he* and a feminine *she*. It is not surprising that children often do not recognize the generic use of *he* when they first encounter it. One child, who had been taught to read, looked at the official communication from the kindergarten to her parents: "Be sure that your child's outer garments are marked with his name." "Mommy," she said, "they think I'm a boy."[13]

What is often ignored is the wide range of uses of *she* where male reference is clearly a possibility. The examples most commonly cited are those involving roles or occupations stereotypically associated with women: *secretary, nurse, model*. For these cases, in which women's predominance is reflected in linguistic usage, the choice of *he* as an anaphoric substitute is taken as reference to a particular male whereas *she* substitutes for indefinite or generic antecedents without connoting female sex. Compare (13a) and (13b):

(13)   a. When the nurse comes, he'll take your blood pressure.
         b. When the nurse comes, she'll take your blood pressure.

Both are well-formed, but (13a) makes reference only to a male nurse whereas (13b) could be used quite correctly in a context where the nurse in question might be of either sex but the speaker was simply making a general statement applicable to whatever nurse happened to come. Note the oddity of (14) as a general characterization:

(14)   ?*The careful nurse will be sure he takes the right medicines to the right patients.

And *teacher*, as a number of observers have noted, tends to take a generic or indefinite *she*, even in communications from individuals who have daily contact with male teachers. The male head of a junior high department with roughly equal number of women and men teachers involved in the self-instruction program, including himself, issued the following department policy statement:

(15)   Students have to check with the teacher regularly so she knows how they're progressing.

The generic feminine is clearly an established usage, and such instances of *she* show that feminine gender must be distinguished from female sex reference.

Some examples of *she* where male reference is clearly not ruled out seem explicable in terms of their occurring in contexts in which the audience is mainly female:

(16)   Behaviorists believe that what a person does is determined by the situation in which she finds herself.

Example (16) occurred in an article in a mass-circulation women's magazine. Other uses probably involve speaker's sex stereotypes:

(17)   Physicians fear—with some reason—that a patient who discovers she can lose weight quickly, without hunger pangs, may fast unwisely on her own.

An interview with a quiz show emcee:

(18)   When I walk down to them and point my fingers and say "you," why that person even forgets her own name in the excitement.

(The show in question did use male contestants.)
   Of special interest are clear oppositions with *he*. A person (male) leading a discussion on teaching techniques had for more than twenty minutes talked about "a student," "the student," "the professor," and the like using *he* as anaphoric substitute. His shift was striking, yet I think it was unnoticed both by him and by most of his audience (a few other women and I exchanged meaningful glances):

(19)   When a student finally says something after sitting silently half the semester, don't intimidate her.

And even a noun like *parent*, wearing its sex neutrality on its sleeve in its primary use to provide a sex-indefinite alternative to *mother* and *father*, can occur with an indefinite or generic *she*.

(20)   When a parent hears her baby cry, she rouses quickly.

A lecture by a distinguished psychologist for whom "a speaker," "a child," and "a subject" were all *he* contained such a generic feminine reference to "a parent."

Use of *she* where male sex reference is possible does, however, require some kind of special explanation more often than not. *She* connotes the special salience of women to the context and the relatively low visibility of men in that context. Whether this special salience arises from cultural stereotypes, a speaker's personal experiences or beliefs, or shared knowledge of social realities does not seem to matter.

3. *He or she*

One increasingly popular reason for using *he or she* is to make explicit mention of the inclusion of women where they were previously excluded:

> (21)   Our department is looking for a new chairperson. He or she will be
>   expected to teach two courses annually at the graduate or undergrad-
>   uate level.

Many feminists have made a self-conscious attempt to abandon the generic use of *he* in favor of *he or she* and their influence is increasingly heard. Speakers often begin by minding their *he*'s and *she*'s, carefully monitoring pronouns and consistently choosing *he or she*, perhaps even *she or he* and sometimes even a shocking *she*, for sex-indefinite or mixed-sex antecedents, yet end up by lapsing into the generic masculine habits of yore. Guidelines to help eradicate sexism from texts advocate use of *he or she* in many cases where *he* was once the order of the day, but such guidelines are consistently adhered to only in carefully edited material.

To understand the masculine generic pattern that this explicitly dual-gender use is intended to replace, examples of opposition of the two patterns in a single context of usage are enlightening. From speakers with an established practice of using generic *he*, an unstudied *he or she* cries for explanation:

> (22)   ...the person feeling hysterical can be in total control. He or she, after
>   all, is the one making them hysterical in character.[14]

This occurred as the only instance of *he or she* in a book in which all other sex-indefinite nouns took an anaphoric *he* replacement. A paper on voting practices contained a number of instances of "the candidate" replaced by *he*, thereby making significant:

> (23)   The voter in the booth knows that he or she can not determine which
>   candidate will win.

Women are certainly not exceptionally dominant as voters, but they appear more highly visible in that role to the author than as candidates.

He or she is not sex-indefinite but explicitly includes both sexes. Where the possibility of a woman's being a referent has been overtly articulated in the discourse, most speakers choose *he or she* rather than *he*:

(24)   But it is also important for a teacher to be aware of the kind of language
          he or she is speaking: if a woman teacher...

This example is useful because it comes from a text whose author explicitly states that the usual rule for pronominal selection picks *he* where the
class is mixed-sex even if "predominantly female." This is the single instance of *he or she* for a sex-indefinite antecedent, and the occurrence of
"woman teacher," explicitly female, of course, in the succeeding discourse
suggests the explanation.

Special salience of women in the context of the sort that gave rise to
generic *she* (note examples in section 2 above) can be expressed with less
violence to the normative canons by use of *he or she*, and this form is
much more commonly encountered in writing than generic *she*.
Institutionalized generic *she*—"a good secretary"—does, of course, occur
frequently in written contexts. Examples abound, but I will cite only
one:

(25)   An economy-minded shopper will adjust her menus to take advantage
          of weekly specials.

The most interesting question is why *he* cannot be used in contexts
such as (26) and (27) without resulting in semantic anomaly:

(26)   If either spouse in a marriage wants a divorce, he or she (*he) should
          consult a good lawyer.
(27)   If either of my parents comes, he or she (*he) will bring a friend.

Cases (28) and (29) are even clearer:

(28)   Either my mother or my father will come next week, and she or he (*he)
          will stay until my birthday. They are going to toss a coin to see which
          one gets to take the trip.
(29)   The boy or girl who painted that picture should be proud of himself or
          herself (*himself).

A disjunction with a specifically female disjunct simply cannot take *he*
as an anaphoric replacement. "Either" of course, explicitly marks an
alternative, and our shared knowledge of marriage[d] and parenthood
accounts for the weirdness of (26) and (27). In the following example, in
order to conceal sex in reference to someone believed to be female, a
speaker avoids dishonesty by choosing *he or she*:

(30)   I will not reveal the identity of the murderer to you yet, my dear Charles,
          but he or she will be behind bars within the week.

These facts are completely inexplicable if *he* is assumed simply unmarked
for gender. *He* is inconsistent with a positively specified female reference.

(31)   *?My mother cooks all his own meals.

---

d. This ignores same-sex marriages, which I simply did not consider as a possibility three
decades ago.

And explicit mention of the possibility of female-reference virtually precludes *he* as in (26)—(29).

4. Singular *they*

They is of course sex-indefinite, unmarked as either FEMININE or MASCULINE. A number of writers have recently noted its widespread use as a sex-indefinite singular pronoun.[15] Examples (26)–(30) could all occur with *they* rather than *he* or *she*, and example (29) is for many speakers more natural with *themselves* than with the disjoined singular reflexives. With indefinite pronouns, all but the most determined purists[e] use *they*:

(32)   Anyone can pass the exam if they try.

Examples with the distributive quantifiers *every*, *each*, and *any* can readily be produced from the works of such authors as Shakespeare, Austen, Shelley, and Woolf as well as from the everyday discourse of almost everyone. *They* is also, however, used in reference to specific individuals:

(33)   Someone phoned you this afternoon, but they wouldn't give their name.

Singular indefinite generics appear possible with *they*:

(34)   When a person eats too much, they get fat.

What is most important for our present analysis is the apparent lack of *they* as anaphoric replacement for the singular definite generic:

(35)   *The child produces many utterances that they could not have heard.

The asterisk denotes the anomaly that many speakers associate with this particular kind of singular *they* anaphora, an anomaly not equally attributed to indefinite generics as in (34) or indefinite singular pronouns as in (33). Sentences like (35) have appeared in the writings of people adopting a policy of promoting singular *they* as a sex-indefinite pronoun just as generic *she* in contexts where *he* is the norm have begun to appear, but such sentences are still highly marked.[f]

---

e. According to Ingrid Tieken-Boon van Ostade, that purism traces back to a grammar of English published by Ann Fisher in the mid-eighteenth century. Fisher was apparently the first to formulate the rule "The *Masculine Person* answers to the *general Name*, which comprehends both *Male* and *Female*; as, *any Person who knows what he says*," although others have attributed its introduction to John Kirkby, who seems to have plagiarized Fisher's popular grammar. See Tieken-Boon van Ostade (2000) for more details on this interesting history.

f. Singular *they* has certainly widened its usage in the past thirty years, occurring not only in speech, as it has done for years, but also in formal writing. Matossian (1997) looks at

Whatever the difficulty with (35), (33) and (34) show that it can not be a matter of singularity or genericness. Even definiteness does not suffice to explain the difficulty:

(36)   The person I hate most in the world told me they would hide my Wheaties.

A possible explanation for the difficulty is suggested by considering anaphoric replacement of a proper name:

(37)   *Jackie went home, didn't they?

A proper name denotes a contextually unique and 'personalized' referent. How are we to understand singular definite generics? Perhaps, like 'Sin' and 'Death' in a medieval morality play, they name person-like beings, created for discourse purposes to represent genuses.

5. Prototypes

A prototype is a paradigmatic instance of some category—fictive or real. Now compare (38) and (39):

(38)   The child learns to use pronouns by the age of four.
(39)   Children learn to use pronouns by the age of four.

Bare plural subjects as in (39) differ from both definite and indefinite singular generics in that they simply replace something like a quantified noun phrase. That is, (39) is more or less equivalent to:

(40)   Most children learn to use pronouns by the age of four.

Example (38) is probably true only if (40) is true,[g] but another pair of examples will help make the contrast between (38), on the one hand, and (39) and (40), on the other, clearer.

(41)   I've canvassed every member of the LSA and found that linguists love pizza.
(42)   ?I've canvassed every member of the LSA and found that the linguist loves pizza.

generic pronouns in naturally occurring speech and finds women using more singular *they* than men, one of the few sociolinguistic studies in the United States finding women ahead of men in usage of a form that is prescriptively denounced. Newman (1997) is another interesting study of actual usage, which finds singular *they* more prevalent than my discussion here might suggest.

g. Bare plural generics are more complicated (and more interesting) than this characterization implies. I would no longer say they are equivalent to quantified noun phrases, but there is the possibility of interpreting them 'statistically' whereas such an interpretation is not available for the singular generics, either definite or indefinite, without further adverbial modifiers like 'often' or 'sometimes'. See McConnell-Ginet (2009) for discussion of the bare plural generic, and for relevant empirical data on interpretation, see Leslie (forthcoming).

The oddity of (42) seems related to the fact that food preferences are simply irrelevant to the linguist *qua* linguist: they play no role in our prototype for determining the reference of *linguist*. Bare plurals refer to sets of individuals rather than a prototype. Example (43) is fine because we can understand it in terms of a prototype.

(43)   The linguist often works with languages for which no writing system exists.

Now consider

(44)   The speaker may argue with his wife.
        *his husband[h]
        ?her husband

Although our shared prototype of a speaker is probably not very specific and indeed may not (in any very interesting sense) exist at all, to use a singular definite generic involves us in the pretense of a person-like prototypical genus representative to be named by that phrase. "The speaker" invites us to hang flesh on the metaphorical bones of one who speaks, bringing to life a prototype to whom we can refer—and whom we can almost hear "arguing with his wife." Singular generics preceded by the definite article are, as suggested at the end of the last section, in some ways like proper names. They function to make an abstract or general property (being a linguist, for instance) more vivid or concrete: *the linguist* can be endowed with a personality, but *a linguist* or *linguists* remain impersonal.

Poets and painters convey messages by incarnating abstract concepts. Sin and Death live as persons in the artist's imagination. Roman Jakobson comments on the influence of grammatical gender on the form such imaginative beings take:

> The Russian painter Repin was baffled as to why Sin had been depicted as a woman by German artists; he did not realize that 'sin' is feminine in German...but masculine in Russian....Likewise a Russian child, while reading a translation of German tales, was astonished to find that Death, obviously a woman...was pictured as an old man....My Sister Life, the title of a book of poems by Boris Pasternak, is quite natural in Russian where 'life' is feminine, but was enough to reduce to despair the Czech poet Josef Rora in his attempt to translate these poems, since in Czech this noun is masculine.[16]

The reason singular *they* is not very satisfactory with definite generics and intolerable with proper names is that both personalize their referents, give them a particular identity, endow them with personality. Personal identity, personality, is in our culture closely tied to sexual identity. *They*

---

h. With men now allowed to marry other men, *his husband* actually does occur, even in such conservative publications as the *New York Times*, in which a July 2, 2000, review by Alice Truax of Edmund White's *An Ideal Husband* with "Did Julien choose his husband well?" My asterisk here reflects judgments of a bygone era.

is sexless, gender-neutral. Live human beings are generally perceived as women or as men, not as androgynes.

Bloomfield was right: our referent for *the doctor, the linguist,* and *the lawyer* must be 'semantically' male. This interpretation is hard to avoid if we pronominalize with a generic masculine *he.* To pronominalize is to personify and to sexualize. Generic feminines must link to a female prototype: note again (16)–(20). Evocation of the prototype may be controlled by any one of a number of different factors: sex of one's audience, experience with actual sex-typing, faith in mythic conceptions of prototypical femininity. The link of generic masculines to prototypical male referents is weaker mainly because normative prescriptions to "use *he* for mixed or indeterminate sex reference" have indeed affected our usage— although we do not in general actually follow that prescription in its formulation. Yet the impossibility of *he* where a female prototype must be considered, the necessity or strong likelihood of *he or she* or *they* in certain contexts that are explicitly not exclusively masculine, suggests that *he* is indeed marked as masculine. Consider again (25)–(29). And the bizarreness of specifically feminine attributes for a sex-indefinite generic usually pronominalized by *he* suggests that only stereotypically feminine generics will be permitted to refer to a female prototype. Since reference to a fully personified prototype is reference to a sexed person, unmarked prototypes tend to become male. Such facts limit women's linguistic visibility to stereotyped contexts and promote masculinization in personalized nonfeminine contexts.

Susan Sontag was right when she claimed that "[g]rammar, the ultimate arena of sexist brainwashing, conceals the very existence of women— except in special situations" (1973, 186).

6. Conclusion

In light of the preceding discussion, it seems appropriate to revise slightly the feature analysis given in table 9.1 and to supplement it with a set of statements indicating roughly the system that underlies production and interpretation of pronouns in context.

First, let us review the results so far:

(1) In reference to specific individuals, attributed sex, or sexuality, agrees with gender of anaphoric pronoun. Only the genderless *they* is neutral on the question of sex attribution.
(2) Where women are particularly visible, *she* can function generically and thus encompass possible reference to males.
(3) Explicit mention in discourse of female reference, or possibility thereof, tends to disfavor use of anaphoric *he,* in some cases virtually requiring for comprehensibility the double-gender *he or she* or the genderless *they.*

(4) A singular generic can refer to either an arbitrary or a typical member of the genus. Singular definite generics appear to function much like proper names, referring to a specific 'persona'. A fictive prototype of this sort has a potentially fuller panoply of personal characteristics than those attachable to an arbitrary representative of the genus.[17]

(5) Personalization tends to promote sexualization and sexualization is in agreement with gender of anaphoric pronoun (see result 1).

(6) Where neither sex is significantly more visible as likely antecedent, speakers can choose *she* in contexts where women are salient for some other reason, as in the context of a feminist utterance, where audience is predominantly female and it is expected by the speaker that they may identify with or imagine themselves as possible referents, and so forth.

(7) *He* need not connote predominance of male referents for antecedents or of males in the context-of-utterance, but it does tend to suggest the nonvisibility of woman (see results 2, 3, and 6).

(8) The rule taught in school prescribing *he*, rather than *he or she* or *they*, for sex-indefinite or mixed-sex singular contexts interferes to some extent with the operation of results 2, 3, 6, and 7. The MASCULINE feature of *he* appears optionally cancellable, although *he* cannot co-occur with a positive specification of the FEMININE feature. Perhaps the classificatory MASCULINE feature ought to be viewed as simply weakened in contexts like these and not as cancelled.

(9) 'Vividness' of singular antecedents is decreased by choice of anaphoric *they*. With proper-name antecedents or definite generics, *they* is virtually impossible. This reflects the central role that sexual identity still plays in personal identity in our culture and the continued significance of sex stereotyping.

(10) In addition to result 8, the relatively greater markedness of *she* may involve a tendency to mark underlying +FEMININE forms as also–MASCULINE. Compare the tendency of feminine activities to be eschewed by males as 'effeminate', 'emasculating'. No parallel avoidance of male activities is culturally prescribed. A 'castrating bitch' threatens some male's masculinity, not her own femininity.

As shown in table 9.2, a classificatory matrix will treat the two gendered pronouns symmetrically. The statements in table 9.3 informally indicate how the underlying meanings are realized. Clearly, both production and interpretation depend on such factors as speaker/hearer sex, extent of feminist sympathies and raised consciousness, age, linguistic conservatism, style and thus, as Labov suggests, extent of conscious attention, and other such features of the speech situation. It seems

Table 9.2

	MASCULINE	FEMININE
He	+	0
She	0	+
They	0	0

Table 9.3

A. Gender tends to be marked (+MASCULINE or +FEMININE) where pronouns refer to specific individuals. If reference is indefinite, the gender-neutral pronoun is sometimes used by some speakers. Where reference is 'vividly' specified (by proper name or by pointing), gender marking is virtually obligatory.

B. Marked gender in specific personal reference attributes sex or sexuality.

C. Visibility of sex in utterance context is associated with marked gender. The strength of the link between FEMININE and FEMALE is stronger than that between MASCULINE and MALE for most adult speakers. Linguistically explicit visibility of both sexes tends to be incompatible with occurrence of a single marked anaphoric pronoun.

D. Gender marking in conjunction with generic antecedents is favored by definitization, which involves reference to a prototype.

E. Vividness of prototype promotes sex attribution, which follows gender markings of anaphoric pronoun, and thus sex typing in portrayal of typical member of the genus.

premature to devise a formalism in which to encapsulate such conditions, but the main point is that considerable variation can be subsumed under a shared system of oppositions.

Pronouns can refer to real people or to fictive prototypes. So long as most of us believe that women and men are what really exist, that androgynes are simply abstract entities, we will tend to sexualize our prototypes as we personalize them. So long as we obey the edicts of prescriptive grammarians and choose *he* for sex-indefinite singular antecedents, we prolong the linguistic and sociocultural invisibility of women.

Notes

1. Many feminists, of course, are as sophisticated linguistically as those who suppose that the notion of linguistic habits sustaining sexism in society is somehow incoherent. Excellent and avowedly feminist accounts of English pronouns are given in Bodine (1975), Martyna (1975), and Nichols (1972). Haugen (1974) and Lakoff (1975) are probably the most sympathetic linguistic critiques of what the Harvard Linguistics Department reputedly labeled "pronoun envy."

2. Mathiot and Roberts (1979) consider oppositions of *he* and *she* with *it*, as well as oppositions of *he* and *she* in reference to nonhuman and nonsexed entities. In a sense, my analysis is aimed at uncovering the actual functioning of the 'non-intimate' pattern Mathiot sets aside as governed by normative rules.

3. See, for example, Weinreich et al. 1968 for an extremely useful discussion of the problem of accounting for linguistic change if variation is not treated as integral to the linguistic system.

4. I have heard Professor Linda Waugh (Cornell) give a lucid account of Jakobsonian semantic theory on several occasions and have discussed some problematic points with her. Although I do not share her commitment to all tenets of the theory, some important methodological points she emphasizes are central to any linguistic theory of meaning. I have tried to confine myself to Jakobsonian classification features to describe the meanings of the personal pronouns, but, as will be apparent, certain problems are not completely solved.

5. Linguists tend to forget that the gender/sex distinction is useful even when one is dealing with a sex-based semantic gender. The linguistic category feminine gender, just like its psychological, sociological, and cultural sisters, need bear only a tenuous relation to the biological category of female sex.

6. That *scip* and *cild* were neuter forms in OE yet take feminine and masculine anaphoric pronouns respectively in modern English makes it difficult to support the view (suggested by Hook 1974) that modern gender pronouns, where they seem 'unnatural', as in the use of feminine anaphoric substitutes as an optional replacement for nouns like *ship*, or somewhat 'arbitrary', as in the use of a masculine substitute for generic occurrences of nouns like *child*, simply constitute some relic of the OE syntactic classes.

7. But see Ervin-Tripp 1962, and note the discussion in section 5.

8. Moore 1921 (91). Quoted in Baron 1971, a generally excellent discussion of the history of gender in English. Example (1) appears in Baron.

9. Whorf 1945 develops the notion of covert grammatical categories and applies it to English gender.

10. Bloomfield 1933 (253).

11. Blair Rudes and Bernard Healy (1979) present a detailed account of different contexts of the use of *she* for male referents gathered in fieldwork in a gay male community. Unfortunately, their discussion was not available to me when this essay was written. See their note 4 for objections to my comments here. The possibility of analyzing uses of *she* in reference to males as expressing a conception of femaleness depends on exploiting the general meaning attached to *she* in all its uses: expression of the cultural significance of female sex, which I have designated by the semantic feature FEMININE. Exactly what that significance is taken to be varies considerably from speaker to speaker and may include both positively and negatively valued attributes. Young boys sometimes use *she* to refer to other males, and this is generally seen as insulting: attributing to the referent some negatively valued trait thought typical of females and unsuitable for males (for example, weakness or emotionality). The fact that the use of *he* for reference to specific females and *she* for reference to specific males is highly restricted may reflect a strong cultural bias against ascribing sex atypicality. More generally, women and men are assumed and expected to be feminine and masculine, respectively.

12. Examples (8) and (9) are from Mathiot and Roberts (1979). Their suggested explanations of the usages seem plausible, but their currency appears too limited to suppose that the meanings in question are part of the semantic system of American English.

13. This example is from Cheris Kramer (now Kramarae), personal communication.

14. This example is from Barrie Thorne, personal communication.

15. Bodine, Martyna, and Nichols all suggest that singular *they* is likely to widen its range, given its availability and the expressed wish for a common-gender pronoun.

16. From Jakobson 1959 (237), quoted in Ervin-Tripp 1962.

17. Ann Bodine, personal communication, suggests that the distinction between the indefinite and definite singular generics may not work as I have suggested to produce a difference in speakers' acceptability judgments for *they* anaphora. Further empirical research is clearly needed, but I want to urge that we investigate a possible link between singular generics and other linguistic devices for creating concrete 'embodiments' of abstract concepts. The situation is undoubtedly considerably more complicated than my brief discussion in this essay would indicate.

References

Baron, Naomi (1971). A reanalysis of English grammatical gender. *Lingua* 27: 113–140.

Bloomfield, Leonard (1933). *Language*. New York: Henry Holt.

Bodine, Ann (1975). Androcentrism in prescriptive grammar. *Language in Society* 4(2): 129–146.

Ervin-Tripp, Susan (1962). The connotations of gender. *Word* 18: 249–261.

Hall, Robert A. (1951). Sex reference and grammatical gender in English. *American Speech* 38: 170–172.

Haugen, Einar (1974). Sexism and the Norwegian language. Paper presented at meeting of Society for the Advancement of Scandinavian Study, Washington, DC.

Hockett, Charles (1958). *A course in modern linguistics*. New York: Macmillan.

Hook, Donald D. (1974). Sexism in English pronouns and forms of address. *General Linguistics* 14(2): 86–96.

Jakobson, Roman (1959). On linguistic aspects of translation. In R. A. Brower (ed.), *On translation*. Cambridge, MA: Harvard University Press.

Lakoff, Robin (1975). *Language and woman's place*. New York: Harper Torchbooks.

[Leslie, Sarah-Jane (forthcoming). The original sin of cognition: Race, prejudice and generalization. *Journal of Philosophy*.]

Martyna, Wendy (1975). Beyond the *he/man* approach: A case for linguistic change (unpublished paper).

Mathiot, Madeleine, assisted by M. Roberts (1979). Sex roles as revealed through referential gender in American English. In Madeline Mathiot (ed.), *Ethnolinguistics: Boas, Sapir and Whorf revisited*. The Hague: Mouton.

[Matossian, Lou Ann (1997). Burglars, babysitters, and persons: A sociolinguistic study of generic pronoun usage in Philadelphia and Minneapolis. PhD diss., University of Pennsylvania.]

[McConnell-Ginet, Sally (2009). Generic predication and interest-relativity. Paper presented at the Non-canonical Predication Workshop, University of Western Ontario.]

Moore, Samuel (1921). Grammatical and natural gender in Middle English. *Proceedings of the Modern Language Association* 36: 79–103.

[Newman, Michael (1997). *Epicene pronouns: The linguistics of a prescriptive problem*. Outstanding Dissertations in Linguistics. New York: Garland Press.]

Newton, Esther (1972). *Mother Camp: Female impersonators in America.* Englewood Cliffs, NJ: Prentice Hall.

Nichols, Patricia (1972). Gender in English: Syntactic and semantic functions (unpublished paper).

[Rudes, Blair and Bernard Healy (1979). Is she for real?: The concepts of femaleness and maleness in the gay world. In Madeleine Mathiot (ed.), *Ethnolinguistics: Boas, Sapir and Whorf revisited.* The Hague: Mouton.]

Sontag, Susan (1973). The third world of women. *Partisan Review* 40(2): 181–206.

[Tieken-Boon van Ostade, Ingrid (2000). Female grammarians of the eighteenth century. *Historical Sociolinguistics and Sociohistorical Linguistics.* Retrieved August 5, 2009, from http://www.let.leidenuniv.nl/hsl_shl.]

Weinreich, Uriel, William Labov, and Marvin I. Herzog (1968). Empirical foundations for a theory of language change. In Winfred P. Lehmann and Yakov Malkiel, eds., *Directions for historical linguistics.* Austin: University of Texas Press, 95–195.

Whorf, Benjamin Lee (1945). Grammatical categories. *Language* 21: 1–11.

10

"What's in a name?"

Social labeling and gender practices

1. Categorizing labels

What do we call one another? How do we identify ourselves? When and how do we label ourselves and others? What is the significance of rejecting labels for ourselves or others? Of adopting new labels? Social labeling practices offer a window on the construction of gendered identities and social relations in social practice.

To get the flavor of some ways that labeling can enter into gender practice, consider the English nominal labels italicized in (1), which are being used to describe or to evaluate, to sort people into *kinds*. These predicative labels characterize and *categorize* people.

(1)   a. He's *a real dork*.
        b. She's *a total airhead*.
        c. I'm not *a feminist*, but...
        d. You are *a fierce faggot*, and I love you.
        e. We're not just *soccer moms*.
        f. What *a slut* (s/he is)!
        g. You're *a dear*.
        h. That blood is the sign that you're now *a woman*.

Examples (1a) and (1b) are both negative characterizations, but they are gendered and they are different: (1a) alleges male social incompetence, and (1b) attributes female brainlessness. (See James 1996 for these and other different semantic categories predominating in insulting labels applied to males and females in her study with Toronto students.) In (1c), the *but* signals that the speaker's rejection of the label is probably linked to acceptance of a negative evaluation that others have placed on those who openly identify with change-oriented gender agendas, often by misrepresenting their actions and attitudes (e.g., presenting feminists as humorless and unattractive man-haters). Another speaker might embrace the alternative label *womanist* as a way of criticizing self-described

This essay appeared in Janet Holmes and Miriam Meyerhoff, eds., *The handbook of language and gender* (Oxford: Blackwell, 2003), 69–97.

feminists who have ignored issues of race and class, effectively equating "women" with "well-to-do White women." (This particular example is discussed at some length in Eckert and McConnell-Ginet 2003, ch. 7.) In (1d), *faggot*, a label that is standardly applied only derogatorily to others by those not so labeled, is being proudly and defiantly reappropriated and joined to a modifier (*fierce*) that completely subverts the weak, wishy-washy image so often associated with the nominal label. The speaker, an 'out' gay man interviewed by one of my students, directly challenges the homophobic attitudes and assumptions that give the label its more usual negative value. A group's appropriation of labels that have been derogatorily applied by outsiders is often a powerful strategy: the word *queer* has been (almost) rehabilitated through this process and can now be used without suggesting prejudice against sexual minorities within certain groups (e.g., academic-based communities of practice) even by those who don't apply the label to themselves. (See McConnell-Ginet 2002 [ch. 11, this volume] for further discussion.) And in (1e), there is an implicit criticism of the gendered political assumptions that are carried by the label, a media invention that marries gender and class privilege. Example (1f) attributes sexual promiscuity to the person so labeled, and, although it is sometimes applied to males these days, it overwhelmingly evokes a female image (see James 1996). Used jokingly, it may mock sexual double standards; in another context, it may reinforce them. The speaker in (1g) is gently stroking the addressee with kind words; to offer this particular form of appreciation is generally to 'do' a certain kind of femininity. And in (1h), the addressee is pushed along a trajectory of gender identity, and a strong link is forged between her menarche and her new status as 'woman'.

As *feminist* in (1c) illustrates, labels often identify social, political, and attitudinal groupings into which people quite self-consciously do or do not enter. Others may, of course, monitor their suitability by refusing to accord them a claimed label: "Well, she's no feminist" can serve in a group defining itself as feminist to criticize the intellectual or political credentials of the person in question, and perhaps to exclude her from membership in the group. Of course, uttering that same sentence in some other group might function as a prelude to welcoming in a new member.[a] In May 2001, the potential potency of embracing or rejecting certain labels was brought home dramatically in U.S. news by the defection of Vermont senator James Jeffords from the Republican Party. "I have changed my party label," he noted, "but I have not changed my beliefs" (*New York Times*, May 25, 2001, p. A20). Jeffords' rejection of the label *Republican*, although it may not have been associated with any change in his beliefs and values, nonetheless set into motion a quite significant chain of events with enormous political repercussions. And as news analysts pointed out, all that was required by the laws of Vermont and

---

a. Intonational features might help discriminate the shunning and the welcoming uses.

the rules of the U.S. Senate for Jeffords to cease being a Republican was for him to reject the label, to say "I am no longer a Republican."

It was reportedly very wrenching for Jeffords to change his party label: being a Republican was not only an important part of how he thought of himself but of his friendships and alliances. It would be even harder for the addressee in (1h) to change or reject the gender label being attached to her. Yet, as we will see, labeling (including relabeling and label rejection) is deeply implicated not only in ascribing gender but in giving content to and helping shape gender identities and in challenging gender dichotomies.

2. Social practice: Local communities of practice and global connections

Although I have offered a sketch of what is probably going on when each of the sentences in (1) is uttered, precisely what each labeling does will depend on how the utterance fits into the other aspects of ongoing social practice. As Penelope Eckert and I have argued in our joint work on language and gender (Eckert and McConnell-Ginet 1992a [ch. 5, this volume], 1992b, 1995 [ch. 7, this volume], 1999, 2003), social identities, including gendered identities, arise primarily from articulating memberships in different communities of practice. A community of practice (CofP) is a group of people brought together by some mutual endeavor, some common enterprise in which they are engaged and to which they bring a shared repertoire of resources, including linguistic resources, and for which they are mutually accountable. Jean Lave and Etienne Wenger (1991) introduced the notion in their work on learning as an ongoing and thoroughly social process, and Wenger (1998) further develops the analytic framework.

Gender is a global social category that cuts across communities of practice, but much of the real substance of gendered experience arises as people participate in the endeavors of the local communities of practice to which they belong and as they move between such communities. The special June 1999 issue of *Language in Society*, edited by Janet Holmes and Miriam Meyerhoff, contains a number of interesting discussions and applications of the idea to language and gender research, and the editors' contribution (Holmes and Meyerhoff 1999) discusses its theoretical and methodological implications for language and gender research. Meyerhoff (2001) details the implications of the CofP framework more generally for the study of language variation and change, comparing the CofP to related constructs and frameworks: the speech community, social networks, and intergroup theory. As Meyerhoff makes clear, much sociolinguistic work that has not used the terminology "community of practice" has nonetheless drawn on similar ideas in attempting to gain insight into the connection between individual speech and broader general social and linguistic patterns. Penelope Eckert (2000) has developed a sustained argument for viewing linguistic variation as social practice, drawing on her extensive sociolinguistic investigations in a Detroit area high school.

Communities of practice are not free-floating but are linked to one another and to various institutions. They draw on resources with a more general history—languages as well as various kinds of technologies and artifacts. Their members align themselves not only with one another but with others whom they imagine share their values and interests. It is not only those we directly encounter who have significant impact on our sense of possibilities for social practice and identity. Benedict Anderson (1983) introduced the notion of an 'imagined community' to talk about national identity, and Andrew Wong and Qing Zhang (2000) talk about sexual minorities developing a sense of themselves as members of an imagined community in which they align themselves with others and thereby affirm and shape their sexual identities. Media, including books as well as newer communicative technologies, feed the imagination and offer glimpses of social practices that may be possible alternatives to those found in one's local communities of practice. Religious, political, and educational institutions also offer more global perspectives and resources, although they often have their main impact on individuals through their participation in connected local communities of practice (particular church groups, political action groups, classroom-based teams).

3. 'Empty' labels: Reference and address

The idea that there might be nothing (or very little) in a name arises most naturally when labels are not used predicatively to characterize, as in (1) above, but are used to refer to or address someone. In (2) and (3), the italicized labels are being used to refer and to address respectively:

(2)   a. *That bastard* didn't even say hello!
       b. When are *you guys* going to supper?
       c. Have you seen *my sister*?
       d. *Jill* said *she'd* talked with *the professors in the department*.
       e. It's *the welfare queens* who undermine the system.
       f. I'd like *you* to meet *my partner, Chris*.

(3)   a. Hey, *lady*—watch where you're going!
       b. Why're you in such a rush, *stuck-up bitch*?
       c. Go, *girl*!
       d. How're you doing, *tiger*?
       e. Frankly, *my dear*, I don't give a damn.
       f. I'll try, *mom*, to make you proud of me.
       g. Be good, *Joanie*.
       h. Wait for me, *you guys*.

Referring is basic to conveying information: we refer to the people we talk about (and also, of course, to other things we talk about). Referring expressions play grammatical roles such as SUBJECT or OBJECT. Typically, they identify the participants in the eventuality designated by the verb: they are what linguists call ARGUMENTS of the verb (or sometimes of another expression, for example, a preposition). Addressing, on the other hand, exists only because of the social nature of linguistic interaction. Address forms tag an utterance with some label for the addressee, the target to whom an utterance is directed. Unlike referring expressions (and the predicative use of labels we saw in (1)), they are not grammatically related to other expressions in the utterance; in English, they are often set off intonationally much as other 'parenthetical' expressions. The expression *you guys* is used to refer in (2b), to address in (3h).

The idea that names don't (or shouldn't) matter—"A rose by any other name would smell as sweet"—is linked to the idea that labeling for referential or address purposes does not characterize an individual or group but simply identifies them: points to the proper entity about whom something is said in the referring case, or indicates to whom an utterance is directed in the addressing case. Indeed, the standard analysis of what referring proper names and pronouns contribute in the way of informational content to sentences like those in (2) fits with this view of things. If my sister is named Alison (and I assume that you know that), then I could ask "Have you seen Alison?" and achieve much the same effect as if (2c) is uttered. Of course, (2c) does attribute the property of being my sister to the individual about whose whereabouts I'm inquiring. If you have some other way to identify the individual in question (perhaps you've recently seen the two of us together and note that I'm carrying and looking at the hat she was then wearing), my utterance might indeed inform you that the individual in question is my sister though that might not have been my intent (I might have been assuming that you already knew she was my sister).

In general, when a referring expression uses a nominal that can be used to characterize or categorize, the speaker is assuming that the referent is indeed categorized by that nominal. But the content of the nominal label—its potential characterizing value—is very often just a way to get attention focused on the particular individual, and other ways might in many cases do equally well. (Not in all cases, however: a matter to which we will return below.) Address forms too can include contentful nominals, and that content is often presupposed applicable to the addressee. Of course, proper names and pronouns do not standardly have content in the same way as ordinary common nouns do. Their relative semantic emptiness precludes their occurring as predicate expressions like those in (1): rather than characterizing, they indicate a person or group. English does, of course, sometimes allow what look like characterizing uses of names and pronouns. In the case of proper names, an ordinary 'common' noun—a category label—can be derived from a proper name, where the content of the noun usually derives from some specially notable characteristics of some particular person bearing that name, as in the first three examples in (4). (The person may be a fictional character as in (4c), where the expression *Lolita* serves to cast young girls as seductive and thus responsible for men's sexual interest in them.) Sometimes, though, a proper name is used just to help personify a typical member of some group or a person with some particular personal qualities; in these cases, the capital letter associated with proper names often disappears, as in the last five examples (but the original gendering of the names contributes to their significance):

(4)   a. Kim's *no Mother Teresa*.
        b. Lee's *a regular Einstein*.
        c. Some of those fourth-graders are already *little Lolitas*.
        d. She's *your typical sorority sue*. [1980s slang at University of North Carolina: Eble 1996]
        e. He's *a nervous nellie*.
        f. She's just *a sheila* I met in Sydney. [Australian English]
        g. He's just *a guy* I know.
        h. The legislators quickest to criminalize prostitutes are often *johns* themselves.

Notice also that some proper names are formally equivalent to labels that do have descriptive content: *Faith, Hope, Rose, Pearl, Iris*, and *Joy* are examples of English names (not coincidentally, all female names) that evoke content. A given girl named *Rose* is not, of course, literally a flower, but her name may suggest the beauty of those fragrant blossoms. I don't mean to imply that men's given names are immune from content associations; the widely increased prevalence of *dick* as a vulgar term for 'penis' and also as an insult has virtually killed off *Dick* as a shortened form of *Richard* among Americans under the age of 40.[b] Here, of course, the content is seen as far more problematic than that associated with the female names mentioned above. Overall, content-bearing names are no longer the norm in English, but they certainly are in many other cultures. Even noncontentful names often link a child to a family history, to someone else who bore the same name in the family or in the family's cultural heritage. Whether that person must be of the same sex as that to which the child is assigned varies. Some languages have devices that can feminize an originally masculine name (e.g., we find English *Georgina, Paulette*, and *Roberta* alongside *George, Paul*, and *Robert*), and there are languages in which there are masculine/feminine pairs of names (e.g., Italian *Mario* and *Maria*), neither of which is derivationally more basic. (There may be cases of masculinizing processes, but I have not uncovered them.) In some cultural traditions, given names are generally contentful, and those naming a child try to pick something auspicious.

---

b. As I was proofreading these pages, I heard a young teenage girl I know express some shock when her father mentioned an acquaintance of his and mine named Dick. "That's not a nice nickname," she said, "and I don't think people should use it."

How names work varies significantly in different cultural settings. Catholic children, for example, acquire a confirmation name, generally with some special significance. Felly Nkweto Simmonds (1995) discusses this and other features of the place of her own different names in her life history. The custom (and onetime legal requirement) in many Western societies of a woman's adopting her husband's surname has meant that women were more likely than men to face name changes during their lives, at least 'official' name changes. Many men leave behind childhood diminutive forms of their given names (*Bobby* becomes *Bob*, *Willie* becomes *Will* or *William*), but many also acquire new nicknames on sports teams or in fraternities or the military, new names that sometimes persist over the rest of the life course. And some men are changing their surnames upon marriage nowadays, hyphenating names or choosing with their partner a name that ties into the heritage of both (e.g., my local paper reported on a couple, one named *Hill* and one with an Italian surname and heritage, who chose *Collina*, 'hill' in Italian, as their common new surname).

Some cultures institutionalize an array of different personal names, others do not use family names as most Europeans understand them, and still others tie names very tightly to life stages. Among the Tamang in Nepal, people of both sexes bear a variety of different names during their lives. Babies are given a name selected by a religious expert to contain appropriate sounds, but those names are seldom used and are generally known only to close family. Young children are typically given rather derogatory labels ('little pockmarked one'), designed to deflect unwanted attention from evil spirits. And adolescents take for themselves joyful sounding names ('Bright Flower') that they use during courtship song festivals and similar occasions in the period between childhood and (relatively late) marriage. Adults, on the other hand, are often labeled in terms of their parental roles ('Maya's mother' or 'father of Mohan') or other kinship relations ('grandfather' or 'youngest daughter-in-law'), seldom being addressed or referred to by what Westerners would count as a name (though close friends from youth may continue to use the courtship-period names, at least in some contexts). (See March 2002 for discussion of Tamang naming.)

Labels for people that identify them only through their relation to someone else—TEKNONYMS—do occur in some English-speaking communities (I was addressed as *Alan's mom* or *Lisa's mother* on many occasions when my children were young), but they are pervasive in some cultures. During some historical periods, Chinese women in certain regions often received nothing but such relational forms, moving from designations such as 'second daughter' and 'oldest sister' to 'Lee's wife' and the like; men, in contrast, were far more often named as individuals (Naran Bilik, personal communication, May 2001; see Blum (1997) for a very useful discussion of naming and other features of address and reference practices among speakers of Chinese). Bernsten (1994) discusses Shona address practices, which construct adult women mainly via their relationships to others. After marriage (when a woman moves to her husband's locale) but before having children, a young woman is generally not called (at least publicly) by her principal childhood name but *amain'ini* (lit. 'little mother'), the term for a young aunt, or, to show respect and recognition of her ancestral ties to another place, by the totem name associated with her natal family or clan. But once she has children, the principal form of address to a woman is *amai* ('mother') + the name of her eldest child. Or at least such teknonymy was the predominant pattern before European colonizers and missionaries came and began to promote Western-style naming practices.

Labeling practices that de-emphasize women's status as very particular individuals can be found closer to home. For example, in American and British history, tombstones have often named male children (*James, Richard, Kenneth, and Thomas*) but not female (*and three daughters*). And *Mrs. John Doe* names a station, whoever the occupant may be, whereas *Mr. John Doe* picks out an individual. This point was brought home to me early in my married life when I came across a box of stationery made for my husband's first wife, bearing what I had until then thought of as 'my' new name. (Stannard 1977 remains a fascinating account of "Mrs. Man"; the epigraph she chooses from a letter Henry James wrote to a friend in 1884 is eloquent: "we talk of you and Mrs you.")

The many ways in which proper names may enter into gender practice is itself the topic for a book. The two critical points for present purposes are that (1) although proper names are not fundamentally characterizing, they nonetheless have considerable significance beyond their picking out particular individuals, and (2) the significance of proper names lies in how they are bestowed and deployed in particular cultures and communities of practice.

There are also occasional characterizing uses of forms identical to pronouns. These are analogous to the occasional transformation of a proper name into a characterizing expression that we saw in (4):

(5)   a. Max thinks he's *a real he-man*.
        b. Bernadette's *a she-wolf*.
        c. I really hope their baby is *a she*.
        d. This *me-generation* has forgotten what it means to care about others.

In (5a–c), *he* and *she* draw on the background gender assumptions they carry in their ordinary referring uses. But they are otherwise lacking in content.

Neither proper names nor pronouns are what people generally have in mind when they speak of *name-calling*. Name-calling is like address in being specifically targeted, but unlike address in that the label itself constitutes a full utterance whose explicit function is to characterize (more particularly, to evaluate) its target. Popular usage speaks of name-calling only when the content of the label applied is overtly disparaging, but I include approving labels in this category as well. In (6) there are some examples. The first two might be hurled at a target by someone intending to hurt, the third is more likely to be used jokingly, whereas the last three might well function as expressions of affection or thanks or appreciative positive evaluation. (Interestingly, it seems significantly harder to omit the pronominal *you* with the positive than with the negative and have a complete utterance.)

(6)   a. (You) *jerk*.   cf. What *a jerk* (you are)!
         b. *Fatso*.
         c. (You) *klutz*.
         d. You *sweetheart*.   cf. You are such *a sweetheart*!
         e. You *angel*.
         f. You *genius*.

Name-calling is directed toward a particular target and ascribes the content of the nominal to that target. What characterizing content amounts to in these cases is evaluation, which can be either (overtly) negative or positive. The strongly evaluative element is why (in English) name-calling is much like uttering a special *wh*-exclamative form, such as "What a(n)—(you are)," or an exclamatory declarative, "You are such a(n)—," where the blank is filled in with some noun phrase. It is the negative cases, of course, that invoke the old playground mantra "Sticks and stones may break my bones but words will never hurt me," chanted by the target of some name in a desperate attempt to prevent further assault by denying its (obvious) power. We can think of name-calling as an utterance of a characterizing expression directed at an addressee, where the whole point of such an utterance is to paste the evaluative label on the addressee.

    Address forms are often used in calls (where the address form may constitute the whole utterance) or greetings or on other occasions to get the attention of the person or persons to whom an utterance is directed: such uses have been called SUMMONS. By analogy with the lines on an envelope that direct the message inside to a particular location, the term ADDRESS suggests the primacy of this attention-getting or 'finding' function of address forms, even though some analysts (see, for example, Schegloff 1972) want to reserve the term for nonsummoning uses. In general, address forms can be parenthetically interjected at almost any point in an ongoing exchange although they are particularly common in greetings or other openings. Many address forms can also be used to refer, and I will sometimes mention differences between address and referring uses of a particular form. And second-person reference, though grammatically distinct from address, raises many of the same social issues. Ide (1990) uses "terms of address" to include both address forms and second-person reference.

4. Address options: Beyond power and solidarity

Address forms are always grammatically optional, but they are often socially required and they are always socially loaded. There are many different ways that analysts have divided the field, but the following two displays give some order to the range of available options in English. Display (7) gives a typology for forms that are individualized in the sense that speaker and addressee consider them names or nicknames that have been specifically attached to this particular addressee. Of course, any given individual may get very different forms from different addressers, and some addressers may use multiple forms. Imagine these preceded by *hey* or *hi* or *hello* or a similar greeting (*yo* is increasingly common among younger Americans):

(7)   Surname plus social title: *Mr./Ms./Miss/Mrs. Robinson*
       Surname plus professional title: *Dr./Prof./Judge/Sen./Capt. Robinson*
       Surname only: *Robinson*
       Title or kinterm plus given name: *Ms. Blanche/Auntie Blanche/Granny Rose/Papa John*
       Bare kin term: *mother/mom/mommy/mama, dad/daddy/papa/pop(s)/ father, sis(ter), bro(ther), son, daughter, aunt(ie), uncle, grandma, grandpa*
       Given name: *Christine/Christopher*
       Standard short form of name: *Chris*
       Special "nicknames": *Crisco*(for *Chris*), *Teddy Bear/Ace/Batgirl*

In general, the choices at the top are used reciprocally between those socially quite separated or nonreciprocally up a hierarchy, whereas the choices at the bottom are used reciprocally between people who are close to one another or nonreciprocally down a hierarchy. But the rankings of the choices may be shifted or other individualized options may be developed in particular communities of practice. Indeed, members of a particular CofP may develop their own practices that do not readily slot into this model. I will discuss some examples of other options and alternative interpretations below. English-speaking children are often instructed as to how they should address (and also refer to) various people. (Blum 1997 observes that address and reference norms are explicitly conveyed for adults as well in many Chinese communities of practice.)

The group of address options given in (8) is more general. Again, it may help to think of them as following some greeting:

(8)   Bare title: *coach, professor, doc(tor), judge, councilor, teach(er)*
       Respect terms: *sir, ma'am, miss*
       Stranger generic names: *Mac, Bud, Buster, Toots*
       General: man, *you (guys), girl (friend), dude, lady, ladies, gentlemen, folks, babe, sexy*; (esp. for children) *tiger, chief, princess, beautiful*
       Epithets/insults: *bitch, ho, slut, prick, bastard, slimeball, nerd, dyke, faggot*
       Endearments (sometimes preceded by *my*): *honey, dear, sweetie, love, darling, baby, cutie*

Although bare kin terms appear in display (7), the category of forms used for addressing particular others (those in the designated relation to the speaker) can also be used more generally, and could have been included in display (8). In the southern United States in the mid-twentieth century (and even more recently), it was very common for White people to use *auntie* or *uncle* to (condescendingly) address Black people whom they did not know. The form *Pops* has been hurled by young toughs at old men whom they are hassling, but the form is now dying out. There are other cultural settings where kinterms equivalent to *aunt* and *uncle* are used to address elderly strangers as respectful forms. And *brother* and *sister* are sometimes used positively among African Americans, often to emphasize shared histories, and in church service contexts among some other groups of Americans. The moral: the significance of particular forms of address lies in the history of patterns of usage within and across particular communities of practice and in the connection between addressing and other aspects of social practice that build social relations and mark them with respect and affection or with contempt, condescension, or dislike.

In neither list is it sufficient to think of a cline from more to less respectful or less to more intimate. This is not to deny that respect and power, on the one hand, and intimacy and solidarity, on the other, are indeed crucial components of interactional meaning. This point was made by Roger Brown and Albert Gilman (1960), in an account of address and addressee reference in European languages with a familiar and a more formal second-person pronoun. Their classic paper, "Pronouns of power and solidarity," focused on what they called the T/V distinction of second-person pronouns found in many Indo-European languages, though absent for centuries now from English. The 'T' form (as in French *tu* or German *du*), which is grammatically singular, is generally described as the more familiar. The 'V' form (as in French *vous* or German *Sie*), grammatically plural (and historically semantically plural as well), is described as the more formal. Canonically, the V form is used reciprocally between distant (nonsolidary) peers and upwards in a (power-laden) hierarchical relation, whereas the T form is used reciprocally between close peers and downwards in a hierarchical relation. Is the V respectful or deferential? Is the T friendly or condescending? This particular polysemy, produced by the interactional tension and connection between power and solidarity, is pervasive, as Deborah Tannen (1994, 2003) has argued.

In the T/V languages, it is not just the pronominal forms themselves that carry the power/solidarity values, but also verb forms. The verbal form of an imperative, for example, agrees in number with the unexpressed second-person pronominal subject, and thus obligatorily indicates a T (*Sors!* 'leave') versus V (*Sortez!*) choice even if there is no overt form referring to the addressee. In contrast, English has only one form for imperatives and even if one has to refer explicitly to the addressee, the second-person pronoun *you* does not make social distinctions. Offering a historical as well as synchronic account, Brown and Gilman observed a progression in the European T/V languages toward increased reliance on the solidarity semantic—increased use of the T form. That progression has certainly continued in the decades since their paper was published, but the distinctions have not vanished, and there are almost certainly still possibilities in some communities of practice using T/V languages for subtle interactions with gender practice in choice of second-person pronouns and verbal form of second-person utterances. Even for the binary T/V split, matters are more complex than the simple split into the power and the solidarity semantic might indicate, especially if our interest is in gender and sexuality.

Historically, in many contexts in which heterosexuality was presumed, it was important to preserve pronominal markings of 'distance'—in other words, nonintimacy—between women and men during the years when they were presumed to be potential sexual partners. For example, children who used mutual T in their prepubescent years might switch as they matured. Paul Friedrich (1972) offered the Russian example translating as "Petya's grown-up now. He says *vy* to the girls." And a man and a woman whose family relations forbade their intimacy—standardly presumed to be at least potentially sexual—were especially careful to stick with mutual V: for example, within families Brown and Gilman report mutual V most common between a married woman and her husband's brother. Because it was women who were expected to police and control intimacy, it was they who were normatively expected to 'give permission' for a move from mutual V-address to mutual T-address. Given the general principle that Brown and Gilman enunciate, that the more powerful member of a dyad is the one able to initiate a move from either mutual V or asymmetric address to mutual T, it is surprising that they do not comment at all on their claim that in cross-sex dyads, it is women who decide whether mutual T is to be permitted. This is, of course, an instance of women's 'power' to dispense or withhold sexual favors, a 'power' often more symbolic than real. Increased egalitarian ideologies with their emphasis on mutual T-relations have undoubtedly eroded these distinctions, but there are still certainly some gender components of T/V usage. Brown and Gilman do note, however, another instance in which the gender and the sexual order introduce some disturbances in their account of the general functioning of the T/V distinction. There is, they say, one particularly "chilling example" that runs counter to their general principle that mutual T, once established, is never withdrawn. German men visiting prostitutes engage in mutual T-address until the 'business' is completed, when they revert to mutual V. Here too, practices may well have changed in the decades since their research, but notice that what address did in such cases was to construct the commercial relationship between customer and sex worker as one of temporary intimacy.

What is important to note is that there are many different 'flavors' of power—of status differentials—and of solidarity—of connections between peers. These flavors are the product of the character of social practice in different communities of practice. They are often linked to gender or to race or ethnicity or class, but they ultimately derive from social practice. As a consequence, address forms from one individual to another often vary significantly, depending on such factors as the CofP in which the two are encountering one another and the nature of the particular interaction in which they are engaged.

To appreciate the different flavors of power and solidarity, consider a few cases of English address that do not really fit on the lists in (7) and (8). For example, there are people who receive a shortened form of their given name from most acquaintances but the full form, generally considered more distant, from a spouse or some other intimate. Presumably, the full form can construct intimacy precisely because most mere acquaintances do not use it. It marks the specialness of the couple's own intimate CofP. Or, consider Leeds-Hurwitz's (1980) report of a woman promoted in a company and creating address distinctions that subtly constructed her new position of ascendancy over former colleagues and (near) equality with former superiors. For her former colleagues, she developed multiple names (signaling more 'familiarity'), whereas they continued simply to use her given name. Her former (male) superiors continued to use her given name, but she dropped the title plus surname forms she had once used to them. She moved to the unusual combination of given name plus surname, perhaps avoiding given name alone either because she had not been explicitly invited to use it, the norm in such changes, or because she found it difficult to break the old taboo. This woman drew on familiar resources but put them together in somewhat novel patterns to help sustain the social challenges of her new form of participation in the workplace CofP.

There are also a number of 'off-the-list' ways to combine intimacy with deference to age. In some communities of practice in the southeastern United States, for example, it is still relatively common for young people to use a social title plus given name for an older woman (*Miz Anne*), a form that combines the 'respect' of the title with the closeness and familiarity implied by the given name. Although the same formula can be used to address an older man, it is somewhat more common to get social title plus some shortened form of the surname. For example, my father, Charles McConnell, was called *Mr. Mac* by college-age friends when he was in his forties and living in North Carolina. This pattern of title plus shortened surname is much less restricted regionally and is frequently used by children to their teachers of both sexes; the initial of the surname is a frequent 'shortening': *Ms. G* (or *Miss G* or *Mrs. G*) or *Mr. G*. Similarly, in some communities of practice, children use *Aunt* or *Uncle* plus first name not only for kin but also for close family friends of their parents' generation or older. A young friend of mine, who's been taught to use respectful titles to adults, recently sent me an e-mail that began "Dear Dr. Sally."

Even when we stay 'on the list', it is obvious that many address forms are canonically gendered but that matters are seldom so simple as restricting application or use of a form to a single sex. In English, first names are often (though not always) gendered, social titles and kinterms are gendered, and there is considerable gendered differentiation in the use of other forms.

Here we will focus on cases that seem to indicate something about ongoing changes in the gender order.

Bare surname, for example, is still far more common among men and boys than among women and girls, but there are changes afoot. (The still prevalent expectation that women will change surnames when they marry probably helps sustain the sense that surnames are more firmly attached to men than to women. But that expectation is certainly weakening, as more women retain birth names or join with partners willing to effect a common change to a new name for the new family unit.) Surnames are not part of address within the nuclear family (not these days, when women no longer use title plus surnames in addressing their husbands, as was the custom in some English-speaking circles in the nineteenth century), and the surname is associated with the move from the nuclear family to other communities of practice and with leaving babyhood behind. It is often used reciprocally as a form of address (and of reference) in communities of practice where relationships focus on camaraderie and collective performance under pressure rather than emotional intimacy. (Nonreciprocal bare surname use is also associated with such communities of practice when they are hierarchically organized. In the military, for example, the higher-ranking individual may use surname to those below and receive title plus surname. Hicks Kennard [2001] offers examples from women in the U.S. Marine Corps.) Reciprocal bare surname address is certainly increasingly used among women; what is noteworthy is that such usage is especially common in communities of practice such as sports teams (or the military) where the relationships called for are those for which such address is especially apt, where there is a friendship of equals and 'sentimentality' is excluded. That this pattern of address is increasing among women, for whom its main provenance in earlier generations seems to have been nursing units, testifies to the increase in women's participation in communities of practice of the sort that promote mutual dependence and teamwork but eschew anything that might suggest vulnerability.

Of course, bare surname address and reference are not completely confined to arenas such as playing fields and hospital floors. A friend of mine refers to her now dead husband this way, and apparently that was how she and almost everyone other than his family of origin addressed and referred to him most frequently. Such cases, however, are exceptional; a young woman whose relationship with a young man moves from simple comradeship to heterosexual romance often finds herself also moving away from initial bare surname address to given name and/or special names and endearments. Bare surname, then, is not simply gendered; the gender differentiation in its use follows from its relation to kinds of social practice and social relations, and changes in the gender patterns of its use are part and parcel of changes in the content of gender practice.

The jocular use of epithets in address—"It's great to see you, you old sonofabitch!"—is in some ways similar to the use of bare surname, especially when the usage is reciprocal. It is, however, more age-sensitive, with peak use among young men, and more situationally restricted, being paradigmatically associated with male locker room or fraternity registers and at least normatively censored in mixed-sex and general public settings (like swearing in general). Like bare surnames (and swearing), however, jocular epithets are becoming more and more commonly used by young women to their close friends and siblings (see, for example, Hinton 1992).

Less jocular (and nonreciprocal) usage of the epithets that are standardly thought of as applied to females is associated with such contexts as male construction workers yelling at female strangers walking by (on street calls generally, see Gardner 1981; Kissling 1991; Kissling and Kramarae 1991). The only instances reported by Leanne Hinton's students surveyed in 1991 of a man's calling a woman *bitch* were from strangers (see also (3b), an example reported to me by a young woman I know)—in other words, the addresser and addressee are not within a common community of practice. Address from strangers to women often also uses 'complimenting' general terms referring to appearance, such as *beautiful* or *sexy*. Just as 'insults' are often really positive marks of intimacy, such 'compliments' are often really negative marks of objectification and condescension. Sometimes hostile 'feminine', as well as specifically homophobic, epithets are used in name-calling as well as in reference by men to harass other men. (See Cameron 1997 for use of epithets with homophobic content in reference to absent men to enforce heterosexual gender conformity.)

Epithets, often quite overtly sexual and classified as obscene, are frequently used for reference in certain communities of practice by men talking among themselves about women. On many all-male sports teams, for example, such references to women are extremely common and may serve both to display a kind of superiority to women and to effect 'bonding' via shared 'othering' and denigration of women. In some such communities of practice, the men using these terms routinely for reference to women would never think of using them in address or in reference in the mixed-sex communities of practice to which they belong. But men are not the only insulters. Abusive referential terms are sometimes used in communities of practice by women talking about other women who are not there to defend themselves. In the woman-woman uses, however, the forms tend to be personally directed, whereas in a number of all-male groups, the forms are used to refer to virtually any woman (at least, any female age-mate). Of course, women do sometimes 'bond' by speaking negatively of men; a brilliant cartoon in a *New Yorker* magazine shows some women gathered around a water cooler, with one saying: "I'd love to join you in saying nasty things about men but I used to be one."

The reports I have gotten of this kind of antimale 'bonding' phenomenon among women speak primarily of labelings that characterize men in general or particular men, many of these characterizations being focused on the men's (alleged) sexual mistreatment of women or their general inconsiderateness. These contrasts point to the somewhat different place of cross-sex hostility in the social practices of all-female and of all-male communities of practice. The negative labeling of women that some groups of men are using to bond tends to be backgrounded, a matter of the default forms of reference some of them use for female individuals of whom they are implicitly dismissive. For women, the negative labeling tends to be more explicitly descriptive or evaluative: they are characterizing the men in a disapproving way, taking men as their topic rather than relegating cross-sex derogation to the background. (These comments are based on reports from my own and others' students as well as on other kinds of informal observations. Systematic study of actual usage in this arena is not easy to undertake, given the relatively 'private' nature of such exchanges.)

In the past several decades there have been a number of studies of abusive terms used to refer to or address women (Schultz 1975 and Stanley 1977 are classic references; Sutton 1995 is a more recent study), many of which note the predominance of words that have sexual allusions. Some studies also look at abusive terms designating men (e.g., Baker 1975; Risch 1987; James 1996). Interestingly, some terms (e.g., *bitch, slut, bastard*) are becoming less strongly gendered in two ways: they can now apply to both sexes, and women use them far more than they once did, both seriously and in joking contexts among themselves. In spite of this, James (1996) still found strong gendered stereotypes for referents and for users of most such epithets, which suggests they still convey gendered meanings, though perhaps more complex and somewhat different ones than they once did. According to Sutton (1995), a significant number of young women report using *ho* affirmatively to one another (a smaller number have also reclaimed *bitch*)—and in jocular contexts, also forms like *slut* and *dork*. These reports fit with the accounts my own students offer of the evolving scene. Most studies have relied on self-reports of usage and interpretation. Just how well such accounts reflect the range of actual practices remains unclear.

Nicknaming can be important in certain communities of practice. Many all-male sports teams or living units such as fraternities bestow special nicknames on new members, names that are virtually always used in the CofP and are often used in encounters between members in other contexts. Some all-female and some mixed communities of practice have such naming practices as well. Some evidence suggests, however, both that the practices are more common in all-male groups and that group-bestowed nicknames are much more frequently used among male teammates or fraternity members than they are in the parallel female or mixed communities of practice. Nicknames are often based on a person's 'real' name (like *Crisco* for *Chris* in display (7)) but can come from other sources, often with a special meaning for a particular CofP.

The general terms in display (8) are often used reciprocally among intimates as well as with strangers. They are much more common from and to men but are beginning to be used among women; *dude*, for example, is by no means any longer confined to male addressees or male addressers, and even *man* is now occasionally addressed to young women (see Hinton 1992). Such forms, most of which began with males as their only referents, seem now to signal casual good will. In the United States, the plural *you guys* is now widely used for group address and second-person reference, no matter what the composition of the group. My mother (in her late eighties) and I (in my sixties) were recently so addressed by a young male server in a restaurant. (The singular *guy* is still pretty strongly male-gendered.) The formality of *ladies* and the frequent condescension of age-inappropriate *girls* may help explain why *guys* has become so popular even for female-only referents.

But women are beginning to turn not only to originally male forms for such casual but friendly, though impersonal, address. For example, in some communities of practice, especially those whose members are mainly African American, *girl* can readily be used to adult female addressees by both other women and men to express a supportive and friendly connection. This use is spreading, probably because of its occurrence in such contexts as U.S. advertisements featuring women basketball stars and popular music lyrics. The form *girlfriend* as a term of address is even more restricted to communities of practice in which African Americans predominate. Among women, it can express affection and ongoing comembership in some emotionally important community of practice. So used, the form is warm but casual. Importantly, the affection being expressed is that of a nonsexual friendship, which depends on the general referential properties of *girlfriend* in American English. Unlike *boyfriend*, which must mean a male romantic interest (and can be so used by both straight women and gay men), *girlfriend* in reference or description can mean either romantic/sexual object (this use is common to straight men and lesbians) or important close friend. This latter use is open only to women—a man who speaks of *my girlfriend* thereby indicates a romantic interest, perhaps because of heterosexual assumptions that relations of men and women are always erotically charged. Although many European American women do use *girlfriend* to refer to their close women friends, they seldom draw on it as an address form. There are attested uses of *girlfriend* by a White lesbian to address her lover, but this use is not the same as the asexual friendship use among African American women. Will this friendship use of *girlfriend* in address spread to other American women, as so many other social and linguistic practices originating in African American communities have? (Note, for example, the appropriation of *yo* and *dude*.) We may eventually see such a spread, but at the moment, the address signals not only warm woman-to-woman friendship but also underscores shared racial heritage. African American men also sometimes use the bare term *girlfriend* in addressing women who may be relative strangers to express good will and to underscore shared heritage; of course, its particular significance depends very much on other features of the setting in which the exchange occurs. It is not surprising, however, that African American men do not use *boyfriend* as a casually friendly form of address to one another; its erotic charge in male-male referential usage spills over to address.

Forms like *honey* and *dear*, classified as endearments in (8), have been widely discussed. Just as epithets do not always insult, so endearments do not always express affection. They can do so, of course, when used in a CofP between intimates, but they can also condescend or be otherwise problematic (see, for example, Wolfson and Manes 1980), especially from a man to a woman he does not know well (or perhaps not at all). Most of them are widely used from adults (especially women) to children, even children they don't know. And older women sometimes use them to much younger men who are strangers to them, in what is often described as a 'maternal' way. But their condescension potential, especially in address from men to women, has been widely noted and thus many men now avoid them outside of genuinely intimate contexts. (Except to very young boys, American men very seldom use them to other males.) There are, however, still English-using communities of practice in Britain where some of these endearments apparently function in much the same way as general terms like *guys* or *dude* or *folks*. They can come from strangers of either sex to addressees of either sex with no suggestion of anything other than lighthearted friendliness (and the absence of 'stuffiness' or undue reserve).

The respect terms *sir* and *ma'am* show considerable local variation in their use. In the American Southeast, they are frequently used by children to parents, a very intimate relation. As respect forms, the terms are not equivalent; not only does *ma'am* compete with *miss*, but neither of these feminine variants has the same authoritative impact that *sir* carries (and *ma'am* is far more restricted than *sir* regionally). The need to mark deference to authority held by females has led to some interesting usages, with women police officers (McElhinny 1995), for example, occasionally receiving the normally masculine *sir*, presumably because the femaleness of the more standard *ma'am* tends to limit its ability to confer real authority on the addressee.

Of course, a taxonomy of the kind given for English, already strained as we have seen in organizing English speakers' address practices, will be even less adequate for other languages. For example, Japanese has the respectful affix *-san*, which can be added to various terms of address (e.g., names, kin terms). It also seems more common in Japan than in English-speaking countries for adults in a family to call each other by the terms designating their parental roles (though one certainly can find in the United States many couples who call each other 'mom' and 'dad' or something equivalent). In addition, Japanese has a number of second-person pronouns, a couple of which (*anata* and *anta*) are used by both women and men, and several that are rather brusque or 'rough' in flavor and used primarily by men. Among married couples, wives are apparently more respectful to husbands than vice versa. Women seem to be avoiding very informal forms such as a plain first name and, as they do generally, the second-person pronouns *kimi* and *omae*. A wife's first name + *-san* to her husband may be matched by his plain first name or even nickname to her, and use of forms like *kimi* and *omae*, which he would be unlikely to use to a peer. Both often use parental terms (*otosan* 'father' and *okasan* 'mother' are most common, but *papa* and *mama* are also used). (Ogawa and Shibamoto Smith 1997 discuss these purported patterns, drawing on Lee 1976, a study based on self-reports by Japanese couples living in the United States, and Kanemura 1993, a survey of Japanese women students reporting on their parents' practices.) Do such gender asymmetries persist among younger married couples in Japan? How do different address choices function in constructing different kinds of marital relationships? Such questions have not yet been addressed, at least not in English-language reports. What Ogawa and Shibamoto Smith demonstrate is that the patterns can be called on outside heterosexual marriage. They examined address (and also first- and third-person references) used in a documentary film by two gay men in a committed relationship, finding that in many ways the two men labeled themselves and the other in much the same ways as do the canonical husband and wife.

Families, including nontraditional families, are of course very important kinds of communities of practice. For many children, they are initially the only community of practice in which the child participates. Hinton (1992) asked entering college students at the University of California, Berkeley, to report on their address to parents and to siblings. The informal but not especially intimate *mom* and *dad* were the overwhelming favorites for addressing parents reported by both sexes (83 percent of women and 89 percent of men reported *mom*, 79 percent of women and 90 percent of men reported *dad*), but the women used both more diminutives (*mommy*, *daddy*) and more of the formal terms (*mother* and *father*, with *father* a vanishingly small usage from both sexes as an address form but *mother* used by about 14 percent of the women as compared to only 4 percent of the men). Both sexes were somewhat more likely to report use of a diminutive form to the other-sex parent, but the striking contrast was sex of user. Of the women, 33 percent and 45 percent reported using *mommy* and *daddy* respectively, whereas only 16 percent and 12 percent of the men admitted to these uses (they were, of course, reporting their current patterns, not recalling earlier uses). Many of the students reported multiple usages; it could be illuminating to see under what conditions a particular form was chosen. There is also an 'other' category, but it is not broken down by sex of speaker or by type of form (first name? endearment?). Hinton did not ask about address from parents, but there certainly are consequences for learning gender practice in a household where a male child is addressed as *son* or *big guy* and his sister is called *honey* or *beautiful*. Given name or a shortened form thereof is the most common form of address to children from adults, including their parents, but other options exist and can enter into social practice within the family in many interesting ways: for example, the full name is sometimes used for 'disciplining' a child who is not doing what the parent wants.

As children move beyond their natal families into other communities of practice, they encounter new address options, but they may also bring with them expectations and interpretations built on their own family's practices. A child who uses *mom* or *mommy* may be shocked by a play-mate's use of first name, apparently assuming a kind of egalitarian rela-tion, or of *mother*, apparently rather 'stiff' or formal. Boys especially may get mocked for *mommy* or *daddy*, learning that *mom* and *dad* are consid-ered more adult and appropriately masculine choices. There can be prob-lems articulating address choices with other family members in a community of practice other than the family itself. A sibling may (unwit-tingly or deliberately) reveal a family pet name that a kid has left at home as too 'childish' for school contexts. And one of my students reported that her mother and father work in the same office, where he uses endear-ments to her whereas she uses his first name only as the fitting choice for the workplace (and finds his endearments somewhat annoying—not sur-prisingly, he is above her in the office hierarchy).

Because address forms are optional and generally admit some variation from a particular addresser to a particular addressee, their occurrence is always potentially significant. Address and addressee-reference options not only very frequently signal gendered identities and relations of inter-locutors, but they often do considerable work in giving content to gender performance.

5. "Enough about you, let's talk about me": Self-reference and gender

In English there are no distinctions of gender or other social relations con-veyed by the first person (*I, me, my*), but this is not the case in all lan-guages. Japanese, for one provides examples of first- and second-person pronouns that are differently used by women and men and are inter-preted as gendered. As Ogawa and Shibamoto Smith (1997) observe, Japanese speakers using first-person pronouns have a number of options, only some of which are gender-neutral. The forms *watakushi* and *watashi* are used by both sexes but the abbreviated *atakushi* and *atashi* are inter-preted as feminine, whereas the abbreviated *washi*, now relatively seldom used (and mainly from older men), is interpreted as masculine (and over-bearing). The forms *boku* and *ore* are listed as used by male speakers, and *atai* as a "lower-class, vulgar" women's form of self-reference. The form *jibun*, often translated as English *self* and used as a reflexive, is also some-times used for self-reference by men and is, according to Ogawa and Shibamoto Smith, associated with military and other strongly hierarchical workplaces. Once again, it is apparent that the real significance of these varied forms of self-reference emerges only from their use in particular communities of practice and their association with particular kinds of social practice. And once again, there is evidence that gender norms are being challenged and changed in various ways. For example, *boku* is increasingly used for self-reference by adolescent girls who are rejecting certain features of traditional normative girlhood, including even the traditional reluctance to compete with boys in school. Reynolds (1990) reports that *boku* has spread to college-age girls and even to adult women in certain contexts. Interestingly, the speakers themselves seem quite aware that their *boku* usage is associated with certain kinds of social practice. Citing Jugaku (1979), she reports, "Girls who were interviewed in a TV program explain that they cannot compete with boys in classes, in games or in fights with *watashi*" (Reynolds 1990, 140).

As Ide (1990) observes, however, the fact that Japanese often dispenses with pronominal forms altogether (it is what syntacticians call a 'pro-drop' language) means that interactions conducted in Japanese often proceed with rather fewer explicit labelings of people than would be found in comparable interactions conducted in English. In addition to imperatives, casual questions in English can omit a second-person subject (*Going to lunch soon?*) and 'postcard register' allows missing first-person pronouns (*Having a wonderful time!*), which are sometimes also omitted by some speakers in casual speech (I've encountered this in phone conversations with certain people). Third-person references are omitted only in severely limited contexts such as answers to questions in which the third-person reference has been explicitly given, a fact about English that is of some importance in considering gendering of person references, discussed briefly in the following section. Languages with no gender distinction in the first-person pronoun but with grammatical gender agreement patterns may produce the effect of gendered self-reference through gender concord: French speakers who want to utter the equivalent of the English "I am happy" must say either "Je suis heureuse" (feminine) or "Je suis heureux" (masculine), thus making it as hard (or perhaps even harder) to speak gender-neutrally of the self in French as it is to speak gender-neutrally of another in English.

Even when pronouns are not themselves gendered, the question of who is 'included' with the speaker by a first-person plural reference can have gender implications. Languages that grammatically mark the distinction between first-person inclusive and exclusive interpretations allow for tracking of affiliations. Meyerhoff (1996) discusses Bislama, a language spoken on the Melanesian islands of Vanuatu, and argues that the choice of the inclusive *yumi* rather than the exclusive form at least sometimes is made to emphasize shared gender identity. Pronominal choice also maps boundary drawing between Melanesian and non-Melanesian and among various family groups within the Melanesian communities.

It is possible to talk about me and you without using explicitly first- or second-person forms. Although third-person expressions generally are used to refer to people (or things) distinct from both the speaker and the addressee of the utterance, they can sometimes be used for speaker reference, as in (9), or addressee reference, as in (10):

(9)   a. *Mommy* wants you to go to sleep now. (uttered by mother to child)
       b. Remember that *Mrs. Robinson* wants you all to send *her* postcards this summer. (uttered by teacher to kindergarten students)

(10)   a. Does *my little darling* want some more spinach? (caretaker to child)
       b. *Joanie* had better be a good girl at school. (caretaker to child)
       c. *His royal highness* will have to make *his* own coffee today. (disgruntled wife to husband)

In most Anglophone communities, such uses occur mainly from adults (especially parents or other primary caretakers and teachers) to children, although they can also occur in jocular contexts between adults (as suggested by (10c)). Since the parent-child model is often called on for romance by English speakers, such usages are also sometimes encountered in the very specialized communities of practice constituted by an intimate couple (straight or gay). They are not unrelated to the playful use of alter personalities in love relations discussed in Langford (1997: 170–171), who comments "on the secrecy and 'childishness' which characterizes these private cultures of love...and their relations to 'adult' love and the 'public' world of 'adulthood.'" In Japanese, however, the use of third-person forms for self- or addressee-reference is apparently much less marked (see discussion above). English speakers too can use third-person forms for self- and addressee-reference without the 'childish' flavor of the above examples. For example, Hicks Kennard (2001) reports female marine recruits being constrained to use third person for both self- and addressee-reference when speaking to their drill instructor, along with the respectful *ma'am* as an address form. In sharp contrast, the senior drill instructor uses the canonical pronominal forms for first- and second-person reference and a (nonreciprocal) surname as an address form:

(11)   R: Recruit Moore [self] requests to know if she [self] can speak with Senior Drill Instructor Staff Sergeant Mason [addressee ref] when she [addressee ref] has time, ma'am [address form].
       SDI: What if I tell you I'm gonna go home, Moore?

In this case, the practice seems to be functioning to depersonalize and subjugate the recruit, to wash her of her own sense of agency.

6. Gendering

Even when the nominal content might seem purely descriptive, there can be much riding on whether or not a particular gendered label is attached to a particular individual. Thirty or more years ago linguists discussed the possibility of understanding a sentence like (12a) as equivalent to either (12b) or (12c); in that era, few people entertained (12c) as a serious possibility:

(12)   a. My cousin is no longer a boy.
        b. My cousin is now a man [having become an adult].
        c. My cousin is now a girl [having changed sexes].

Although the possibility of sex change is far more salient now than it was
then, most people still fail to entertain (12c) as a possible interpretation of
(12a). Judith Butler points out that the gendering process often starts with
a doctor's uttering a sentence like (13a), a process that "shifts the infant
from an 'it' to a 'she' or a 'he'" (Butler 1993, 7). Either (13a) or (13b) is
expected as an answer from new parents to that common question, (13c):

(13)   a. It's a girl.
        b. It's a boy.
        c. What is it?

The expected answers to (13c) strongly suggest that a baby's gender label
is taken to be of primary importance in characterizing it: answers like
those in (14) are virtually unthinkable in most social contexts:

(14)   a. It's a baby who scored 10 on the Apgar test.
        b. It's my child.
        c. It's a two-month-old.

In English and in many other languages, the first labels applied to a child
attribute gender to it. Thus begins the ongoing process of 'girling' (or
'boying'), with relatively little space for creating just 'kids'. There is some
resistance, however. A recent birth announcement card has "It's a" and a
picture of a baby on the front with a marker covering its genitals; inside
the card continues with "baby."

   English, of course, enforces a gender distinction in third-person singular
pronouns. One thing this means is that use of a singular personal pronoun
carries a presumption of sex attribution. I say to a colleague, "One of my
students missed the final because of a sick kid and no babysitter available."
The colleague responds, "Well, did you tell her that is not acceptable?" My
colleague is assuming that the student is female. If I ascribe maleness to
the student and want to make that clear I might say "It's a *he*, actually,"
perhaps implying a rebuke to my colleague for the apparent assumption
that anyone responsible for childcare is female. On the other hand, if
there is no conflict between my colleague's presumption of sex and my
assessment of the situation, I may well fail to point out that there was a
presumptive leap made and thus may contribute in some measure to sustaining the gendered division of labor that supports that leap.

   It is actually very difficult in English and other languages with gendered
third-person pronouns to talk about a third person without ascribing sex
to them—and virtually impossible to do so over an extended period. This
is why Sarah Caudwell's wonderful mystery series featuring Professor
Hilary Tamar, to whom sex cannot be attributed, had to be written with
Hilary as a first-person narrator. (See Livia 2001 for discussion of this and

many other interesting literary cases in which gender attribution is an issue.) Many proper names and nominals ascribe sex, but it is the pronouns that really cause trouble because continued repetition of a name such as *Hilary* or a full nominal such as *my professor* generally seems odd. Linguists have suggested that such repetition often implies a second individual, which is one reason why people standardly use pronouns for at least most later references. There is some use of *they* as a singular pronoun; it is quite common in generic or similar contexts, as in (15a, 15b), and is increasing its use in reference to specific individuals, as in (15c, 15d):

(15)   a. If *anyone* calls, tell *them* I'll be back by noon and get *their* name.
        b. *Every kid* who turned in *their* paper on time got a gold star.
        c. *Someone with a funny accent* called, but *they* didn't leave *their* name.
        d. *A friend of Kim's* got *their* parents to buy *them* a Miata.

It is still unlikely to be used for a specific individual in many circumstances: if, for example, both interlocutors are likely to have attributed (the same) sex to that individual.

The choice of referring expressions plays an important role in gender construction. For example, kin terms in English (and many other languages) are mostly gendered. *Wife* and *husband* are much more often used in the course of everyday practice than *spouse*, and *brother* and *sister* are far ahead of *sib(ling)*. The gender-neutral *kid*, *child*, and *baby* are pretty common and can be used with a possessive to refer to someone's offspring (*Lee's kid* or *my baby*), but *daughter* and *son* are probably more common, especially since they can be freely used for adults, unlike the colloquial gender-neutral forms, which tend to suggest youth. *Mother/mom* and *father/dad* are much more common for singular reference than *parent*; *aunt, uncle, niece,* and *nephew* have no gender-neutral alternatives; and *cousin* names the only kin relation for which English offers only a gender-neutral form. There are, of course, languages that have much more richly elaborated kinship terminology. Distinctions of relative age may be marked in sibling terminology, and there may be different expressions for mother's sister and father's sister or mother's brother and father's brother. And, as is well known, it is the social relations and not the strictly biological that count most in some languages: an expression more or less equivalent to English *aunt*, for example, might designate not only sisters of one's parents but other women tied to the family in some way and construed as having somewhat similar kinds of rights and responsibilities for one. Even in English, the social relations typically prevail in families in which children are adopted or in which children come from different marriages. (We noted above some extended uses of kin terms in English address.)

There are not many systematic studies of how often references to people are gendered and what difference this makes, but there is some relevant research. Barrie Thorne (1993) observed that *boys and girls* was far and away the most common general group form of address in the two elementary schools where she conducted ethnographic research, and that many of the teachers made heavy use of the gendered labels. She also cites research by Spencer Cahill (1987) that suggests that the gendered terms are used by school staff in opposition to the gender-neutral (and disapproving) *baby*: "You're a big girl/boy now, not a baby." Thus Cahill argues that children learn to claim the gendered identities as part of claiming their new relative maturity. Thorne herself observed that "[b]y fourth grade the terms 'big girl' and 'big boy' have largely disappeared, but teachers continue to equate mature behavior with grown-up gendered identities by using more formal and ironic terms of address, like 'ladies and gentlemen'" (Thorne 1993, 35). Of course, the sex-neutral *kid* is fairly common and may in some communities of practice outpace *girl* and *boy* for referring to children or young adults. For adults, however, *woman* and *man* are much more commonplace than *person* (which, unlike *kid*, is not only gender-neutral but also age-neutral) for referring to particular individuals.

In the 1970s there was considerable discussion of the use of *girl* for mature females and the condescension it frequently conveyed (as in "I'll have my girl call your girl"). There are many common practices that conspire to link femaleness with childishness (e.g., Goffmann 1976 argued that the male-female relation was modeled on the parent-child in media depictions), and it is probably no accident that the word *girl* once simply meant 'child'. Nonetheless, the use of the label *girl* to refer to adult females (and, as we saw above, to address them) is by no means always inappropriately juvenilizing. In some communities of practice, *gal*, originating from a variant pronunciation of *girl*, is being used to try to provide a female equivalent of *guy*, a form appropriate for casual conversation that can happily apply to a teenager but can equally well be used to refer to a middle-aged or older man. Says science writer Natalie Angier, obviously not wanting to choose between the more serious-sounding *woman* and the sometimes too youthful *girl*, "I write with the assumption that my average reader is a gal, a word, by the way, that I use liberally throughout the book [on women's biology], because I like it and because I keep thinking, against all evidence, that it is on the verge of coming back into style" (Angier 1999, xv). In spite of Angier's hopefulness, *gal* still tends to be regionally and stylistically restricted, and some readers (including me!) found her liberal use of it rather jarring. Of course the fact that the plural *guys* may be widely used for female referents and addressees complicates the picture. Even in the plural, *guys* is restricted: someone who asks "How many guys were there?" is not inquiring about the number of people in general but about the number of men.

The bottom line is that it is still somewhat easier to be relatively age-neutral and informal when speaking of or to males than when speaking of or to females. Will *guys* become more completely sex-indefinite and bring counting and singular uses under a sex-indefinite umbrella? Or will some label like *gal* widen its range?

The issue of sex attribution that pronominal choice forces in English can become particularly charged when there are challenges to conventional binary gender dichotomies. Transgendered and transsexual people generally want to be referred to by the pronoun consistent with the identity that they currently claim. Those resisting moves from initial gender attributions (former friends or colleagues, unsympathetic family members) may do so by persisting in the pronominal choice consistent with the early attribution. Stories that others tell of such lives must make choices: to use the pronoun consistent with the person's publicly claimed identity at a particular time may well lead to use of different pronouns at different stages, thus visibly/audibly fracturing personal identity. When the identity an individual claims is not the identity others are willing to recognize, pronouns are one turf on which such conflicts get played out. Even those who simply resist gender conformity in their dress or behavior may find others commenting critically on that resistance by derisively using *it* in reference to them. Of course, people who are resisting gender norms can themselves use pronouns creatively as part of constructing alternative identities. Some years ago, Esther Newton (1972) noted that male drag queens often spoke of one another using *she* and *her*, the pronoun fitting the performed identity. Like the Hindi-speaking *hijras* studied by Kira Hall and Veronica O'Donovan (1996), they could also insult one another by using male forms of address and reference.

Hindi is a language with grammatical gender, which offers further gendering possibilities that go beyond the pronominal and nominal labels on which this essay has focused. Livia (1997) offers a compelling account of the importance of grammatical gender as a resource for transsexuals who face a dilemma in articulating new identities within the communities of practice to which they belong (or aspire to belong). Drawing on several autobiographies of French-speaking male to female transsexuals, Livia notes that each of the authors, although asserting a lifelong femaleness, "alternates between masculine and feminine gender concord with regard to herself, indicating that the situation was in fact far more complex" (Livia 1997, 352). In the original French edition of Herculine Barbin's (1978) memoir, grammatical concord in the first person is predominantly feminine in the earlier sections and progressively becomes more masculine over the course of the 'discovery' of Herculine's 'true' masculine identity.

7. Conclusion

Labeling enters into gender construction within and across communities of practice in a host of different and complex ways, and no single essay (or even book) could possibly really cover this topic. I have tried, however, to point to some of the possibilities that should be kept in mind in investigating the linguistic texture of gender construction by specific individuals or in particular communities of practice or institutions. As we have seen, the particularities of the linguistic resources and practices readily available to speakers are critical for how labeling connects to gender. At the same time, the function of particular labels depends on how they are deployed in social practice generally and their connection to gender practice in particular.

Of course, speakers do many creative things. The following exchange comes from an interview conducted by an undergraduate student of mine with a gay male friend of his in the spring of 2001 (used with permission of both parties):[c]

> INTERVIEWER: Do you realize that you call me and other gay friends *girl* a lot?
>
> INTERVIEWEE: Yes, but it is special for a few of you guys. And it's spelled differently.
>
> INTERVIEWER: Yeah?
>
> INTERVIEWEE: With a "U." G-U-R-L. (clapping hands happily)
>
> INTERVIEWER: Awesome.
>
> INTERVIEWEE: And whatever, because it doesn't mean you are like a female. It's for someone who is a fierce faggot.
>
> INTERVIEWER: "Fierce faggot?" (laughing hysterically)
>
> INTERVIEWEE: Hell yeah. You know what I mean. A fierce faggot. Someone who is that fabulous and fucking knows it.

References

Anderson, Benedict (1983). *Imagined communities: Reflections on the origin and spread of nationalism*. New York and London: Verso.

Angier, Natalie (1999). *Woman: An intimate geography*. Boston and New York: Houghton Mifflin.

Baker, Robert (1975). "Pricks" and "chicks": A plea for "persons." In Robert Baker and Frederick Elliston (eds.), *Philosophy and sex*. New York: Prometheus Books, 45–64.

Barbin, Herculine (1978). *Herculine Barbin, dite Alexina B., presente par Michel Foucault*. Paris: Gallimard.

Bernsten, Jan (1994). What's her name? Forms of address in Shona. Paper presented at Cultural Performances: Third Berkeley Women and Language Conference, Berkeley, CA.

Blum, Susan D. (1997). Naming practices and the power of words in China. *Language in Society* 26(3): 357–380.

Brown, Roger, and Albert Gilman (1960). Pronouns of power and solidarity. In Thomas A. Sebeok (ed.), *Style in language*. Cambridge, MA: MIT Press, 253–276.

Butler, Judith (1993). *Bodies that matter*. New York: Routledge.

Cahill, Spencer E. (1987). Language practices and self-definition: The case of gender identity acquisition. *Sociological Quarterly* 27: 295–311.

Cameron, Deborah (1997). Performing gender identity: Young men's talk and the construction of heterosexual masculinity. In Sally Johnson and Ulrike Hanna Meinhof (eds.), *Language and masculinity*. Oxford: Blackwell, 47–64.

Eble, Connie (1996). *Slang and sociability: In-group language among college students*. Chapel Hill and London: University of North Carolina Press.

---

c. Readers will note that example (1d) is inspired by this interview.

Eckert, Penelope (2000). *Linguistic variation as social practice: The linguistic construction of social meaning in Belten High.* Oxford: Blackwell.

Eckert, Penelope, and Sally McConnell-Ginet (1992a). Communities of practice: Where language, gender and power all live. In Kira Hall, Mary Bucholtz, and Birch Moonwomon (eds.), *Locating power: Proceedings of the Second Berkeley Women and Language Conference.* Berkeley, CA: Berkeley Women and Language Group, University of California, 89–99.

—— (1992b). Think practically and look locally: Language and gender as community-based practice. *Annual Review of Anthropology* 21: 461–490.

—— (1995). Constructing meaning, constructing selves: Snapshots of language, gender and class from Belten High. In Kira Hall and Mary Bucholtz (eds.), *Gender articulated: Language and the socially constructed self.* New York: Routledge, 469–507.

—— (1999). New generalizations and explanations in language and gender research. *Language in Society* 28(2): 185–201.

—— (2003). *Language and gender.* Cambridge: Cambridge University Press.

Friedrich, Paul (1972). Social context and semantic features: The Russian pronominal usage. In John J. Gumperz and Dell Hymes (eds.), *Directions in sociolinguistics.* Oxford: Blackwell, 270–300.

Gardner, Carol Brooks (1981). Passing by: Street remarks, address rights, and the urban female. *Sociological Inquiry* 50: 328–356.

Goffman, Erving (1976). Gender advertisements. *Studies in the Anthropology of Visual Communication* 3(2): 69–154.

Hall, Kira, and Veronica O'Donovan (1996). Shifting gender positions among Hindi-speaking hijras. In Victoria Bergvall, Janet M. Bing, and Alice F. Freed (eds.), *Rethinking language and gender research: Theory and practice.* London and New York: Longman, 228–266.

Hicks Kennard, Catherine (2001). Female drill instructors and the negotiation of power through pronouns. Paper presented at the Annual Meetings of the Linguistic Society of America, Washington, DC, January 2001.

Hinton, Leanne (1992). Sex difference in address terminology in the 1990s. Paper presented at Locating Power: Second Berkeley Women and Language Conference, Berkeley, CA.

Holmes, Janet, and Miriam Meyerhoff (1999). The community of practice: Theories and methodologies in language and gender research. *Language in Society* 28(2): 173–184.

Ide, Sachiko (1990). Person references of Japanese and American children. In Sachiko Ide and Naomi H. McGloin (eds.), *Aspects of Japanese women's language.* Tokyo: Kurosio, 43–62.

James, Deborah (1996). Derogatory terms for women and men: A new look. Paper presented at Gender and Belief Systems: Fourth Berkeley Women and Language Conference, Berkeley, CA.

Jugaku, A. (1979). *Nihongo to Onna [Japanese and women].* Tokyo: Iwanamisyoten.

Kanemura, Hasumi (1993). Ninsho Daimeishi Kosho. 5-gatsu Rinji Zokango: Sehai no Joseigo Nihon no joseigo. *Nihongogaku* 12: 109–119.

Kissling, Elizabeth Arveda (1991). Street harassment: The language of sexual terrorism. *Discourse and Society* 2(4): 451–460.

Kissling, Elizabeth Arveda, and Cheris Kramarae (1991). "Stranger compliments": The interpretation of street remarks. *Women's Studies in Communication* (Spring): 77–95.

Langford, Wendy (1997). "Bunnikins, I love you snugly in your warren": Voices from subterranean cultures of love. In Keith Harvey and Celia Shalom (eds.), *Language and desire: Encoding sex, romance and intimacy*. London and New York: Routledge, 170–185.

Lave, Jean, and Etienne Wenger (1991). *Situated learning: Legitimate peripheral participation*. Cambridge: Cambridge University Press.

Lee, Motoko Y. (1976). The married woman's status and role as reflected in Japanese: An exploratory sociolinguistic study. *Signs: Journal of Women in Culture and Society* 1(1): 991–999.

Leeds-Hurwitz, Wendy (1980). *The use and analysis of uncommon forms of address: A business example*. Working Papers in Sociolinguistics, vol. 80. Austin, TX: Southwest Educational Development Laboratory.

Livia, Anna (1997). Disloyal to masculine identity: Linguistic gender and liminal identity in French. In Anna Livia and Kira Hall (eds.), *Queerly phrased: Language, gender, and sexuality*. New York and Oxford: Oxford University Press, 349–368.

—— (2001). *Pronoun envy: Literary uses of linguistic gender*. Oxford and New York: Oxford University Press.

March, Kathryn (2002). *"If each comes halfway": Meeting Tamang women in highland Nepal*. Ithaca, NY: Cornell University Press.

McConnell-Ginet, Sally (2002). 'Queering' semantics: Definitional struggles. In Kathryn Campbell-Kibler, Robert Podesva, Sarah Roberts, and Andrew Wong (eds.), *Language and sexuality*. Palo Alto, CA: CSLI, 137–160.

McElhinny, Bonnie S. (1995). Challenging hegemonic masculinities: Female and male police officers handling domestic violence. In Kira Hall and Mary Bucholtz (eds.), *Gender articulated: Language and the socially constructed self*. New York and London: Routledge, 217–243.

Meyerhoff, Miriam (1996). My place or yours: Constructing intergroup boundaries in Bislama. Paper presented at Gender and Belief Systems: Fourth Berkeley Women and Language Conference, at Berkeley, CA.

—— (2001). Communities of practice. In J. K. Chambers, Peter Trudgill, and Natalie Schilling-Estes (eds.), *Handbook of language variation and change*. Oxford: Blackwell, 526–548.

Newton, Esther (1972). *Mother Camp: Female impersonators in America*. Englewood Cliffs, NJ: Prentice-Hall.

Ogawa, Naoko, and Janet Shibamoto Smith (1997). The gendering of the gay male sex class in Japan: A case study based on "Rasen no Sobyo." In Anna Livia and Kira Hall (eds.), *Queerly phrased: Language, gender, and sexuality*. New York and Oxford: Oxford University Press, 402–415.

Reynolds, Katsue Akiba (1990). Female speakers of Japanese in transition. In Sachiko Ide and Naomi H. McGloin (eds.), *Aspects of Japanese women's language*. Tokyo: Kurosio, 129–146.

Risch, Barbara (1987). Women's derogatory terms for men: That's right, "dirty" words. *Language in Society* 16: 353–358.

Schegloff, Emanuel (1972). Sequencing in conversational openings. In John J. Gumperz and Dell Hymes (eds.), *Directions in sociolinguistics*. Oxford: Blackwell, 346–380.

Schultz, Muriel R. (1975). The semantic derogation of women. In Barrie Thorne and Nancy Henley (eds.), *Language and sex: Difference and dominance*. Rowley, MA: Newbury House, 64–75.

Simmonds, Felly Nkweto (1995). Naming and identity. In Delia Jarrett-Macauley (ed.), *Reconstructing womanhood, reconstructing feminism*. London: Routledge, 109–115.

Stanley, Julia Penelope (1977). Paradigmatic woman: The prostitute. In David L. Shores and Caitlin P. Hines (eds.), *Papers in language variation*. Montgomery: University of Alabama Press, 303–321.

Stannard, Una (1977). *Mrs Man*. San Francisco: Germainbooks.

Sutton, Laurel A. (1995). Bitches and skankly hobags: The place of some women in contemporary slang. In Kira Hall and Mary Bucholtz (eds.), *Gender articulated: Language and the socially constructed self*. New York and London: Routledge, 279–296.

Tannen, Deborah (1994). The relativity of linguistic strategies. In Deborah Tannen (ed.), *Discourse and gender*. Oxford: Oxford University Press, 19–52.

——— (2003). Gender and family interaction. In Janet Holmes and Miriam Meyerhoff (eds.), *The handbook of language and gender*. Malden, MA: Blackwell.

Thorne, Barrie (1993). *Gender play*. New Brunswick, NJ: Rutgers University Press.

Wenger, Etienne (1998). *Communities of practice*. Cambridge: Cambridge University Press.

Wolfson, Nessa, and Joan Manes (1980). Don't "dear" me! In Sally McConnell-Ginet, Ruth A. Borker, and Nelly Furman (eds.), *Women and language in literature and society*. New York: Praeger, 79–92.

Wong, Andrew, and Qing Zhang (2000). *Tonqzhi men zhan qi lail:* The linguistic construction of the *tongzhi* community. *Journal of Linguistic Anthropology* 10(2): 248–278.

11

'Queering' semantics

Definitional struggles

In a famous passage from Lewis Carroll's *Through the Looking Glass*, Humpty Dumpty explains to Alice why un-birthdays should be celebrated.

> …and that shows that there are three hundred and sixty-four days when you might get un-birthday presents—'
> 'Certainly,' said Alice.
> 'And only ONE for birthday presents, you know. There's glory for you!'
> 'I don't know what you mean by 'glory',' Alice said.
> Humpty Dumpty smiled contemptuously. 'Of course you don't—till I tell you. I meant 'there's a nice knock-down argument for you!''
> 'But 'glory' doesn't mean 'a nice knock-down argument',' Alice objected.
> 'When I use a word,' Humpty Dumpty said, in rather a scornful tone, 'it means just what I choose it to mean—neither more nor less.'
> 'The question is,' said Alice, 'whether you CAN make words mean so many different things.'
> 'The question is,' said Humpty Dumpty, 'which is to be master—that's all.'

Many students of language have drawn their own morals from this passage. In this essay, I argue that both Humpty Dumpty and Alice are partly right. Alice understands that we can't make words mean whatever we want them to: there are substantial constraints that arise from past history and from what is involved in trying to mean something. At the same time, there is room for shaping and reshaping word meanings. Humpty Dumpty understands that tugs over meaning can be struggles for power. But the stakes go far beyond who wins. Different meanings promote the pursuit of different kinds of social action, cultural values, intellectual inquiry. Meanings, I argue, can indeed facilitate mastery in a variety of arenas.[a]

This essay derives from the plenary address I gave in 2000 at the first International Gender and Language Association (IGALA) meeting at Stanford. The published version appears in Kathryn Campbell-Kibler, Robert Podesva, Sarah Roberts, and Andrew Wong, eds., *Language and Sexuality: Contesting Meaning in Theory and Practice*, (Stanford, CA: CSLI, 2002), 137–160.
    a. McConnell-Ginet (2008) offers more on the power of word meanings.

1. 'Queer'

The word *queer* is my starting point. I highlight this particular word because it is such a powerful example of semantic indeterminacy, shift, and, most important, contestation. The word *queer* has figured prominently in recent years in political and theoretical discourse centered on issues of sexuality, especially sexual diversity, and its complex relation to gender. Annamarie Jagose (1996, 1) puts it quite nicely:

> Once the term *queer* was, at best, slang for homosexual, at worst, a term of homophobic abuse. In recent years, *queer* has come to be used differently, sometimes as an umbrella term for a coalition of culturally marginal sexual self-identifications and at other times to describe a nascent theoretical model which has developed out of more traditional lesbian and gay studies. What is clear is that queer is very much a category in the process of formation. It is not simply that queer has yet to solidify and take on a more consistent profile, but rather that its definitional indeterminacy, its elasticity, is one of its constituent characteristics....[P]art of queer's semantic clout, part of its political efficacy, depends on its resistance to definition, and the way in which it refuses to stake its claim.

In a real sense, I want to argue, many words are queer; that is, they resist definition and it is their definitional intractability that gives them much of their real bite, their efficacy as tools for thought and action. What is the source of such malleability? Like all words, *queer* figures in discursive history, a history that is never fully determinate and that looks back to sometimes conflicting assumptions and forward to a range of alternative possibilities. Noting the importance of the history of its deployment, Judith Butler (1993, 228, 230) claims that the semantic indeterminacy of *queer* is essential to its political utility:

> If the term *queer* is to be a site of collective contestation, the point of departure for a set of historical reflections and futural imaginings, it will have to remain that which is...never fully owned, but always and only redeployed, twisted, queered from a prior usage and in the direction of urgent and expanding political purposes....[T]he term *queer* has been the discursive rallying point for younger lesbians and gay men and, in yet other contexts, for lesbian interventions and, in yet other contexts, for bisexuals and straights for whom the term expresses an affiliation with anti-homophobic politics.

As the passages from Jagose and Butler demonstrate, queer theorists are unlikely to be surprised by my two main claims. (1) Particular meanings are better or worse suited for various kinds of enterprises: to use Jagose's language, 'semantic clout' can be significant but it is variable. To put it a different way, questions of semantics are often not 'just' semantics. (2) The historically contingent character of meaning—its dependence on discursive practice in a range of contexts—is critical to its power. Many linguists and philosophers of language, however, may find these claims initially puzzling, indeed quite queer. In this essay, I sketch a skeletal framework for thinking about the interconnections of linguistic meaning and discourse. The aim is to further understanding of the role language plays in human plans and projects, especially but by no means only those of our plans and projects that connect directly to gender and sexuality.

Let us begin by examining some sample attempts to define *queer*. Table 11.1 has definitions from several different dictionaries or similar volumes, slightly abridged in some cases.

For many speakers of English, the word *queer* seems pejorative, and several of the entries describe its application as 'derogatory.' Random House puts no such label on any of the uses it describes, and in 1985 *A Feminist Dictionary* noted that the word was sometimes used 'appreciatively', though also noting its 'depreciative' uses. Obviously, what is derogatory depends on who is using the word of whom and from what kind of position. The citation in *A Feminist Dictionary* is from a 1975 piece by Charlotte Bunch:

> One of the ways to understand better [what heterosexism is]…is to 'think queer', no matter what your sexuality. By 'think queer', I mean imagine life as a lesbian for a week. Announce to everyone—family, roommate, on the job, everywhere you go—that you are a lesbian. Walk in the street and go out only with women, especially at night. Imagine your life, economically and emotionally, with women instead of men. For a whole week, experience life as if you were a lesbian, and you will learn quickly what heterosexual privileges and assumptions are, and how they function to keep male supremacy working.

There is a long tradition of disagreement over whether *queer* is a label to embrace or to shun. Historian George Chauncey (1994) reports that *queer* was the preferred term of self-reference in New York City in the early part of the twentieth century for men whose primary identification was their sexual interest in other men. And yet the *Encyclopedia of Homosexuality* (Dynes 1990) forecast the imminent death of the word *queer*. The encyclopedia did note that *queer* was still the preferred self-designator for some gays, although its entry indicates some incredulity that the term could be seen as 'value-free'.

Certainly, until the late 1980s *queer* as a positive term was nearly invisible to people outside communities with a focus on same-sex desire. Before the term *gay* spread widely as a nonclinical designator of homosexuals, *queer* did have some currency among some American heterosexuals as 'politer' than words like *faggot, fruit, fairy, dyke*, or *butch* and, of course, less clinical than *homosexual*. This is not to say that it was positive in those uses. In the early 1970s, a former colleague of mine, a straight-identified woman, described another former colleague, a man, as "queerer than a two-dollar bill." In doing so, she was certainly condescending and homophobic, and I recall vividly my shock that she would say *queer* rather than *homosexual*. At the same time, however, she clearly saw herself as simply

Table 11.1. 'Queer'

queer adj. 1. Deviating from the expected or normal; strange. 2. Odd or unconventional in behavior; eccentric. 3. Arousing suspicion. 4. *Slang.* Homosexual. 5. *Slang.* Fake; counterfeit. —n. *Slang.* 1. A homosexual. 2. Counterfeit money. —tr. v. 1. To ruin or thwart. 2. To put into a bad position. [Perhaps from German *quer*, perverse, cross....See *terkw-*.]

terkw- To turn. 1. Variant form *t(w)erk- in Germanic **thuerh*, twisted, oblique, in a. Old High German *dwerah, twerh*, oblique: QUEER. *American Heritage Dictionary* (1969).

queer adj. and n. A. adj. 1. Strange, odd, eccentric; of questionable character, suspicious. early 16th c. 2a. Bad; worthless. mid 16th. b. Of a coin or banknote: counterfeit, forged. *Criminals' slang.* mid 18th c. 3. Out of sorts; giddy, faint, ill. 4. Esp. of a man: homosexual. *slang derog.*, late 19th c. B. n. 1. Counterfeit coin. Also (US) forged paper currency or bonds. *Criminals' slang.* early 19th c. 2. A (usu. male) homosexual. *slang derog.* Early 20th c. Special collocations and combinations [of particular relevance]: **queer-basher** *slang* a person who attacks homosexuals; **queer-bashing** *slang* physical or verbal attack on homosexuals; **queerdom** n. (*slang, derog.*) the state of being a homosexual mid 20th c. **queerness** n. (a) strangeness; (b) (*slang, derog.*) homosexuality: late 17th c. *The New Shorter Oxford English Dictionary* (rev. ed., 1993).

[Note: the 1971 edition of the full OED gives nothing explicitly connected to sexuality in either the main entry or the appendix. It gives essentially the etymology of the AHD, though expressing some skepticism as to the validity because of *queer*'s early 16th c. appearance in Scots.]

queer adj. 1. strange or odd from a conventional viewpoint; unusually different; singular. 2. of a questionable nature or character; suspicious; shady. 3. Not feeling physically right or well; giddy, faint, or qualmish. 4. mentally unbalanced or deranged. 5. *Slang* a. homosexual. b. bad, worthless, or counterfeit. v.t. 6. to spoil; ruin. 7. to put (a person) in a hopeless or disadvantageous situation as to success, favor, etc. 8. to jeopardize. n. *slang* 9. a homosexual. 10. counterfeit money. *Random House Dictionary* (1966).

queer almost archaic. The word's declining popularity may...reflect today's visibility and acceptance of gay men and lesbians and the growing knowledge that most of them are in fact quite harmless ordinary people. [Although in 20th c. America] *queer* has been the most popular vernacular term of abuse for homosexuals, even today some older English homosexuals prefer the term, even sometimes affecting to believe that it is value-free. *Encyclopedia of Homosexuality* (1990).

queer Perhaps from German *quer*, 'crosswise' in the original sense of 'crooked,' 'not straight,' to modern English via Scots beggars cant. Means singular, strange, odd, differing from what is 'ordinary.' Generic slang term used depreciatively and appreciatively to mean homosexual (also means 'counterfeit' as in *queer as a two-dollar bill*). *A Feminist Dictionary* (1985).

'telling it like it is' as opposed to engaging in overtly hostile 'name-calling' as she would have been if she'd used *faggot* or *fruit* or *fairy*. Her use of *queer* probably reflected a growing discomfort with other available terms, a discomfort that was manifest both among antihomophobic activists and among vaguely 'progressive' straight-identified people. Jagose (1996, 75) quotes James Davidson, writing in the *London Review of Books* in 1994: "*Queer* is in fact the most common solution to the modern crisis of utterance, a word so well-traveled it is equally at home in 19th-century drawing-rooms, accommodating itself to whispered insinuation, and on the streets of the Nineties, where it raises its profile to that of an empowering slogan."

As the Random House entry in table 11.1 indicates, the term tended to be used primarily for men. One fear many self-described lesbians and other nonstraight women have expressed is that this androcentric pattern will persist even as other features of the term's use shift. Certainly the related term *gay* has often not been construed gender inclusively, as the frequent conjunction *gays and lesbians* in all kinds of public discourses indicates. In spite of such fears, however, *queer* has become very widespread in self-reference among political activists as an umbrella term for gay men, lesbians, bisexuals, transgender and transsexual people, and others who challenge heteronormative views of sexuality. A turning point was the birth of Queer Nation, with its in-your-face politics and its defiant and memorable slogan: "We're here; we're queer; get used to it." Interestingly, definitions of *queer* are missing from some places one might expect to find them. For example, Part IV of *Bi any other name: Bisexual people speak out* (Hutchins and Kaahumanu 1991) is titled "Politics: A queer among queers," and the overview to that section begins with the following quotation from Autumn Courtney, a bi activist speaking in 1988 at the San Francisco Lesbian Gay Freedom Day Parade Celebration:

> Hey queer! Hey you are queer aren't you? What kind of queer are you? QUEER—you know what it means—odd, unusual, not straight, gay. I am queer, not straight. And...I am odd. Odd in the fact that I have been an *active open out-of-the-closet Bisexual* in the lesbian and gay world for the last seven years. We must unite to fight common enemies; we must not squabble among ourselves over who is more queer or more politically correct.

The editors and other contributors to this very interesting book clearly recognized *queer* as a word applicable to self-identified bisexual people. In spite of that, the short glossary at the end of the book does not include *queer*, even though it does tackle such difficult to define expressions as *bisexual*, *homophobia*, *patriarchy*, and *sexism*. Part of the problem for the editors in defining *queer* might have lain in the tension between the kind of identity politics represented by some contributors to the volume and the dis-identity politics that theorists have so often associated with *queer*. Queer theorists tend to emphasize difference and to challenge the ideological processes that help constitute identity, even 'queer' identities.

2. 'Gay'

How does *gay*, now probably the most widely used 'umbrella' term, differ from *queer*? To 'outsiders', *gay* was somewhat less familiar than *queer* as a label for a sexual identity until the gay liberation movement began in the late 1960s. It became increasingly prominent in both speech and print during the 1970s and 1980s as gay liberation became a real political force. As a label of self-identification for men, Chauncey (1994) reports that *gay* entered the New York City scene in the 1920s and 1930s and became increasingly common during the wartime period. Kennedy and Davis (1993) report that it became more prevalent as a generic term for lesbians in Buffalo, New York, during the 1950s than it had been earlier. Table 11.2 contains some dictionary entries for *gay*.

Gay as a designator for homosexuals had many fewer negative associations in the minds of those outside the homosexual community than *queer*. This is partly because it was less familiar in such uses and partly because its other uses were generally more positive than the other uses of *queer*. It is probably for such reasons that it very quickly established itself as the most general 'polite' form for outsiders to use in referring to self-identified homosexuals. By the 1990s even mainstream politicians were talking publicly about 'gays', especially in contexts where they wanted to be seen as inclusive. Even in 2000, however, *queer*, though widely used by academic theorists and political activists, was still taboo in contexts like presidential candidates' speeches. [And in 2010, *queer* is still mostly avoided except by academics and activists, whereas *gay* is commonplace.] And large numbers of people who do not identify themselves as belonging to sexual minorities still assume that *queer* is fundamentally 'derogatory', although they might use it among familiars as a 'milder' form than some others available.

3. 'Lesbian'

In contrast to *queer* and *gay*, the term *lesbian* has no generally familiar uses outside the domain of sexual identity and politics. It has, however, for a very long time been used in speech and in writing as the least marked way to refer to women whose sexual desires are primarily directed toward other women. More accurately, *lesbian* has been the least marked designator outside communities of such women. Elizabeth Kennedy and Madeline Davis (1993, 6–7) comment on terms of self-reference among the women they interviewed for their groundbreaking ethnohistorical study of the working class lesbian community in Buffalo, New York, from the 1930s through the 1950s:

> We use the term 'lesbian' to refer to all women in the twentieth century who pursued sexual relationships with other women. Narrators, however, rarely used the word 'lesbian,' either to refer to themselves or to women like

Table 11.2. 'Gay'

Gay a. 1. Showing or characterized by exuberance or mirthful excitement. 2. Bright or lively, especially in color. 3. Full or given to social or other pleasures. 4. Dissolute; licentious. 5. *Slang*. Homosexual. [Middle English *gay, gai,* from Old French *gai,* probably from Gothic *gaheis* (unattested), akin to OHG *gahi,* sudden, impetuous.] *American Heritage Dictionary,* 1969.

Gay a., adv., & n. ME [(O)Fr. *gai,* of unkn. origin.] A adj. 1. Full of, disposed to, or indicating joy and mirth; light-hearted, carefree. ME. b. Airy, offhand, casual. late 18th c. 2. Given to pleasure; freq. *euphem.,* dissolute immoral. Late ME. b. Leading an immoral life; *spec.* engaging in prostitution. *slang.* Early 19th c. 3. Good, excellent, fine. Now chiefly *dial.* Late ME. c. In good health, well. *dial.* Mid 19th c. 4. Showy, brilliant, brightly colored. Also, brightly decorated *with.* Late ME. b. Of a woman: beautiful, charming, debonair. Long *arch.* & poetic. Late ME. c. Finely or showily dressed. Now *rare.* Late ME. c. Superficially attractive; (of reasoning, etc.) specious, plausible. Late ME-Late 18th c. (now obsolete) 5. Of a quantity or amount: considerable, reasonable, fair. Chiefly Sc. Late 18th c. 6. Of an animal: lively, spirited, alert. Early 19th c. b. Of a (dog's) tail: carried high or erect. Early 20th. 7. (Of a person, sometimes *spec.* a man) homosexual; of or pertaining to homosexuals; (of a place, etc.) intended for or frequented by homosexuals. Chiefly *colloq.* Mid 20th c. *Special collocations & phrases:* **gay cat** *US slang* (a) a young tramp, *esp.* one in company with an older man. **gay dog** a man given to revelling or self-indulgence. **gay deceiver** (a) a deceitful rake; (b) in *pl. (slang),* shaped pads for increasing the apparent size of the female breasts. **Gay Lib, Liberation** (the advocacy of) the liberation of homosexuals from social stigma and discrimination. **gay plague** *colloq.* (sometimes [!] considered *offensive*) AIDS (so called because first identified amongst homosexuals), **get gay** *US slang* act in an impertinent or overfamiliar way. C. n. 3 A homosexual; sometimes *spec.* a male homosexual. Chiefly *colloq.* Mid 20th c. *The New Shorter Oxford English Dictionary* (rev. ed., 1993).

Gay is a Middle English word derived from the Middle French term GAI (gai). It is defined in British dictionaries as 'joyful, akin to merry, frivolous, showy, given to dissipated or vicious pleasure'. GAI became popularized in the Middle French burlesque theatre's description of effeminate, pretentious male character roles.…English theatre began to use the word GAY to describe 'saucy, prostituting, or sexually promiscuous' characters. Since women were not at that time allowed on stage in either country, these mock feminine roles were always caricatured by men. The Scottish tradition of the word GAI (guy) was more distinctly used to describe someone different…an astrologer, forester, or recluse. (E.g., 'I say, he is a bit gai!'). This tradition originally was not negative, but merely implied 'different or queer from the norm.'…It is interesting to note that the word GAY was not used to describe 'homosexual' women until it found its way to the Americas. Today the terms LESBIAN and SAPPHIC are still the tradition in Europe. In the 1920s and 1930s the word GAY surfaced in the underground homosexual subculture as a term of identification among homosexual men. Expressions such as 'You're looking gay tonight,' or 'That's a gay tie you have there' were used to establish mutual identity in social situations. Finally, in the late 1990s, the term GAY was taken up by the Gay Liberation Movement in its attempt to affirm 'a truly joyous alternative lifestyle' and throw off the sexually objectifying term 'homosexual'. Entry quoted from Jeanne Cordova (1974) in *A Feminist Dictionary,* 1985.

themselves. In the 1940s the terms used in the European-American community were 'butch and fem,' a 'butch and her girlfriend,' sometimes a 'lesbian and her girlfriend.' Sometimes butches would refer to themselves as 'homos' when trying to indicate the stigmatized position they held in society. Some people...would use...'gay girls' or 'gay kids' to refer to either butch or fem. In the 1950s, the European-American community still used 'butch' and 'fem' [but other] terms became more common. Sometimes butches of the rough crowd were referred to as 'diesel dykes' or 'truck drivers.' They sometimes would refer to themselves as 'queer' to indicate social stigma. In the African-American community 'stud broad' and 'stud and her lady' were common terms, although 'butch' and 'fem' were also used...The term 'bull dagger' was used by hostile straights as an insult, but was sometimes used by members of the African-American community to indicate toughness.... [L]anguage usage was not consistent and a white leader in the 1950s says that she might have referred to lesbians as 'weird people.'

(This discussion makes it clear that it is within particular communities of practice that patterns of language usage develop and that it is important to consider localized as well as broader patterns; see Eckert and McConnell-Ginet 1992, 1995, for discussion of the notion 'community of practice' in application to language and gender research.)

As Kennedy and Davis point out 1993, 7–8), at least four distinct kinds of erotic relationships existed between women in the nineteenth and twentieth centuries: (1) women who passed as men, some of whom were erotically involved with other women; (2) middle-class married women with intense passionate friendships with other women, some erotic (though few genital); (3) middle-class unmarried women who "built powerful lives around communities of women defined by work, politics, or school"; (4) "women...who socialized together because of their explicit romantic and sexual interests in other women." Does/should *lesbian* apply to all these women? For some, the word was unavailable; only those in group (4) were likely to think that the word might apply to them (although they may not actually have used it). Such questions are among those that have animated discussion of the term during the past several decades.

Standard dictionary entries don't go much beyond the Isle of Lesbos, where Sappho lived in the sixth century BC, and the idea of same-sex desire among females. There has been, however, considerable dispute about how to construe *lesbian*. Is it a sexual or a political identity, or does it point to a continuum of woman-identified practices and attitudes? Does it allow for diverse sexual practices or is it normativizing? Are fems *really* lesbians—or, conversely, are they the only *genuine* lesbians? Is there a transhistorical notion of *lesbian*, or does the term presuppose consciousness of sexual preferences and practices being constitutive of personal identity, a consciousness that arguably developed as a real possibility only in the late nineteenth century? Table 11.3 includes a number of entries from *A Feminist Dictionary* that give some idea of the range of these disputes. As with *gay*, the entry leads with a quote from Jeanne Cordova's 1974 article 'What's in a Name?'.

Table 11.3. 'Lesbian'

lesbian

"The word LESBIAN comes to us as a British word derived from the Greek 600 BC Isle of Lesbos and 'the reputed female homosexual band associated with Sappho of Lesbos' (*Webster's Seventh New Collegiate Dictionary*). Etymologically speaking, the word LESBIAN, rather than the word 'gay,' is the more correct term when speaking of women-identified women." (Jeanne Cordova, 1974)

Mary Daly…prefers "to reserve the term LESBIAN to describe women who are woman-identified, having rejected false loyalties to men on all levels. The terms *gay* or *female homosexual* more accurately describe women who, although they relate genitally to women, give their allegiance to men and male myths, ideologies, styles, practices, institutions, and professions." (Mary Daly, 1978)

"A lesbian is the rage of all women condensed to the point of explosion." (Radicalesbians, 1970)

"I, for one, identify a woman as a lesbian who says she is." (Cheryl Clarke, 1981)

"Lesbian is the only concept I know of which is beyond the categories of sex (woman and man), because the designated subject (lesbian) is *not* a woman, either economically, or politically, or ideologically." (Monique Wittig, 1981)

Those who "have a history of perceiving them Selves as such, and the will to assume responsibility for Lesbian acts, erotic and political." (Janice Raymond, 1982)

"One who, by virtue of her focus, her attention, her attachment is disloyal to phallocratic reality. She is not committed to its maintenance and the maintenance of those who maintain it, and worse her mode of disloyalty threatens its utter dissolution in the mere flicker of the eye." (Marilyn Frye, 1983)

lesbian continuum includes "a range—through each woman's life and throughout history—of woman-identified experience; not simply the fact that a woman has had or consciously desired genital sexual experience with another woman." Adrienne Rich wants to expand the concept of lesbian to "many more forms of primary intensity between and among women, including the sharing of a rich inner life, the bonding against male tyranny, the giving and receiving of practical and political support." (Adrienne Rich, 1980)

lesbianism means that "you forget the male power system, and that you give women primacy in your life—emotionally, personally, politically." (Rita Mae Brown, 1976)

"Feminism is the complaint, and lesbianism is the solution." (Jill Johnston, 1975)

Joan Nestle challenges this slogan, on the grounds that it invalidates lesbian herstory. Pre-Stonewall lesbians, though not lesbian feminists as currently defined, were nevertheless feminists. "Their feminism was not an articulated theory, it was a lived set of options based on erotic choice." Further the playing out of butch-fem roles, now considered oppressive, was actually a mode of adventuring produced by their social and sexual autonomy from mainstream culture. (Joan Nestle, 1981).

"For most women—especially of my age—it is not a choice. Being attracted to women sexually is a unique and precious response." (Chrystos, 1981)

lesbian politics of naming

"The attempt to criminalize lesbianism through a clause in the 1921 [UK] Criminal Law Amendment Bill (to place it on a par with the 1885 criminalisation of male homosexuality) foundered on the conviction that drawing attention to the existence of a practice unknown to most women might itself incite the practice." (Lucy Bland, 1983)

"The denial of lesbians is literally Victorian. The Queen herself was appalled by the inclusion of a paragraph on lesbianism in the 1885 Criminal Law that sought to penalize private homosexual acts by two years' imprisonment. She expressed a complete ignorance of female inversion or perversion and refused to sign the Bill, unless all reference to such practices was omitted." (Blanche Cook, 1977)

"It is not ethical to call yourself a feminist when you mean lesbian, or to use those words interchangeably." (Thyme Siegel, 1983)

Although the choice between *gay* and *homosexual* certainly has political overtones, neither of those words has been the site of as much ideological struggle as *lesbian*, with its connections not only to antihomophobic but also to antisexist politics. Indeed, there is a tendency, as noted in some of the citations in table 11.3, to conflate feminism and lesbianism. The quotes from Mary Daly and from Marilyn Frye take being a lesbian to require not only defiance of male dominance but also a focus of attention on women in all areas of life. On this kind of view, *lesbian* certainly resists assimilation into some gender-neutral 'gay' category. Some lesbian theorists (e.g., Jeffreys 1993), have even seen gay men as more invested in patriarchy than straight men, arguing that their erotic preference for men stems from a thorough-going misogyny. In my view, although gay men, like some women, are not immune from misogyny, this particular charge seems profoundly misguided. Not only have many men been active in gay liberation, but they have also been active in antisexist efforts. It is also clear that erotic preferences are far more complex than the equation of a man's male-directed desires with his disdain for women would allow.

This is not to deny that gender and sexual oppression are linked in many different ways. Heterosexual desire (or at least norms promoting such desire) can lead women to cooperate in their own subordination, especially in cultural contexts that eroticize female vulnerability and male strength. These connections are part of what has led some to see lesbianism as the only path to female emancipation. Opting out of what Barrie Thorne (1993) and Penelope Eckert (1996) call the 'heterosexual marketplace' can be a liberating move for some girls and young women. And being independent of men sexually can make it easier to avoid other kinds of dependence on them (and also the deference that dependence often brings). But equating lesbianism and feminism risks obscuring the specificity both of sexualities and of gender dynamics. The equation can be particularly problematic because it resonates all too well with persisting conflation in the dominant culture of heterosexual eroticism with male dominance and female subordination. Many feminists, among them many lesbians, want to open up more discursive space for sexual desire and erotic activity involving strong female agency no matter whether the sexual object might be female or male. Farwell (1988) treats definitions like Daly's and Fry's as 'simply' metaphoric since they treat genital sexual activity between women as insufficient for applying the label *lesbian* and require a certain (feminist) stance toward men and male dominance. I return below to this and other metaphoric uses of identity labels, but at this point I simply want to note that such uses, even if seen by all as special and 'nonliteral', are nonetheless often implicated in attempts to promote certain kinds of social norms and values or pursue certain kinds of political strategies.

Even if we stay with sexualities, the citations make clear that there have been many disputes on just what being lesbian might amount to. Is it a matter of sexual behavior or of sexual desire or of sexual identity? Is it impossible to be lesbian if one does not embrace that identity whole-heartedly? Can someone whose sexual fantasies include both other women and men be lesbian? Can someone who engages in sexual activity with both women and men be a lesbian? Can a woman become a lesbian at the age of 50 or stop being a lesbian at the age of 30? Questions like these have been actively debated and were particularly prominent during the 1970s and 1980s. Although they are by no means dead, they have faded somewhat in importance as activists have tended to move away from identity politics.

4. Comparisons of *queer*, *gay*, and *lesbian*

Both *gay* and *lesbian* have tended to focus on identities, often modeled on ethnic identities. In contrast, *queer* has been mobilized in the past decade or so to cut across a range of sexual identities. One aim has been to bring together those who *dis*-identify with heteronormativity; in other words, those who challenge sexual norms that assume potentially reproductive sexual encounters as a standard, with other kinds of sexual activity at best a substitute for the 'real thing' or, more often, somehow distasteful or morally wrong. Unlike the self-affirming uses of *gay* and *lesbian*, however, the reclamation of *queer* is pretty much limited to gay-affirmative groups or to academic contexts like this book. As noted earlier, the word is not used by presidential candidates in their speeches or in *New York Times* reporting on gay rights issues. A number of my students have reported not knowing that *queer* could be used to speak about diverse sexualities without thereby derogating them. Thus the reclamation of *queer* is certainly still not a complete one, being limited to certain communities of practice.

In contrast to *queer*, both *gay* and *lesbian* are widely seen as nonjudgmental terms, quite useable in contexts where they might be heard by those they designate. Of course, this does not mean that there is no 'taint' of homophobic attitudes associated with these words. Those of my students who thought that *queer* was always somewhat negative and that *gay* and *lesbian* were the preferred neutral terms were nonetheless familiar with the relatively recent use of *gay* as an all-purpose derogatory descriptor, roughly glossable as 'uncool' or 'gross'. This use, very common among elementary school kids, is not reflected in the dictionary entries above. It seems quite likely, however, that the third graders' sneering "That's so gay" ultimately has arisen from contemptuous talk about gay sexuality, even though the third graders themselves generally do not make a connection to sexual orientation (and may never even have heard the kind of homophobic talk that gave birth to their own usage).

So we have here a cluster of related words—*queer*, *gay*, and *lesbian*—each of which has a cluster of (more or less) related senses or patterns of use, and each of which has a history not just of change from earlier patterns but of ongoing tension among them. There are many more words that are related to these: for example, *homosexual, heterosexual, monosexual, bisexual,* and *straight.* In his influential *Keywords,* social theorist Raymond Williams pointed to the sociocultural significance of distinct but connected interpretations for particular words. His entry for the word *culture* contains the following discussion (Williams 1983, 91, 92):

> Faced by this complex and still active history of the word, it is easy to react by selecting one 'true' or 'proper' or 'scientific' sense and dismissing other senses as loose or confused....It is clear that, within a discipline, conceptual usage has to be clarified. But in general it is the range and overlap of meanings that is significant. The complex of senses indicates a complex argument about the relations between general human development and a particular way of life, and between both and the works and the practices of art and intelligence....[T]he range and complexity of sense and reference indicate both difference of intellectual position and some blurring or overlapping. These variations, of whatever kind, necessarily involve alternative views of the activities, relationships, and processes which this complex word [i.e., *culture*] indicates. The complexity, that is to say, is not finally in the word but in the problems which its variations of use significantly indicate.

Similarly, the complexity we find in *queer* and its kin points to the wide array of issues involved in thinking about sexual practices, sexual identities, sexual norms, and values.

5. Word meaning and social practice

What I want to do in the rest of this essay is explore some of the mechanisms through which the shaping and reshaping of word meanings emerge as part and parcel of the shaping and reshaping of social and political practices. There are four independent but related ideas about language and word meaning I want to draw on. (1) Natural languages are in important ways like formal linguistic systems or logics in which basic expressions—the word-like units—are not given fixed meanings but must be assigned interpretations when the system is used. (2) The cognitive structure underlying the concept a (content) word labels is less like a definition or a prototype than like a theory (or family of theories) in which that concept plays a key role. (3) Interpretations draw on preceding discourse understandings and on projections of future plans. (4) Linguistic communication involves bringing about some kind of change in the discourse-produced picture of how things are (or might be or should be or...).

5.1 Words as 'empty' forms

The first idea—that a natural language is in many ways very like a formal linguistic system—is common to a number of approaches to semantics in linguistics and philosophy. Formal semantic theories offer considerable insight into combinatorial semantics—how word meanings fit together to express thoughts. There is significant work done on the semantics of function words like *and, not, if, every,* and *the*. From a slightly different but also relatively formal perspective, there is very illuminating investigation of such features of word meaning as the argument structure of verbs—for example, the role of a verb's direct object or its subject. Formal semantics has also offered insight into the meaning of plurality, tense and aspect, possessives, and other grammatical morphemes and constructions. But formal semantics has rather little to say about the meanings of the basic content-ful expressions, about words like *woman* or *tree* or *water* or *laugh* or, of course, expressions like *queer, gay,* and *lesbian*. There may be some things to be noted about truth-conditional relations among words; for example, perhaps *Kim is a lesbian* entails *Kim is a woman*, which in turn entails *Kim is not a man*. Such connections, however, are limited and do not offer us much insight into the conceptual complexity of basic vocabulary items. (I will return to the question of why and how sometimes even such entailments seem to be missing.)

Among the more contentful analyses of lexical items are those that identify semantic features on the basis of contrasts: for example, *woman* contrasts with *man* in being +FEMALE, with *girl* in being +MATURE, and so on. The idea that what a word means is, at least in part, a matter of how it contrasts with certain other words in the same semantic field is an important one that informs many empirical explorations of word meaning.[b] The status and utility of semantic features or components is a matter of some dispute, but there is no question that lexical contrasts have to figure in any guide to word usage and that speakers must incorporate them somehow in their understanding of linguistic practice.

There are also, of course, other ways to shed light on word meanings. So-called cognitive semantics looks less at particular words and more at metaphorical patterning, at the recurrence of certain abstract identifications. For example, Caitlin Hines (2000) explains the evolution of dessert terms to refer to women in terms of such identifications as WOMEN ARE SWEET, ACHIEVING A DESIRED OBJECT IS GETTING SOMETHING TO EAT. And George Lakoff (1987) has an interesting discussion of the complex and changing conceptual structure(s) associated with the word *mother* as reproductive technologies and women's increased participation in the waged labor force allow more varied kinds of relations between women and children. The evolving and competing meanings he identifies are, of course, embedded in evolving and contested social practices of reproduction and parenting. (Note that the recent emergence of *parent* as a verb is part of feminist-inspired moves to involve men more actively in responsibility for childcare.)

---

b. See chapter 9 of this volume for use of semantic features in analyzing pronominal semantics.

An approach in which word meaning is relatively empty and is filled in as part of ongoing discursive processes can indeed draw on insights from cognitive semantics or from componential analysis into semantic features. What is important is that the empty vessel view of words does not assume that there will be available anything like a necessary and sufficient set of conditions for applying the word. Nor does it assume that the word's meaning is somehow encapsulated in something like a prototypical exemplar. On the view I am proposing, words do not really *have* (much) meaning—word meanings are underspecified—but they are given meaning as they are deployed to do things in ongoing discourse. Humpty Dumpty was on the right track.

5.2 Words anchored by 'theory'

But now we must turn to the remaining ideas I mentioned. Of course, words are not as completely 'empty' as I may have seemed to suggest, free to be used in just any old way. People do attach some kind of concepts, some sort of cognitive structures, to the content words of their language. And, just as important, people often take their uses of those words to be 'regulated' in certain ways that may go beyond what is in individual users' heads, their individual lexical concepts. What has been called the 'theory-theory' of lexical concepts draws on recent work in psychology and also on some ideas from the philosophy of language. In his influential "The meaning of 'meaning'," philosopher Hilary Putnam (1975) posited a 'linguistic division of labor' for regulating our use of words. Putnam notes that many English speakers might have both the words *elm* and *beech* in their lexicons, knowing nothing about them other than the fact that they are trees. To know whether someone has spoken truly if she says "Hildegard's yard has two elms in it," speakers turn to those with botanical expertise. We use others to access the scientific theory that elucidates the distinction between elms and beeches. In this attenuated sense, then, tree-theory underlies these lexical concepts, but particular individuals may know only that there is a relevant tree-theory, whereas others may have some mental representation of this theory (though perhaps even then deferring to experts on fine points). At the same time, Putnam suggests, individual language users may access a 'stereotype' that guides them fairly well in regulating their own usage. For example, even people who believe that certain bodily features are 'really' criterial for applying the terms *woman* and *man* to individuals may rely on things like clothing, hairstyles, facial hair, and linguistic and behavioral style to guide their own labeling of people as women or men. Putnam's basic idea has been adopted by a number of cognitive and developmental psychologists. Keil (1989), for example, notes that the child seems to shift from an early belief that the stereotypical features are what count to later recognition, at least for biological kinds, that there is stuff 'below the surface' that counts more than what is readily apparent.

What neither Putnam nor the psychologists influenced by him point out is that the stereotype may be allied with a theory of social norms: this is how women 'should' dress, wear their hair, speak, and act. Such norms can then be drawn on for helping to interpret expressions like *womanly*. Even generic statements about *women* are often not simple statistical generalizations but generalizations that mark those who deviate from them as somehow deficient as women, as not 'true' women, as 'queer' in some way or other.[c] Socially normative theories may be in competition with one another, and language users may recognize a number of alternative uses of a word, each of which 'fits' better with some theories than with others. The standard 'theory-theory' does not consider the possibility of competing theories. It might be that for some lexical concepts like tree names, ceding semantic authority to scientific experts is unproblematic. Who is master matters much more, however, when we turn to words and concepts that play a more central role in our informal, everyday theories of ourselves and our social worlds, our cultural values and ideologies. What I propose is that words may be associated with a family of theories, some of which are in direct competition with one another, others of which are simply deployed for alternative purposes. 'Theory' may weight the balance too much toward notions of scientific expertise. Perhaps it might be better to say that words are associated with families of discursive practices that give them their real force.

5.3 Words shaped by history

The third idea is that interpretations draw on the past and project to the future. One might be introduced to the word *lesbian* by being told that it's a term for female homosexuals, but the concept would be enriched and complicated in many different ways. Social stereotypes of various kinds can get added. As one of my self-identified lesbian students said sarcastically, "Of course we're all Birkenstock-wearing vegetarian dykes with extremely short hair who hate men." And, as the citations in table 11.3 show, political and moral attitudes of various sorts also get loaded in. The lexical concept in some sense organizes potentially accessible discursive history. Some parts of the history are seen as grounding 'literal' meaning (perhaps quasi-scientific theories of women's erotic attraction to other women), and others are seen as having a different kind of connection, relating to the role the word plays in various other kinds of theories and debates.[d]

---

c. Recent work on generics supports this idea. See, e.g., McConnell-Ginet 2009 and Leslie (forthcoming).

d. McConnell-Ginet 2008 proposes the term 'conceptual baggage' for content that, although not part of meaning as such, is often brought into discourse when words are used: stereotypes often fit here.

Where Humpty Dumpty went astray was in assuming that he could do anything at all with any word. When Humpty Dumpty says something to Alice, he is entitled to assume that they can both access (1) a linguistic system and certain words in it, (2) patterns of using those words to do particular things, (3) background beliefs and other attitudes, (4) assumptions about the current situation and some of its likely developments. It is through a (more or less) shared discursive history that (1)–(3) are guaranteed—it is a common past that is important. If Humpty Dumpty and Alice have not had much prior personal contact, the assumptions they can make about access to patterns of word use and to background beliefs and other attitudes will be limited to what they have reason to think is relatively conventional or at least very widespread in discursive practices in the larger society to which they belong. On the other hand, if they are longtime coparticipants in some local community of practice, they may well be able to assume access to many more distinctive word uses and particularized attitudes. What (4) involves includes not only standard assessments of current surroundings and why linguistic exchange is occurring but also appraisals of interlocutors' social relationship to one another and their relevant capacities and interests and resources. So, for example, even though *queer* might have long carried a presumption of derogation and an air of gay-bashing in the discursive history of most interlocutors, those who heard activists chanting "We're here, we're queer, get used to it!" were not thereby misled into thinking that these folks using *queer* to refer to themselves were abjectly confessing to self-hatred. Rather, it was clear that by publicly and assertively using the term in self-reference, queer activists were explicitly challenging the contempt and the attempts to control them that had fueled others' use of *queer* as a term of abuse. Indeed, the challenge would not have been so insistently issued had they used a word that did not have a readily accessible history of use in gay-bashing. "We're gay; get used to it" or "We're homosexual; get used to it" or "We're not straight; get used to it" would have been far less effective. And of course it was not just the history of *queer* in homophobic practices but also its suggestions of 'strange' and 'odd' and 'not ordinary' that helped give the slogan its punch, its in-your-face effectiveness. *Queer* can insist on the 'specialness' of those so labeled. (Some may have also appreciated the fact that English *queer* sounds a lot like French *cuir* 'leather', creating a bonus joke for those in the know; my colleague Nelly Furman reminded me of this cross-lingual wordplay.)

Examining a very different cultural context, Andrew Wong and Qing Zhang (2000) discuss the appropriation of the word *tongzhi*, widely employed in Chinese revolutionary discourse and usually glossed as 'comrade', as a term for members of the 'imagined' queer community being constructed by a Chinese gay and lesbian magazine. The word *tongzhi* brings its Chineseness and its revolutionary associations with it; it does not have the clinical feel of the medical term *tongxinglian zhe* 'homosexual', allowing it to emphasize ties with others rather than some kind of deviance. Its use in the magazine creates a quite different sense of community than would the use of imported Western terminology like *queer*, translated into Chinese as *ku-er*, literally something like a 'cool person'. The word *tongzhi* did have some negative associations from its history in Communist discourse, but the new uses managed to ameliorate the word and reclaim it as an appropriate self-designator for members of a homegrown queer community. But amelioration was by no means completely successful. As Wong (2002) shows, the term in its recently acquired sexual identity uses is undergoing new pejoration. The word *tongzhi* is now also used in the mainstream press to apply to Chinese gays and lesbians, but a large proportion of those uses are negative. Not only is sexual orientation often highlighted inappropriately, but there is frequently a kind of 'mocking' of the *tongzhi* and their relationships to one another. These detailed case studies illustrate beautifully that what words can convey and the impact they can have is firmly rooted in their connection to past histories and to conceptions of future possibilities. They also show how different and competing perspectives on social practices and values affect linguistic practice. The pejoration of *tongzhi* occurs in opposition to attempts to push toward a future of sexual tolerance and inclusiveness and get beyond the still predominant idea of deviance that infects talk and thinking about Chinese sexual minorities.

5.4 Words as tools for acting

This brings us to the final and central idea—namely, that linguistic communication is a kind of action. More specifically, to say something is generally to attempt to bring about a change in the mutually available picture of how things are or might be or should be. This important insight is at the heart of the picture of meaning and communication developed by the philosopher Paul Grice (Grice 1989 collects most of Grice's papers on meaning and related issues). Humpty Dumpty claims that when he said "There's glory for you," he meant 'There's a nice knock-down argument for you'—in other words, that he intended to get Alice to recognize that the possibility of 364 gift days rather than just a single one provided an irrefutable argument in favor of celebrating unbirthdays. Unlike the Queer Nation activists, however, Humpty Dumpty was not able to draw on a rich context that would make it clear that this is what he intended to do. Just wanting *glory* to mean 'nice knock-down argument' is not enough to endow it with that meaning: the past history plus the present context must support what a language user tries to do with words. Of course, Humpty Dumpty is right that we do occasionally simply stipulate that we are using old words in new ways, but if stipulation is needed, a reliable communicator will preface her comments with the stipulation. Without stipulation, which is always a rather special move and of course a part of establishing the current context, interlocutors must rely on what can be accessed from discursive history and readily accessible features of the current context. These features include assumptions about the others' knowledge, cleverness, and so on. It is clear that Humpty Dumpty did not think Alice could actually figure out what he had meant (nor could he reasonably have done so). On the Gricean account of what it is for a speaker to mean something to an addressee, Humpty Dumpty could not really have meant to Alice 'there's a nice knock-down argument for you'. Humpty Dumpty can expect Alice to ignore past discursive history only if he has explicitly asked her to do so for purposes of the current exchange. And even then, it's pretty hard to get interlocutors to stick to a stipulative definition of a familiar word. But the Queer Nation slogan shows that there are indeed questions of 'mastery' or power involved. To use *queer* both to affirm difference from heterosexual norms and to refuse efforts to eliminate or reduce such differences is to claim a kind of 'mastery', to refuse the conjunction of abuse and attribution of homosexuality so prominent in the discursive history of the word *queer*. At the same time such moves typically meet with resistance. It is hardly surprising that we do not find a general 'acceptance' of *queer* as affirmative.

Notice that we can have metaphorical interpretations that arise contextually and contribute to discursive history but do not have the same kind of effect on default interpretations as, for example, the gay-affirming uses of *queer*. For example, when Monique Wittig says "A lesbian is not a woman" (see table 11.3), she is not really challenging earlier discourses that put particular lesbians in the category *woman*. She is not, for example, saying that a lesbian does not have two X chromosomes or does not have ovaries or a vagina. As she goes on to say, her point is that "economically, politically,…a lesbian is not a woman." Similarly, Lord Baden-Powell is reputed to have said, after meeting with a group of African political leaders one of whom was female, "the only man in the room was that woman." His point, of course, was that she was the only one who showed the kind of courage and intelligence he took as characteristic of men and not of women. He was not commenting on her bodily configuration or that of her male companions. So we might still maintain that language users 'know' that *being a lesbian* entails *being a woman*, which entails *not being a man*, even though we can understand Wittig and Baden-Powell when they deny those entailments. We recognize their uses of *lesbian*, *woman* and *man* as special, as nonliteral and metaphorical, mainly because their utterances do have something of a shock value—and are clearly intended to seem paradoxical. Wittig is forcing us to confront various aspects of men's control over wives and female lovers and to see lesbianism as breaking such bonds. Baden-Powell is heaping contempt on the African men who did not seem to live up to his standards and doing so by comparing them invidiously with their female compatriot, whom he lauds but in a somewhat problematic way. Such metaphorical uses can, of course, become literalized, as in the words *womanly* and *manly*.

Marilyn Farwell (1988) has discussed *lesbian* as a metaphor for female creative energy. As Farwell says (110), the metaphor "remains within the tradition that highlights sexuality as the core of creativity, but because it privileges a female sexuality that does not need or want male energy, it radically revises the symbolic order." Adrienne Rich's writings have been especially influential and also very controversial in developing this metaphor: "It is the lesbian in us who is creative, for the dutiful daughter of the fathers in us is only a hack" (Rich 1979, 201). This use is not far from the definitions of Daly and Frye, discussed earlier, which see the lesbian as the one who has turned attention toward women and away from 'the fathers'. In her very important article introducing the notion of the 'lesbian continuum', Rich highlights "forms of primary intensity between and among women" (see table 11.3) and seems at times to erase sexuality from the picture. We take Wittig's claim that a lesbian is not a woman as metaphorical in the sense that it is supposed to have a certain shock value and to direct us to the pervasive and debilitating dependence of women upon men in all kinds of realms. Similarly, we take Rich's focus on the nonerotic to be intended to direct our attention to a positive kind of ideal of women-centered activities and concerns and, at the same time, to infuse fresh and positive meaning into the term *lesbian*. Is it also an exhortation to women whose sexual desires center on other women to pay more attention to women's needs and interests in other domains? Probably, though it is probably more widely addressed and intended to push all women toward increased concern for one another. Can we read Rich as exhorting women who care about women's welfare to direct their erotic energy only toward other women? This seems much less clear, and interpreters have not agreed (nor have they always read her as 'exhorting' rather than 'describing').

Ferguson, Zita, and Addelson (1981) each discuss what Farwell has called Rich's metaphoric lesbian. Ferguson seems to take Rich to be speaking literally and criticizes her use of *lesbian* as ahistoric and problematically desexualized, rendering it unable to discriminate among contemporary forms of sexual identity. Zita agrees that Rich may have strayed too far from sexuality in her conception of the lesbian continuum. At the same time, Zita thinks that Ferguson fails to appreciate the power of heterosexism as an institution and has missed the challenge that Rich's notion offers to polarized heterosexist conceptions. Like Rich, Zita takes women's bonding to be crucial to their resistance to male dominance. Addelson (195) finds the notion of the lesbian continuum useful for examining "the past (and present) not in terms of hierarchical institutions but in terms of women's own understandings within the historical contexts of life patterns they were creating," although she disagrees that effective resistance to male dominance has always involved women bonding with one another. She points out that by its nature *lesbian* will be understood from (at least) two perspectives. In the dominant culture, it (still) designates a 'deviant' identity, one that is institutionalized as 'abnormal', whereas lesbian communities themselves have a positive perspective and a critique to offer of the dominant view. But she also offers a cautionary note (199): "the terms defining willingness to [engage politically in resistance to both heterosex- ism and male dominance] should not be made into a procrustean bed against which to measure the resistance of women throughout history or throughout our own society."

As Addelson makes clear, disputes over interpretations show the ways in which alternative theories and ideologies and strategies get enmeshed with how words are understood. It is because words are used to do things, to have effects, that people often endorse or promote one construction of a word over alternative ways that they also recognize of construing it. So though some people use *queer* as simply equivalent to 'gay male or les- bian', politically there can be real utility in creating alliances with other people outside heterosexual norms: for example, those who identify themselves as bisexual or transsexual. Queer activism promotes such alli- ances. What seems an obvious difference of the word *queer* from compound designators like *lesbian and gay* or *lesbian, gay, bisexual* or *lesbian, gay, bisexual, transsexual* is that it does not draw definitive boundaries. It leaves room to welcome those who identify with none of the standard categories of sexual minorities but nonetheless feel excluded by dominant hetero- sexual norms. In some contexts it even embraces those who just want to promote sexual tolerance or nonrestrictiveness, though their own sexual dispositions might seem to categorize them as *straight*. Such inclusiveness is often seen as a political advantage. It can, however, also be seen as a shortcoming: namely, such a sweeping use of *queer* obscures the special burden borne by those whose sexual inclinations are heavily stigmatized. A rather different political objection to *queer* as an umbrella term is that it does not fit well with an assimilationist gay politics since it seems to insist on the peculiarity, the difference, of those who do not identify as straight.

Queer theory grew out of lesbian and gay studies, and several of the papers in the volume in which this essay first appeared address its rele- vance to linguistic inquiry. Teresa de Lauretis is often credited with coin- ing the term in a special 1991 issue of *différences: A Journal of Feminist Cultural Studies*, but the thinking it embodies goes back considerably further. Queer theory questions—queries?—the notion of essential or innate sexual identities. It points to the historical and cultural specificity of sexual practices and categories, criticizing the assumption that the world 'naturally' splits into homosexual and heterosexual people. It treats both gender and sexual identities as 'performative', constituted through discursive histories of repeated acts of self- and other-identification. It often emphasizes the ongoing 'polymorphous perversity' of sexual desire and practice. It examines the constraining effects of naming and the effects of identity formations. There is, of course, not a single queer theory but a family of related queer theories. And the possibility of accessing these theories is part of what underlies the lexical concept of *queer* for many of us academics who are trying to explore productive ways for feminism and queer theory to meet.

I have emphasized the elusiveness and elasticity of *queer*. Do we always want such fuzziness in our concepts? For certain kinds of purposes, rigid-ifying interpretations can be useful. This is why we find specialized uses of everyday words so often in theoretical discourses. In linguistics, for example, we try to impose on our students an understanding of *dialect* in which everyone speaks a dialect, even though in ordinary uses *dialect* is reserved for language varieties that are seen as either defective or at best suited only for certain kinds of informal uses. Sometimes of course new terminology is introduced for technical purposes, but even when this hap-pens, there can be an ongoing process of trying to develop definitions that will elucidate the patterns in which the investigators are interested, with one way of marking out the patterns often more useful than another. A classic article of the 1930s is called "On defining the phoneme." For both *lesbian* and *feminist*, there have been extensive arguments about what kind of 'definition' best fits both the needs of intellectual (esp. historical) inquiry and of current political strategizing. (For *lesbian*, see, e.g., Rich 1980; Ferguson, Zita, and Addelson 1981; Farwell 1988. For *feminist*, see Offen 1988.)

6. Defining

Defining is often an attempt to direct thought along certain theoretical lines, to push a particular strategy for political action.[e] Definitions draw boundaries around a concept. When the concepts involved are ones connected to personal identities, some people are included and others excluded by defining. Defining is seldom 'just' semantics but is conse-quential precisely because words are key resources for thought and action, central players in theory and in politics. Kulick (2000) argues that 'queer linguistics' is too slippery a notion to be useful in sociolinguistic inquiry, that the elasticity so celebrated by queer theorists promotes confusion and equivocation when used in studies of linguistic phenomena. Certainly, any particular study that aims to enrich our understanding of how talk enters into the construction of sexual identities will need to offer some explicit discussion of the people and practices being examined. But that kind of particularized explicitness is not inconsistent with seeing the study as part of a broader (and not clearly bounded) inquiry into 'queer linguistics'.

Queer certainly does in many of its uses recognize openness and indeterminacy in interpretation. At the same time, it recognizes the need to continue questioning names and strategies as they change their direc-tions in the course of discursive history. Humpty Dumpty's dream of being fully 'master' is illusory, but shifting alliances can indeed use words to mean and to do new things.

e. McConnell-Ginet 2006 offers a fuller discussion of defining.

References

Butler, Judith (1993). *Bodies that matter: On the discursive limits of 'sex'*. New York: Routledge.

Chauncey, George Jr. (1994). *Gay New York: Gender, urban culture, and the making of the gay male world, 1890–1940*. New York: HarperCollins.

Dynes, Wayne R. (1990). *Encyclopedia of homosexuality*. New York: Garland.

Eckert, Penelope (1996). Vowels and nail polish: The emergence of linguistic styles in the preadolescent heterosexual marketplace. In Natasha Warner, Jocelyn Ahlers, Leela Bilmes, Monica Oliver, Suzanne Wertheim, and Melinda Chen (eds.), *Gender and belief systems: Proceedings of the Fourth Berkeley Women and Language Conference*. Berkeley, CA: Berkeley Women and Language Group, 183–190.

Eckert, Penelope, and Sally McConnell-Ginet (1992). Think practically and look locally: Language and gender as community-based practice. *Annual Review of Anthropology* 21: 461–490.

—— (1995). Constructing meaning, constructing selves: Snapshots of language, gender, and class from Belten High. In Kira Hall and Mary Bucholtz (eds.), *Gender articulated*. London and New York: Routledge, 469–507.

Farwell, Marilyn R. (1988). Toward a definition of the lesbian literary imagination. *Signs: Journal of Women in Culture and Society* 14(1): 100–118.

Ferguson, Ann, Jacquelyn N. Zita, and Kathryn Pyne Addelson (1981). On 'compulsory heterosexuality and lesbian existence': Defining the issues. *Signs: Journal of Women in Culture and Society* 7(1): 158–199.

Grice, Paul (1989). *The ways of words*. Cambridge, MA: Harvard University Press.

Hines, Caitlin (2000). Rebaking the pie: The 'WOMAN AS DESSERT' metaphor. In Mary Bucholtz, Anita Liang, and Laurel Sutton (eds.), *Reinventing identities: The gendered self in discourse*. New York and Oxford: Oxford University Press, 145–162.

Hutchins, Loraine, and Lani Kaahumanu (eds.) (1991). *Bi any other name: Bisexual people speak out*. Boston: Alyson.

Jagose, Annamarie (1996). *Queer theory: An introduction*. Melbourne: Melbourne University Press; New York: New York University Press.

Jeffreys, Sheila (1993). *The lesbian heresy: A feminist perspective on the lesbian sexual revolution*. Melbourne: Spinifex Press.

Keil, Frank C. (1989). *Concepts, kinds, and cognitive development*. Cambridge, MA: MIT Press.

Kennedy, Elizabeth Lapovsky, and Madeline D. Davis (1993). *Boots of leather, slippers of gold: The history of a lesbian community*. London and New York: Routledge.

Kramarae, Cheris, and Paula Treichler with assistance from Ann Russo (1985). *A feminist dictionary*. London: Pandora Press.

Kulick, Don (2000). The future of 'queer linguistics'. Paper presented at the International Gender and Language Association, Stanford University, Palo Alto, CA.

Lakoff, George (1987). *Women, fire and dangerous things*. Chicago: University of Chicago Press.

[Leslie, Sarah-Jane (forthcoming). The original sin of cognition: Race, prejudice and generalization, *Journal of Philosophy*.]

[McConnell-Ginet (2006). Why defining is seldom 'just semantics': M 'marriage', and other minefields. In Betty Birner and Gregory War Drawing the boundaries of meaning: Neo-Gricean studies in pragmati semantics in honor of Laurence R. Horn. Amsterdam: John Benjamins, 22. Shortened version anthologized in Deborah Cameron and Don Kulich Language and sexuality: A reader, 227–240. London: Routledge.]

[——— (2008). Words in the world: How and why meanings can matter. La 84(3), 497–527.]

[McConnell-Ginet, Sally (2009). Generic predication and interest-relativity. presented at the Non-canonical Predication Workshop, University of We Ontario.]

Offen, Karen (1988). Defining feminism: A comparative historical approac Signs: Journal of Women in Culture and Society 14(1): 119–157.

Putnam, Hilary (1975). The meaning of 'meaning'. In Keith Gunderson (ed.), Language, mind, and knowledge. Minneapolis: University of Minnesota Press, 131–193.

Rich, Adrienne (1979). 'It is the lesbian in us...' On lies, secrets, and silence: Selected prose, 1966–1978. New York: Norton, 199–202.

——— (1980). Compulsory heterosexuality and lesbian existence. Signs: Journal of Women in Culture and Society 5(4): 631–660.

Thorne, Barrie (1993). Gender play: Girls and boys in schools. New Brunswick, NJ: Rutgers University Press.

Williams, Raymond (1983). Keywords: A vocabulary of culture and society, rev. ed. London: Fontana Paperbacks; New York: Oxford University Press.

Wong, Andrew (2002). The semantic derogation of tongzhi: A synchronic perspective. In Kathryn Campbell-Kibler, Robert Podesva, Sarah Roberts, and Andrew Wong (eds.), Language and sexuality: Contesting meaning in theory and practice. Stanford, CA: CSLI, 161–174.

Wong, Andrew, and Qing Zhang (2000). The linguistic construction of the tongzhi community. Journal of Linguistic Anthropology 10(2), 248–278.

Coda

My closing chapter, "Breaking through the 'glass ceiling'," offers a more practical look at issues of language, gender, and sexuality. It grew out of a talk in a conference that included many nonacademics whose view of such matters had less to do with theory than with practical questions of everyday experience, mainly (though not only) about women's achievement (or lack thereof) in various kinds of workplaces. The essay brings together some of the ideas in earlier chapters and work in social psychology to argue that linguistic practice, though only part of the picture, helps keep in place the glass ceiling limiting women's advancement in high-level positions.

I offer this as an example of ways in which both social and content meaning can have real material consequences. Readers will, I hope, explore other areas where linguistic practice affects the basic conditions of people's lives, some of them mattering far more than competition among elite women and men for workplace visibility and success. As Nicholas D. Kristof and Sheryl WuDunn remind us in their recent book, *Half the sky: Turning oppression into opportunity for women worldwide* (Knopf, 2009), women in the developing world are oppressed in ways most of us Western feminists can barely imagine: they are beaten daily, subjected to genital cutting, sold into sexual slavery, gang-raped, and deprived of food and medical care and education. At the same time, Kristof and WuDunn let us hear from women who have not only endured violence and deprivation but have gone on to become effective agents of social change. They found schools for girls, for example, or small businesses that open up opportunities not only for them but for family and friends.

Could 'linguistic awareness' be relevant for addressing moral and, as Kristof and WuDunn stress, economic issues of this magnitude? Their own powerful rhetoric shows some ways that it can. They don't gloss over horrendous practices with euphemistic labels like *female circumcision* or *honor killings*, and they don't hesitate to use labels like *sexual slavery* and *gang rape*. Most important, however, they recognize and support the extraordinary efforts of some of these women. In listening to and retelling their stories, amplifying the voices that so many others have ignored, Kristof and WuDunn are themselves helping effect social change from within. They resist the temptation of resorting to familiar well-intentioned but ultimately 'patronizing' and 'paternalistic' efforts to import 'reform', emphasizing instead locally-based liberation movements.

It remains critically important, however, to continue working to understand and confront injustice linked to gender and sexuality in our own local communities of practice. Even for privileged young American women, there is no 'postfeminist utopia', and gay-bashing continues across the United States. Issues of language also still matter. For example, Jaclyn Friedman and Jessica Valenti, editors of the "feministing.com" blog, have written *"Yes" means 'yes': Visions of female sexual power and a world without rape* (Berkeley, CA: Seal Press, 2008). The essay in this coda explores some of the petty linguistic stuff that impedes women's achievement in academia and related areas.

Of course, language is never the whole story. But it matters in more ways than we usually realize.

12

Breaking through the 'glass ceiling'

Can linguistic awareness help?

0. Introduction

Linguistic awareness involves paying explicit attention to who says what, how and when they say it, and, critically, to what effect. Linguistic awareness is enhanced by the kind of scholarly work on the gender dimensions of discursive practices represented in Holmes (2000). Such work can, I will argue, help dismantle male advantage in professional achievements. But, I will also argue, linguistic awareness is only part of the picture. Not only does any individual woman need strategies for effective action, there must also be collective action to effect the systemic social changes that are needed if those strategies are to work reliably.

In August 1998, Rita Rossi Colwell became director of the National Science Foundation (NSF), an independent agency of the United States government that provides support for research and education in science, mathematics, engineering, and technology. Immediately prior to becoming NSF director, Dr. Colwell was president of the University of Maryland Biotechnology Institute and professor of microbiology at the University of Maryland, positions she had held since 1991 and 1972, respectively.

As the first woman to head the NSF, Dr. Colwell has frequently been interviewed on her views of women's participation in science and, more generally, in research and education. She has remarked on noticing at meetings that women's comments and proposals, her own included, often get attributed to men who have picked them up for repetition. Although the women then do not get 'credit' for their ideas, she goes on, worrying about who gets credit diverts us from getting things accomplished. Since Dr. Colwell did indeed eventually get tapped for leadership positions, it is obvious that somewhere along the line she finally did get some 'credit'.

This essay began life as a talk I gave in 1999 in Wellington, New Zealand, at a conference on language and gender organized by Janet Holmes. The written version was published in Janet Holmes, ed. *Gendered speech in social context: Perspectives from town and gown* (Wellington: Victoria University Press, 2000), 259–282.

   Stories like Rita Colwell's have been heard from virtually every
American woman who has recently achieved prominence in a professional
or high-powered business position. These women have somehow managed
to become successful in spite of finding themselves sometimes unfairly
ignored. The 'sometimes' is important here: no one whose contributions
are always ignored becomes a leader in her line of work. So it is possible
for a woman eventually to make herself heard and acknowledged, even if
she may often have trouble doing so. But for every woman who has made
it in the face of such barriers, there is almost certainly another woman
who has lost out to a man who is objectively no better on the job than she
is (and sometimes not as good). There is another woman who has accepted
the implicit devaluation of her capabilities that such ignoring conveys,
and who has consequently stopped making the requisite effort, and
trimmed back her aspirations. (Uta Lenk's discussion of job advertisements in Holmes 2000 points to other discursive practices that could
limit aspirations before women even get into the workplace.) And there
are women who never allowed themselves any such aspirations and thus
never got the credentials needed for professional achievement. They
decided in girlhood to focus their energy and talent in domains where
females predominate: at home taking care of other family members and
in various kinds of jobs that provide support to high-achieving profes-
sionals and executives.
   In this essay, I explore some of the linguistic texture of the social practices and institutions that support the 'glass ceiling' that limits women's
aspirations and achievement. The glass ceiling is, of course, the invisible
barrier that seems to keep even some exceptionally capable women from
ascending to the top in the many professions dominated by men. Its
companion, the glass elevator, is the invisible leverage that propels even
relatively mediocre men upward in female-dominated occupations. Both
are created and sustained by gender practices of various kinds, including
many that involve language. What are some of these practices, and where
do they fit in the more general picture of language and the gender order?

1. A practice-theory approach to language and gender

In joint work, Penelope Eckert and I have been developing a practice-the-
ory framework for thinking about the interaction of language and gender.
(See Eckert and McConnell-Ginet 1992a, 1992b, 1995, 1999, 2003.) I will
explain what this entails by first contrasting it with some of the approaches
many of us first brought to this area, and which continue to be useful for
certain purposes. Early research on language and gender took social structure, in particular the gender order, as given and then tried to correlate
language with preexisting gender categories and relations. This is not surprising. Commonsensically, there are 'women' and 'men', categories that
sort people generally into two nonoverlapping classes. There is a gender

order that is patriarchal, in the sense of being characterized by male advantage, the concentration of social prestige and power in male hands. Approaching language and gender research in this way, the obvious way forward is to explore correlations that might exist between the socially given distinctions and language. Language itself is also typically viewed as given, a system to take off the shelf, use, and then reshelve. So, on this approach, what we try to match to society are elements of a linguistic system. Typically these elements are linguistic expressions, where these might be structured from sound units, morphosyntactic units, or semantic units. The linguistic forms are tagged, then, as associated with women or with men, with the socially subordinate or the privileged.

It can be quite useful to think of gender in structural terms. Virtually all societies provide for a binary categorization of people into sex classes. They also have a gender order, an array of social institutions and structures that link to the sex-class categories. Sociologist Robert W. Connell (1987) has introduced a useful tripartite classification of the gender order: in addition to allocation of power and prestige, already mentioned, Connell identifies the division of labor, and the regulation of cathexis. CATHEXIS is originally a Freudian term that deals with the direction of libidinal energies, especially sexual. It can also somewhat more expansively cover the whole range of likes and dislikes, including but not confined to erotic desire and gender-based derogation of others. As Connell also points out, however, these different aspects of the gender order are interrelated, and, most important for our purposes, they are created and sustained by social practices of various kinds.

As linguists are well aware, it can also be very useful to view a language as a static structure with a grammar. That grammar includes phonology and phonetics, systematic sound patterns. It includes morphology, princi-ples of word formation and inflection. It includes syntax, categorizations of words and principles for combining them into larger phrases and sen-tences. It includes a lexicon of words and other meaningful units that specifies for each unit its grammatical characteristics, its sound structure (and how it is written), and its basic meaning (which may be 'underspeci-fied', i.e., not completely fixed). Lexical semantics and syntactic structure feed into combinatorial semantics, principles for assigning meanings to complex structures on the basis of the meanings of their constituent parts. Japanese, English, and Finnish speakers have access to quite different grammars. But it is social conventions of linguistic practice that are the real basis of our saying that, for example, Japanese have access to or 'use' a grammar in which pronouns are gendered in all persons, whereas English speakers access a grammar in which pronouns are gendered only in the third-person singular, and Finnish speakers access a grammar in which pronouns are not gendered at all. In other words, what counts as the grammar (or grammars) accessed by a particular population—what lan-guage or languages they speak—depends on ongoing and always poten-tially shifting social practices in communities.

If we confine attention to language and gender as static systems, it is difficult to understand either interactions between them or possible changes in each system. A focus on the structural systems of gender and of language obscures the role of human agency and actions, including purposive uses of language, in creating and sustaining the gender order and in effecting gender and other social change. Staying at the structural level also obscures the role of agency and action, including that focused on gender distinctions and relations, in linguistic change of various kinds. Agency is completely external to both social and linguistic structures. What bridges the gap between structure and agency is social practice. Social (including linguistic) practice is constituted by the interplay between social (including linguistic) structure and our own actions. Social practice includes both the way we do things as individuals and the way in which such individual actions fit into the larger scheme of things. Ultimately social practice encompasses the effect of individual agency on social structure and the constraints social structure puts on individual agency.

So in a practice-theoretic approach to language and gender, the focus is on the place of language in the social practices that construct a gender order and the place of gender in the social practices that construct particular linguistic systems as those used by a population. In this essay I focus on some of the ways in which language figures in the social practices that create and sustain male advantage in power and prestige. When our interest is social practice, it is immediately apparent that decontextualized linguistic forms will give us only limited information. We have to consider not only who is speaking and with whom, where the interactants are and when the interaction is taking place, but also which utterances are attended to, and which ideas are taken up. In other words, we have to look at how others interpret and respond to what is said. Whether a particular person's talk and other actions affect many or few, it is the unfolding over time of a structured totality of situated acts that creates meaning in and for society. The meaning of gender unfolds continually, gradually modified by large and small acts. And that meaning is produced in social interaction, which involves actions and reactions in ongoing exchange. DISCURSIVE PRACTICE is a useful label for the generation of social meaning in practice, and GENDER DISCOURSE for discursive practice as it pertains to gender. We should keep in mind, however, that discursive practice in this sense goes far beyond what people say or understand others to say.

Early studies of language and gender distinguished sharply between two topics. One was the study of how men and women speak, what were sometimes called 'genderlects' or 'gendered styles'. The other was the study of how women and men are spoken of, a topic that includes, for example, 'sexist' language. (See, for example, the introductions to Thorne and Henley 1975; McConnell-Ginet, Borker, and Furman 1980; Thorne, Kramarae, and Henley 1983.) On a discursive practice approach, however, we can see that the two topics are intimately connected: the effects intended and produced by any utterance depend not only on the linguistic form proffered, but also on the place of that utterance in gender discourse, which draws on past history and involves who utters it to whom, and the reactions it evokes (or fails to evoke, as in the case of the women whose meeting comments seem to be ignored or misattributed). Discursive practice draws especially heavily on the kinds of face-to-face exchanges people have with one another in the course of their ongoing mutual engagement in various activities. For example, work colleagues constitute an ongoing group that develops a shared history of linguistic practices, including interpretations and evaluations of what different individuals bring to the group's exchanges. Drawing on work by Jean Lave and Etienne Wenger, Penny Eckert and I have emphasized the importance of understanding linguistic practices in light of their place in such groups, what Lave and Wenger call 'communities of practice'. (In addition to the Eckert and McConnell-Ginet references provided above, see Lave and Wenger 1991 and Wenger 1998.) Each individual's relation to discursive practice generally and gender discourse in particular depends on the various local communities of practice to which they belong and their forms of membership in those communities, relations of those communities to one another and to various institutions, and so on.

2. Engagement, content, and personas

In constructing language and gender, people collaboratively construct (1) discursive engagement, (2) discursive content, and (3) personas. In constructing engagement, people make social moves involving speech actions and activities, they manage interactions, and they connect themselves and others to ongoing discourse. Making suggestions or offering evaluations, getting and keeping the floor, building on what you or others have said earlier, acknowledging and developing others' contributions, asking questions of clarification or issuing challenges: such practices construct discursive engagement. Not surprisingly, much work on language and gender has focused on the terms of engagement. Being able to engage effectively is essential to achieving virtually any of the aims one might have. The woman who keeps talking even after a man (or perhaps another woman) has tried to interrupt her is shifting, however slightly, the gendered terms of discursive engagement.

In constructing discursive content, people label and categorize, and they invoke and convey all kinds of background assumptions. How we categorize not only ourselves but all of experience is critical to discursive practice. In the United States, there is talk of the 'mommy track' in certain professions but there is as yet no parallel 'daddy track'. We talk about 'working mothers' but not 'working fathers', of 'career women' as a special group but not 'career men'. News stories about successful women highlight their families (or comment on the absence of a spouse and children). Behind such construction of gender content there lies, of course, a host of implicit gender assumptions that might well be rejected if made explicit. Increased linguistic awareness can bring the gender content of discursive practice into sharper focus, thus helping to change that content. And of course content that is not directly 'about' gender may nonetheless be critical to gender discourse. Evelyn Fox Keller (1992), for example, has argued that scientific discourses have been gendered in interesting and important ways. A 'masculine' discourse of control and destruction dominated physics during the first two-thirds of the twentieth century; a more 'feminine' discourse of collaborative engagement and life-creating forces came into biology during the last decades. Does the increasing importance of the life sciences really make women more welcome participants in scientific enterprises? Perhaps, though the story is undoubtedly quite a complicated one. Still, it is clear that discursive content is of critical importance in all kinds of workplaces. Exactly what kind of content is constructed depends in part on how engagement is constructed, and both of these also depend on how participants' personas are constructed.

In constructing personas, people use language choice and variation to negotiate the linguistic market, and they make social meaning visible through their stylistic choices. My presenting myself as a linguistics professor and getting others to ratify that presentation, to take me seriously in that persona, involves my speaking in certain ways and not in others, and involves others responding to what I say appropriately. At the same time, the collaborative construction of me as a woman relies on a different array of practices. A colleague may start our meeting by commenting, perhaps quite approvingly, on my clothes or some other aspect of my physical appearance. There may be appreciative little jokes about how meetings have been 'toned up' since women joined the working group, and perhaps also a little reminiscing about the 'dirty talk' that earlier characterized workplace meetings. I may assume a somewhat diffident and 'modest' style in advancing my ideas in order to forestall harsh judgments of me as an overly ambitious or self-aggrandizing and thus unfeminine woman. Perhaps I will smile frequently and use intonational patterns that suggest I am seeking others' input rather than trying to impose my ideas on them. Or maybe I will rely mostly on nonverbal actions to construct myself as feminine: certain kinds of clothing, postures, jewelry. Occasionally gender identities may be completely irrelevant, but this is still less common than might be supposed. In most contexts, including most workplace contexts, gender attributions are not only made but have a fairly significant effect on perceptions of what people are contributing and evaluations of their work. Constructing gendered personas has implications, of course, for constructing discursive engagement and content and vice versa.

As I noted at the outset, linguistic awareness can be of some help in breaking through the glass ceiling and eventually, I hope, in removing the ceiling and the elevator altogether. I should make clear, however, that there is no quick purely linguistic fix for gender inequities to be found. In her very interesting *Talking from 9 to 5: How women's and men's conversational styles affect who gets heard, who gets credit, and what gets done at work,*" Deborah Tannen (1994) has argued that the glass ceiling is a "wall of words," suggesting that conversational styles are at the root of women's failure to achieve authority and rewards commensurate to their skills and efforts. She is certainly right that language use enters centrally into our construction of gender and occupational status, but not, I think, in the implied suggestion that knowledge of different styles is the real key to women's breaking through the glass ceiling. That implication is often interpreted as meaning that women need to remedy deficiencies in their communicative styles in order to advance on the job, an interpretation that Tannen tries at points to forestall, but which is now well institutionalized in a variety of programs aimed at teaching women to 'improve' their communication skills. Tannen herself argues that it is not that women's styles are deficient, but that men do not understand or appreciate them. But she does not adequately acknowledge that many of the differences she discusses are part and parcel of the social practices that maintain men's advantage over women in the workplace: they are not minor cosmetic differences in individual style but connect to socially substantive matters of values and interests that sustain sexual inequality. There are at least two issues. First, the problem that Tannen does acknowledge, which is the double-bind to which linguist Robin Tolmach Lakoff (1975) first drew attention: women are faced with the dilemma that open verbal displays of their competence or authority can undermine their social attractiveness, especially their perceived heterosexual desirability. And second, there is the related problem that tacit and often quite unrecognized assumptions about gender can lead to women being undervalued no matter how they speak. Nonetheless, I agree with Tannen that attention to what we and others say, how it is said, and how others respond can be helpful in developing general strategies to get women the kind of recognition and rewards that their talents and work should but do not consistently bring. It is important, however, not to see the glass ceiling as 'merely' a wall of words, readily broken through by training individuals in linguistic difference and tolerance. And our focus should not be on helping token individuals break through, but on collective action to remove the ceiling for women generally and also for men who are disadvantaged by race, ethnicity, class or some other characteristic that ought to be, but is not, irrelevant to their chances for achievement.

3. Gender schemas

The best discussion I know of the difficulties women have faced and continue to face in professional life is Virginia Valian's excellent (1998) book, *Why so slow? The advancement of women.* Although Valian's data on how women fare in academia and related high-status jobs come pretty much

exclusively from U.S. studies, I suspect that similar data could be found
for New Zealand, Australia, the United Kingdom, and most of Western
Europe. The particular details will vary in different countries, in different
institutions, in different workplaces. And the details are important. But
there do seem to be some recurrent general patterns that we can usefully
discuss.

Valian argues that the distorting lenses of gender schemas—by which
she means our expectations of people on the basis of the sex to which we
have assigned them—are not just distorting but actively operate to wom-
en's disadvantage in public arenas where competence and achievement
are at stake. She cites a host of empirical studies that show that both
women and men tend to expect men to function more effectively in high
power jobs. In explaining achievements, both women and men tend to
credit men with skill and hard work and see women as having had good
luck, an easy task, or having exerted phenomenal effort. Men's successes
tend more to confirm expectations, to bring to mind their other successes;
women's tend to run counter to expectations and also tend not to redound
to their credit. In explaining failures, both women and men tend to see
women's failures as evidence of their lack of ability whereas men's failures
are more likely to be explained in ways that do not bear on future accomplishments: the task was very hard, he had some bad luck, he didn't try as
hard as he should have. Men tend to be compared to other men, no matter
what the task, whereas women tend to be compared to other women only
when doing 'feminine' tasks. In tasks seen as masculine, women who fail
are seen as doing so *because* they are female. In tasks seen as feminine,
men often are seen as succeeding *because* they are male. Valian cites a host
of empirical studies that show this pattern, a pattern of which most of us
are unaware because gender content is so often implicit. Noting one's
own and others' explanations of successes and failures is an important
first step to changing these gender-biased patterns.

More generally, Valian argues that gender schemas influence evaluations to women's detriment, in turn making it difficult for women to
accumulate advantage at the same rate as men, and she goes on to suggest
several ways to nullify the negative professional consequences of gender
schemas and to equalize men's and women's ability to accumulate
advantage (1998, 303). She does note that gender schemas can be detri-
mental to women's self-confidence and their capacity not only to present
their achievements in the best possible light but actually to achieve at the
level of which they are capable, in other words, that individual women
may often benefit from taking steps to change their own attitudes and
behavior. But, in sharp contrast to Tannen, and also to the cottage industry
that has sprung up to train women in asserting and displaying themselves,
Valian is quite clear that there is a systemic problem:

> No woman should think that if she just does everything 'right' she will suc-
> ceed. No woman should think that any modifications she may make in her

everyday demeanor will guarantee success. Observers' views of women as a class constitute an entire structure that no individual woman can change. It is that structure that needs changing. (1998, 322–323)

Of course this does not mean that individual women's efforts are irrelevant. Structural change necessarily involves individual-level changes, and women can indeed engage in 'self-improvement' programs that do help them in their lives, both personal and professional. But the critical point emerging from Valian's research is that it is not women or their differences from men that is the major problem. The sex differences that matter most and that almost certainly make a major contribution to the hypothesized sex differences in personalities and interests and the disturbing documented sex differences in workplace achievement still found are differences in how people are judged and evaluated, the 'advantages' they receive, depending on the sex to which they have been assigned (certainly these results fit with what Olsson 2000 reports on women's workplace narratives: women find their biggest problem to be how others, especially but not only men, treat them). Both women and men expect different things of women and of men, and these expectations lead them to respond to and evaluate women and men quite differently, often in professional contexts undervaluing women's talents and work and overvaluing men's. This happens in various ways even from people who are sincerely committed to promoting gender equity.

Valian uses the example of meeting dynamics to which Rita Colwell alluded to illustrate how very small differences in advantage or disadvantage can add up to major differences in position over the long term, just as tiny differences in savings or debt can be dramatically multiplied by the compounding of interest. Speaking and having your contributions recognized are part of constructing engagement, of positioning yourself and being positioned by others in ongoing discourse. As Valian notes, not only are some comments not taken up, participants in the group also tend to register who is credited and who is not and form expectations for future creditable performance on this basis. The person whose contributions are ignored or not credited this time may find even less receptivity in the audience the next time around. Her prestige has suffered, albeit slightly, whereas the male colleague who got credited for her suggestion has enjoyed a slight increase in prestige. Part of constructing men as more capable and knowledgeable than women in affairs of consequence is treating their comments as more worthy of attention, more credit-worthy. Their getting the floor may be easier in some contexts, but, even more critically, they seem to find it easier to get their suggestions and ideas taken up by others—and, importantly, taken up as *their* ideas. Sometimes of course there may be belated recognition that many of the most influential ideas that have affected the practices of some particular community have actually originated with some woman rather than with the men who initially got the credit for them. But such delayed recognition does not always come, and women and men interested in seeing women achieve on an equal basis with men need to devise ways for getting credit to women who deserve it. This does not mean that women themselves need to be preoccupied with whether they get credit. As Colwell notes, such preoccupation can actually impede making credit-worthy contributions. What it does mean is that everyone concerned about equity issues needs to be alert to the need for appropriate crediting. If Mary's idea is picked up by John and then later called John's idea, either John or another of Mary's colleagues, Linda perhaps, can point out that the idea really came first from Mary. Simply alerting those responsible for personnel evaluations to the well-documented tendency to differentially attend to women's and men's contributions can help effect a shift to more equitable patterns of giving credit.

Male advantage in constructing engagement does not begin in business or research meetings. It is already well attested in research on elementary and secondary schools and has sometimes been observed in university classrooms as well. Even cartoonists have noted the phenomenon. Gary Trudeau in his "Doonesbury" cartoon strip has a sequence in which Alex, a very bright computer-wise young girl, is shown in the classroom trying to get the teacher to notice her raised hand as boy after boy is called on and praised for stumbling and confused comments. "Maybe I should lose weight," Alex speculates. Alex's counterparts are in many classrooms, even ones in which teachers consciously believe in gender equity. *Punch* had a cartoon some time ago showing a professor addressing the class after a young woman has just spoken: "That's an interesting point, Miss Jones; perhaps we can get a man to make it now."[a]

In scholarship, the equivalent is citation practice; men do not cite women in the same proportion that other women do, though both sexes tend to undercite women. A particularly notorious scientific case is that of Rosalind Franklin, whose data were essentially stolen by Francis Crick and James Watson and used with quite minimal credit in their Nobel-winning work on the structure of DNA. A number of analysts have observed that Franklin might well have been first to light on the helical structure had her best X-ray picture not been shown to Watson and Crick without her permission and that they certainly could not have made their breakthrough without access to her data. Watson's (1968) book on the race to understand DNA spoke condescendingly of 'Rosy' and commented quite patronizingly on her painstaking work and even about her personal appearance and her 'nervous' interactional style. In the second edition (1980), published after Franklin's tragically early death from cancer, Watson apologized for having underestimated her and her work, noting

a. In July 2010 I bought a card based on a Punch cartoon that shows a man at the head of a conference table with four other men and a woman; he says "That's an excellent suggestion, Miss Triggs. Perhaps one of the men would like to make it." Same joke, recycled.]

that he had not earlier appreciated the obstacles faced by women in science. Of course, the apology came too late for Franklin. A happier ending is the story of Barbara McClintock (see Keller 1983), a biologist denied a regular research job and somewhat dismissively regarded as a bit of a crank until others' work showed the tremendous importance of her ideas and led to her receiving a Nobel Prize toward the end of her long and productive life.

Professional advancement, Valian observes, depends on being able to parlay small gains into big ones:

> If everyone understood explicitly what some people understand implicitly—that success comes from creating and consolidating small gains—no one would counsel women to ignore being ignored. The concept of the accumulation of advantage lets us see that the well-meaning advice often given to women—not to make a mountain out of a molehill—is mistaken. That advice fails to recognize that mountains *are* molehills, piled one on top of the other. Fairness requires appreciating the importance of each molehill of advantage and disadvantage and taking steps to ensure that molehills do not accrue to individuals on the basis of their group membership. (1998, 4–5)

Colwell's advice, then, to focus on getting things accomplished and not to worry about getting 'credit' is problematic. It *is* important not to get diverted from one's main goals by minor setbacks: for some women, a focus on getting things accomplished plus a certain amount of good luck may eventually led to their accruing advantage and ultimately to their advancement. But so long as they remain a small group of 'exceptional' women, the glass ceiling will stay in place.

Angier 2000, a *New York Times* feature on the 'glass ceiling in the sky' that women in astronomy continue to encounter, reports on recent surveys on gender arrangements in astronomy departments in the United States. Dr. C. Megan Urry, an astronomer who has been very active in spearheading such studies, says that, despite perceptions to the contrary, women did not really share in the rapid expansion of the field during the 1990s. Their numbers rapidly decline as one goes up the academic ladder, in spite of the fact that there have been distinguished women astronomers for centuries. Is it overt discrimination? David Gelernter, a computer scientist at Yale, has argued that it is women's lack of abilities or interest that has impeded their advancement in the sciences:

> If women aren't being kept out of science by force, they must be choosing not to enter, presumably because they don't want to, presumably because (by and large) they don't like these fields or (on average) don't tend to excel in them, which is nearly the same thing. They're also less prone to the intense cut-throat aggressiveness that usually marks the successful research scientist or engineer.

As Dr. Urry points out, Gelernter's view completely misses the cumulative effects of small slights and disadvantages that mount up over time. There are much subtler kinds of things going on, as a look at what is written about or said to women clearly demonstrates. The article cites some anecdotes that recently appeared in *Status*, a biannual report on women in astronomy published by the American Astronomical Society. One letter of recommendation for a female applicant for a postdoctoral position emphasizes twice how tiny, sweet, and charming the applicant is, and gives a specific example of how amusing and cute it is to watch the applicant in the laboratory wrestling with astronomical equipment larger than she is.

A woman graduate student in astronomy reports having just passed her PhD oral exam. A well-intentioned senior male faculty member approached her with a handshake and remarked, "I am very proud of your accomplishment, knowing how hard astronomy and physics is, especially for a woman...." Another young woman astronomer tells of approaching two male colleagues in her field at a conference, one of whom was a senior astronomer whose work was very close to hers. The pair of men were talking about a scientific issue with which she was quite familiar and continued their conversation until the senior astronomer finally acknowledged her presence by saying, "Ah, but we are boring this sweet young girl. What can I do for you, dear?" That such experiences persist into the new millennium suggests that molehills are still often piling up into mountains for women scientists, who face kinds of skepticism about their abilities and commitment that male scientists do not encounter.[b]

4. Gender discourse and 'backstage semantics'

Gender discourse applies what psychologist Helen Haste (1993) calls the 'sexual metaphor' to gender attributes, activities, and even things. The sexual metaphor uses the female-male contrast to organize thinking about a host of other binary contrasts and, typically, to present those binary contrasts as polar opposites, as incompatible with one another. Rationality and instrumentality, for example, are constructed as masculine, whereas emotionality and affectivity are constructed as feminine. (Let me note parenthetically that language and gender research reports have contributed to this aspect of gender discourse.) Women who venture into 'masculine' realms such as science can thereby jeopardize their perceived femininity. Some women use the strategy of ostentatiously constructing themselves as feminine on other dimensions to get around this obstacle: they use makeup, wear feminine clothes, practice many 'feminine' virtues, and smile a lot as they continue to pursue success in traditionally masculine preserves. A recent obituary for a very successful Chicago lawyer spent some time on how kind she was to clients and colleagues, while at the

---

b. Lawrence Summers's comments in section 6 of chapter 1, this volume, are relevant here.

same time noting that she had achieved a kind of prominence shared by few other women. Some women make it clear that being seen as 'feminine' simply does not concern them: this is most likely from women who are not, for whatever reasons, concerned to be seen as heterosexually attractive.

For a variety of reasons, lack of concern about being seen as heterosexually attractive is rare among adolescent or young adult women. Few women at that vulnerable life stage feel that they can afford not to worry about whether men will find them attractive or, more generally, will admire them. Many a teenaged girl in an American high school still keeps quite silent (or lies) about her achievements in the highly rational and thus highly masculine areas of science and mathematics. She does so for fear of seeming less than desirable to her male peers. In the 1950s, wearing eyeglasses was seen as a sign of intellectual seriousness, and the slogan was "Boys don't make passes at girls who wear glasses." The slogan itself is dated, but recent reports suggest that rationality is still gendered masculine, and nested within it are types of intellectual activity like science and mathematics that inherit masculine gender. A true story from the late 1990s can illustrate. A young woman whom male peers found quite attractive surprised them all by winning the high school's physics prize. She had not spoken out in class, and she had concealed her perfect test scores. Next thing she knew, comments that "she must have slept with the physics teacher" or that "her dad or brother or boyfriend must have helped her" were filtering back to her. She had been trying to keep her 'unfeminine' achievements invisible from her peers; when those achievements got broadcast, they also got denied and her success either attributed to her 'feminine' attractions, or transferred to males. How did this young woman come to believe that some might see intellectual competence, especially in a science like physics, as inconsistent with attractiveness to men? Perhaps she heard someone say "Linda is at the top of her physics class but quite good-looking," thus presenting Linda's combining excellence in the physics classroom with good looks as somehow surprising, especially remarkable. The same speaker might also have said "Jim is at the top of his math class and quite good-looking," making it clear that for Jim the combination of good looks and outstanding performance in math is not especially remarkable. Speakers are often unaware that they have said *but* rather than *and*, and the choice may be only faintly registered by their hearers. Nonetheless, words like *but* and *even* and other presuppositional triggers do have effects, albeit often very subtle ones. Of course, the process is far more complex than this: it is a whole discursive history that leads a young woman to try to construct herself as desirable by constructing herself as (somewhat) incompetent, at least in traditionally masculine areas. The response to the revelation of her competence will itself enter gender discourse: perhaps it will anger and galvanize her into abandoning her policy of hiding her talents, leading her to work hard and openly for success in the sciences. Or perhaps the response might simply confirm for her the wisdom of her self-deprecating policy and lead her to turn away from scientific endeavors altogether. This high school experience is closely linked to the kind of minor harassment so many women encounter on the job, for example, excessive and unwanted attention to their appearance ("You look so pretty today") unmatched by similar attention to male colleagues or inappropriate expressions of interest in their personal lives ("Stay out late last night?"). Women astronomers who get so far as completing PhDs have undoubtedly been tripping over such molehills for many years.

Gender schemas are typically constructed very early. Parents, teachers, and other children busily convey messages to a child about differing expectations for females and for males. Sometimes the messages are pretty explicit. I remember hearing a little Scottish boy tell my two-year-old daughter, who was happily playing with her Matchbox miniature cars and trucks, that "Wee lassies shouldna' play wi' wee motors." Sometimes different expectations are conveyed rather more subtly. Both my son and my daughter picked up on my use of *shit* as an occasional expletive when I was particularly annoyed by something. A neighbor reported to me that another neighbor, on hearing this word from my daughter's mouth, had gently remonstrated "Oh dear—such a pretty little mouth shouldn't say such an ugly word." To my son, the correction was "I don't like to hear that word." Both children got the message that the word was somehow taboo, but it was suggested to the girl that speaking that way might jeopardize her 'prettiness' and to the boy only that he should be careful of the audience. At just about the same time my kids were getting this kind of feedback in response to their use of 'bad' language, the professors in a leading academic department in a major U.S. university were discussing whether to hire their first woman. The candidate was a very distinguished scholar in the field, and many of the faculty were keen to have her as a colleague. What carried the day, however, was the sentiment of those who said that hiring a woman would mean "cleaning up our language at lunch and meetings" and that collegiality would be seriously impaired. This was back in the late 1960s, and few if any would advance the 'freedom to talk dirty' argument when discussing an academic hire any more—at least not in a general departmental meeting from which it might be more widely reported. Nonetheless, the threat to camaraderie and "emotional unity" of introducing women into their numbers continues to be taken seriously in the twenty-first century by the traditionally all-male Viennese Philharmonic Orchestra, many of whose members still insist that their distinctive and much admired ensemble playing is jeopardized with women as peer colleagues.

Gender schemas that potentially distort judgments of women and men are still being actively constructed, though often without explicit recognition. A couple of years ago I happened to see a news clip about a program that used professional sports stars to help encourage kids to read. The clip showed a large American football player talking with a boy of about six or seven. The boy was actually engaged in reading a book, and the sports star looked over his shoulder. "Oh," he said, "that book's about a girl. Why don't I help you find something more interesting?" The news commentator who introduced the clip did not comment at all on this gender message, but the kid certainly must have registered that his hero did not think girls or their activities of much interest. The athlete did not say explicitly that girls are relatively boring, but that message was certainly conveyed by what he did say. And not too long ago there were studies that showed males figuring much more prominently than females in school textbooks, and more often doing things while females observed or cheered them on. In these cases, a message is conveyed by a general *pattern* of what is and what is not said. That is, no one need say explicitly that females are or are supposed to be passive, and males are or are supposed to be active: this is a generalization that emerges from the general pattern of talk about women and men, girls and boys, and it is a generalization that figures in gender discourse, and thus plays a role in gender schemas even when it is not overtly acknowledged.

More often than not, gender schemas are conveyed covertly, their tenets often not explicitly recognized even by those who help to convey them. Even gender-liberal parents in the United States tend to give their children sex-specific names and dress them in sex-specific ways (after all, one of the first questions parents are asked about a newborn is "Is it a girl or a boy?"), to steer their girls more than their boys toward preparing for household responsibilities and for nurturing roles ("when"—not "if"—"you get married and have kids …"), to push their boys but not their girls to develop math and technology skills, and in a host of different ways to reinforce the message that sex is of paramount importance to personal identity and to the division of labor. Adults often speak of *girls and boys* rather than *kids*, cast kids' opposite sex-friendships in romantic terms ("Oh, Scott is Lisa's boyfriend!"), and suggest that Michael play with cousin John rather than with cousin Betsy, even though Betsy is nearer Michael's age and shares more of his interests. In late September 1999, a *New York Times* article on home decor reported a mother objecting to her three-year-old son's preference for a 'Spice Girls' motif in his bedroom, trying to get him to go for football-adorned bedclothes instead. Adults have not given up pushing gender and sexual conformity, even though they may be less frequently overt about it.

Still, there are many more communities of practice now than there used to be in which there is an explicit commitment to gender equity. Teachers in some U.S. schools encourage young boys to play with dolls and girls to build with blocks; they read children stories about men taking care of children and about women fighting fires or having exciting adventures on their own rather than waiting for princes to come to their rescue. This does not mean that gender discourse is completely neutral in these communities, but such practices have certainly had some effect. Not only are U.S. girls becoming quite involved in competitive sports, but high-powered career aspirations are far more common for them at this time than they were in the 1950s or 1960s. Discourses of gender egalitarianism, especially directed toward children and advanced by people recognized as leaders and authorities, can go some way to promoting egalitarianism.

In addition, there have been dramatic changes created by equal opportunity legislation and its implementation in the late 1960s and the 1970s. As the twentieth century ended, women in the United States held about 45 percent of managerial and executive jobs (compared to under 17 percent in 1970), they constituted about 42 percent of college faculty (29 percent in 1970), they were 46 percent of economists (11 percent in 1970), 44 percent of pharmacists (12 percent in 1970), 62 percent of psychologists (39 percent in 1970), 33 percent of veterinarians (5 percent in 1970), and 18 percent of architects (4 percent in 1970). They outnumbered men among entrants at several of the top medical schools and accounted for 41 percent of medical degrees overall as well as 44 percent of law degrees; they were the vast majority of graduates in pharmacy and veterinary science (both, it should be noted, relatively low paying fields). For every 100 men graduating from college, 123 women got degrees. (Figures from the U.S. National Center for Education Statistics and from the Bureau of Labor Statistics, cited in Hacker 1999.) These are all changes that have not only strengthened women's credentials for professional and executive jobs but have also increased women's desire for such jobs.

Yet in 2000 only three of the one thousand largest U.S. corporations were headed by women.ᶜ At my own university, there are still only a handful of women with named chairs or six-figure U.S. dollar salaries, a much lower proportion than of men. Overall, U.S. women still earn under 80 cents on average for every dollar men earn. It is still assumed that issues like childcare and eldercare are 'women's issues' rather than general social issues. Men may 'help' with the children and the household chores, but women continue to assume the primary responsibility in most cases. One study reported that both women and men think their arrangements are 'equitable' even when women spend about twice as much time as men in taking care of family needs. Women begin to feel overworked only when their share rises to 70 percent or more, whereas men feel overworked when they are doing 35 to 40 percent of the job.

Interviews with successful women often ask them how they manage to combine family and career (or else mention that the woman involved does not have a family). Interviews with successful men do not usually ask those questions. As a college senior, some time before it was illegal in the

c. The May 4, 2009, issue of *Fortune* magazine reported that there are now fifteen Fortune 500 companies with women at the top and twenty-eight in the Fortune 1000, up from twelve in the Fortune 500 the preceding year and twenty-four in the Fortune 1000. So the trend is certainly up, but there is still a large disparity at the top.

United States to ask about women's childcare arrangements or similar matters, I was interviewed for a Woodrow Wilson (WW) Fellowship, then given for people contemplating a career in college or university teaching. I do not know the proportion of women who applied—I think it was in the neighborhood of 30 percent—but recipients included only 10 percent women. I was a nervous 20-year-old, who had given rather little thought to how I might indeed combine a career and family, or even whether I wanted to. The interviewers said, "Well, you're an attractive young woman and you'll probably get married. How do you plan to manage a family and a career in college teaching?" (I should add the obvious: the interviewers did not ask that same question of my male classmates who were interviewed the same day.) "Well," I said, "I'll probably marry someone who is also a professor [as indeed I did], and we'll be able to arrange our schedules so that we can take turns taking care of the children." Little did I know how much more might be involved! For example, I ended up asking to switch my fellowship from Harvard to Ohio State because that was where my husband was working; neither of us even thought about his trying to find a job near Harvard while I worked on my PhD. It was not that we said to ourselves that we needed to stay where his job was, but rather that we never considered any other option. It was some years before it occurred to us that we had simply assumed that his job would determine where we lived. When my transfer request arrived, I suspect that someone at the WW Foundation office said something like, "That's why these things shouldn't go to women." For some time now, however, I have wished that when the interviewers asked me about how I would manage family responsibilities, I had thought to smile sweetly and say, "How do you gentlemen manage?" Of course, I would then probably not have been awarded the fellowship, but it would have been satisfying. The point of this anecdote is that the Woodrow Wilson interviewers and I both helped construct a gender discourse in which women have primary responsibility for children and the personal needs of their husbands and other household members, whereas men have primary responsibilities in the public world of work.

Gender schemas are mainly conveyed through what I sometimes call 'backstage semantics'. That "How do you plan to manage a family and a career?" could be seen as a reasonable question to direct to a female but not to a male indicates that it was, and often still is, simply taken for granted that women's primary responsibilities lie in the domestic domain rather than in the world of paid employment, and thus that their career commitment may be at issue. Men's focus on career even at the expense of family is similarly assumed. These messages need never be explicitly conveyed, but they are part of what helps us make sense of the explicit linguistic actions that we do encounter—not just individual actions but their overall patterning. In other words, meaning depends not just on particular utterances but on their being situated in a rich discursive history. Gender discourse results in powerful and influential gender schemas in part because so much of the content of gender schemas is constructed covertly.

I mention to a colleague, for instance, that a student who had been doing splendidly on the in-course work had fallen apart on the exam. The colleague responds, "Did you suggest that she practice by taking old exams?" My colleague is presupposing, taking for granted, that this student is female. If that is not the case, I might say something like "Well, actually, this student is male, but I think your advice might be good for him." Or I might just say "No, I didn't but I will," leaving intact the assumption of femaleness. If the student is indeed female, I am quite likely indeed to say simply "No, I didn't but I will," a response that does not explicitly confront the presumption that females are more likely than males to fail in high-pressure performance situations. Neither I nor my interlocutor may notice explicitly that we have just implicitly ratified that presumption, strengthening a gender schema that may have negative consequences for women. Such assumptions can lead, for example, to suggesting that one of the male members of the research team present a paper, while 'protecting' female members from that kind of pressure situation and thus from that chance for increasing their professional visibility. 'Chivalry' of this kind ultimately harms rather than helps women's chances for professional advancement.

Gender discourse is saturated with gender content that is seldom if ever made explicit. In constructing content, much work is done 'backstage' as the examples with 'but' and the unwarranted 'she' illustrate. One thing we can do is train ourselves and others to notice such backstage semantic moves, to bring them to our own and others' explicit attention and thus help reduce their potency. The 'change the sex' test is often useful for making glass ceiling supports visible. When discussing Mary and her work, do we say the same kinds of things we would say if Mary were Jim and vice versa? Do we mention Mary in the same kinds of situations in which we would mention Jim, and, if so, how do we talk about her as compared to him? How do we respond to her as opposed to him? Do we hesitate to offer her substantive criticism because we fear she 'can't take it'? Do we promote her brother because 'it means more to him'? Do we pay her less so that her husband won't feel he's failed?

It can be useful to let people know that women may do more to facilitate others' contributions to conversation than men, and that they may be far less comfortable than men in offering or facing direct challenges. Those responsible for evaluating women and men on the job can be alert to these possible differences and can try to take steps to ensure that they do not result in unfair advantage for men. But it may be even more important for evaluators to realize that it is *expectations* of profound differences of women in general from men in general that lead to biased evaluations of individual women and men. This means it is very important to make sure that our own findings about how gender differences are constructed linguistically are properly contextualized and do not strengthen problematic aspects of currently dominant gender discourses. Just as the fact that the average height of men is greater than the average height of women does not tell us anything about the relative heights of a particular male and female, so findings that women orient themselves more collaboratively toward conversational interaction do not mean that a given woman does not or should not care about being credited for her discursive contributions. Similarly, we should not take it as given that a man does not or should not care about the communal good or is unwilling to take direct responsibility for meeting the personal needs of others with whom he shares a household. Of course we may well want not only to change gender discourse but also to change the discourse of achievement so that nurturing and support are given more recognition than they now are. An important first step, though, is to take and give credit where appropriate and more generally to work collectively on making visible the gender schemas supporting the glass ceiling so that we can begin to curtail their effects.

References

Angier, Natalie (2000). For women in astronomy, a glass ceiling in the sky. *New York Times*, February 15, 2000: F5.

Connell, Robert W. (1987). *Gender and power: Society, the person, and sexual politics*. Stanford, CA: Stanford University Press.

Eckert, Penelope, and Sally McConnell-Ginet (1992a). Communities of practice: Where language, gender, and power all live. In Kira Hall, Mary Bucholtz, and Birch Moonwomon (eds.), *Locating power: Proceedings of the Second Berkeley Women and Language Conference* 1: 89–99.

—— (1992b). Think practically and look locally: Language and gender as community-based practice. *Annual Review of Anthropology* 21: 461–90.

—— (1995). Constructing meaning, constructing selves: Snapshots of language, gender and class from Belten High. In Kira Hall and Mary Bucholtz (eds.), *Gender articulated: Language and the socially constructed self*. London: Routledge, 459–507.

—— (1999). New generalizations and explanations in language and gender research. *Language in Society* 28: 185–201.

[—— (2003). *Language and gender*. Cambridge and New York: Cambridge University Press.]

Hacker, Andrew (1999). The unmaking of men. *New York Review of Books* XLVI, 16 October 21, 1999: 25–30.

Haste, Helen (1993). *The sexual metaphor*. New York and London: Harvester Wheatsheaf.

Holmes, Janet (ed.) (2000). *Gendered speech in social context: Perspectives from town and gown*. Wellington: Victoria University Press, 259–282.

Keller, Evelyn Fox (1983). *A feeling for the organism: The life and work of Barbara McClintock*. New York: W. H. Freeman & Co.

Keller, Evelyn Fox (1992). *Secrets of life, secrets of death: Essays on language, gender and science*. New York and London: Routledge.

Lakoff, Robin Tolmach (1975). *Language and woman's place*. New York: Harper & Row.

Lave, Jean, and Etienne Wenger (1991). *Situated learning: Legitimate peripheral participation*. Cambridge: Cambridge University Press.

McConnell-Ginet, Sally, Ruth Borker, and Nelly Furman (eds.) (1980). *Women and language in literature and society*. New York: Praeger. Reissued in 1986 by Greenwood.

Olsson, Su (2000). The 'Xena' paradigm: Women's narratives of gender in the workplace. In Holmes 2000, 178–191.

Tannen, Deborah (1994). *Talking from 9 to 5: How women's and men's conversational styles affect who gets heard, who gets credit, and what gets done at work*. New York: William Morrow.

Thorne, Barrie, and Nancy Henley (eds.) (1975). *Language and sex: Difference and dominance*. Rowley, MA: Newbury House.

Thorne, Barrie, Cheris Kramarae, and Nancy Henley (eds.) (1983). *Language, gender and society*. Rowley, MA: Newbury House.

Valian, Virginia (1998). *Why so slow? The advancement of women*. Cambridge, MA: MIT Press.

Watson, James D. (1968). *The double helix: A personal account of the discovery of the structure of DNA*. New York: Atheneum. Revised 1980, ed. by Gunther S. Stent. New York: Norton.

Wenger, Etienne (1998). *Communities of practice*. Cambridge and New York: Cambridge University Press.

Index

Abel, Elizabeth, 169
abstraction, as problem in
    sociolinguistic research,
    93–95, 97–99, 120, 125n15
abuse terms. *See* epithets
academia, careers in, 269–270
access, as factor in linguistic
    variation, 67–69
accommodation. *See*
    presupposition
acquisition, language, 42, 82–85.
    See also children
Addelson, Kathryn Pyne, 255, 257
address, 48, 83, 96
    distinguished from
        reference, 210–215
    forms of, 48, 70, 72, 82,
        215–226
    and titles, 81–82
African American Vernacular
    English, 15
African-Americans, 11, 45, 67–68,
    87n7, 217, 223
age, 98, 100–102, 202, 217, 219.
    See also children
agents, linguistic, 40, 56–57.
    See also speaker
Alice (fictional character), 237,
    252, 253–254
Amazon Indians, 44
American English. *See* English
American Indians, 44, 107
American Sign Language, 65
American Southeast, 216–217,
    219, 224
Americans, 15, 97, 112

anaphoric replacement, pronouns
    as, 198, 199
anatomy, voice affected by, 111.
    See also biology
Anderson, Benedict, 19, 210
androcentricity, 109, 116, 121,
    123, 186, 241
androgyny, 121, 201
Angier, Natalie, 231, 273
Anglo-American culture, 7, 228
Appiah, Kwame Anthony, 11
Aries, Elizabeth, 101
Aronovitch, Charles D., 123n5,
    124n11
Atkins, Bowman K., 43, 45
attitude, illocutionary, 49, 109,
    121. *See also* speech acts
Austin, John L., 50, 69
Austin, William, 113
authenticity, and social/stylistic
    meaning, 25–27. *See also*
    identity
autonomy, from institutional
    control, 133, 136

Bach, Kent, 51, 75n7, 171
Baden-Powell, Lord, 254
Baker, Robert, 222
Barbin, Herculine, 232
bare plural. *See* generic, bare
    plural as
Baron, Dennis, 40, 50
Baron, Naomi, 204n9
Barrett, Rusty, 15
Belten High School, 129–163
Bem, Sandra L., 174, 129

discursive practice, 266–267, 268
diversity, within sex and gender.
   See also intersectionality;
   ethnicity; race; class, social
   39, 42, 98–99, 102
division of labor, linguistic, 54–55,
   250
dominance, 53
  male, 37, 43, 47, 85, 93, 107,
    109, 116 , 135, 156, 161,
    246, 255–256
Doonesbury, 272
drag queens, 15, 232
Drakich, Janice, 175nb
Dravidian languages, 43, 186
Dubois, Betty Lou, 45, 86n1
Dutch, 49
dynamics, of gender, 98, 103, 246
dynamism, intonational, 91,
   114–117, 122, 124n8,
   124n14, 125n19
Dynes, Wayne R., 239

Eakins, Barbara Westbrook, 174
Eakins, R. Gene, 174
Eble, Connie C., 117, 212
Eckert, Penelope, 16, 18–19, 208,
   244, 246, 267
  collaboration with Sally
   McConnell-Ginet, 17,
   93–106, 129–163,
   209–210, 264
Edelsky, Carole
  and conversation, 51, 175
  and intonation, 75n8, 119,
   125n14
  and stereotypes of language, 45,
   87n6
egalitarianism. *See also* linguistic
   egalitarianism, principle of
  and high school, 133
  in second-person pronoun use,
   218
  sexual and gender-based, 121,
   278
Eisenhart, Margaret A., 149

Eisenstein, Hester, 169
Ekka, Francis, 43
emotion, 115–117
  speaker, 121
Encyclopedia of
   Homosexuality, 239
endearment
  as address option, 82, 216, 220,
   224–226
  terms of, 216, 220, 224, 226
engagement
  constructive, 271–272
  discursive, 267–269
English, 6, 20, 39, 69, 181
  American, 44–45, 46,
   108, 114, 121, 122,
   204n12
  gendering of reference in,
   229–232
  history of gender in, 186–187,
   189–192
  Middle, 191
  Old, 190, 204n6
  and pronouns, 10, 55, 198ne,
   265
  and self-reference, 226–228
entailment, 249, 254
epithets
  abuse terms, 222
  in address, 220–221, 224
equal opportunity legislation,
   changes linked to, 278
equity, gender, 271–272
Erickson, Donna, 112
Ervin-Tripp, Susan, 123n1, 204n7,
   205n16
Eskimo, 186
ethnicity, 98, 100–102, 130,
   218, 269
ethnography, as essential to
   sociolinguistics, 99
euphemism
  as aspect of 'women's
   language', 44
  and sexism in language, 70
Europe, 112, 213–214